The Political Economy of the Japanese Financial Big Bang

The Political Economy of the Japanese Financial Big Bang

Institutional Change in Finance and Public Policymaking

Tetsuro Toya

Jennifer Amyx,
Consulting Editor

OXFORD
UNIVERSITY PRESS

OXFORD
UNIVERSITY PRESS

Great Clarendon Street, Oxford OX2 6DP

Oxford University Press is a department of the University of Oxford.
It furthers the University's objective of excellence in research, scholarship,
and education by publishing worldwide in

Oxford New York

Auckland Cape Town Dar es Salaam Hong Kong Karachi
Kuala Lumpur Madrid Melbourne Mexico City Nairobi
New Delhi Shanghai Taipei Toronto

With offices in

Argentina Austria Brazil Chile Czech Republic France Greece
Guatemala Hungary Italy Japan Poland Portugal Singapore
South Korea Switzerland Thailand Turkey Ukraine Vietnam

Oxford is a registered trade mark of Oxford University Press
in the UK and in certain other countries

Published in the United States
by Oxford University Press Inc., New York

Originally published as a Japanese translation. Toya, Tetsuro (2003)
Kin'yu Biggu Ban no Seiji Keizai-gaku: Kin'yu to Kokyo Seisaku Sakutei ni
Okeru Seido Henka (The Political Economy of the Financial Big Bang:
Institutional Change in Finance and Public Policymaking), Tokyo:
Toyo Keizai Shimposha. Translated by Masahiko Aoki and Riina Toya.

The moral rights of the author have been asserted
Database right Oxford University Press (maker)

First published 2006

British Library Cataloguing in Publication Data
Data available

Library of Congress Cataloging in Publication Data
Data available

Typeset by Newgen Imaging Systems (P) Ltd., Chennai, India
Printed in Great Britain
on acid-free paper by
Biddles Ltd., King's Lynn, Norfolk

ISBN 0–19–929239–6   978–0–19–929239–4

10 9 8 7 6 5 4 3 2 1

Foreword

This book is a case study of structural reform in the Japanese financial sector. Tetsuro Toya adopts a novel approach, combining rational choice analysis from the field of political science with comparative institutional analysis from the field of economics. Notably, Toya uses a nuanced variety of rational choice analysis, developing assumptions more robust and in touch with reality than those often utilized by rational choice theorists—whose work tends to elicit criticism from scholars more grounded in empirics. In doing so, Toya goes beyond simply using rational choice analysis as a tool to making his own significant contribution to the rational choice literature. His study is proof that the assumptions of a rational choice analysis need not be so stylized as to depart from reality.

Toya takes great care to observe high standards in social science research in his case selection, his generation of plausible hypotheses, the testing of these hypotheses, and in seeking out ways to gauge the generalizability of the main argument. As a result, the study is valuable not only because of what it tells us about the origins of the Big Bang and how Japanese politics is changing, but also because it is an outstanding example of a particularly well-thought out and executed research project.

Toya's central hypothesis is that Japanese politics and policymaking has changed. This change has been induced by a combination of policy failures and scandals, as well as the emergence of the possibility of a change in government, following thirty-seven years of uninterrupted LDP rule. The Big Bang was initiated as a result of the change in these policymaking dynamics, when the Ministry of Finance was forced to prioritize organization survival over all other organizational goals and when actors were able to bypass traditional policymaking mechanisms. In making this argument, Toya solves the puzzle of why a ministry would seek to institute reforms that seemingly reduce the ministry's own regulatory authority.

Toya provides evidence that there has been significant change in two institutions fundamental to financial policymaking prior to the mid-1990s: a policymaking mechanism referred to as "bureaupluralism" (Aoki 1988) and the Finance Ministry's "convoy approach" to financial regulation. Through his case study of the Big Bang, he provides convincing documentation of changes in these two areas and argues that the public—largely excluded from the bureaupluralism mechanism—now plays a much more prominent role in policymaking. Toya's analysis of the new role of the Japanese public in policymaking and of the concrete implications of this development is a key contribution of the study.

The book's analysis should aid the reader not only in better understanding Japan's Big Bang financial reforms, but also in better understanding the political motivations surrounding the numerous reform initiatives put forward by the current Koizumi administration. The prime minister's championing of these reforms appears puzzling on the surface because most have as their goal the change in—or even elimination of—the very institutions that have historically provided both votes and campaign contributions to the Liberal Democratic Party (LDP), Koizumi's own party. Yet, Koizumi's attempts to tackle these reforms have won him unprecedented public support; without such initiatives, it is unlikely that the LDP would still be in power. Newspaper and magazine accounts of how these initiatives came about confirm that the traditional policymaking mechanism of bureaupluralism is being bypassed repeatedly in many different policy areas today, just as Toya argues was the case in the Big Bang reforms.

Importantly, the emergence of reform initiatives does not equate with their successful implementation; neither is change in policymaking dynamics necessarily evidenced by more desirable policy outcomes. Japan's political economy remains in transition, having moved away from one defined state but not yet settled on a new one. Few have analyzed the nature of this transition as skillfully as Toya, however; or so capably provided a link between detailed case study analysis and the "bigger picture" in the political economy.

This book represents an edited version of the Toya's doctoral dissertation by the same title, submitted in 2000 to the Department of Political Science, Stanford University. It was my privilege to edit and prepare the manuscript for publication, as a tribute to the author.

Jennifer Amyx

Tokyo, Japan
June 2004

Preface

In 1996, the Japanese government introduced a policy package initiating massive deregulation and liberalization in the nation's financial sector. Referred to as Japan's Financial "Big Bang", this set of reforms extends across the banking, securities, and insurance industries, as well as to foreign exchange and accounting standards. The impact on Japan's financial landscape since the commencement of the Big Bang reforms in April 1998 has been huge. The lifting of regulatory constraints gave rise to the development of new financial products and opened the doors to market newcomers. More importantly, the reforms spurred financial firms to significantly alter their strategies in anticipation of heightened competition. The unthinkable in the 1980s and early 1990s has materialized: inter-*keiretsu* alliances are forming *en masse* and foreign takeovers of domestic financial institutions have become commonplace.

The emergence of the Big Bang poses a challenge to conventional interpretations of Japanese politics. Despite the disruption in 1993 of nearly forty years of uninterrupted single-party rule by the Liberal Democratic Party (LDP) and the emergence of large-scale policy failures and scandals in the bureaucracy in the 1990s, many observers continue to stress continuity in Japanese politics. They argue that recent political and economic reforms represent gradual rather than fundamental change (Curtis 1999; Vogel 1999). And, those who make the claim that Japanese politics has changed significantly focus almost exclusively on the Lower House electoral reforms of 1994 as the catalyst for change, emphasizing the way in which the new single-member district alters electoral incentives of politicians (Rosenbluth and Thies 1999).

Through an examination of the political economy of the Big Bang, this book argues that Japanese politics has been changing significantly since 1995, but for reasons other than a change in electoral rules. The gradualism widely observed until the mid-1990s does not hold in the case of the Big Bang. These financial reforms are wider in scope and deeper in degree than past financial reforms. The Big Bang covers five areas of finance and includes measures that endanger the survival of some financial firms—a sharp departure from the previous "convoy approach" to regulation that ensured the survival of even the weakest firms. Given the pivotal role of the financial system in Japan's political economy, significant change in this area has necessarily had a ripple effect across the political economy as a whole.

The Big Bang initiative also deserves attention because it did not evolve from the same informal bargaining process among actors that has long characterized public policymaking in postwar Japan. This process has been conceptualized as "bureaupluralism" (Aoki 1988), wherein public policies are produced from a consensus-making process organized by the bureaucracy but involving the regulated industries and affiliated LDP politicians ("tribesmen" or *zoku giin*).[1] Bureaupluralism centers on such policymaking bodies as the deliberative councils in the government and the LDP Policy Affairs Research Council (PARC). Yet, the political process that produced the Big Bang largely circumvented these bodies. The Big Bang initiative first came to be known publicly when Prime Minister Ryutaro Hashimoto announced it two weeks after the LDP victory in the Lower House elections of October 1996, taking many by surprise.

These observations about the distinctive nature of the Big Bang reforms, and the decision-making process that gave rise to them, are intricately related to three additional puzzles. First, evidence suggests that the Ministry of Finance (MOF) was more than willing to launch this initiative. The MOF began discreetly preparing the reforms in early 1996, and proposed its plan to Hashimoto, who adopted it as his Initiative. Yet, this Initiative brought about negative consequences for the finance ministry. Not only did it strip away many of MOF's regulatory tools, but it also severed the ministry's close ties with the financial sector by introducing fierce competition into finance and undermining the prospects of survival for many financial institutions. These ties had served as avenues for gathering information from the private sector, facilitated public administration, and ensured retirement positions for former ministry officials. Conventional accounts of bureaucratic behavior that focus on the bureaucracy's maximization of budget size, regulatory jurisdiction, or breadth of discretion (Niskanen 1971; Kato 1994; Vogel 1996; Amyx 1998) would lead us to expect MOF to resist—or at least to forestall such reforms.

---

[1] Similar conceptualizations include "patterned pluralism" (Muramatsu and Krauss 1987), "compartmentalized pluralism" (Sato and Matsuzaki 1986) and "bureaucratic-inclusive pluralism" (Inoguchi 1983).

Second, many scholars have pointed to the great influence of the financial industry in Japanese politics (Rosenbluth 1989; Calder 1993). Indeed, it appears that the "weaker" financial institutions, the securities firms, and the long-term credit and trust banks in particular, successfully prevented past attempts by the MOF to launch financial reforms (e.g. the 1979–82 banking reforms and the 1991–93 financial reforms). Why were the financial industries unable to forestall the Big Bang as they had done with other reforms similarly threatening the viability of weaker firms?

Third, many scholars have noted a strong alliance between the ruling LDP and the permanent bureaucracy over the 1955–93 period of one-party dominance by the LDP (Aoki 1988; Okimoto 1989). While the Big Bang was launched by the LDP Prime Minister and received the full support of the LDP and the MOF, parallel developments in finance suggest this alliance had undergone a major change. These developments included the transfer of authority over financial supervision from the MOF to a new Financial Supervisory Agency (FSA) and the devolution of monetary authority from the MOF to the Bank of Japan (BOJ). How can we explain the LDP's support of the Big Bang alongside such decisions that drastically undermined the MOF's presence in finance? In other words, what happened to the seemingly stable LDP–MOF alliance of the postwar era?

To solve the puzzles delineated above, this book adopts a rational actor approach to show that there has been institutional change, or a shift in the shared expectations about how finance works in Japan. Stability, cooperation, and continuity characterized the system of financial regulation over the postwar period but no longer accurately describe the post-1995 world. The study identifies two factors that have led to decay in the public policymaking mechanism of bureaupluralism: the emergence of performance failures and scandals attributed to the bureaucracy and an increased likelihood of a change in government where such a possibility once seemed remote. These new factors are likely to affect other policy areas as well, meaning that decay in the financial policymaking process is likely to lead to change throughout the political economy.

In making the above argument, this book attempts to provide a realistic image of post-1995 financial politics by improving on existing behavioral assumptions of actors. It demonstrates that the Big Bang can be best understood as an outcome of the strategic interaction of state actors. More specifically, the Big Bang is the product of interaction between the LDP and MOF, each pursuing organizational survival through cooperation, competition, and confrontation. To explain the causal mechanisms behind developments in financial politics, the study constructs a framework of institutional change and a typology of financial reforms. "Failures" (financial crisis and scandals)—caused by the emergence of a gap between the faster pace of environmental changes and the slower pace of institutional adaptation—and "change in the institutional environment" (namely, the change of government in 1993) have together produced institutional change by altering the players, the formal rules, informal patterns of interaction, and the shared expectations among actors. Using a four-by-two typology, constructed from the diversity in the coalition patterns and the interaction patterns of state and societal actors, the Big Bang is shown to be a product both of "defection" and "public interest politics."

Broader theoretical insights also emerge from the study's analysis of the Big Bang: entrenched actors may not always be as entrenched as they may seem, and bureaucrats may not always maximize tangible tokens of organizational power. Moreover, the public may be more influential than commonly thought, because not only politicians but also bureaucrats and interest groups have reasons to pursue public support to enhance their respective political influence. As a consequence, well-organized groups may not always prevail over the unorganized public.

The assistance of many individuals was indispensable to the completion of this study. I am greatly indebted to the advisers of my dissertation: Daniel Okimoto, Masahiko Aoki, and Barry Weingast. Daniel Okimoto guided me through every stage of the process—choosing the topic, carrying out empirical research in Japan, and writing up the dissertation. I am indebted to him as well for the encouragement to pursue doctoral studies at Stanford, and for offering inspiring advice, based on his deep knowledge and understanding of Japan. I would never have made it through the program without his guidance, and I consider myself lucky to have had an advisor with such personal warmth as his.

Masahiko Aoki equipped me with the tools to tackle my research puzzle. I only hope that I did justice to his innovative framework of institutional change that builds on the Comparative Institutional Analysis (CIA) perspective, in my attempt to demonstrate its promise in analyzing real world issues. I learned a great deal about how social science works by witnessing his devotion to a better explanation of the world through a continuous improvement of his theory. Barry Weingast provided useful comments that helped me relate my work better to the general literature beyond the study of Japanese politics. His incisive feedback at various points in the research forced me to focus and better organize the main argument of the dissertation.

Sharp comments from Stephen Krasner, although difficult to take at times, helped me to formulate the basic problematique for this research. Walter Powell also kindly served on my oral examination committee and provided helpful suggestions for improving the dissertation. Interaction with the following scholars at Stanford further contributed to this research project: David Brady, Judith Goldstein, Torben Iversen, Ronald McKinnon, Roger Noll, Jean Oi, and Michael Thies. I would also like to thank the participants in a workshop on Japan's economic crisis held at the Stanford Asia/Pacific Research Center (A/PARC) on October 29, 1999 for their helpful feedback.

The wisdom of the talented current and former students of Japanese politics at Stanford facilitated my studies in many ways. Harukata Takenaka helped me survive the whole process by serving as a mentor and pioneer in the challenging task of completing a Ph.D. while serving as a government official. Jennifer Amyx shared valuable research data with me and gave me an opportunity to present my research findings in her course on Japanese politics at Stanford. Yves Tiberghien provided me with many helpful suggestions and useful documents; this research topic would not have emerged had Yves not proposed that I give lectures for the Rise of Industrial Asia course for which we served as teaching assistants. Mariko Yoshihara, with her warm personality, encouraged me as I prepared for the challenge of simultaneously tackling the Ph.D. program and marriage. I would also like to acknowledge the input of Philipp Riekert, Amy Searight, and Masaru Kohno. Friends in the Department of Political Science as well as peers in Stanford's Asia Pacific Scholars Program helped me through the project by making life in graduate school more pleasant than it otherwise would have been.

The faculty and staff at the Stanford Asia/Pacific Research Center (A/PARC) and the Asia Pacific Scholars Program greatly facilitated my research. In particular, my thanks go to Yumi Onoyama, Greet Jaspaert, Claire McCrae, Maria Toyoda, and Romola Breckenridge. I also wish to thank Susan Stevick, who provided invaluable editorial assistance on the dissertation.

I am grateful to those I interviewed for generously giving their time to answer my questions. Four individuals even went further, offering me their wisdom about life in general (career, marriage, etc.), turning the interviews into a truly memorable educational experience: Shijuro Ogata, Eisuke Sakakibara, Yasuhisa Shiozaki, and Katsuhiro Nakagawa. My thanks also extends to Kazuhito Ikeo, Hideki Kato, Yutaka Kosai, Kiyoshi Mizuno,

Yoshimasa Nishimura, and Yukio Noguchi, as well as to other government officials and individuals working in the financial sector who prefer to remain anonymous. In particular, friends at the Ministry of Finance (MOF) and at the Ministry of International Trade and Industry (MITI) helped me better grasp how government works by sharing their *honne* (true feelings) with me.

Partial research support was provided by a Book Grant on Japanese Studies and the Japan Fund, both from the Institute of International Studies at Stanford University. The Stanford Asia Pacific Scholars Program and the Long-Term Study Abroad Fellowship of the National Personnel Authority of Japan also provided partial financial support during my studies at Stanford. I am immensely grateful for the generosity of the Ministry of Finance of Japan, which sponsored my Ph.D. studies at Stanford. However, the views expressed in the dissertation [and book] should not be attributed to any organizations with which I have been affiliated.

Three professors at the University of Tokyo opened my eyes to the excitement of academic work. Hiroshi Watanabe introduced me to the study of politics and first directed my attention to the importance of perceptions in the political world. Kahei Rokumoto first introduced me to works in social science. Shiguehiko Hasumi, the first teacher I had in college and later the President of the University of Tokyo, left me with no choice but to engage in the pursuit of knowledge from day one of my college life.

Finally, I would like to express gratitude to my family, whose encouragement and feedback on the project were invaluable. My parents, Hiromichi and Kiyoko Toya, provided their uncompromising love and support. My brother, Hiroaki Toya, consistently provided me with his wisdom and protection as the older sibling. Riina Toya, *née* Tomita, made a significant contribution to this research (extending to the choice of the research topic), besides becoming my fiancée and then wife over the course of the project. As promised on our engagement day, the dissertation is dedicated to her.

TT

Stanford, California
May 2000

Contents

Contents

List of Figures

List of Tables

List of Abbreviations

ARPH	Administrative Reforms Promotion Headquarters, LDP
BOJ	Bank of Japan
CLB	Cabinet Legislation Bureau
CPJ	Communist Party of Japan
DKB	Daiichi Kangyo Bank
DPJ	Democratic Party of Japan
EPA	Economic Planning Agency
FILP	Fiscal Investment and Loan Program
FRC	Financial Reconstruction Committee (established following the 1998 Financial Diet)
FSA	Financial Supervisory Agency (established in June 1998); Financial Services Agency (from July 2000, when merged with FRC)
FSRC	Financial System Research Council, MOF
FTC	Fair Trade Commission
FY	Fiscal Year
IBJ	Industrial Bank of Japan
IC	Insurance Council, MOF
IFB	International Finance Bureau, MOF
LDP	Liberal Democratic Party
LTCB	Long-Term Credit Bank of Japan
MAFF	Ministry of Agriculture, Forestry, and Fisheries
MHW	Ministry of Health and Welfare
MITI	Ministry of International Trade and Industry
MMD	Multi-Member District (electoral system)
MOC	Ministry of Construction
MOF	Ministry of Finance
MPT	Ministry of Posts and Telecommunications

NCB	Nippon Credit Bank
PARC	Policy Affairs Research Council, LDP
PT	Project Team (of the ruling coalition)
RCC	Resolution Collection Corporation
SDPJ	Social Democratic Party of Japan
SEC	Securities and Exchange Council, MOF
SESC	Securities Exchange Surveillance Commission, MOF
SMD	Single-Member District (electoral system)
SPJ	Socialist Party of Japan
WG	Working Group (producing the Ikeo Report)
WT	Working Team (at MOF)

1

Did Japanese Politics Change in the 1990s?

Change or Continuity?

Did Japanese politics change in the 1990s? Numerous changes were evident in the political economy over the course of the decade. Most notably, the economy was no longer depicted as the wonder of the world, and, in 1993, the Liberal Democratic Party (LDP)—the ruling party since 1955—saw an end to its uninterrupted hold on power. The bureaucracy, once perceived as a power center of the activist state, also came under heavy fire amidst numerous policy failures and scandals, giving rise to the first major reorganization of the central government ministries since the postwar reforms of the 1940s. The list of major changes could go on and on.

Some observers nonetheless stress continuity in Japanese politics. Those skeptical of change point to the limitations of reforms implemented by longstanding institutions. When achieved, reforms were gradual—they argue—despite the need for deep-seated structural reform (Curtis 1999; Vogel 1999). On the other hand, those who concede that change has occurred tend to attribute the impetus for change to the 1994 electoral reforms, which introduced single-member election districts, thereby altering the electoral incentives of Diet members (Rosenbluth and Thies 1999).

Of course, elements of change and continuity coexist in any political economy. A primary empirical goal of this study is to establish which aspect—continuity or change—best explains outcomes in Japanese politics in the 1990s and which characterization provides the best basis for judging where Japanese politics is likely to head in the future. The study argues that Japanese politics has changed significantly since 1995, but due to reasons other than the 1994 electoral reforms. To make this point, we examine financial politics in the 1990s and the emergence of the Big Bang financial reforms in 1996.

The Japanese Financial Big Bang was a policy package introduced by the Japanese government in 1996, initiating massive deregulation and liberalization in the financial sector. Affected areas include the banking, securities, and insurance industries, as well as foreign exchange and accounting standards. Prime Minister Ryutaro Hashimoto unveiled the initiative in November 1996, and the Ministry of Finance (MOF) announced the detailed plan in June 1997. The reforms were to be carried out over a three-year period, starting in April 1998 with the deregulation of the control on foreign exchange, and to be completed by the year 2001 (See Table 1.1).

Table 1.1 The Big Bang initiative: a summary

Fields: *private finance*
Includes

- Banking (MOF Banking Bureau)
- Securities (MOF Securities Bureau)
- Insurance (MOF Insurance Department in Banking Bureau)
- Accounting (MOF Securities Bureau)
- Foreign exchange (MOF International Finance Bureau)

Excludes

- Fiscal Investment and Loan Program (MOF Financial Bureau)
- Postal savings (Ministry of Posts and Telecommunications)
- Pension fund (Ministry of Health and Welfare)

(*Note*: ministerial jurisdiction in parentheses)

Chronology: *a five-year plan, launched in 1996*

- *Nov. 1996* Hashimoto announces the Initiative (scope and deadline)
- *June 1997* MOF announces detailed plan for banking, securities and insurance
- *April 1998* 1st phase begins with the liberalization of foreign exchange controls
- *2001* Planned completion date

The Measures: *free, fair, and global*
1) Enhanced competition and reduced government control

- Liberalization of international capital transactions
- Product liberalization (securities, investment trusts, derivatives, loan securitization)
- Deregulation of cross-entry among banking, trust banking, securities, and insurance
- Removal of the ban on financial holding companies
- Liberalization of fixed brokerage commissions

2) Market development, fairness, and transparency

- Harmonization of accounting standards with international practices
- Stricter disclosure rules for banks and securities firms
- Creation of safety net for securities and insurance firms

Parallel Reforms in Finance:

- Creation of the FSA (Break-up of MOF)
- Full revision of the BOJ Law (increased central bank independence)
- Change in the style of financial administration (towards a rules-based system)

Many observers have stressed the pivotal importance of the financial system in the Japanese political economy,[1] and financial deregulation under the auspices of the Big Bang clearly had a significant impact on Japan's financial landscape in the latter half of the 1990s. The lifting of regulatory constraints resulted in a number of new products as well as newcomers to the market.[2] More importantly, financial firms altered their strategies significantly in anticipation of increased competition. While it was understood that financial liberalization would bring such changes at some time in the future, not many would have predicted—even as late as 1995—that the changes would occur at this time, be so broad in scope, or be carried out at such a rapid pace. Given the importance of finance to the political economy, drastic change in this sector has translated into significant change across the broader political economy. Although "continuity" seems to continue to overshadow "change" in policy areas such as agriculture and construction, even these sectors have been affected by the developments in financial politics emanating from the Big Bang.

Numerous accounts of the Big Bang have emerged both in Japan and abroad, reflecting the significance of this reform. Most accounts focus on the economic aspects of the Big Bang and on the projected impact of the reforms. In contrast, the present study seeks to explain the origins of the Big Bang, utilizing a political economy perspective that focuses on the incentives of the political actors in deciding economic policies with distributional effects.

Among existing arguments for why financial liberalization takes place are those that point to structural factors in the environment, such as an aging population, the global integration of national economies, and technological innovation. While such structural factors no doubt operated in the background of the drive for financial reforms in Japan, they alone cannot explain more specific dimensions of the Big Bang reforms, such as its timing (1996–97), scope (the "Big Bang" approach—encompassing private finance, yet excluding public finance), pace (completion by 2001—a specific deadline), or sequence (foreign exchange first, before proceeding to other areas). Actors in the political economy alter their behavior to reflect environmental changes but choices regarding many important details do not follow naturally from structural changes. The lack of consensus in Japan's policy world about the Big Bang initiative reflects this fact. Few contested the need for financial liberalization in Japan, but there were many conflicting views over the appropriate means of achieving it. Skeptics of the Big Bang package

---

[1] See for example, Zysman (1983) and Aoki and Patrick (1994).

[2] Asset management accounts were introduced, for example, and banks began selling investment trusts, a market traditionally dominated by the securities industry.

raised numerous concerns. Some argued that the timing of the Big Bang would "hit financial institutions while they were down," imposing hardships just as these firms were at their weakest and struggling to resolve their bad debt problems. Others protested that the scope of the Big Bang reforms was insufficient, the pace of reforms too slow, or that their sequencing would result in the massive outflow of assets from Japanese individual investors and thus lead to the "hollowing out" of the Japanese financial market.[3]

To understand why the Big Bang materialized at this time and with its particular scope, pace, and sequence, it is necessary to focus on the political questions of "Who gains?" and "Who loses?" Some actors may have seen the potential for economic gain via the Big Bang, while others may have seen the Big Bang as a means for the attainment of political goals. Who brought about the Big Bang? Answering this question requires us to delve into an even more fundamental question: what is so significant about the Big Bang? The Big Bang caused major changes in the financial landscape, but so did numerous regulatory reforms over the past thirty years, including the liberalization of the capital account and the opening up of the financial sector to foreign competition.[4]

The political, economic, and financial context of the Big Bang distinguished this package of reforms from those reforms that preceded it. The context, in turn, had a major impact on the final form the deregulation package took. Japan had a successful political economy for thirty years until the 1980s, achieving consistently higher economic growth rates than most other industrialized nations, as well as maintaining a stable political system. This achievement was based on a set of distinct, basic institutions in the political economy. In the economic realm, these included the main bank system, *keiretsu*, and lifetime employment; in the political realm, these institutions included one-party dominance by the LDP between 1955–93 and a large presence for the bureaucracy in policymaking. Japan experienced economic crisis in the 1990s, however. The economy stagnated, despite a short recovery in 1995–96, falling into negative growth in 1998. Unemployment steadily rose, and financial system problems led the banking sector to verge on total collapse in 1997–98.

Many changes in the financial system prior to and paralleling the Big Bang also contributed to the emergence of the new reform initiative. Let us briefly review the course of events. Beginning in the mid-1980s, financial liberalization was carried out gradually under the careful guidance of MOF,

---

[3] See Saito (1997), Suzuki (1997), Horiuchi (1998), and Nishimura (1999) on these points.
[4] See economist Yukio Noguchi's view, presented in Chapter 8.

whose main concern was to maintain financial system stability. In practical terms, this meant that the ministry's primary concern was with preventing bank failure at all costs. Piecemeal liberalization centered on interest rates and the corporate bond market, eliminating some of the rents that the banking industry enjoyed under the postwar regulatory system that had essentially allowed no financial institution to fail. Dubbed the "convoy system," this system was meticulously maintained by MOF through the compartmentalization of the financial sector into separate banking, securities, and insurance business areas—and additional segmentation within the banking and insurance sectors—even in the face of globalizing pressures. A half-hearted effort to break down the barriers separating business areas in finance only emerged in 1993 (Ikeo 1995; Horiuchi 1998).

As a result, heavily regulated financial firms lost incentives to innovate and became largely inefficient during the 1990s, compared to their counterparts in the United States and the United Kingdom, where deregulation efforts were carried out earlier, faster, and more comprehensively. The "hollowing-out" of financial services followed, with market players leaving the Tokyo market for New York, London, Hong Kong, or Singapore. The banking industry also failed to come to terms in a timely manner with its bad lending and investment decisions made during the bubble economy of the 1980s, and delays in addressing the bad debt that resulted with the bursting of the bubble led to the further accumulation of huge amounts of bad loans.[5] Inadequate monitoring of financial firms further exacerbated problems, as the MOF lacked the ability to enforce adequate regulations, including prudential regulation (Ueda and Fukao 1996; Horiuchi 1998).

The Japanese financial system became increasingly unstable from 1995, with the emergence of bank failures, policy failures, and scandals. In the summer of 1995, the failure of several small financial institutions reflected the instability in the financial system. In the fall of 1995, huge losses incurred by a bond dealer in New York evolved into a cover-up scandal by Daiwa Bank that extended to the MOF, when ministry officials failed to promptly notify US authorities of the situation. The result was the eviction of Daiwa from the US market and heavy public criticism of MOF. In the winter of 1995–96, the first decision to inject public money to deal with a financial mess created by housing loan companies,[6] banks and agricultural

---

[5] The bad debt was centered primarily in industries that attracted speculative investment, such as real estate and construction.

[6] Housing loan companies are non-bank financial firms that originally specialized in making housing loans to individuals, but became heavily involved in real estate development loans during the bubble years of the 1980s.

cooperatives spurred great political debate and led to the Housing Loan (*Jusen*) Affair. The result again was a public uproar—this time against MOF, the LDP, and the banking industry. Meanwhile, wining and dining scandals enveloped MOF and were widely reported in the mass media. Trust in the financial system hit an all-time low, leading to a universal call for structural reforms in finance.

Many observers of the Japanese political economy have put forth explanations of the aforementioned developments (Gibney 1998; Horiuchi 1998; Curtis 1999; Vogel 1999).[7] Most provide a story line that emphasizes the forces of institutional inertia and entrenched political interests and might be summarized as follows. The basic institutions that supported the economic success of the high growth period and political stability were kept essentially intact with only very incremental reforms introduced in hopes of overcoming the economic slump—deemed to be temporary. Economic stagnation persisted, however, in spite of these gradual reforms, eventually lending credence to the view that problems in the political economy were deep-rooted rather than mere reflections of temporary adjustment problems. Japan needed drastic, structural reforms rather than incremental, gradual reforms. Even so, far-reaching reforms were slow to emerge because of such structural impediments as institutional inertia and entrenched interests. The bureaucracy and/or the LDP posed the greatest impediments, being concerned above all with maintaining the status quo and the privileged status of their respective organizations.

The present study takes issue with the aforementioned interpretation in two respects. First, we contest the way in which change in Japanese finance is equated in this depiction with "correcting" the Japanese system's deviation from market economy principles. We offer instead an alternative depiction of change drawing on the Comparative Institutional Analysis (CIA) approach. This approach delves into the reasons behind the diversity of economic systems around the world and thus departs from the neoclassical view that implicitly assumes the convergence of all economies into the "market economy" model (Aoki 2001). The institutions that comprise Japanese finance existed for particular reasons in their heyday; while these institutions may be changing, we need an interpretive framework to explain this change that does not rely purely on *ex post* blame of actors for failing to bring about the necessary "regime change" (Horiuchi 1998) in finance at an earlier time. As mentioned previously,

---

[7] Similar views are also widespread in the journalistic literature. See, for example, Hartcher (1998) and Katz (1998).

while the pro-liberalization direction of reform may have been clear throughout the process, the question of how to proceed was much less clear. Thus, an analysis of the politics of financial reforms is necessary to understand why particular outcomes resulted. We need an alternative causal framework that allows us to make sense of the causal interaction between the Big Bang and the environment.

Our second objection is raised against the image of non-change widely shared among observers of Japanese politics. While regulatory reforms were indeed gradual and the bureaucracy and the LDP did not act to introduce drastic reforms until the mid-1990s, drastic, structural reforms transforming numerous basic institutions took place thereafter. The Big Bang experience suggests that state actors—namely, politicians and bureaucrats—displayed patterns of behavior after 1995 different from those observed over most of the postwar era. Instead of seeking the perpetuation of the status quo, as might be expected given their image as entrenched actors, the MOF and LDP pushed for drastic reforms. This shift may have important implications for future regulatory reforms in other fields of the political economy and for reform in countries outside Japan. What makes actors behave in such a way? If institutional inertia and entrenched interests can be expected to hinder drastic regulatory reforms in general, then the Big Bang is clearly a rare case of drastic reform and the conditions that enabled the emergence of this reform package deserve attention.

The remainder of this introductory chapter proceeds as follows. The next section introduces the research puzzles that arise from the political actors' behavior observed in the Big Bang. We then turn to the methodology employed in the study and briefly summarize the main research findings. The chapter concludes with an overview of the structure of the book.

Research Puzzles

The Big Bang poses an anomaly to the conventional understanding of the Japanese political economy that sees gradualism in reforms. The gradualism widely observed until the mid-1990s does not seem to hold in two respects. First, while the Big Bang initiative was carried out largely under the guidance of MOF, as in past financial reforms, it was wider in scope than past reforms, spanning across five financial areas, and reached "deeper," including measures that drastically hurt the prospect of survival for some financial firms.[8] Previous reforms, such as those implemented in 1991–93, centered only on banking and securities and resulted in incomplete, gradual cross-entry by financial firms into new business areas.

Second, and more importantly, the initiative did not evolve from the informal bargaining process among actors which characterized public policymaking in postwar Japan—a steady pattern that observers conceptualized as "bureaupluralism" (Aoki 1988), "patterned pluralism" (Muramatsu and Krauss 1987), "compartmentalized pluralism" (Sato and Matsuzaki 1986), and "bureaucratic-inclusive pluralism" (Inoguchi 1983). The Big Bang initiative first came to be known publicly when Prime Minister Hashimoto announced it within two weeks of the LDP victory in the Lower House elections of October 1996, taking many by surprise. Thus, the initiative did not originate from what we call the institution of "bureaupluralism," where public policies are produced from a consensus-making process organized by the bureaucrats, involving the regulated industries and the affiliated LDP politicians ("tribesmen"), centering around such policymaking bodies as the deliberative councils in the government and the LDP Policy Affairs Research Council (PARC) apparatus.

These observations lead us to ask what made the Big Bang different from past attempts to reform the financial system. This can be developed into four questions, each related to one of the key actors in financial politics: the bureaucracy, financial firms, politicians, and consumers of financial services.

First, evidence suggests that MOF was more than willing to launch this initiative. MOF discreetly prepared for it beginning in early 1996, and presented a proposal to Hashimoto, who adopted the ministry's plan as his Initiative. Notably, this initiative was expected to bring about negative consequences for MOF in two respects. First, it stripped away from the agency many regulatory tools. These tools were of more than nominal importance, holding historical importance and including tools of control over foreign exchange and over entry into the securities business. The Big Bang was also expected to sever MOF's close ties with financial firms, which long served to provide information, facilitate cooperation in public administration, and provide positions for retiring ministry officials. By introducing fierce competition into finance and undermining many financial institutions' prospects for survival, these ties would no doubt be disrupted.

---

[8] For example, the reforms included the liberalization of brokerage fees, which threatened the previously guaranteed profits of brokerages, and abolished legal quasi-cartels in the casualty insurance industry.

If we follow conventional accounts of bureaucratic behavior, which focus on the bureaucrats' maximization of tokens of power—such as the budget, regulatory power, or discretionary power—(Niskanen 1971; Kato 1994; Vogel 1996; Amyx 1998), we would expect MOF to resist, or to at least forestall such reforms that diminish its regulatory and jurisdictional power. What made MOF willing instead to launch the initiative?

Alternately, we might hypothesize that the Big Bang was a plot by the Ministry of International Trade and Industry (MITI). Some, including developmental state proponents (Johnson 1982), describe this ministry as pushing for all-out deregulation of the Japanese economy from the early 1990s. Might the Big Bang be a product of MITI trying to pry into MOF's jurisdiction over finance?

Puzzle 1) Why was MOF willing to propose and carry out the Big Bang? More generally, what makes a bureaucracy willing to abandon tokens of organizational power such as regulatory power and beneficial networks? Or, was the Big Bang MITI's plot and essentially the manifestation of a bureaucratic turf war?

Second, many point out the great influence of financial institutions in Japanese financial politics (Rosenbluth 1989; Calder 1993). Indeed, the weaker financial institutions (as opposed to the powerful, large city banks), especially the securities firms and the long-term credit and trust banks, appeared to successfully forestall past attempts by MOF to launch financial reforms (e.g. the 1979–82 banking reforms, the 1991–93 financial reforms). Because increased competition negatively affects these weaker financial firms that were the beneficiaries of the heavy segmentation of finance, their positions on financial reform might be expected to remain constant. What made the Big Bang different from financial reforms in the past?

Puzzle 2) Why were financial industry actors unable to forestall the Big Bang as they had past reforms?

Third, there appears to have been a steady alliance between the ruling LDP and the permanent bureaucracy during the one-party dominance period between 1955 and 1993 (Aoki 1988; Okimoto 1989). While the Big Bang was launched by the LDP Prime Minister and received the full support of the LDP and MOF, paralleling developments in finance—such as the breakup of MOF and the creation of the Financial Supervisory Agency (FSA) in June 1998, as well as the revision of the Bank of Japan (BOJ) Law in 1997 giving greater independence from MOF to the central bank—suggest that the once steady alliance between the LDP and MOF underwent a major change. In the past, the LDP was known to endorse wildly unpopular proposals by MOF even at the risk of electoral defeat. The twenty-year process that led to the introduction of the consumption tax in 1989 attests to this fact (Kato 1994). This time, however, when MOF suffered from a bad reputation among the general public as a result of various scandals and its economic mismanagement in the mid- to late-1990s, the LDP decided to part ways with the ministry.

Puzzle 3) How can we explain the LDP's behavior of supporting the Big Bang while making decisions that drastically undermined MOF's presence in finance? What happened to the seemingly stable LDP–MOF alliance of the postwar era?

Fourth, the Big Bang may represent a pivotal change in Japanese public administration in that it explicitly benefits consumers over producers—or, more specifically, the users over the providers of financial services. The Japanese political system has often been seen as one in which the interests of the providers are over-represented at the expense of the interests of the consumers or the general public (Okimoto 1989; Vogel 1999). Here, the "users" who may benefit from more efficient financial services can be either non-financial firms or the general public. There may be a possibility that the non-financial firms saw their interests effectively represented by MITI, forming a counter-coalition against the financial sector and MOF. Or, it may be that the general public found ways to effectively represent their interests through a mechanism that overrides, substitutes, or supplements the "bureaupluralism" model of interest representation. Might this influence of the public come via elections, as a result of the newly introduced single-member district (SMD), as some proponents of electoral rational choice such as Rosenbluth and Thies (1999) might claim?

Puzzle 4) How can we understand the new, user-friendly orientation of the Big Bang vis-à-vis "bureaupluralism" against the backdrop of the provider-friendly model of the past? Is the Big Bang a victory of a counter-coalition of the corporate sector and MITI over the financial sector and MOF? Or, does it represent a victory for the consumers, brought about by the 1994 electoral reforms? Or, is there another better explanation?

Methodological Approach and Theoretical Framework

The methodology we use to tackle the aforementioned research puzzle has 3 pillars. The first is a rational-actor approach, which considers the (boundedly) rational calculations of actors as the main explanatory factor of political outcomes resulting from the strategic interaction of actors. This approach starts from the simple assumption that organizations seek survival and conducts analysis at the level of organizations and sub-organizational groups. To explain organizational behavior, we introduce the distinction between organizational survival as the "ultimate" goal, and other "ceteris paribus" goals such as the maximization of tokens of organizational power. Our focus is on the interaction of actors rather than on a fixed pattern of domination, such as bureaucratic dominance. We introduce a model of strategic interaction that distinguishes the state actors (politicians and bureaucrats) and the societal actors (firms and interest groups, and the public) according to whether they enjoy direct or indirect access to governmental power. We propose that both politicians and bureaucrats seek the support of the two sets of societal actors. In so doing, we challenge assumptions underlying conventional theories of the bureaucracy, noted earlier, and theories of regulation, wherein politics is driven by organized groups.[9]

Second, unlike many past works focused on the apparent stability of Japanese politics, we focus on change by developing a framework of institutional change. We define institutions in terms of collective perceptions about "how the world works" and characterize institutional change as an evolutionary process leading to a shift in shared perceptions. We then link this framework to politics, or to distributional conflicts among actors, examining what drives institutional change ("failures"), what leads actors to change their perceptions (their "forecasts" and "distributional calculations"), as well as how a status quo coalition can be displaced ("defection" from the inside or emergence of a "counter-coalition" from the outside).

Under this overarching framework, we develop several theoretical frameworks. We introduce the logic of organizational survival, in which sub-organizational groups with different views and interests about institutional change compete for the control of their organizations, and we use this logic to explain the behavior of the LDP and MOF. Moreover, we construct a typology of how financial reforms can take place. This guides the empirical analysis. A new look at the role of the public in politics is proposed, where "public support," rather than objective "public interest," plays a larger role in not only influencing politicians through elections but also bureaucrats and interest groups.

---

[9] We refer here to economic theories of regulation, such as the theory depicted by Peltzman (1998). See Chapter 2 for details.

·Third, we seek to improve the link between theory and empirical data through three means: comparison, analytic narrative, and alternative explanations. To this end, we present a longitudinal comparison of financial reforms: three cases prior to the Big Bang and one case that follows the Big Bang. Doing so enables us to construct an image of change across cases sharing many similarities, including the same actors and institutional settings. We also construct an analytic narrative (Bates et al. 1998) by offering a preliminary theoretical account, then revising it through a dialog between theory and data. We contrast our account against alternative explanations, derived from the existing literature, in an effort to increase the plausibility of our explanation.

We begin the empirical analysis with the case of the Big Bang, focusing on the November 1996 initiative announced by Prime Minister Hashimoto and on the June 1997 detailed plan announced by MOF. After analyzing the emergence of the Big Bang initiative and the implementation process that followed, we introduce three cases of financial reforms in the 1980s and 1990s to show how the two worlds (i.e. before and after 1995) differ from one another.

Having obtained general observations about political developments surrounding regulatory reforms in private finance, we compare and contrast these observations with features of another case in the realm of financial policymaking that took place after the Big Bang: the Financial Diet of 1998. Although focused on financial crisis management rather than on regulatory reforms, this Diet session represented a major step towards the resolution of the bad debt problem in the Japanese banking sector by producing schemes for the nationalization and forced re-capitalization of troubled banks. This case enables us to confirm the assertion that the public policymaking process observed in the Big Bang reflects a new post-1995 trend of drastically changed dynamics, rather than a mere one-time deviation from past policymaking patterns.

To further strengthen the link between theory and our empirical cases, we develop a four-by-two typology of financial reforms, focusing on the evolution of coalitions and the way state actors interact with societal actors. The evolution of coalitions yields four categories (status quo, inclusion, defection, and replacement) along a continuum, regarding who can participate in public policymaking. In "status quo," "insiders" remain in charge; in "inclusion," some "outsiders" see their interests incorporated while the policymaking process itself remains intact; in "defection," some "insiders" switch strategies and "go around" the established policymaking process; and in "replacement," "outsiders" take over, eliminating the

Interaction of state and societal actors

		Interest group politics (I)	Public interest politics (P)
Evolution of coalition patterns	Status quo (S)	**Past financial reforms** *(Domestic financial firms)*	
	Inclusion (C)	**Postwar LDP politics** *(Non-banks and foreign firms)*	
	Defection (D)	*(Some financial firms)*	*The Big Bang (LDP and MOF)*
	Replacement (R)	*(Corporate sector)*	*(LDP thrown out)*

Notes:

In Parentheses: "Who Brought About the Big Bang?"
Shaded: Institutional change (departure from bureaupluralism)

I: state actors act as a result of interest group pressure
P: state actors act independently of interest group pressure

S: same policymaking process, insiders only (e.g. domestic financial firms)
C: same policymaking process, inclusion of outsiders (e.g. non-banks)
D: different process, led by insiders switching strategies (e.g. LDP and MOF)
R: different process, outsiders displacing insiders (e.g. change of government)

Figure 1.1 Typology of financial reforms

status quo policymaking mechanism. We find two patterns of state actors' interaction with societal actors: "interest group politics," in which state actors act based on the exchange of goods and services with interest groups, and "public interest politics," in which state actors act independently of interest group pressure (see Figure 1.1). The empirical analysis of the case studies establishes that within our four-by-two typology of financial reforms, the Big Bang fits the one that combines "defection" ("insiders" such as MOF and the LDP in charge) and "public interest politics" (as opposed to "interest group politics"). This enables us to offer insights with relevance to other cases of regulatory reforms.

Argument in Brief

The book's main contention is that Japanese politics has changed since 1995. There has been an institutional change, or a shift in the shared expectations about "how the world works," in two pivotal institutions in financial politics developed over the postwar era. The Convoy System in finance has broken down, and the public policymaking mechanism of bureaupluralism is in decay. Accordingly, cooperation, stability, and continuity have ceased to prevail in the post-1995 world. Moreover, the decay in bureaupluralism is likely to extend to the wider political economy, as the causal factors of changes in financial politics, "performance failures and scandals," and "possibility of change in government," are salient to other policy areas as well.

The book also argues that the Big Bang was the product of strategic interaction between the LDP and MOF and an increased role played by the public in policymaking. In making this argument, we contend that the Big Bang initiative was *not*:

1) A pre-designed and coordinated initiative by a single bureaucratic agency;

2) The result of financial institutions' domination of financial politics;

3) The result of politicians overcoming or subduing bureaucrats;

4) The result of the non-financial firms (and MITI) gaining the upper hand of MOF and financial industries; or

5) An achievement by the LDP backbenchers promoting consumerism as a result of the 1994 electoral reform introducing a SMD.

Rather, the LDP and MOF brought about the Big Bang, seeing political gains in obtaining public support independently from the exchange of goods and services with their constituents. Their strategic interaction through the logic of organizational survival explains the process of financial politics in 1995–96. As the loss of public trust amidst performance failures and scandals (e.g. the Housing Loan Affair) was what brought the threat to their survival, the LDP and MOF sought to recoup public trust by enhancing public interest over constituents' interest. The views held by the sub-organizational groups within the LDP and MOF that won in the policy contest were those rewarded by the environment (continued public criticism due to recurrent failures; and increased probability of change of government). As long as survival was the ultimate goal for all members, whatever was perceived to increase the prospect of survival eventually became organizational policy. Our framework stressing the strategic interaction of actors enables us to understand the complexity of the relationship between the LDP and MOF in 1995–96: cooperation (the Housing Loan Affair), competition (the Big Bang), and conflict (MOF reforms). The timing of the Big Bang reflected Hashimoto's reform agenda at the beginning of his second Cabinet; the pace and the scope reflected the fact that MOF planned the content; and, the sequence reflected the field in financial policymaking controlled by the "reformers" within MOF and the "mavericks" within the LDP.

The domestic financial institutions were, on the whole, unable to effectively oppose the reforms, which threatened their survival through increased competition. This becomes clear through a comparison with previous financial reforms. While financial industry actors influenced the pace of the Big Bang reforms, they failed to significantly influence the timing (commencement in April 1998 and complete implementation by 2001) or the scope (such as the inclusion of the insurance sector). Because those who conceived of the Big Bang bypassed the regulated industry actors in the planning phase, financial firms were only able to respond to the Initiative once it had already been made public. Political leadership by Hashimoto made it hard for industry organizations to campaign through the LDP and public support of the reforms markedly raised the cost of assembling a counter-coalition. The financial scandals drastically weakened the political clout financial industries might otherwise have drawn on to forestall the reforms. The subsequent scandals propelled the Big Bang further because the initiative became symbolic of a move away from the Convoy System, which by then was discredited by the financial crisis.

Our empirical analysis of various financial reforms in the 1980s and 1990s finds that the essence of the new developments in financial politics since 1995 (including the Big Bang) is that the public now matters as a determinant of financial politics in a world of financial crisis where changes of government can occur. The most significant change in financial politics since 1995 is not so much the altered financial landscape itself (after all, alterations in the landscape occurred to varying degrees in the past), as it is the shift in the public policymaking process towards greater inclusiveness. Public policymaking once carried out via the mechanism of bureaupluralism—a mechanism that excluded "outsiders"—has increasingly permitted these "outsiders" to bypass this mechanism when they are able to obtain public support.

A third major contention of the book is that there has been institutional change in financial politics since 1995 and that this change is represented by the breakdown of the Convoy System and the decay of bureaupluralism. Both were institutional cornerstones of the pre-1995 system. The Convoy System was one in which all financial institutions proceeded at the same speed as the slowest firm, just as in a naval convoy. The Convoy was maintained via regulatory rules segmenting financial businesses and restricting entry and exit, the reliance on informal policy tools for governmental regulation, and shared expectations that cooperation and stability

15

would prevail. "Cooperation" refers here to relations between such insiders as the MOF, the LDP, and domestic financial firms, while "stability" refers to the continuity of existing arrangements. Bureaupluralism was a steady bargaining process involving a stable pattern of informal interactions among the same set of actors over time—the bureaucracy, financial firms, and the LDP—but guaranteed and reinforced by formal rules and sustained by shared expectations of "continuity" or that the policymaking process would always remain the same.

Change in these two institutions came about when they were slow to respond to rapid exogenous developments, such as technological innovation and financial globalization, leading to the emergence of performance failures and scandals in finance. This development occurred on the backdrop of simultaneous change in the institutional environment, represented foremost by a change of government in 1993 and a more prominent role for the public in politics. The result was institutional change in finance and public policymaking. With the Convoy System, this meant a shift in the fundamental principles recognized by all actors as objective characteristics or normative values of the institution. The shift was from "cooperation and stability" to "competition and transparency." The Big Bang triggered and was triggered by—as well as reinforced by—other shifts in the same direction of breakdown occurring in the Convoy System in finance.

In the area of public policymaking, bureaupluralism is clearly in decay. Reflecting the collapse of shared expectations of "continuity," actors have started to question the worth of this institution. While it remains to be seen whether full-scale institutional change will emerge here or not, we predict, based on our causal framework, that institutional change is likely for two reasons. First, experiments in bypassing this policymaking mechanism have been on the rise and the conditions that make the role of the public more salient in politics persist—namely, the presence of "failures" and the potential for a change in government. Thus, the shared expectations of continuity are likely to further weaken, leading bureaupluralism to erode over time.

The study's findings provide a number of insights into regulatory reform in other contexts. First, they suggest that entrenched actors may not always be as entrenched as they initially seem. Our analysis shows that such seemingly "entrenched actors" as the LDP and MOF willingly engaged in efforts of deregulation when faced with a new set of incentive structures (the loss of public support and threat to organizational survival). The image of the past may be misleading, as the past does not necessarily prohibit future shifts in strategy.

The study's introduction of a hierarchy of goals (where survival is ranked above all others) helps establish this truism and leads to more realistic behavioral assumptions for the bureaucracy. One may, of course, expect an internal struggle within an organization prior to a major policy shift. Yet, the logic of organizational survival sheds light on the mechanism through which a single organizational policy is formed, enabling us to account for the seemingly puzzling behavior by MOF, which planned the give-away of its regulatory power, or by the LDP, which engaged in a complex relationship with MOF in the financial politics of 1995–97.

Second, the findings given previously suggest that the public's control over politicians through elections may not be the only way the public influences politics. Elections certainly matter to political parties: the Big Bang experience confirms this generally accepted view, as it emerged partly out of the LDP's strategy for dealing with tough competition from its rivals in the 1996 elections. However, we stress that not only the politicians, but also bureaucrats and regulated industry actors have incentives to cater to the general public to boost public support. "Failures" lessen public support for the organization at the level of competence ("performance failures") and ethics ("scandals"). It is when "failures" occur and organizations become "public enemies," such as in the case of polluting firms or corrupt bureaucrats and politicians, that such incentives to promote the public interest become salient. When organizational survival is in danger, actors will pursue this ultimate goal. The public need not engage in direct action, such as a boycott or mass protests, to wield political influence. This is because politicians, bureaucrats, and industry actors risk losing political influence regarding matters in their respective interests when they become "public enemies."

In these ways, our model of strategic interaction among actors gives us an improved characterization of the role of the public in politics. It questions the conventional assumption that societal interests can only have significant political influence through organized groups. It also sheds light on modes of public influence other than through the principal-agent relationship linking voters and legislators.

The study's development of a four-by-two typology of financial reforms, focusing on the evolution of coalitions and the way state actors interact with societal actors, further deepens our understanding of the strategic interaction among actors, inside and outside of the Japanese context. We show that the evolution of coalitions yields four categories (status quo, inclusion, defection, and replacement) along a continuum, with regard to who can participate in public policymaking. In "status quo", "insiders" remain in charge; in "inclusion", some "outsiders" see their interests incorporated while the policymaking process itself remains intact; in "defection", some "insiders" switch strategies and "go around" the established policymaking process; and in "replacement", "outsiders" take over, eliminating the status quo policymaking mechanism. Two patterns emerge for state actors interaction with societal actors: "interest group politics", in which state actors act based on the exchange of goods and services with interest groups, and "public interest politics", in which state actors act independently of interest group pressure (see Figure 1.1).

Finally, the study's findings suggest that such factors in domestic politics as "failures," "public visibility," and "electoral vitality," along with such economic factors as "technological innovation," "global integration," and "institutional environment," may help us determine the likelihood of economic reforms in other issue areas. While our findings may be more relevant to areas of economic regulatory reforms rather than to areas more directly related to budgetary politics, the study nonetheless produces candidates for determinants of economic reform in general by constructing a rudimentary two-level model of domestic politics and the economic environment that may be employed outside the area of financial policymaking.

Structure of the Book

Part I (Chapters 2–4) provides conceptual tools and background information in preparation for later analysis. In Chapter 2, we offer a survey of the existing literature on Japanese politics, financial politics, and the Big Bang, from which we derive our approach and the concerns to be addressed. We outline our methodology in response and build alternative explanations concerning the question of "Who brought about the Big Bang?" for later use in Part II.

In Chapter 3, we have two tasks. First, we introduce our theoretical frameworks of institutional change and organizational survival that we utilize in later chapters to make sense of the development in financial politics. Second, we construct possible scenarios regarding financial reforms, by identifying the actors and deriving their preferences based on observed behavioral regularities. We will see how our starting assumption—that organizations seek survival—applies more broadly to actors in the political economy in general. These actors include political parties, bureaucratic agencies, and firms and interest groups. Through this process, we identify the institutions in Japanese finance (the Convoy) and public policymaking (bureaupluralism) that prevailed until the first half of the 1990s.

In Chapter 4, we explore the projected economic impact of the Big Bang at the time the Initiative was announced. The chapter discusses what the initiative included and what it implied for actors in the financial market. This leads us to grasp the distributive impact of the reforms, or who the "winners" and the "losers" were perceived to be. We will see that the Big Bang was expected to bring negative results to almost all domestic financial firms, who comprised an important "insider" component of the formerly stable policymaking process of bureaupluralism.

Part II (Chapters 5–7) provides an empirical analysis of financial politics. Chapter 5 analyzes the politics surrounding the emergence of the Big Bang through November 1996, when the initiative was first launched. The question of "Who brought it about, and why?" is the focus of our inquiry. We show how the logic of organizational survival worked to bring it about: MOF and the LDP—in cooperation, competition, and confrontation with one another in financial politics—saw political benefits to be reaped from the reforms and thus acted to move forward the initiative.

In Chapter 6, which analyzes the process in which the initiative of November 1996 was embodied and implemented, the Big Bang is contrasted with three cases of past financial reforms (1991–93, 1992–94, and 1979–82) to assess the extent of change the Big Bang has brought about. The focus is on the influence of regulated industry actors—the economic "losers" from the Big Bang—on public policymaking. We assess how much influence they had on the outcome as well as explain their inability to reverse the Big Bang reforms, given their past record of exercising significant political clout.

In Chapter 7, we proceed from financial reforms to financial politics in general, to find out what can be said about the new developments in financial politics since 1995. To achieve this goal, we examine the case of the Financial Diet of 1998, an extraordinary legislative session held to deal with the bad debt problem in banking. Doing so enables us to confirm that the new developments observed in the case of the Big Bang represent a more general trend in financial politics, evident since 1995. This trend is one in which the public matters more than ever before in the policymaking process.

Part III (Chapters 8 and 9), our concluding section, seeks to make sense of the developments analyzed in Part II by returning to the analytical frameworks developed in Part I. Chapter 8 situates the Big Bang in finance and in the political economy in general. We utilize the framework of "institutional change," introduced in Chapter 3, to understand the larger changes taking place in finance. We show the causal mechanism through which the observed changes in financial politics occurred, while demonstrating how the components of the Financial Convoy related to one another, triggering the breakdown of the Convoy. In the end, we observe the breakdown of the Convoy and the decay of bureaupluralism, and offer a prediction on the future of the latter.

Chapter 9 probes the applicability of our findings to other cases in the political economy, generating hypotheses about the determinants of regulatory reform in general. It also discusses the policy implications of the analysis and identifies further issues ripe for additional research.

Part I

Analytical Framework

2

A Rational Actor Approach

This chapter expounds upon ideas introduced in Chapter 1 and begins to lay a more formidable theoretical groundwork for the empirical analysis contained in Part II. The chapter first provides an overview of the existing literature on Japanese politics, with our case of interest—Japanese financial politics in the 1990s—in mind. We identify three issues of contention in the various approaches to Japanese politics and explain how these debates help inform the study's research design. We then provide a brief review of the literature that focuses more specifically on Japanese financial politics and the Big Bang financial reforms, noting five sets of concerns or questions that emerge from these studies. These help to further inform the present study's methodological approach. The chapter closes by suggesting five alternative explanations for the emergence of the Big Bang reforms, against which we weigh our explanation in later chapters.

Three Contentious Issues in Japanese Politics

Three main issues of contention may be identified in the various approaches to the study of Japanese politics. First, the literature reveals a tension between actor-oriented and institution-oriented studies; second, the literature reveals a tension between those studies focused on change and those focused on stability; and, third, the literature reveals a tension between those studies that emphasize dominance and those that emphasize interaction of a less hierarchical nature.

Actor-oriented vs. Institution-oriented Studies

Studies of institutions in the social science literature typically begin analysis at the level of individual actors (an actor-oriented approach) or begin instead with the analysis of institutional structures (an institution-oriented approach).[1] In actor-oriented approaches, the actors and their preferences are considered beyond the scope of explanation, and the social scientist seeks to explain the institutions that shape human behavior. This methodological orientation, dominant in the study of economics, can be seen in the rational choice analysis of political institutions: the emphasis is on how the institutions reflect actors' interests and structure their incentives and strategies, while the preference of actors is taken as given.[2] In institution-oriented approaches, on the other hand, the institutional structures are what explain the actors and their behavior. Historical institutionalism in political science adopts this latter position, often shared in sociological studies. Here the emphasis is on how institutional structures shape actors' preferences and constrain their behavior.[3]

In the study of Japanese politics, the latter approach has traditionally dominated. Many theorists place historically developed institutional structures at the center of their explanatory frameworks (Johnson 1982; Samuels 1987; Calder 1988).[4] Typically, these scholars put forward an analytical concept that summarizes the essence of the complex set of institutional structures (e.g. Johnson's "developmental state" or Samuels' "reciprocal consent"). A typology of possible arrangements, such as Johnson's "plan rational" and "market rational" categorizations is also sometimes offered. Then, a detailed process tracing of the historical development of one or more cases is used to establish the validity of such conceptualizations. The emphasis in such studies is on delving into causal complexity rather than on determining a single cause for the observed outcome. Thus, the analytical orientation is more inductive than deductive.[5]

The principal strength of such an approach lies in its empirical accuracy: the methodology dictates that the researcher grasps his/her cases very thoroughly in making theoretical assertions. This attention to historical,

---

[1] For the distinction between the two approaches, see Steinmo, Thelen, and Longstreth (1992), Scott (1995), Bates et al. (1998), and Krasner (1999).

[2] For a rational choice analysis, see for example, essays in Alt and Shepsle (1990). Levi (1997) provides a summary of this methodology's strengths and weaknesses. In economics, the actor-oriented neoclassical approach has dominated the field for a long time. See Scott (1995: Chapter 1).

[3] For historical institutionalism in general, see for example, Steinmo, Thelen, and Longstreth (1992), Katzenstein (1978), Skocpol (1985), and Karl (1997). The new institutionalism in sociology shares this institutions-oriented approach. See, for example, essays by Meyer and Rowan, and DiMaggio and Powell, collected in Powell and DiMaggio (1991).

[4] See also Calder (1993), Woodall (1994), Vogel (1996), Pempel (1998), Katzenstein (1978), and Zysman (1983).

[5] For example, Samuels (1987: 285) rejects mono-causal explanations and argues that multi-causal explanations "predict little but explain much."

social, cultural, and other contexts reduces the risk of making erroneous assertions based on false empirical data: the reliance on extensive archival research and interviews protects against significant deviation from empirical realities. Nonetheless, this approach has several weaknesses. First, because the emphasis is on detailed case studies and the analysis is inductive in nature, the theoretical findings are often applicable only to the specific case at hand and have little potential for generalization to other cases. Second, while the theoretical findings may indeed provide a realistic image of how things evolved to the present, the causal mechanism and the micro-level incentive structures are often left unclear because of the very emphasis on causal complexity. The inductive nature of the theory may also mean the scholar fails to clearly specify the causal mechanism, making the findings less amenable to verification by others. Behavioral assumptions about actor objectives and their incentive structures under strategic settings are often ill-defined, making them vulnerable to *post hoc* explanation. Third, a corollary of vagueness in the causal mechanism is that such studies often have little potential to provide the basis for predictions about future outcomes or behavior. Prediction is a difficult task for all social scientists; nonetheless, prediction does enable the academic to have more relevance to the policy world.

Actor-oriented approaches in the study of Japanese politics first appeared in the 1990s, in the form of rational choice analysis (Ramseyer and Rosenbluth 1993; Cowhey and McCubbins 1995; Kohno 1997).[6] Applying the principal-agent framework developed in transaction cost economics and the rational choice analysis of American politics, theorists would seek to explain such topics as electoral politics, postwar party politics (Kohno 1997), and the legislative control over the bureaucracy and/or the judiciary in public policymaking (Ramseyer and Rosenbluth 1993; Cowhey and McCubbins 1995). The theoretical emphasis is on the individual actors' incentive structures, which are derived from behavioral assumptions such as that politicians pursue reelection in strategic settings, which are defined by the formal and informal institutions that comprise the "rules of the game." These institutions include laws, constitutions,

---

[6] In economic analyses of the Japanese political economy, the actor-oriented approach is, of course, the norm. Economic studies of Japanese finance include, for example (in English) Hamada and Horiuchi (1987), Aoki (1988), Aoki and Patrick (1994), Aoki, Kim, and Okuno-Fujiwara (1997), and Hoshi and Kashyap (1999); (in Japanese), studies include Ikeo (1995), Ueda and Fukao (1996), and Horiuchi (1999). However, relatively little attention has been placed on the political struggle between actors. In other words, the politics of distributional conflict is largely absent from all but a few. Exceptions include Aoki, Kim and Okuno-Fujiwara (1997).

seniority rule and so forth.[7] The orientation of this approach is deductive: the behavioral assumptions and the constraints set by the institutions lead the theorist to deduce a set of hypotheses, which are confirmed (or disconfirmed) via a narrative of empirical cases. In this approach, such causal factors as electoral rules (e.g. single- versus multi-member districts—SMD versus MMD), regime types (presidential or parliamentary), or the veto power of legislators over bureaucrats is purported to explain the political outcomes. These "rules of the game," which actors try to manipulate to pursue their own goals, define the incentive structures of these actors. In this way, the rules of the game determine the outcomes of strategic interaction.

The strengths of the rational choice approach are the weakness of the historical institutionalist approach and vice versa. The first strength of the rational choice approach is that its theoretical frameworks are better suited to generalization across cases. The universalistic behavioral assumptions and micro-level analysis of individual incentives (e.g. politicians pursue reelection, which can be expected to hold across democracies), with little emphasis on country-specific historical, social, or cultural context, make the findings from the analysis easier to connect to cases in other countries (but this can be a weakness as well: see later). For example, if the behavioral assumptions do not vary significantly across cases, then, the variations in political outcomes could be attributed to variation in political institutions. Second, rational choice analysis excels in theoretical rigor and clarity. The assumptions, as well as the process of deriving the hypotheses through deductive logic, are well delineated: this makes it easier for others to check the theory's validity. The causal mechanism is often made clear: for example, one can easily see that "electoral rules" and "regime type" are the two explanatory factors of various outcomes in Cowhey and McCubbins (1995). Third, because the causal mechanism is made clear, this approach is well suited to offer predictions: for example, if "electoral rules" are shown to matter, then the change of electoral rules would likely alter outcomes.

There are also shortcomings to rational choice analysis, however. First, the behavioral assumptions of actors are often problematic. In rational choice, "the trick is in defining the preferences in general, ex ante to a particular application" (Levi 1997: 24). However, without knowing for sure what the actors are pursuing, one cannot offer a plausible explanation of the strategic interaction. How accurate is the assumption that politicians

---

[7] This view of institutions is strongly influenced by the new institutionalism in economics. North (1990: 1), for example, defines institutions as "the rules of the game in a society," or "the humanly devised constraints that shape human interaction."

seek reelection? This problem becomes all the more acute for the bureaucrats, as their behavioral goals are much less clear: what do they pursue?[8]

Second, this ambiguity about the veracity of the assumptions, combined with the minimal attention to historical, social, and cultural contexts and emphasis on deductive logic, increases the risk of theorists making inaccurate claims.[9] Because empirical cases tend to be used merely to "confirm" rather than to test hypotheses, there tends to be less contribution to "theory-building" and empirical research need not be as extensive as in historical institutionalism. Many studies employing the rational choice approach fail to provide detailed empirical evidence to support arguments. This aspect leads to a greater risk of making inaccurate (or misleading) statements, which more extensive empirical research might prevent. For example, erroneous assertions such as "the Supreme Court only includes recent LDP appointees" (Ramseyer and Rosenbluth 1993: Chapter 8) are less likely to emerge from other approaches with more emphasis on detailed case studies and less emphasis on the application of theories developed elsewhere.[10]

We have given an overview of the two different approaches to institutions in Japanese politics. This difference in focus need not be viewed as a dichotomy, and the two approaches might instead be seen as complementary.[11] The weaknesses mentioned previously are not inherent in the approaches and therefore may be avoided if the researcher proceeds with caution. For

---

[8] Of course, it depends on what the theorist seeks to explain. Career advancement (Tullock 1965), budget maximization (Niskanen 1971), and discretionary power (Kato 1994) are examples of plausible assumptions. However, these works fall short of explaining the principal case of interest in our study, the Big Bang financial reforms, where MOF willingly shed its regulatory power.

[9] Levi (1997: 21) states, "rationalists are almost always willing to sacrifice nuance for generalizability, detail for logic, a forfeiture most other comparativists would decline." This point seems to be central to criticisms of rational choice studies of Japanese politics. See Johnson and Keehn (1994) and Curtis (1999).

[10] The assertion that the LDP remains in ultimate control because it appoints the Supreme Court justices must also be more closely scrutinized. Justices selected from the bar are typically those who have managed the highly independent Japanese Bar Association, whose progressive policies lie far from the conservatism of the LDP. The LDP may control the cabinet, which appoints the justices, but whether the LDP has a say in the appointment process must be explored and confirmed through deeper empirical research, rather than assumed. Merely asserting the existence of a control mechanism based on deductive logic is insufficient for making a persuasive case. Scholars err by simply projecting the partisan practice of judiciary appointment in the United States onto the Japanese polity.

[11] Proponents of rational choice and historical institutionalism alike seem to be increasingly aware of this fact. See Steinmo, Thelen, and Longstreth (1992) and Thelen (1999) for the historical institutionalist view on this point, and Levi (1997) and Bates et al. (1998) for the rational choice viewpoint.

example, generalizability and theoretical clarity may be strengthened in historical institutionalism by making more explicit the assumptions, nature of incentive structures, and causal mechanisms. Similarly, rational choice analysis may achieve greater empirical accuracy by paying more attention to contexts other than the formal "rules of the game," such as constitutions and electoral laws.

Keeping the strengths and weaknesses of the two approaches in mind, we adopt the actor-oriented approach in this study. This deliberate choice reflects our belief that works of political science on current issues ought to aim for greater policy relevance, if they are to be of greater use to society.[12] Unfortunately, the presence of political scientists in the policy debates on issues of political economy is minimal, especially in the Japanese context.[13] In our view, this state in part reflects the way academic works of political science are presented to policymakers. If, as in studies of economics (which invariably adopt an actor-oriented approach), research findings link particular causal factors with particular outcomes, then researchers are able to develop more helpful policy recommendations. On the other hand, if, as in numerous past studies of Japanese politics, the academic shows that the Japanese system is complex with interacting causal factors and that the historical (or socio-cultural) development of the basic institutions make things hard to change, what are the policymakers to do? While analyses telling us how complex the world is contribute to our understanding of politics, we aim in this study for more by adopting a rational-actor approach, constructing a framework that enables us to identify the causal factors that provide clues to prediction and policy recommendations.

The aforementioned discussion on the weaknesses of rational choice analysis points us in the way to proceed. We will strive for empirical accuracy while operating within the rational choice paradigm by paying attention to aspects of the policy context other than the formal "rules of the game" and by developing more realistic assumptions.

Stability vs. Change

The second issue of contention in the study of Japanese politics is one between analytical frameworks of "stability" and "change." Reflecting the

---

[12] This, we believe, contributes to the advancement of social science, as more resources are likely to be invested in efforts that have greater relevance to what is happening in the "real world."

[13] This may also be true in international organizations dealing with political economy issues. Note, for example, how few political scientists the International Monetary Fund (IMF) employs.

apparent stability of the postwar political economy, many works of Japanese politics, particularly those that appeared through the 1980s, have sought to explain the perceived stability of bureaucratic dominance, LDP one-party dominance, or patterns of interaction between the public and private sectors (Johnson 1982; Sato and Matsuzaki 1986; Muramatsu and Krauss 1987; Samuels 1987; Okimoto 1989). One common strategy for theorists was to characterize the Japanese state, or the arrangement that governs the interplay of politics, economics, and society, with a single phrase, such as the "developmental state" (Johnson 1982), "societal state" (Okimoto 1989), or "patterned pluralism" (Muramatsu and Krauss 1987).

This attention to stability was warranted up until the early 1990s. LDP rule collapsed in 1993, however. How are the theorists to deal with these developments? In the face of the seemingly unstable political reality of the 1990s, there are those who continue to stress the continuity from the past and stability in the political system, arguing that little has changed in Japanese politics in the 1990s (Curtis 1999; Vogel 1999). According to this view, there is a large gap between the reform rhetoric of Japanese political leaders and the reform policies of the Japanese government: in the decade, little has been achieved by the numerous attempts to reform the political system and the public policymaking process. If policy change occurs, these scholars believe it will be incremental, rather than radical.[14]

On the other hand, there are those scholars who argue that change is taking place in Japan. As Kohno (1997) suggests, the stable aspects of the postwar era such as LDP one-party dominance had the potential to change at any moment (as was the case in 1993). In this way, the image of stability may be misleading in that it gives the false image that things were predestined to be stable from the start. Pempel (1998) argues from an institutions-oriented approach that a significant public policy redirection and coalitional adjustment occurred in Japan in the 1990s (compared to that of the 1960s), just short of a complete "regime shift."[15] As we will see later, some works on Japanese finance, such as Amyx (2000 [and 2004]) and Rosenbluth and Thies (1999), also suggest that there was a significant departure from the traditional patterns of policymaking in finance in the 1990s.[16]

[14] See Curtis (1999: 234–42).

[15] Pempel (1998) distinguishes between different types of "regime shifts." According to Pempel, a "third-order" regime shift occurs when socioeconomic coalitions, political institutions, and the public policy profile (which together comprise a "regime") shift en masse. Pempel contrasts this with the "second-order regime shift" observed in Japan in the 1990s.

[16] Note that the aforementioned division between actor-oriented and institutions-oriented approaches does not necessarily coincide with this division. Both can generate theories of

The single-phrase characterizations of the Japanese political system, common in past studies (as mentioned previously), have a shortcoming in the sense that they are based on assumptions of stability, or of continuity and non-change. By adopting analytical strategies focused on explaining a stable system at work, these scholars find it hard to identify signs of change until well after that change takes place. Of course, change is a relative concept, and one can easily find evidence at any time for both change and continuity. Determining which is the more salient dynamic requires weighing the primacy of each against empirical reality at a given point in time.

Many actor-oriented approaches also tend to focus on explaining equilibrium states (Green and Shapiro 1994). Yet, stability is merely one of the many possible outcomes of strategic interaction among actors. While an equilibrium state may provide actors with disincentives to shift their strategies, changes in the environment may induce actors to adopt different strategies, thus disrupting "stability." Thus, we adopt the actor-oriented perspective but use it to question the appearance of stability.[17] We utilize a framework of "institutional change," developed in the next chapter, to challenge the findings of those who argue for the prevalence of stability and the absence of change. We show that "change" indeed best characterizes developments in the Japanese political economy since 1995. In the areas of finance and public policymaking, Japanese politics has departed from the past patterns of gradualism and status quo maintenance.

Dominance vs. Interaction

A third issue of contention in the literature on Japanese politics may be whether one focuses on the dominance of one set of actors (e.g. bureaucrats, politicians, or interest groups) over others or, instead, focuses on the patterns of interaction among actors.[18] Among those who fall into the former camp are those who assert the dominance of bureaucrats over other actors

"stability" and theories of "change." For example, while rational choice approaches have tended to center on the analysis of equilibrium states (see Levi (1997) or Green and Shapiro (1994)), others have shown that this approach can apply to the question of institutional change (see, for example, North (1990)). As we will see later, Aoki (2001) grapples extensively with this question of institutional change. Select works in the historical institutionalist tradition have sought to deal with change, such as those on social revolutions or democratic transition. See, for example, Skocpol (1979) and O'Donnell and Schmitter (1986).

[17] In this respect, our approach resonates with that taken by Kohno (1997) in his study of Japanese political parties.

[18] The triumvirate or "Japan Inc." view and the Marxist approach are additional perspectives but have become more peripheral to debates in the field of Japanese politics in recent years.

(Johnson 1982).[19] A bureaucratic dominance approach posits the primacy of a "pilot agency" (be it MITI or MOF) over that of politicians or interest groups. In contrast, other scholars argue for the dominance of interest groups in the political economy. From an actor-oriented point-of-view, financial institutions would be expected to dominate Japanese finance (Rosenbluth 1989); or, from a more institutions-oriented perspective, long-term credit banks and *keiretsu* enterprise groups might be seen as key to Japan's "strategic capitalism" strategy of economic development (Calder 1993). A third group of scholars stresses the dominance of politicians over the bureaucracy by adopting a rational choice approach (Ramseyer and Rosenbluth 1993; McCubbins and Noble 1995), or by adopting a framework of pluralism, adding such adjectives as "patterned" (Muramatsu and Krauss 1987) and "compartmentalized" (Sato and Matsuzaki 1986).[20]

On the other side of the spectrum, there are those who deemphasize dominance and focus instead on less hierarchical forms of interaction among actors. Okimoto (1989) and Amyx (1998 [and 2004]) focus on the relational networks linking the actors by delving into their informal inter-action patterns. They show how such networks enabled or constrained the state's ability to pursue economic goals. In a similar vein, Samuels (1987) found that "reciprocal consent" was the dominant interaction pattern between the state and the private sector in the transformation of the industrial structure in the energy sector.

Needless to say, one's theoretical focus is often determined largely by the state of academic discourse when research is undertaken. Given the large impact of the bureaucratic dominance view (largely to the credit of Chalmers Johnson), many works that appeared in the 1980s naturally focused on the question of dominance. However, in the end, as Curtis (1999: 60) notes, there has been an increasing convergence regarding the state-society relationship among theorists, towards an image of "an activist state interacting with strong social institutions."[21] We endorse this view. Some models stressing dominance are set up to determine the pattern of dominance even before testing the theory with reality.[22] If one

[19] See also Zysman (1983) and Vogel (1996).

[20] Reference here to the concept of pluralism is to the conceptualization developed by Dahl (1971). Note that this concept of pluralism can also be used to stress the dominance of the bureaucracy, as was done by Inoguchi and Iwai (1987).

[21] Curtis calls this more activist state a "refractive state" and cites "patterned pluralism" as one characterization that represents this growing consensus (see later).

[22] Thus, we do not find fault with some theories of pluralism that assert dominance based on the results of empirical analysis (Muramatsu and Krauss 1987; Inoguchi and Iwai 1987), although our actor-oriented approach diverges from these institution-oriented approaches.

a priori defines the policymaking model so as to incorporate the preeminence of a "pilot agency" in the political system, how can one account for the loss of bureaucratic dominance? The pattern of dominance may or may not be stable over time, and thus it may be more fruitful to search for a trend in which the pattern of domination evolves, rather than to try to identify a permanently dominant actor.

Similarly, some works adopting the rational choice approach contain an *a priori* assumption of dominance by politicians over bureaucrats. The mechanism of political control has been portrayed in a number of different ways. Some depict control as veto power "over anything bureaucrats do" or as control over the promotion of bureaucrats within their respective organizations (Ramseyer and Rosenbluth 1993). Others have depicted it with the metaphor of "fire-alarm" oversight (McCubbins and Schwartz 1984), wherein interest groups report to the politicians when actions taken by the bureaucracy fail to support their interests. And, still others have asserted the thesis of dominance by rebutting the hypothesis that politicians abdicate power to bureaucrats (McCubbins and Noble 1995).

Two factors undermine the validity of such theories as explanations for Japanese policy outcomes. First, some lack sufficient grounding in empirical evidence. For example, some pointing to the mechanism of "fire-alarm" oversight by politicians of bureaucrats mistakenly claim that deliberative councils serve the information needs of the LDP (McCubbins and Noble 1995: 70).[23] Second, excessive attention to the formal "rules of the game" leads these scholars at times to confuse theory with practice. Consider the "veto power" argument. In theory, the Japanese Constitution guarantees the primacy of the legislative branch, legal statutes assure cabinet ministers of their leadership positions, and the ruling party can always veto the bureaucrats' proposals. If we assume that theory translated directly into practice, however, then we have trouble explaining the extreme frustration by many politicians over how difficult it is to overcome bureaucratic resistance.[24]

The "veto power" supposedly held by the LDP fails to work as predicted by theory. One can skirt the issue by choosing to define abdication by politicians as a situation in which "the agent has complete discretion over policy choices and the principal has no control," asserting that "relative

<hr/>

[23] The writer's interviews with LDP and bureaucratic officials suggest that there is little evidence that the LDP obtains information from the deliberative councils.

[24] For example, Masaharu Gotoda, chief cabinet secretary under the Nakasone government in the 1980s, spoke of his difficulties in moving forward with administrative reforms as a result of bureaucratic resistance in Otake (1997a).

amounts of abdication imply that the principal is able to influence the agent's choices to at least some extent" (McCubbins and Noble 1995: 74). However, the creation of a dichotomy between "abdication = zero control" and "control = some control" obfuscates the crucial question. Whether or not politicians have *some control* over the issues is not the subject of contention; rather, the point at question is how much *substantive control* they have.[25] To help bridge the gap between theory and reality, we must pay attention to constraints extending beyond the formal "rules of the game" that set the outer limits of bureaucratic behavior, to include informal patterns of interaction, digging into the substance of the relationship between politicians and bureaucrats. While we do not dismiss the relevance of the search for "dominance" *per se*, we reject theories with built-in dominance assumptions.

In sum, the examination of three issues of contention in the current literature on Japanese politics leads us to adopt an actor-oriented approach to institutional analysis, which seeks to account for—as well as to establish—that change has occurred in the Japanese political economy since 1995. To do this, we focus on the patterns of interaction between actors rather than on the dominance of a particular set of actors. Moreover, we extend our scope of analysis beyond formal "rules of the game" to include informal patterns of actor interaction.

Works on Japanese Financial Politics and the Big Bang

We now turn to the works on the specific field of our interest within the Japanese political economy, financial politics (or the political process of the public policymaking concerning private finance), and the Big Bang. In the study of financial politics, many analysts have emphasized the gradual nature in which reforms take place (Rosenbluth 1989; Vogel 1996; Amyx 1998). Thus, such works would have difficulty coping with the Big Bang. In comparison to the 1991–93 reforms, the planning was much quicker, the content was much more far-reaching (i.e. creating obvious losers), and the schedule of implementation was largely pre-fixed by the reform initiative (instead of being left to later negotiations).

---

[25] The "rules of the game" certainly matter, as bureaucratic initiatives cannot become laws unless they are in the "win-set" of legislators. Consider, however, a case in which the bureaucratic agent negotiates with interest groups, drafts the bills, informs the legislators in the broadest terms, and in this way enjoys a large amount of discretion in choosing policy outcomes, as well as in setting the timing, scope, and schedule of the initiatives.

Work by economists on financial reforms, while important, tends to focus on the gap between the most desirable policies that might be pursued from an economic standpoint and actual policies implemented, but offer little insight on the political interaction among actors which gives rise to such a gap. More often than not, MOF or the LDP—whichever actor is assumed to be in charge of financial policymaking—is simply blamed for this failure (Ikeo 1995; Horiuchi 1999; Hoshi and Kashyap 1999). If there are optimal economic policies, what hinders them from being adopted?

This question leads us to consider the validity of a view held by many analysts of Japanese politics of the bureaucracy/ MOF/ and/or the ruling party, LDP, as actors that hinder or forestall much needed economic deregulation when they promote organizational interests over those of the nation (Vogel 1996; Keehn 1998; Pempel 1998; Curtis 1999).[26] If so, who brought about the Big Bang? Is it that some other actors who benefit from financial reforms (e.g. domestic or foreign financial institutions) pushed for it, overriding MOF and/or the LDP? Or, is it that MOF and/or the LDP somehow decided to change their minds and actively push for the reforms? Were the "entrenched actors" (the LDP and MOF) as "entrenched" as was typically believed?

Certainly there are numerous accounts of the Big Bang that tell us what it contains and what the expected economic consequences were, and some such works include valuable narratives of the interplay of actors (Tahara 1998; Otake 1999).[27] Nevertheless, few works systematically treat the political process of the Big Bang in the context of the accompanying changes in financial politics. How can we understand such diverse developments in finance as the breakup of MOF (Mabuchi 1997), the Housing Loan Affair (Rosenbluth and Thies 1999), and the Financial Diet of 1998 that represented the first aggressive response by the government to the bad debt problem in the banking sector (Amyx 2000 [and 2004]), *and* the Big Bang financial reforms? What is the relationship between these developments? Is there a framework that gives us a sense of the causal mechanism at work across cases?

In analyzing the relationship between the actors in financial politics, scholars tend to stress either the dominance of MOF (Vogel 1996;

---

[26] This view is held by those who embrace the "revisionist" view of the Japanese state, including van Wolferen (1990), Johnson and Keehn (1994), and Hartcher (1998).

[27] For economic analyses, see for example, Dekle (1997), IMF (1997), and OECD (1997). For journalistic accounts, see for example, Asahi Shimbun (1997), Nihon Keizai Shimbun (1997), and Mainichi Shimbun (1997).

Keehn 1998), dominance of financial institutions (Rosenbluth 1989), or the paralysis of MOF bound by its relational networks with the banking sector (Amyx 1998 [and 2004]). In the financial politics of 1995–96, as we will see in Chapter 5, MOF and the LDP cooperated in the Housing Loan Affair (related to the bad debt problem), competed in the planning of the Big Bang, and confronted each other on issues of MOF reform. How can we possibly grasp such a complex situation by utilizing a framework of dominance? If we focus on interaction, what type of explanatory framework can satisfactorily explain the fact that the bad debt problem remained unresolved in the late 1990s, as Amyx suggests, while financial reforms, that worked against the interests of many financial institutions, were introduced suddenly in 1996? If the relational ties prevented state actors from taking action, why was this effect seen in banking reforms but not in the Big Bang?

Lastly, we may note that the role of the public is unclear in many works on financial politics (as well as works on Japanese politics in general), despite the fact that Japan is a liberal democracy, where the public is assumed to be "ultimately" in charge.[28] Works tend to focus on the interplay of such elite actors as politicians, bureaucrats, and interest groups, paying little attention to the role of the public. An exception to this generalization is work in the rational choice vein which incorporates the voting public as the ultimate principal in chains of principal-agent relationships leading first to the politicians and then to bureaucrats.[29] Empirically-based studies such as Kabashima (1986) suggest, however, that not only politicians but also other elite actors (bureaucrats and interest groups) are influenced by public opinion, largely via the mass media.[30] What is the public's role in Japanese politics? Might the change of government in 1993 have given a greater role to the voting public? While voting provides the public with an avenue for influence over politicians, are there not other means of policymaking influence by the public? How might the public influence the behavior of bureaucrats and interest groups?

---

[28] For example, see such representative works on financial politics of the 1980s and 1990s as Rosenbluth (1989), Calder (1993), Vogel (1996), Mabuchi (1997), and Amyx (1998). See also representative works on politics in other sectors of the economy, such as Johnson (1982), Okimoto (1989), Samuels (1987), and Calder (1988).

[29] For works that address the role of the public in the rational choice vein, see Ramseyer and Rosenbluth (1993), Cowhey and McCubbins (1995); for those that deal with financial politics, in particular, see Rosenbluth and Thies (1999).

[30] See also Muramatsu, Ito, and Tsujinaka (1992) on this point.

The Study's Methodological Approach and Research Design

To address the concerns raised previously, the present study adopts the following three-pronged approach, introduced briefly in the previous chapter (See Table 2.1).

Rational Actor Approach Focusing on the Nature of Strategic Interaction Among Actors

We begin our analysis with the assumption that actors are rational in their pursuit of goals. Our analysis proceeds at the level of organizational and sub-organizational groups. The relevant actors are political parties, bureaucratic agencies, and firms and interest groups, as well as the public. Clearly, how the incentive structures within the organizational actors work vis-à-vis their individual members also needs to be taken into account. Organizations can utilize both formal and informal reward and punishment to ensure compliance with organizational policy, as decided

Table 2.1 Response to five concerns identified in existing works on Japanese financial politics and the Big Bang

---

Q1) What happened to the gradualism in the financial reforms of the past? Does this gradualism persist? Why did the pattern of financial reforms change between 1991–93 and 1996?

- Adopt a framework of "change"
- Carry out a comparison of cases of financial reforms

Q2) Who brought about the reforms? Financial institutions? MOF and/or the LDP?

- Adopt an actor-oriented approach
- Make better behavioral assumptions
- Utilize the logic of organizational survival
- Develop a typology of financial reforms

Q3) How can we establish a link between the Big Bang and other parallel developments in finance?

- Utilize a framework of institutional change

Q4) Does dominance or a less hierarchical form of interaction best capture the nature of the relationship among actors?

- Adopt a model of less hierarchical interaction among actors
- Adopt a rational actor approach
- Employ the logic of organizational survival

Q5) What is the public's role in Japanese politics? How has the change of government in 1993 changed this role? Are there means of public influence over policy other than that exercised through elections?

- Role of the unorganized public in politics (in the model of interaction among actors)
- Patterns of financial reforms
- Role of public support in the analysis of organizational survival and financial reforms

---

by internal decision-making bodies.[31] Thus, we do not offer an extensive scrutiny at the individual level, but instead assume that organizations such as political parties and firms have incentive structures that make it rational for individuals to go along with the organizational policy observable from outside.[32] However, we allow for possibilities that some groups of individuals within the organization compete for control over the organizational policy, thus operating at the suborganizational level.

Our analysis is organized from the rational choice perspective, assuming the actors to be rational (in the sense of means-end efficiency) in the pursuit of their goals, however these goals are defined. We view actors as having bounded rationality in that they face constraints regarding their reasoning ability and available information, but are rational in intent, or "subjective rational."[33] In the discussion of institutional change in Chapter 3, we will see that the institutions in fact help the actors understand how the world works, conveying information in compressed forms to the subjectively rational actors. While we base our analysis on the rational choices made by actors *ex ante*, we do not contend that these choices alone produced institutional change. The existence of multiple equilibria makes the analysis of historical information necessary; random events, mistakes, and unintentional fits, as well as *ex post* rationality (or the rationalization by actors, after events take place) are also important in the process of institutional change.[34]

With regard to actor goals, we start from a simple assumption that *organizations seek survival*. There may be many other goals but this is the ultimate goal—the goal that overrides all others. We introduce a rank ordering of goals between the ultimate goal, the pursuit of survival, and other *ceteris paribus* goals. The latter includes such goals as budget, profit and power maximization.[35] The assumption of survival as the ultimate

[31] For example, a firm can demote (or fire) individuals who do not comply with organizational policy decided by the steering board. Or, a firm's president may utilize the threat of demotion or the promise of promotion to ensure support of his or her views. Political parties can expel or place other sanctions on members who do not comply with party policy, as decided by such bodies as the LDP's Executive Council. The LDP's political leaders can utilize the threat of demotion (or the withholding of funds) or the promise of positions within the party or the government to ensure compliance. The same holds for the bureaucracy, although the law protects bureaucrats from being fired at will.

[32] Because our behavioral assumptions about bureaucrats depart from conventional wisdom, we delve more extensively into the individual incentive structures of this set of actors.

[33] See Simon (1979) on bounded rationality. In the study of Japanese politics, our definition of rationality is very similar to that used by Kato (1994).

[34] See Aoki (2001). See also Fujimoto (1997), where the behavioral patterns surrounding the emergence of a new system are analyzed in a study of the Toyota production system.

[35] This is not to deny the likelihood that such factors are subject to the law of diminishing returns or other laws. The point here is to distinguish "ultimate" from "ceteris paribus" objectives.

goal is not uncommon in other fields. For example, the assumption that nation-states prioritize survival above all else is widely accepted in the study of international relation.[36] To avoid tautology, we refer to the Japanese political economy in general in deriving our behavioral assumptions, rather than limiting our scope to Japanese financial politics. In so doing, we see how this assumption of survival fits the observed empirical regularities concerning the goals pursued by political parties, bureaucratic agencies, and firms.

With regard to the nature of interaction among actors, we adopt a stance that the strategic interaction among actors does not necessarily result in the dominance of one actor over the others. However, we recognize that there is a distinction between state actors—that is, the political parties and the bureaucratic agencies—and other actors such as firms, interest groups, and the general public. The former have direct access to governmental power, while the latter enjoy only indirect access through influencing the former. Put simply, politicians can make laws, and bureaucrats can make administrative decisions, but firms, interest groups, and the public cannot wield governmental power by themselves: they have to influence state actors through inducement, coercion, and other means. Thus, in our world of politics, there are two state actors: politicians and bureaucrats. And, there are two societal actors: firms and interest groups, and the public.[37] Each state actor is supported by two sets of societal actors: constituencies (firms and interest groups) and the public. For state actors to pursue their ultimate goal of survival, they have to rely on the resources provided by these societal actors.

While a common theory of deregulation assumes that interest groups drive politics,[38] thereby focusing on the need for state actors to rely on the resources provided by constituents, organized groups need not determine the politics of regulation. State actors may also promote deregulation, as a means for vying for the support of the unorganized public, and independently of any inducement from organized interests—especially if survival is at stake.

[36] Here, we refer to the so-called neo-realist literature that followed Waltz (1979), as well as to such neoliberal perspectives as those introduced by Keohane (1984) that share the "survival" assumption.

[37] In this way, we extend the framework of "bureaupluralism" provided by Aoki (1988) to state actors in general. This interpretive paradigm holds that bureaucrats seek to cater to both "jurisdictional constituents" and public interest but politicians simultaneously pursue these two sets of interests as well.

[38] See Peltzman (1998) and Noll (1989) for this approach. Rosenbluth (1989) and Noll and Rosenbluth (1995) provide examples of the application of this approach to Japanese politics.

Focusing on Change: Institutional Change, Organizational Survival, and Patterns of Reform and Public Support

We focus on patterns of interaction among actors rather than on the dominance of any one set of actors, and on explaining change rather than stability. To this end, we utilize a theoretical framework of institutional change and organizational survival. Chapter 3 develops and discusses this framework in detail. In the discussion that follows, therefore, we provide only a brief introduction.

Dissatisfied with the existing rational actor literature on Japanese politics, which focuses too much on "rules of the game"—especially formal rules such as the constitution, electoral rules, and veto points—we adopt a view on institutions developed on the comparative institutional analysis (CIA) perspective.[39] We reach beyond the emphasis on "the rules of the games" to adopt a view of institutions as "equilibria" and concentrate more on explaining the formation of these institutions. Moving beyond the exclusive attention on formal rules, and learning from other approaches with more attention to context, we include an examination of informal patterns of interaction among actors. We also ask what factors give rise to these patterns and rules? Here, we find that institutions are best represented in terms of shared expectations, as the fact that actors collectively believe such institutions are in place is what fundamentally supports the existence of these institutions.[40]

Following Aoki (2001), we define institutions as *shared, stable, summarized expectations about how the world works, which may not be unique*, developed via a feedback mechanism between the shared expectations and the validation of such expectations by objective reality. Our study analyzes institutions at four levels: players, formal rules, informal interaction patterns, and the shared expectations that reinforce, and are reinforced by, the other three levels.

We build our framework of institutional change, linking Aoki's framework to politics, or the distributional conflicts among actors, of the economic reforms. In our framework, institutional change is essentially a shift in shared perceptions about how the world works through a collective

---

[39] See Aoki (2001) for a delineation of this approach.

[40] Even if there are formal rules or the accumulation of informal patterns of interaction, "institutions" that shape and constrain human behavior do not emerge if the actors collectively believe that these rules or interaction patterns are irrelevant. Imagine that there is a widely accepted practice by all actors, such as the wining and dining of officials. While it was known that laws and past court decisions treated this practice as bribery, it was only after collective beliefs shifted from seeing the practice as "acceptable" to "unacceptable," that such practices began to be punished as prescribed by law.

learning process based on the evolutionary selection mechanism of strategies. This change is caused by the gap between the faster pace of environmental changes and the slower pace of adaptation in domestic political and economic institutions. This gap appears in the form of "failures," or "performance failures and scandals," which lead the actors to question the taken for granted aspect of the institutions. "Nature"—that is, environmental changes in technology or institutional environment—eventually determines the outcome of the competition between institutions by rewarding actors' strategies: the successful strategies will increase their share in the population. Yet, a political struggle takes place between those actors who see the process as "resilience" of the institutions and/or have stakes in preserving the status quo on one hand, and those actors who see "change" taking place and/or see their interests as being enhanced by the new institutions. This political struggle is facilitated by symbols derived from such sources as history, foreign practice, ideology, and leadership. In the process, "reformers" may displace "conservatives," either via a "counter-coalition" (from the outside) or via "defection" (from within). When a critical mass of the agents shifts their views about how the world works and the new institutions become taken for granted, "institutional change" results.

Upon this backdrop, we derive the logic of organizational survival. While all individuals in the organization may start from the same goals (survival), their views about the future and/or the stakes they have in the status quo may differ. This may lead to a split within the organization: a competition for the control of the organization may result. Eventually, "nature" rewards one group over the others: observing this, the "losing" groups revise their strategies. As long as all the individuals share the ultimate goal of survival, eventually, the group that calls for an organizational strategy that seems the most promising for organizational survival will control the organizational policy.

After deriving the actors and their behavioral assumptions from observed regularities, we construct a typology of financial reforms from our framework of institutional change. Based on the patterns of coalition evolution and on the interaction patterns between state and societal actors, we arrive at a four-by-two typology that we later use in Part II to guide the empirical analysis. Throughout the discussion of organizational survival and patterns of financial reforms presented in our empirical analysis in Part II, we emphasize the role of the public. We will see that in both dimensions, public support is a critical factor that constrains not only the politicians who face elections, but also the bureaucrats and the financial industries in terms of the political influence they command. In a liberal democracy, no single actor can sustain itself while being labeled as "public enemy," due to the accompanying loss of public support. If an actor finds itself in the situation of "public enemy" as a result of "failures," that actor has strong incentives to recover the lost support to ensure survival.

Improving the Link between Theory and Empirical Validation: Longitudinal Comparison, Analytic Narratives, and Alternative Explanations

We seek to cure the shortcomings of rational actor approaches by adopting the following three strategies that improve the link between theory and empirical validity in Part II: longitudinal comparison, analytic narratives, and the use of alternative explanations.

As we saw in Chapter 1, our first empirical objective is to show a realistic picture of the Big Bang, including what and who brought it about. In order to strengthen our approach, we rely on a comparison with the past cases of financial reforms. While a thorough comparison by John Stuart Mill's Method of Difference is impossible in this complex world, we seek to assimilate this method by trying to select cases with the most commonalities—those that essentially share the same set of actors, the same political and economic settings, and the same fields of reform. In this sense, we carry out a longitudinal comparison.[41] Our analysis is about the politics of the regulatory reforms in finance with particular focus on their distributional effects. Thus, we are interested in past cases of financial reforms, which had many similarities with the Big Bang, but different results. Contrasting our case against these past cases raises the plausibility of our thesis stressing "change."

Second, we seek to improve our rational actor analysis by learning from the "analytic narrative" approach, developed by rational choice theorists (Bates et al. 1998). This approach advocates an iterative process between theory and empirical data in theory building, recognizing that theories are shaped by case materials, departing from a conventional notion of hypothesis testing of deductive theories and blurring the line between deduction and induction.[42] We find this approach attractive, as it helps us cure the conventional ills of actor-oriented approaches—namely, insufficient attention to context. Thus, we seek to build an analytic narrative,

---

[41] See Ragin (1987) for a discussion of comparative methods, including longitudinal comparison. This method is similar to one adopted by Skocpol (1979) in her contrast of the success of the Russian Revolution of 1917 to the failure of 1905. In her study, as well, similar settings produced different results.   [42] See Bates et al. (1998: 13–18).

41

based on an understanding of "the actors" preferences, their perceptions, their evaluation of alternatives, the information they possess, the expectations they form, the strategies they adopt, and the constraints that limit their actions (Bates et al. 1997: 11).

Yet, by adopting this approach, empirical validation of the theory becomes problematic and another means of confirmation is needed. Thus, the third component of our research design tests our explanation against alternative explanations to increase the plausibility of our account.[43] While there may be multiple explanations for a single observed phenomenon, one may assess the strength of one explanation relative to another (Kohno 1997).

Table 2.1 summarizes how our methodology responds to the five concerns identified in the previous section as emerging from the existing literature.

Possible Alternative Explanations

We close this chapter by suggesting possible alternative explanations to our main argument. We derive these explanations from the existing literature surveyed earlier and weigh the robustness of these explanations with our own in Part II of the book.[44] While the diversity of the literature cannot be captured in its entirety, we organize the alternative explanations along the lines of "dominance" as our main concern regarding the Big Bang (as identified in Chapter 1) is to ask the essentially political question of who brought these reforms about. We obtain five different views. The first three derive from explanations based on common "dominance" views, while the other two represent two more nuanced explanatory paradigms.[45]

First, one might imagine that a single bureaucratic agency, be it MITI or MOF, was the mastermind of the Big Bang, as the literature of bureaucratic dominance might suggest. In this scheme, MITI as the pilot agency of the economy (Johnson 1982) or MOF as the regulator of finance (Vogel 1996) would plan and coordinate the process, while pursuing the enhancement of its own goals, or the maximization of regulatory power over the financial industries. If MITI or MOF, acting as a single unitary actor, can be

---

[43] See Bates et al. (1998). Note that this strategy is hardly limited to the analytic narrative perspectives. See Kohno (1997) for an example of such a methodology in Japanese politics.

[44] The alternative explanations as presented here should be understood more as counterfactuals, as we ask how each theory might have explained the observed outcome, rather than engaging in a criticism of the theories themselves.

[45] There are likely many other variations of possible explanations than these five, but we limit the alternative explanations to this number to keep the analysis manageable.

shown to have gotten its way in interaction with politicians and the private sector, this explanation would hold.

Second, studies positing the dominance of financial firms in financial politics (Rosenbluth 1989; Calder 1993) suggest that perhaps domestic financial institutions drove reforms by influencing politicians or bureaucrats. Such firms could be banks, including the city banks around which *keiretsu* centered, or long-term credit banks that played a key role in postwar industrial finance. Alternately, these firms might be securities firms that might gain from an accelerated shift away from indirect toward direct financing that would result from financial deregulation. Or, the insurance industry—especially the life insurance firms that bought up assets all over the world with their financial might in the 1980s—might be seen as the main drivers of reforms. Finally, we might posit that the political source of deregulation emerged out of the rise of new interest groups, such as foreign financial firms and Japanese non-financial firms seeking to enter the financial industry. Perhaps these "financial outsiders" displaced the "financial insiders," to control the political process. The formation of a coalition involving the financial firms ("insiders" or "outsiders") on the one hand and state actors on the other hand, to induce the latter to work for the benefit of the former, would confirm this line of explanation.

Third, studies that emphasize the dominance of politicians over bureaucrats in Japanese politics (Sato and Matsuzaki 1986; Muramatsu and Krauss 1987), suggest that the Big Bang might have been the politicians' victory over the bureaucrats. After all, the Big Bang initiative to deregulate was announced by Prime Minister Hashimoto, who was also the President of the LDP. Might we find that politicians, pursuing deregulation for some reason, emerged triumphant over the bureaucrats, who naturally resisted such reforms encroaching on their bureaucratic power? Or, we might adopt the rational choice perspective (Ramseyer and Rosenbluth 1993) and stipulate that the bureaucrats anticipated their political masters' wishes. If this was the case, then we would not expect to see much conflict between politicians and bureaucrats across issues in financial politics.

We may add two other possible explanations for the question of who brought about the Big Bang by combining the previously cited reasons. A fourth explanation might be that a counter-coalition formed outside of finance, as the theory of regulation might lead us to predict (Noll 1989). Non-financial firms, seeking better financial services, might have spearheaded the drive for deregulation in alliance with MITI, which was happy to encroach onto MOF's jurisdiction over finance in its pursuit of bureaucratic power. Was the Big Bang essentially an interest-group dominance story coupled with a bureaucratic turf war? The formation of a counter-coalition and the struggle between the two coalitions would confirm this explanation.

Fifth and last, we might consider an explanation that questions the assumption of the continuation of the "producer economy," wherein producer groups see their interests better represented than consumers, who tend to be less well-organized (an assumption common to all of the previously given explanations). Rational choice explanations focusing on formal electoral rules (which we will refer to as "electoral rational choice" to distinguish from our rational actor explanation) might see the Big Bang as a victory of consumers, brought about by the introduction of the single-member electoral district in 1994 (Ramseyer and Rosenbluth 1993; Rosenbluth and Thies 1999).[46] Perhaps the LDP shifted from its bank-coddling practice to pursue a victory for the consumers, as has been suggested was the case in the resolution of the Housing Loan Affair of 1995 (Rosenbluth and Thies 1999). If so, then the Big Bang initiative, announced weeks after the first election following the 1994 electoral reforms might be attributed to electoral reform. This line of explanation places emphasis on the principal-agent relationship linking consumers, LDP backbenchers, and the LDP leadership to explain a rise, at last, in consumerism.

Table 2.2 lists the five alternative explanations, which correspond to the empirical puzzles introduced in Chapter 1. Note that the "dominance" view may lead to conclusions in favor of either change or stability, depending

Table 2.2 Five alternative explanations for the Big Bang and related developments

a) A pre-designed and coordinated initiative by a single bureaucracy (MOF or MITI)
  • Bureaucratic dominance (Johnson 1982; Vogel 1996)

b) The result of the domination of financial institutions ("insiders" or "outsiders")
  • Interest group dominance (Rosenbluth 1989; Calder 1993; theory of regulation)

c) The result of politicians overriding bureaucrats
  • Political dominance (Muramatsu and Krauss 1987; Ramseyer and Rosenbluth 1993)

d) The result of the non-financial firms and MITI gaining the upper hand of financial industries and MOF
  • A variant of interest group dominance (theory of regulation)

e) An achievement by LDP backbenchers promoting consumerism as a result of 1994 electoral reforms that introduced a single-member district
  • Electoral rational choice (Ramseyer and Rosenbluth 1993; Rosenbluth and Thies 1999)

---

[46] Also, see Cowhey and McCubbins (1995).

on how one evaluates the significance of the Big Bang. Our account of the emergence of the Big Bang as well as our general observation about financial politics since 1995 will be weighed against these alternative explanations in Part II. Before moving on to this component of the analysis, however, we first develop our theoretical framework in Chapter 3.

3

How do Systems Change?

Actors, Preferences, Strategies, and Institutions in Financial Politics

This chapter seeks to achieve two tasks in preparation for our analysis of Japanese financial politics. First, we introduce the theoretical framework utilized in later chapters to make sense of developments in financial politics. Second, we sketch the strategies and possible scenarios for financial reform, by identifying the actors and deriving their preferences, based on observed behavioral regularities. To achieve this, we first introduce the concept of an institution as a strategic equilibrium (Aoki 2001). Upon this concept, we build our theoretical framework of institutional change and organizational survival. Here we show how our starting assumption—that organizations seek survival—applies to political parties, bureaucratic agencies, and firms. Through this process, we identify two institutions that prevailed in Japanese postwar finance and public policymaking through the first half of the 1990s: the public policymaking dynamic of bureaupluralism and the convoy system of financial supervision (hereafter, the Convoy). We then discuss the key actors involved in the politics of financial reform and the preferences of each vis-à-vis these reforms. Finally, we draw on these insights to sketch possible reform scenarios.

Introduction of Conceptual Tools for Institutional Analysis

Institutions

What is an institution? One may identify roughly three different views of "institutions" represented in actor-oriented approaches.[1] First, institutions

---

[1] See Chapter 2 for a discussion of two different approaches to "institutions" in political science (actor-oriented and institution-oriented).

may be depicted as the "players of the game," or as organizations such as firms, political parties, and bureaucratic agencies, which group individuals.[2] Second, they may be defined as "rules of the game" or informal and formal rules that constrain and shape human behavior by reducing uncertainty (North 1990). In this conceptualization, rules are determined exogenously. For example, in North's framework of economic analysis, the "rules of the game" that regulate economic behavior are decided in the polity, and thus exogenously.[3] While this type of theorization often provides a powerful explanation for the stability of existing institutions, it neglects any account of the evolution of these rules. Third, institutions may be defined as an equilibrium of actors' strategies that arises out of strategic interaction. Here the equilibrium is a Nash equilibrium, where no actor has incentives to change strategies (Aoki 2001; Calvert 1995; Greif, Milgrom, and Weingast 1994).

Because our primary interest is in how institutions change, we adopt the third view of institutions, which might be dubbed the "equilibrium approach." This approach provides a way to incorporate the formation of "rules of the game" into the analysis, while also allowing us to incorporate both the formal and informal patterns of interaction among actors and the collective perceptions about how these rules and interaction patterns are governed. Within the equilibrium approach, we draw more specifically on the comparative institutional analysis (CIA) perspective developed by Aoki (2001).[4] In this perspective, institutions are conceptualized as representing shared expectations about the state of the world, which arise out of the stable reproduction of behaviors and interactions over time.[5]

Thus, institutions emerge out of feedback between the objective and subjective worlds. An institution is (1) an equilibrium that arises from the repeated, strategic interaction of actors in the objective world, as well as (2) a summary representation of such an equilibrium that is collectively shared by actors as subjective beliefs. The feedback mechanism between the two makes institutions self-sustaining. Actors observe the equilibrium

---

[2] Following the examples of many in the field of actor-oriented approaches to institutions, we sometimes refer to the terminology of "game" as used in game theory to facilitate conceptual understanding.

[3] For example, see North (1990: 110).

[4] This framework was developed from evolutionary game theory and dynamic adaptive learning models of large populations composed of subjectively rational actors. See Young (1998) for a methodological discussion of this approach.

[5] In Aoki's terms, institutions are "*collectively shared, self-sustaining system of beliefs* regarding a salient way in which the game is repeatedly played." What follows in this section is an effort to represent the conceptual thinking developed by Aoki in a summarized, somewhat cursory, manner without using the language of game theory, while adding some interpretation and examples of our own. See Aoki (2001), especially Chapter 1.

in the objective world, and being subjectively rational, compress it into specific expectations about how the world works (e.g. "If actor A takes action X, then actor B will take action Y").[6] Such rules come to be collectively shared by all actors as the representation of the objective world, when they are repeatedly validated by the stable equilibrium—which is, in fact, the same strategic interaction reproduced repeatedly. Notably, multiple equilibrium may exist and these may or may not be Pareto-rankable.[7]

This definition of institutions gives rise to four observations. First, under our definition, codified forms of "rule of the games," such as laws, contracts, routines, and operating procedures, represent existing shared beliefs about how the world works. Accordingly, they may stop being institutions if actors stop believing that they effectively represent how the world works. Second, uncodified practices may be institutions if such practices are consistently reproduced over time and expected to continue into the future. In Aoki's terms, such practices remain institutions "as long as the agents believe in them as relevant representations" of how the world works.[8]

Third, once actors become aware of the existence of an institution, then the new concept itself acts as a symbol or "focal point" to facilitate the reinforcement of the actors' shared beliefs in the institution as a representation of "how the world works." Examples include ideology, such as militant nationalism in 1930s Japan, and historical tradition, such as social systems present in pre-modern Japan and invoked in reference to the "Japanese Economic Model" of the 1980s.

Fourth, the shared expectation helping uphold the existence of an institution both derive from the stable reproduction of observable features of the institution ("what has happened / will happen") and represent normative values or priorities that actors come to hold about what *should* happen, based on observations to the present. Consider the institution of lifetime employment in postwar Japan. This practice originated out of purely economic considerations, but the practice acquired a normative character after its stable reproduction over time gave rise to shared expectations about the way employment practices should be. Thus, while

[6] In this sense, institutions reduce transaction cost, as in the transaction-cost perspectives (North 1990).

[7] That is, all actors are better off in institution α than β; or actor A may be better off than actor B in α, and vice versa for β. Note that institutions α and β are still Nash equilibria. The definition of a Nash equilibrium is that no single actor has the incentives to alter his own strategy, given the other actors' strategies.

[8] The "main bank system" in Japan, an accumulation of practices in banking and industrial sectors and the government, is given by Aoki as an example of such institutions. See Aoki (2001). For more on the Japanese main bank system, see Aoki and Patrick (1994).

the practice does not have particularly deep historical roots, it heavily constrains the employer's ability to fire employees. Even though the legal right to fire employees is stipulated in labor contracts, shared expectations give rise to widespread social condemnation if this legal right is, in fact, exercised.[9]

Institutional Complementarity

An institution has an institutional environment in the sense that the strategic interaction of actors takes place outside one's own "institutional field."[10] Institutional complementarity arises in cases where actors see their institutional environments as "parameters" beyond their control.[11] At the objective level, actors in one institutional field both affect the institutional environment and are constrained by this environment. Actors only consciously recognize the latter, however, due to bounded rationality in the face of a complex world. In this way, actors conceive institutions to be "parameters" affecting the institutional field in question. This phenomenon may give rise to interdependence among institutions: an institution may only become viable in the presence of other institutions in the institutional field, and vice versa.

Aoki (2001) shows that this type of institutional interdependence, or "institutional complementarity," gives rise to multiple viable institutional arrangements. Aoki defines institutional complementarity as a situation that occurs across two or more institutions when a specific condition obtains regarding the relative preferences of actors in one particular field given the existence of an institution in other fields (and vice versa).[12] In

[9] For more on lifetime employment in Japan, see Aoki (2001) and Noguchi (1995). According to Sakakibara (1993), "anthropocentrism" such as employee sovereignty in firms assumed a normative character over time.

[10] See Aoki (2001) where the synchronic linkage of institutions is discussed. The "institutional fields" correspond to what he calls the "domains" in which the games take place. Aoki's "domains" are classified into four categories along the characteristics of the strategic interaction (the availability of "exit" and actor symmetry); however, in our framework, we call the domain in which strategic interaction takes place an "institutional field," without making such a distinction among fields.

[11] Aoki (2001) develops this concept in a thorough and formalized manner.

[12] Suppose that there are two institutional fields (A and B); actors have two options in each field (a1, a2; b1, b2); actors have identical payoff functions regarding their choices in each field. If all actors choose a1 in A, institution A1 arises in A (likewise, a2 gives rise to A2). Similarly, b1 (b2) in B gives rise to institution B1 (B2). The actors in one field may have differing preferences over the institution in the other field: for example, some actors in A1 may prefer B1 in B, others B2 in B. In each field, strategic complementarity obtains: when an institution (= equilibrium) has not arisen and actors are making their choices, each actor always sees his/her own marginal gains of switching choices increase, when any other actors make the same shift. When the following two conditions hold ("super-modularity"), multiple

such a situation, even if a Pareto-superior institutional arrangement is possible where every actor would be better off, Pareto sub-optimal institutional arrangements may be stable over time.[13]

On the one hand, the concept of institutional complementarity sheds light on the stable reproduction of Pareto sub-optimal institutional arrangements. When the existence of one institution is predicated on the existence of others, change in either may become less likely, and institutional arrangements may therefore tend to be "sticky" over time. On the other hand, if the environment (including the institutional environment) drastically changes to bring change in one institution, the bias toward stability may be overcome: the altered state of one institution may start a chain reaction, leading all institutions to be affected and giving rise to a new institutional arrangement.

Institutional Change[14]

For the purposes of this study, an institution only exists when the actors engaging in strategic interaction believe it to represent an equilibrium state. This definition, in turn, helps inform our definition of institutional change. The fundamental trait of institutional change is the shift in collective beliefs of a critical mass. Thus, it matters not whether institutional change takes place by conscious design, such as through the passage of laws, nor whether institutional change takes place via decentralized experiments carried out by policy entrepreneurs or other actors operating at the margins of the institutions.

Institutions may be robust to minor deviations from standard behavior, as long as the current strategies bring about satisfactory results and such deviations do not result in markedly better outcomes. Adjustments can be made at the margins to incorporate any minor but successful strategies that deviate from the norm. However, if particular environmental changes drastically alter the objective world, the effectiveness of the institution

---

equilibria arise. First, all the actors in A see that the marginal benefit derived from choosing A1 over A2 increases, if the institutional environment is B1 rather than B2. Second, all the actors in B see that the marginal benefit derived from choosing B2 rather than B1 increases, if the institutional environment is A2 rather than A1. Under this condition, two Nash equilibria in terms of institutional arrangements arise: (A1, B1) and (A2, B2). When such multiple equilibria arise, fields A and B are said to be institutionally complementary, and institutions A1 and B1 (A2 and B2) are complementary institutions.

[13] Alternatively, the institutional arrangements may not be Pareto-rankable in that some actors may prefer the status quo while others prefer a new institutional arrangement.

[14] For more on concepts of "institutional change," see the chapter on diachronic linkages of institutions in Aoki (2001).

"as a summary representation of how the world works" may be undermined and result in a "perceptual crisis" (Aoki 2001). For example, technological innovation may make new actions feasible or alter the consequences of the same action. A crisis due to such developments as war, famine, foreign competition, or demographic change may also threaten the survival of a nation, leading all actors to come to realize the need for drastically improving their performance and creating a "window of opportunity" for institutional change. Alternatively, the accumulated interaction among actors may bring about a crisis—for example, by leading to drastic distributional gaps. The institutional environment may also undergo a shift due to external shocks, triggering institutional change.

When environmental changes give rise to misalignment between objective reality and the subjective representation of how the world works, actors may begin to doubt the effectiveness of institutional arrangements and be encouraged to experiment with strategies that diverge from the norms prescribed by the institution. If such strategies are rewarded by success and then emulated by other actors, these strategies may become increasingly prominent. A new institution emerges when a critical mass of agents shift their views on how the world works to a new collectively shared view and this view is perceived to yield desirable results.

In this process, symbols or focal points facilitate convergence of actor beliefs about optimal institutional alternatives. Examples of such symbols include ideology, historical tradition, and foreign practice. Recall the role played by communism in facilitating the Russian Revolution, the role played by democratic ideals in bringing down the socialist regime in Eastern Europe, the images of Czarist Russia or eighteenth-century Poland invoked in the demise of these countries' respective socialist regimes, or the role played by foreign practice in the "third wave of democratization" since the 1970s (Huntington 1991).

A Theoretical Framework for Institutional Change

Political and economic institutions are known to be "sticky" not only because of the stable reproduction of behaviors over time, but also because the powerful actors who benefit from the status quo are often in privileged positions and able to prevent unwanted changes from happening. This framework provides insight into how institutional change may occur even in the face of "stickiness" caused by a political bias of entrenched state actors towards the status quo: new collective perceptions about how the world works emerge through an evolutionary selection mechanism that rewards successful strategies (with respect to the objective world) and results in the reproduction of these strategies among the populace.

How does this evolutionary mechanism work in the political economy? Might privileged actors preferring the status quo interfere in the process, hindering the evolutionary mechanism? Clearly, the "victory" of alternative strategies is not pre-determined—that is, they may be evaluated as successful ex post, but not ex ante. Thus, we can see how political conflict might arise between those preferring the status quo and those experimenting with alternative strategies. What are the conditions for the "victory" of the alternative strategies over the old ones and the concomitant rise of a new institution?

To better understand the politics of—or the distributional conflicts that arise over—institutional change, we must link the issue of institutional change to a discussion of the power and interests of actors. With this goal in mind, we turn next to develop a theoretical framework of institutional change in the political economy, building on the concepts provided in the last section. Here we focus on two questions: (1) What makes actors re-examine their strategies?; and, (2) How does the process of competition among institutions work—that is, what determines which side "wins"? Although the framework that follows is developed in an effort to answer these questions in the context of Japan of the 1990s, it is also general enough to be applied to other cases of institutional change, inside and outside of Japan.

Factors that Make Actors' Re-examine their Strategies

In the conceptualization of institutional change introduced previously, a misalignment between objective reality and subjective perceptions spurs actors to re-examine their strategies. How does such a misalignment arise? The framework of institutional change introduced earlier suggested that it comes about in the presence of exogenous shocks such as technological innovation, through the emergence of huge distributional inequalities, or via change in the institutional environment. If such shocks or new situations were quickly accommodated by changes in institutions, then misalignment would not happen. As suggested earlier, however, institutions are sticky for various reasons such as the presence of entrenched actors, forces of inertia, or investment of sunken costs. Thus, we may expect a gap to be formed between the speed of environmental changes and the pace of institutional adaptation. This gap may be characterized as a "failure," since the institution fails to prescribe strategies that yield expected results given its objective or exogenously determined constraints.

"Failures" may appear in the form of performance failures, where actors are unable to yield expected results, or as "scandals," where actor behavior is exposed as diverging from what is expected of by the institution. In the political economy, potential areas for performance failure include economic growth, production volume, profit, or political stability. Scandals, in contrast, arise through the infringement of laws or social standards (what the public collectively regards as right or wrong). Legal breaches may occur because large gaps emerge between what the law prescribes and what is taking place in the real world, such as was the case in the recurrent scandals of political financing in Japan, Italy, and Germany.[15] The loss compensation scandals in Japan in the early 1990s provide an example of a breach in social standards. In this case, securities firms provided an implicit guarantee to VIP clients against losses. When the practice was exposed, the top management of many firms compensated for losses were forced to resign. Although the practice was technically not a legal breach at the time, the public resented the preferential treatment of prominent individuals.

Performance failures and scandals often go hand-in-hand. Performance failures may lead actors to question the taken for granted aspect of institutions. When economic growth, inflation, unemployment, political stability, or other performance indices decline significantly, scandals may accelerate an erosion in collective beliefs about institutions by providing the symbols or focal points for alternative strategies or views. When things go well, as with the Japanese economy of the late 1980s, the Asian economies of the early 1990s, or the US economy of the late 1990s, scandals tend not to surface. And, even if they do, they often are not perceived as representing the pathology of institutional arrangements in the economy.[16] However, once things start to "fall apart," as did the Japanese economy in the 1990s and many of the other Asian economies in 1997–98, scandals become increasingly salient for institutional change. In this way, scandals by themselves are insufficient for causing a shift in collective beliefs about institutions. However, in the presence of performance failures, we may expect recurrent scandals, which in turn accelerate the erosion of collective

---

[15] Another example might be the drastic changes of the political and/or the economic system that occurs in such situations as "democratization" or "revolution."

[16] In this example, what is actually taking place in the real world is the real "institution," according to our definition.

beliefs about the institutions in question. "Failures"—namely, performance failures and scandals—shake up actors' beliefs that an institution effectively represents how the world works and spur actors to question whether an institution should continue to be used as a reference point for determining strategies.

The Mechanism of Evolutionary Selection

In this framework, the dynamics of evolutionary selection reward the "best response" strategy, and the share of that strategy in the population increases as its success leads other actors to emulate it. However, this characterization bears an "auto-pilot" flavor. How the process relates to the political struggle of actors needs to be further specified, if we are to identify any signs of institutional change *ex ante*, in the hopes of offering clues for prediction.

Let us start from "performance failures and scandals," which lead some actors to re-think how the world works and adopt alternative strategies. A competition between two (or more) sets of strategies arises: one is prescribed by the dominant "institution" and the rest are alternative strategies, adopted by a few "mavericks." At this point, "institutional change" has not yet taken place since institutions are usually resilient to minor deviations. There may be attempts to change; however, if these attempts fail, institutional change is not observed *ex post*, and institutions persist. On the other hand, if the alternative strategies of the first "mavericks" succeed, the use of such strategies increases in society. Once a critical mass of the actors adopt the new strategies and accepts the new views about how the world works, we can call it "institutional change."[17] What determines which strategy wins? Why do new strategies sometimes fail? How does the experimentation (or mutation or mistake) go from being a minority to a dominant strategy and thus help comprise part of the newly shared perceptions about how the world works?

Here is where the political struggle comes in. Exogenous conditions such as technological innovation, crisis, or change in the institutional environment may dictate which side ultimately wins or loses by determining how successful each strategy is. Yet, we may gain insight into how this process works by considering what differentiates actors' strategies and how

---

[17] For example, a common characterization of the Japanese political economy in the 1980s was a country with "first-rate economics and third-rate politics," a cliché representing the collective beliefs of the 1980s that troubles were confined to politics. In contrast, not many characterized the economy as "first-rate" in the 1990s.

coalitions form. For the sake of simplicity, let us suppose that there are two sets of institutions, the status quo institutions (α) and the alternative institutions (β). Let us further suppose that the population is composed of two sets of actors, insiders (I), or actors with privileged positions in the institution that provide an entry point to the political process, and the outsiders (O), or actors without institutional resources. At the starting point, the equilibrium is α: every actor prefers this institution (by definition, an institution is a Nash equilibrium). We call those who prefer α "conservatives," and those who prefer β "reformers." Thus, all actors begin as "conservatives."

WHAT DIFFERENTIATES ACTORS' STRATEGIES?

We may posit two possibly divergent concerns that drive a change in actor strategies. The first concern is whether actors anticipate the outcome of "institutional resilience," that is, a return at some point to the institutional status quo, or whether actors anticipate more permanent "institutional change." The second concern relates to the distributional effect of institutional change. This effect may lead the actors to prefer either α (the status quo) or β (the alternative), depending on whether the institutional change is Pareto-rankable. Note that the first concern affects the second: if one thinks that "change" is happening due to exogenous developments and/or adaptation of other actors, one is more likely to shift preferences from α to β. Institutional change (the shift from α to β) may or may not have distributional effects: if α and β are not Pareto-rankable, then α may be beneficial to some, while β may be beneficial to others, however, if they are Pareto-rankable (e.g. the shift from α to β is beneficial to both A and B), the shift is not constrained by the political struggles between A and B.

Suppose nature "moves," and some environmental changes shake the taken for granted aspect of the institution. Now α holds dominantly with some scattered observation of β in the population: some "mavericks" start to experiment with alternative strategies, joining the ranks of "reformers." Such developments are likely to be suppressed by the "conservatives" and the political struggle between the two groups that ensues is part of the process of institutional change. If such efforts to suppress change succeed, we observe "institutional resilience."

In this process, symbols (focal points) invoked by actors—both in favor of continuity and of change—may enhance the legitimacy of their views about how the world works. History, or common historical experience, can be both a source for conservatism (such as in the case of patriotic wars) or reform (such as in the case of an imperial past). Similarly, foreign practices may lead to calls for emulation at home or justify the preservation of existing practice.[18] Ideology, such as communism or democracy, may furnish another focal point influencing actor behavior. Leadership or personal charisma may also provide symbols for continuity or for change. Consider, for example, the role of Mao in upholding the status quo in post-1949 China versus his role pushing for change in prewar China.

PATTERN OF COALITION FORMATION

Thus, we may see a struggle between two or more coalitions of actors in the process of institutional change. How does this struggle play out? Distinguishing between "outsiders" and "insiders" is helpful here: in the discussion cited previously, "outsiders" are more likely to become "reformers" than "insiders," all else being equal, as the former have fewer stakes in preserving the status quo. Two patterns emerge in which the "conservatives" may be displaced: the formation of "counter-coalitions" or "defection." The formation of a "counter-coalition" is a scenario in which the outsiders turned into "reformers" form a coalition among themselves against the insiders or "conservatives," while "defection" is one in which some among the insiders defect to become "reformers" and band together against the remaining insiders or "conservatives."

To relate these concepts to real world examples in political economy, we may think of revolutions and regime changes "from outside" and "from within." Counter-coalitions can be found in the Russian Revolution, which was marked by the emergence of "outsiders" with different strategies, the Bolsheviks. On the other hand, defection may be found in many instances of democratization in Latin America and Southern Europe since the 1970s. In the latter case, exogenous changes such as democratization in other countries, defeat in war, or economic depression spurred a split between the hard liners and the soft liners within the ruling elite in authoritarian regimes, to start democratization (O'Donnell and Schmitter 1986). Or, to rephrase, some among the "insiders" began to adopt different strategies. Later we will return to these concepts, using them to project possible scenarios of financial reforms.

Summarizing our Theoretical Framework of Institutional Change

Institutional change is essentially a shift in shared perceptions about how the world works through a collective learning process based on an evolutionary

---

[18] The process may be compressed into one short event that rapidly unfolds.

selection mechanism of strategies derived from the actors' subjective beliefs about how the world works. It is caused by the gap between the faster pace of environmental changes (including the institutional environment) and the slower pace of adaptation in domestic political and economic institutions. This gap appears in the form of "failures," or "performance failures" and "scandals," which lead actors to question the "taken for granted" aspect of the institutions. "Nature"—environmental changes such as in technology or in the institutional environment—eventually determines the outcome of the competition of the institutions by rewarding various strategies of actors: successful strategies become increasingly employed in the population. Yet, political struggle takes place between those actors who see the process as institutional "resilience" and/or have stakes in preserving the status quo, and those actors who perceive that "change" is taking place and/or perceive that their own interests are being enhanced by the new institutions.

The distributional concerns of institutional change come in only when the old and new institutions are not Pareto-rankable. Political struggle is facilitated by symbols derived from such sources as history, foreign practice, ideology, and leadership. In the process, "conservatives" may be displaced by "reformers" via either the formation of a "counter-coalition" (from outside) or through "defection" (from within). When a critical mass of the agents shift its views about "how the world works" and the new institutions become taken for granted, "institutional change" has occurred. Institutional complementarity often makes institutional change in one institutional field difficult; however, once change happens in one institution, it is likely that actors will be forced to reassess surrounding institutions, thus starting a chain reaction of change.

Figure 3.1 summarizes the theoretical framework of institutional change presented in this section. Note that the process of institutional change can be reversed at any point in the process. Once "failures" appear, the shared expectations about how the world works come to be increasingly questioned by "mavericks." We may refer to this situation as institutional "decay," where an increasing number of actors conclude that something is amiss. However, if "nature" signals the return to the status quo or if the "conservatives" crush the few "mavericks," then this "decay" may be halted. The latter scenario would be another instance of "institutional resilience," wherein the institution shows its robustness against minor deviations.

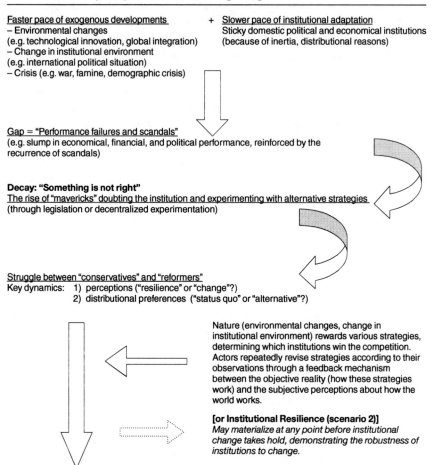

Faster pace of exogenous developments
– Environmental changes
(e.g. technological innovation, global integration)
– Change in institutional environment
(e.g. international political situation)
– Crisis (e.g. war, famine, demographic crisis)

+ Slower pace of institutional adaptation
Sticky domestic political and economical institutions
(because of inertia, distributional reasons)

Gap = "Performance failures and scandals"
(e.g. slump in economical, financial, and political performance, reinforced by the recurrence of scandals)

Decay: "Something is not right"
The rise of "mavericks" doubting the institution and experimenting with alternative strategies (through legislation or decentralized experimentation)

Struggle between "conservatives" and "reformers"
Key dynamics: 1) perceptions ("resilience" or "change"?)
               2) distributional preferences ("status quo" or "alternative"?)

Nature (environmental changes, change in institutional environment) rewards various strategies, determining which institutions win the competition. Actors repeatedly revise strategies according to their observations through a feedback mechanism between the objective reality (how these strategies work) and the subjective perceptions about how the world works.

[or Institutional Resilience (scenario 2)]
May materialize at any point before institutional change takes hold, demonstrating the robustness of institutions to change.

Institutional Change (scenario 1)
Enough objective reality supports the alternative strategies derived from the new subjective notion about how the world works. A shift in the actors' collective notion of how the world works takes place. A new institution is taken for granted and replaces the old.

Two patterns of displacement of "conservatives"
1) Counter-coalition (from outside: "outsiders" displace "insiders")
2) Defection (from within: defecting "insiders" displace the remaining "insiders")

Figure 3.1 Theoretical framework of institutional change in the political economy

The Dynamics of Organizational Survival

By further examining how "defection" works in our framework of institutional change, we may capture the dynamics at work concerning the "entrenched actors" (the "insiders" in our terminology) and "organizational survival." Entrenched actors, such as the LDP in Japan, are conventionally expected to be the jealous guardians of their secured interests under the status quo, and thus are typically assumed to oppose institutional change. However, they may not be as "entrenched" as they often appear to be: some among them may adopt alternative strategies as a result of reevaluation based on an altered situation (e.g. changing environment and a shift in the distribution of the strategies adopted by the population), and become "reformers." In other words, a stable reproduction of strategies by some actors with privileged positions in one institutional arrangement does not prohibit such actors from becoming "reformers" later on. They are only more likely to be "entrenched" when change threatens to make them lose their privileged positions in the status quo. Thus, we may expect, *ceteris paribus*, that "entrenched" actors will be slower to join the reform camp. However, this does not preclude the possibility that some who once served as guardians of the old institutional arrangements later become strong proponents of institutional change.

Taking the process of institutional change to the sub-organizational level, we may conceptualize an evolutionary selection mechanism that propels an organizational strategy prioritizing survival above all else. At the starting point, under a stable institution, all actors (i.e., individual members of the organization) are "conservatives." However, "nature" moves, environmental changes spur the increasing emergence of alternative strategies. At this point, a split appears within the organization—that is, a conflict takes place between two sets of sub-organizational actors, wherein each side seeks to maximize prospects for organizational survival according to its own views about how the world works and/or according to its own interests.

On the one hand, "conservatives" see the process as one in which the institution in question is resilient. These actors may also have their own stakes in the preservation of the institution. Thus, their prescription for the organization is to adopt the same strategies as adopted in the past. "Conservatives" tend to include those who have large stakes to lose if change occurs. Such actors include the "insiders" within the organization, or those with relatively more power resources within the organization. "Reformers," on the other hand, see the process as one in which environmental changes spur institutional change. Thus, they recommend that the organization alter its strategies to adapt to the new institution—or even participate in creating the new institution. Because "reformers" may have gains to be made with the creation of new institutions, this group tends to comprise those more on the margins rather than at the center of the power structure of the organization.

Both sides recommend the strategy they think increases the prospect for organizational survival, the "ultimate" goal shared by all actors. "Nature" (technological constraints and changes in the institutional environment) moves and rewards one of the strategies. All actors, observing which strategy better leads them closer to the goal of survival, then revise their views accordingly. Through this reiterated process and selection mechanism, either "conservatives" or "reformers" emerge as the winner and gain command over the organizational strategy.

We will utilize this conceptual framework in Chapter 5 to show how the loss of public support drives politicians and bureaucrats to engage in a complex strategic interaction, involving competition, cooperation, and conflict. Before proceeding to that stage of the analysis, however, we must first introduce the relevant actors in Japanese politics and examine their preferences. Four sets of actors emerge: political parties, bureaucratic agencies, firms and interest groups, and the public. We distinguish state actors who enjoy direct access to public policy tools (laws and administrative tools) to influence the private sector from societal actors who influence state actors to obtain preferred policies. The former include politicians and bureaucrats while the latter include firms and interest groups, as well as the public. In the case of state actors, we start from a Downsian assumption that "every government seeks to maximize political support" (Downs 1957: 11). However, in contrast to Downs, who equates "government" with politicians, we see two sets of state actors as important: politicians and bureaucrats.[19] In our framework, state actors seek to maximize political support from two sources: constituencies and the general public. In the following four sections, the goals of each set of actors will be derived from a discussion of their behavioral regularities in the context of the Japanese political economy. For the state actors (politicians and bureaucrats), the sources of political support will be discussed as well.

State Actors (1)—Political Parties

Politics in postwar Japan has been characterized by the dominance of one party, the LDP, a conservative party continuously in power from 1955 through 1993. Prior to Lower House elections in 1993, some of the party's lawmakers defected from the party over the issue of electoral reforms—the

---

[19] This focus on both bureaucrats and politicians draws on Aoki's (1988) framework of "bureaupluralism."

most prominent component of which was the introduction of a single member district (SMD). The defection led to an eight-party non-LDP coalition government.[20] The coalition broke down in 1994, however, with the defection of the Socialist Party of Japan (known as the Social Democratic Party of Japan from January 1996 (SPJ; SDPJ)) and the Sakigake Party. A coalition government centered on the LDP has ruled Japan since 1994 to the time of this writing. The Socialist and Sakigake Parties were members of the LDP-led coalition government between 1994 and 1998. The first Socialist Prime Minister since 1947, Tomiichi Murayama, held office from 1994 to January 1996, as the policy package dealing with the Housing Loan Affair was about to reach the Diet and our account of the Japanese Financial Big Bang begins. LDP President Ryutaro Hashimoto succeeded Murayama as prime minister, and presided over the passing of the legislation related to the Housing Loan Affair and the Big Bang initiative (see Chapter 5).

To make better sense of these political developments in the 1990s, we start from the assumption that organizations seek survival. When applied to political parties, this translates into the assumption that political parties seek to maximize the number of electoral seats.[21] Political parties in a liberal democracy compete to maximize political influence, and in Japan, this influence is exercised through the party's presence in the Diet, the nation's bicameral parliament.[22] While early observations on Japanese politics may have questioned whether true inter-party competition existed in Japan under the dominance of the LDP, we have the benefit of being able to observe the development of the 1990s, where party alignment constantly shifted. Thus, we are confident that competition was present at least in Japanese politics of the 1990s, if not for the whole postwar era.[23]

Political parties maximize their chances of organizational survival by winning elections.[24] A withering political party with fewer electoral seats

[20] See, for example, Kohno (1997) and Pempel (1998) for the political process before and after 1993. Also, see Reed and Thies (1999) for the electoral reforms since 1955 including the origin of the 1994 reforms.

[21] As noted above, this is in line with the Downsian tradition that assumes that "every government seeks to maximize political support," that "the government exists in a democratic society where periodic elections are held, and that the government's goal is "reelection." (Downs 1957: 11)

[22] Japan has a bicameral system: the Lower House (*Shugiin*), with priority over the election of the prime minister as well as votes on budget and treaties, and the Upper House (*Sangiin*).

[23] See Kohno (1997: 12–13) on this issue. We agree with Kohno's assertion that the outcome of one-party rule by the LDP does not necessarily mean the lack of competition among political parties in the postwar era.

[24] Note that "winning" does not necessarily involve gains in electoral seats. For example, in the 1993 elections, the Komeito party seemed to adopt the strategy of keeping as many seats as possible, by limiting the number of their candidates: victory may also be defined as a party having most of its candidates elected.

cannot be expected to wield power; at its worst, such a party must fear extinction.[25] Our assumption of organizational survival through the maximization of electoral seats is based upon the behavioral goals of the individual politicians, who are assumed to pursue their own reelection.

Our analysis mostly focuses on the LDP for the following reasons. First, the LDP has been the largest and most influential party over the postwar period and throughout the 1990s, whether it was in power or in opposition. As a reflection of its long period of dominance, interaction between the government and the private sector in the Japanese political economy has largely come to be structured around this party. Second, the LDP was in power throughout our period of analysis (1995–98), after holding power for more than forty years prior, with the exception of a short interval of less than a year. This is not to say that the LDP saw its chance of electoral survival unaffected by party competition, as we will see that the LDP was clearly threatened by rival parties in our period under analysis.

The non-LDP parties—those in coalition and in opposition—will be discussed in Part II as they enter into the political process. The coalition parties are obviously important in influencing policy outcomes, as they are incorporated into the policymaking process (or the process in which a legislative proposal passes through the public policymaking bodies of the bureaucracy and the ruling parties before it reaches the Diet; see later). The opposition parties are basically excluded from the policymaking process, and can participate in decision-making only after bills reach the Diet. Under a parliamentary democracy with strong party discipline, as in Japan, the opposition can hardly affect the passage of bills through their votes, unless they resort to some kind of boycott such as refusing to attend Diet deliberations, refusing to move to vote, or engaging in delaying tactics.[26] However, opposition parties can have a significant role in the policy-making process if the LDP loses its majority in the Upper House. When the control of the Lower House and the Upper House belong to a different party (or coalition), the one which controls the Lower House will be in power, by electing the Prime Minister; however, the opposition will have

---

[25] See the fate of the Sakigake Party: once a prominent coalition member for the 1993 non-LDP government and the 1994–98 three party LDP-coalition, it was disbanded in 1999 with only a few Diet members left.

[26] This led to bargaining behind closed doors between the LDP and non-LDP party officials in charge of Diet affairs, and in these interactions, the non-LDP parties did possess a certain degree of bargaining power. However, when both houses were under LDP control, the opposition party did not appear to wield a significant degree of power. See Sato and Matsuzaki (1986: Chapter 7).

increased access to political decision-making, as those in power need to compromise if they wish to pass their proposals.[27]

Parties need two kinds of resources to maximize their goal of organizational survival through electoral victory: votes and money. Constituencies (or interest groups) and the public provide these essential resources. Constituencies such as agriculture, labor or big business provide blocks of votes and/or campaign contribution via cooperatives, labor unions or large firms grouped into pro-business groups and industrial associations. In return, these constituencies may request particularistic favors from those in power, such as favorable budget measures or regulatory protection. Alternately, constituency support may be untied to specific policies but linked to more general policy platforms, such as pro-business or pro-labor positions. When the public votes in elections, it does so not so much in anticipation of special policy favors, but more so on the basis of general policy concerns, such as the nation's overall economic health or pollution concerns. In this way, the public's support can be characterized as "generalized voter support."[28]

State Actors (2)—Bureaucratic Agencies

The Japanese bureaucracy has played an important political role in postwar Japan. Such bureaucratic agencies as the MITI and the MOF have wielded considerable influence over economic policy decisions, especially since the commencement of LDP one-party dominance in 1955. As mentioned in Chapter 2, we are interested not so much in whether the politicians or the bureaucrats dominate the policymaking process as we are in the pattern of their interaction. As dominance fails to capture an important aspect of political interaction, both actors matter in our theoretical framework. These two state actors are the only ones with direct access to the exercise of governmental power through legislation and its administrative execution.

What do bureaucratic agencies pursue? Some argue that bureaucrats pursue budget maximization (Niskanen 1971), while others say revenue

---

[27] The Japanese Constitution guarantees the primacy of the Lower House over budget proposals and treaties but the approval of both houses is required for the passage of ordinary legislation.

[28] This phrase comes from Okimoto (1989), who offers a discussion of the types of exchanges of goods and services ongoing between the LDP and the members of its support coalition. Note that the power to grant particularistic policy favors has been almost monopolized by the LDP since 1955 (with its structured process of distributing such favors developed over the years).

maximization (Brennan and Buchanan 1980). In works on Japanese politics, Ramseyer and Rosenbluth (1993: 99–120) argue that bureaucrats seek to please their political masters, who have veto power, alternative sources of information, and control over their individual careers (via control over promotion and retirement options). Kato (1994) focuses on the maximization of discretionary power in her study of tax politics in Japan.[29] Vogel (1996), meanwhile, sees a "regime orientation" toward the maximization of regulatory control to be prevalent among Japanese bureaucrats.[30]

The empirical validity of such behavioral assumptions needs to be confirmed, however. When we check the aforementioned assumptions against the reality of Japanese politics and the case of the politics of financial reforms, we find that they fall short in a number of respects. First, the assumption that bureaucrats seek foremost to "please their political masters" ignores the potential conflicts that may arise between bureaucrats and politicians. Just because politicians possess ultimate veto power does not mean that they can use it freely. A number of social, political and other constraints may interfere with their actual exercise of this veto. One can point to many past instances in which political initiatives were successfully stymied—perhaps most notably the many past attempts at administrative reform. It is clear that such assumptions provide little utility in explaining a number of important outcomes.[31]

Second, assumptions centered on maximizing tokens of organizational power—such as budgets, revenue, discretionary authority, or regulatory control—overlook cases in which bureaucrats see it in their interests to oppose the aggrandizement of such tokens or even actively seek to reduce such tokens of power. If regulatory reforms occur, or when regulatory control or discretionary power is reduced, proponents of this school of thought interpret the outcome as a sign that either politicians or interest groups gained the upper hand over resisting (or acquiescing) bureaucrats. Yet, the reduction of regulatory power may be a plausible goal for

---

[29] How Kato defines discretionary power, according to Amyx (1998: Chapter 1), which uses a similar behavioral assumption, is unclear. Discretionary power as used in this study, is the power to decide when or when not to enforce rules.

[30] Whether this is the starting assumption, or the conclusion, or both is somewhat unclear.

[31] For instance, the analysis of administrative reforms in the 1980s by Otake (1997a), and documented through interviews with politicians, suggests that bureaucratic resistance importantly influenced outcomes. Otake's interview with former chief cabinet secretary, Masaharu Gotoda, in particular, fails to support the assumption that politicians can freely exercise their veto powers. Gotoda recalls the hardship he endured in trying to overcome the bureaucracy's resistance to these reforms.

bureaucratic agencies to pursue. Actors have priorities and some goals are more important than others. Those focused exclusively on the assumptions discussed previously overlook the most fundamental goal of bureaucratic actors: organizational survival. We argue that Japanese bureaucrats pursue organizational survival, or the maximization of organizational prestige, of their respective agencies more than any other objective, and that they pursue this goal within the incentive structures defined by the institutional settings in which they operate. In the discussion that follows, we show how this assumption is derived and contrast our approach against those approaches stressing the bureaucratic maximization of tokens of organizational power. In the context of regulatory reforms, we refer to the latter assumption as one centering on the maximization of "regulatory power," as measured by jurisdiction and discretion.

It is well understood that individual incentives for bureaucrats may consist of many things, including promotion, job security, political influence, social status, and material gains. As Amyx (1998 [and 2004]) demonstrates in her study of MOF's internal organization, the personnel system is structured in such a way that job promotion serves as a proxy for all these individual incentives combined into one. The personnel system is based on continued employment commencing immediately after university graduation until the *de facto* forced retirement approximately thirty years later. An official typically remains employed by one ministry, although he or she may be temporarily assigned to positions in other agencies over the course of his or her career. Job promotions are carried out with attention to both seniority and meritocratic considerations. Those who join the ministry in the same year (an official's "peers") are generally promoted at the same speed; however, whether one reaches a higher rank in the bureaucracy usually depends on how well one does in early competition among peers. While the rank and salary of each assignment does not vary across a class of peers, the status and power attached to the assignments distributed across this class differ and decisions made about these appointments are based on an individual's reputation within the organization.

In the second stage of a bureaucrat's career, the official typically retires from the ministry to assume a position in the private sector or a public corporation related to the agency. This practice has been referred to as *amakudari*, or "descent from heaven." It is well-known that the status, prestige and financial incentives attached to the position one occupies in the second stage depends on how far one climbs up the bureaucratic ladder before leaving the ministry: the higher one makes it within the bureaucracy, the higher position one lands in retirement.[32] Given the personnel structure, competition among peers for promotion is very fierce. This process also serves to inculcate loyalty to one's agency (Pempel and Muramatsu 1995: 49). Thus, the personnel system serves to ensure that those who seek to enhance organizational interests are selected for higher positions, occupying the mainstream positions within the agency.

Thus, promotion works to integrate individual incentives and organizational goals. How does this work to make organizational survival the top priority? Keep in mind that there may be many goals being pursued simultaneously by the organization. On the one hand, officials may wish to maintain their regulatory power. As long as one's continued employment is incorporated into the expectations of individual bureaucrats, officials also have reasons to wish that the *amakudari* practice is maintained, so as to keep alive their second career opportunities. One of the reasons that firms receive retired officials is that they may expect favorable treatment, such as better access to information from regulators. Thus, officials are likely to have stakes in protecting regulatory control or discretionary power over industry—authority that tends to generate demand for retirement positions. On the other hand, the agency's social status, as well as its political influence, at the level of shared expectations among all actors (i.e., within the nation as a whole) may also be important goals to pursue, given the uncertain future of one's individual promotion. Therefore, the pursuit of an intangible resource such as "prestige," is important as well.

While many times all of these goals go hand-in-hand, there may be situations in which the maximization of organizational prestige takes on greater importance than the maximization of regulatory power or when the two goals directly conflict with one another. The maintenance or enhancement of the agency's prestige, for example, is likely to matter more than such quantifiable or tangible measures as budget, jurisdiction, or regulatory powers, when uncertainty about the future increases and as the possibility for future internal promotion or *amakudari* postings decreases. Moreover, in a situation in which regulation comes to be seen by all actors as hampering the "public interest" due to changed trends in economic thought, the latter goal of enhancing organizational prestige may be expected to dominate, as this goal is crucial even for those who

---

[32] The highest rank that a career official can reach is the position of administrative vice-minister. Until 2001, politically appointed positions in the ministry included the cabinet minister and one or two parliamentary vice-ministers.

are concerned about regulatory power. The agency's ability to influence the private sector is, after all, determined by more than the regulatory power the agency possesses. High prestige enables the agency to enjoy influence vis-à-vis actors other than its regulatory constituency, and this influence, in turn, enhances the agency's leverage vis-à-vis the private sector. Thus, if an agency's prestige is dealt a blow and the agency is perceived as weak, industry actors may reassess the costs and benefits of employing retired bureaucrats and decide that the benefits are insufficient to justify the high salaries paid to these individuals. In this way, the power of an agency vis-à-vis its regulatory constituencies and the material benefits accrued by retired officials may be adversely affected by a drop in organizational prestige.[33]

This reasoning leads us to posit that the goal of organizational survival is the most important goal that bureaucrats pursue. We define "survival" of a bureaucratic agency as the maintenance or enhancement of the agency's presence in politics, economics, and society—not necessarily measured by tangible tokens of organizational power, but rather, measured in terms of the agency's prestige, or the social status and political influence that the agency enjoys vis-à-vis other actors such as political parties, firms, and the public.

This distinction of "prestige" from "power" corresponds to our placing greater emphasis on "shared expectations" than on "formal rules" in the theoretical framework of institutional change: organizational survival, or the maximization of prestige, matters more than the preservation or expansion of an agency's regulatory jurisdiction, as defined by legal statutes.[34]Given the institutional setting in which the Japanese bureaucracy operates, wherein a single agency's personnel management is charged with overseeing the continuous employment of its officials, bureaucrats are likely to resist downsizing of their employing organization, such as the split of an agency into two (or more) pieces. However, we should interpret this resistance as being due less to worry over the loss of organizational jurisdiction *per se* and more to the attempt to encroach on

---

[33] For more on *amakudari*, see Inoki (1995). Also Aoki (1988: Chapter 7), Okimoto (1989: 161–5), Ramseyer and Rosenbluth (1993: 115–22), and Amyx (1998 and 2004: Chapter 3). The tie between a retired official and the bureaucracy does not end when the official leaves the ministry. Most bureaucrats move on to a new *amakudari* position every few years, with each move typically made in line with a recommendation from one's former ministry.

[34] Our discussion on "power" parallels the contrast often drawn in international relations literature between material resources that actors command and intangible influences over other actors. See Gilpin (1981: 31), which distinguishes power (material capabilities) from prestige, or the reputation of power, which is the "everyday currency of international relations." Also see Keohane (1984: Chapter 2) for a review of the concepts of power.

the agency's prestige. The MOF's resistance to reforms of its organization, detailed in Chapter 5, serves as a case in point.

In some cases, bureaucrats may perceive gains to be made by sacrificing jurisdictional territory. For example, an agency may be willing to sacrifice some of its authority in one area to capture a more strategic position (and thus prestige) within the government as a whole. Similarly, while bureaucrats generally welcome an increase in jurisdiction, the consolidation of multiple agencies into one to achieve that end may mean that each official has to compete against a larger number of individuals for higher positions. If those in an agency are confident of capturing a strategic position in the newly formed agency and of being able to seize the organizational initiative, then they are likely to be more willing to accept such a reorganization than otherwise.[35]

Lastly, what do bureaucratic agencies pursue to secure the survival of their organization? Although bureaucrats do not pursue votes and money in the same way as political parties do, we may be able to identify similar sets of interests by following the framework of "bureaupluralism" developed by Aoki (1988). In this framework, regulatory constituencies and the public occupy particularly important positions.[36] Jurisdictional constituents—that is, regulated industries—may provide goods and services to the bureaucracy in the form of valuable information, cooperation with administrative measures, and retirement positions for employees of bureaucratic agencies. The agency's reputation among the general public is also a determinant of the chances of organizational survival. By highlighting their positive contributions to the well-being of the nation, bureaucratic agencies can expect better acceptance for their policy measures, maximize the societal status they enjoy, and hence better secure the prospect of continued existence.

Societal Actors (1)—Firms and Interest Groups

The conventional characterization of firms' behavioral regularity in the economics literature is the maximization of profit. This characterization

---

[35] See Eda (1999) for a proposal by Prime Minister Hashimoto's private secretary (from MITI), towards MITI assuming a role over macroeconomic policy by merging into the Economic Planning Agency (EPA). Given the relative power relationship between MITI over EPA (e.g. in personnel practice), it may not be surprising if MITI's strategy towards administrative reforms under the Hashimoto government included the concern mentioned here.

[36] In Aoki's language, these two factors determine the political stock that the bureaus command. While we assume, as Downs (1957: 11–12) does, that "every government seeks to maximize political support," we define "government" not as "governing party" but rather as "state actors," or "politicians and bureaucrats with direct access to governmental power."

reflects a corporate governance structure that emphasizes the control of the shareholders, or the "owners" of the firms, over corporate management. While "shareholder capitalism" may well capture the dynamics of economic systems such as the one that operates in the United States, the Japanese economy in the postwar era developed a very different "stakeholder capitalism." In Japan, stakeholders such as management, employees, and creditors other than shareholders, exercise a large amount of control in addition to shareholders.[37] Interrelated practices, such as lifetime employment, cross-shareholding, and the main bank system also largely undermine the assumptions of "shareholder capitalism."[38] In Japan's economic system, as in other capitalist systems, firms pursue profit. However, just as was the case for the bureaucracy, other goals also coexist. This is particularly the case given the prevailing firm-level practices of lifetime employment, a seniority wage system, and the recruitment of management from within the corporation. Management may also be interested in the continued employment of core workers, which can be best provided by the continuous prosperity of the organization, or through the survival of the organization.

Most of the time, firms pursue both profit and the continued employment of core workers (part-timers generally enjoy less job security). Yet, just as bureaucratic organizations have priorities, firms have priorities. When the goals of profit maximization and the continued employment of core workers come into conflict with each other, as they may with a downturn in corporate performance, then the priorities rise to the surface. If profit maximization is the ultimate priority, then the management will choose the solution of "lay-off." If, on the other, maintaining continuous employment is seen as the ultimate priority, then the management will sacrifice profit while retaining a potentially redundant labor force.

It has been widely observed that Japanese firms, especially large Japanese firms, have operated with the latter concern foremost in mind, prioritizing jobs of core workers over profit maximization. According to Fukao (1999), the shareholders for large public firms have less control over residual rights than do core employees. Clearly, corporate profit acts as a parameter that determines whether a firm can continue to exist: if a firm approaches failure, it will fire its employees. However, in the Japanese context, such

---

[37] Note that this distinction may be the result of how one defines corporate governance: "the control of suppliers of finance over corporation" or "the design of institutions that induce or force management to internalize the welfare of stakeholders" (Tirole 1998). For example, contrast Shleifer and Vishny (1997) from the former approach, against the "stakeholder" approach in Tirole (1998). As we are interested in the Japanese political economy, we adopt the latter view.   [38] See Aoki (1988: 2001), Sakakibara (1993), and Aoki and Patrick (1994).

practice can only be observed well after other attempts, such as salary cuts of board members and employees, fail. Firms also refrain from firing employees even when the profit for a particular term turns negative, as long as the firm is able to retain some internal savings (Fukao 1999: 175–82).

Given the existence of an inflexible labor market in postwar Japan, such concern for the continued employment of core workers translated into the pursuit of organizational survival. Many firms, particularly those in sectors heavily protected by government regulation, such as broadcasting and finance, faced a situation of segmented or limited competition in the postwar period due to government regulation. The participants in these sectors remained the same over time, given the rare entry into the market by new actors and rare exit out of the market by existing actors. In this context, firms tended to pursue the maximization of market share or sales volume over short-term profits. Doing so helped maintain the need for the services of their core employees.[39] Thus, stability or order within the industry as a whole came to be valued more than was the kind of competition that had the potential to result in a failure (or "exit") of a firm, and thus a loss of jobs. While the competition for market share was often intense, the restriction on entry and exit helped give rise to a stable distribution of market share among a set of large firms dominating a given sector.

Firms wield their political influence through the exchange of goods and services with politicians and bureaucrats. While individual firms may engage in such exchanges, firms usually organize themselves into interest groups for this purpose.[40] Organized interest groups offer political contributions as well as blocks of votes to politicians in Japan, as is the case all around the world. In the Japanese context, as observed by Okimoto (1989), firms are organized into industrial associations, which aggregate individual company interests, build intra-industry consensus, and serve as a vehicle of communication between industry and government. The formation of sector-specific industrial associations may be attributed to the need for individual firms to increase their bargaining power vis-à-vis the government or

---

[39] See Yoshida (1993: 63–5). See also Yoshitomi (1998: Chapter 6), which shows how the "purpose" of the Japanese firms are markedly different from that of the US firms. However, this trend is also undergoing a change, as some "mavericks," such as Yoshihiko Miyauchi of Orix Corporation, who openly adhere to the dictates of "shareholder capitalism," are on the rise. See *Nikkei Bijinesu* (October 18, 1999: 148–51), where Miyauchi debates against Toyota Motors Chairman, Hiroshi Okuda. Okuda professes that his company sees priority in pursuing "the balance among such stakeholders as shareholders, employees, and customers" and that "there is a responsibility for firms to provide continued employment, given the inflexible labor market."

[40] The reasons (e.g. to increase bargaining power vis-à-vis the less organized actors, such as the public) why firms organize themselves into interest groups need not concern us much here. See Noll (1989) for a survey of the interest-group theory of regulation in economics.

other interest groups (Aoki 2001). Compared to sector-specific industrial associations, the national business associations, such as Keidanren, do not wield much power. As a rule, these associations refrain from taking a stand on industry-specific issues, concentrating instead on macroeconomic and societal issues. With respect to regulatory reforms, in particular, such peak associations have trouble adopting a policy position, since they include both competitive and protected sectors among their membership and the development of a policy consensus is therefore difficult.[41]

Societal Actors (2)—The Public

Finally, we add the public to our list of actors in the Japanese political economy. Within the framework of liberal democracy, where citizens are guaranteed personal freedom, the public has the ultimate power to decide political outcomes. One powerful way for the public to exercise that power is through the election of political leaders. This channel of influence has naturally been one of the centers of attention in the study of politics by political scientists and economists alike. However, there are also other means by which the public may influence political parties, bureaucratic agencies, and firms in an industrialized democracy. These other means may include mass protests, boycotts, and civil disobedience. Nevertheless, for numerous reasons, the public does not typically wield political influence of this type. For example, the public may not be well-organized vis-à-vis other groups, such as interest groups. The public may also not care to know what the issues are because of the cost that must be incurred to obtain such information.[42] These observations are as relevant to Japan as they are to any liberal democracy.

In our framework, the public has two ways to influence political outcomes. First, the public may be "actors" who engage in direct action to translate their preferences. Examples of such actions include voting, wherein influence is directed at politicians, as well as mass protest and boycott directed against other actors. Elections occur infrequently, however, and, many studies raise the question of whether the public's preferences actually translate into policy results. Mass protests or boycotts may be influential but tend to be rare.

Second, and more importantly, the public may serve as a kind of "parameter" that determines the behavior of other political actors such as

[41] See Okimoto (1989: 165–71), Aoki (2001), and Vogel (1999).
[42] See Downs (1957), Olson (1965), and Peltzman (1998).

political parties, bureaucratic agencies, firms, and interest groups. For the politicians, this link may be obvious: they face elections and thus constantly must care about what the public thinks. However, the public may be similarly important for bureaucrats and firms. Bureaucrats need the support of the public in addition to that of their jurisdictional constituencies, as their ability to act as the delineator of the national interest vis-à-vis other actors is largely affected by public support (Aoki 1988). As for firms, becoming a "public enemy" may have dreadful consequences: mass protests or boycott may result, and their political activities such as lobbying for a particular cause, may be significantly constrained by such developments. For example, polluting companies in postwar Japan such as Chisso Corporation (in the Minamata Pollution Case), have paid hefty prices for becoming public foes. As we will see, banks and securities firms faced a similar situation in the post-bubble years.

Thus, while we do not ignore the first pattern of "direct action" via elections, mass protests, or boycotts, we focus on the second pattern of more indirect action, wherein the public is depicted as a "parameter" of actors' strategies. Political actors observe the public, and decide their strategies based on what they perceive will maximize "public support"—or at least avoid losing "public support."[43]

In incorporating the often underemphasized public into our analysis, it is necessary to raise two concerns before proceeding. First, the public may matter in some instances, such as in a social revolution, but not in others. Thus, when we assert that "the public matters," we must also specify the conditions under which such an assertion holds. This will be one of our central concerns in later chapters. Second, due to limitations on reasoning capacities and available information, the public is unlikely to know what is "objectively" good for it. Public interest is not necessarily equal to public support. In the remainder of this section, we discuss this second concern.

What is Public Interest?

What is "public interest"? Where does the public interest lie in regard to economic policy? One answer may be to add up all actors' utility functions. A common way to do that is to add the welfare of producers (firms) and that of the consumers and decide that the maximization of the aggregate welfare, or the most efficient outcome, must be where the public interest

---

[43] This framework not only applies to the concept of the public as a "parameter," but also to influence via "direct action," as "public support" is an important determinant of elections, mass protests, and boycotts.

lies. Following this line of thought, increasing economic efficiency requires remedying the tendency of producers' interest to be over-represented by increasing consumers' benefits. The inefficiency of existing institutions in the political economy may also be explained by interest-group capture of the regulatory process. Alternately, it might be explained from the trans-action cost perspectives with emphasis on the institutional structures in which actors strategically interact.[44]

Another way to define public interest may be to equate it with improve-ment in indicators such as growth in the national economy. Thus, policies perceived as leading to more economic growth may be labeled as policies in the public interest. Alternately, noting that these positions have implicit biases towards efficiency concerns, we may introduce non-economic goals such as distributive justice (equality), social stability, and the like.

More often than not, such goals as economic efficiency, economic growth, equality, and social stability go hand-in-hand, as seen in the devel-opment process of many of the East Asian countries (World Bank 1993). The issue becomes problematic, however, when the goals come into conflict with each other. For example, as in postwar Japan, economic growth may be achieved through a producer-led economy with an under-representation of consumer interests, resulting in a loss in efficiency. When the Japanese nation as a whole was in consensus about the pursuit of a higher gross national product (GNP), where did the public interest lie? Would it really have been better served if, as some economists argue, inefficient sectors as agriculture were dismantled? Alternately, we may think of a case in which maximizing economic efficiency and growth resulted in a widening gap in the distribution of wealth, leading to a rise in social turmoil. In such a case, we may wish to sacrifice efficiency and growth in favor of such concerns as social stability. Any comparison of the different approaches adopted in employment policies in the United States and continental Europe makes it clear that the definition of public interest varies from country to country.

Vogel (1996: 15) aptly notes, "there is no single public interest: disputes over the definition of the public interest lie at the heart of political debate." Indeed, actors often manipulate the definition of public interest to match their economic goals. In Chapter 4, we will see, for example, that in the debate surrounding financial reforms, domestic financial institu-tions argued that the preservation of financial order and the avoidance of

[44] For example, see Grossman and Helpman (1994), Noll (1989; 1999), and Peltzman (1998) for interest-group theory of regulation; see Laffont and Tirole (1991) and Dixit (1996) for transaction-cost perspectives.

73

confusion among the public was in the public interest. In contrast, foreign financial firms argued that public interest was served by increased efficiency in the financial markets and an expansion of choices for customers. It is not surprising that each group's definition of public interest matched with the economic interests of its members, as these interests pertained to financial reforms.

Based on this discussion, we adopt an approach to the public interest that in many ways mirrors our approach to institutions. Just as we saw a feedback mechanism operating between the objective and subjective worlds in the creation and maintenance of institutions, we envision a similar feedback mechanism running between "public interest" (or the objective aggregation of the public's social and economic welfare) and "public support" (or the subjective support received from the public). Our definition of "public interest" differs from "constituency interests," as it includes concerns for the unorganized consumers and the nation in general, such as aggregate economic output; in contrast, "constituency interests" represents the interests of firms and industries as articulated by interest groups.

Our definition of public interest operates at the level of "shared expectations" of the institutions. The "organizing principle" of an institution, developed through stable reproduction over time, may acquire normative value for actors in the institution, as was the case with lifetime employment in Japan. The definition of an organizing principle or of public interest may also shift over time. What the actors collectively perceive to be an organizing principle may be where the public interest resides but this depends on the initial conditions across time and space. Take the case of Japan. Starting from a condition of poverty, due to wartime destruction, the nation's top priorities after the war became "high growth" and "catching up with the West." Potential distributional conflicts between producers and consumers were of lesser concern. However, as the nation's economic performance began to approach that of the West, greater priority began to be given to "quality of life" issues. Today, the desire of consumers for cheaper prices is more important than ever before, and thus the definition of public interest in Japan may be expected to shift accordingly.

While acknowledging that defining public interest requires a value judgment, we start from an economic definition of "public interest" in our exploration of the origins of the Big Bang and related changes, expanding and questioning the definition as the analysis progresses. As will be seen in Chapter 4, everyone could not be a winner in the Big Bang. It was expected to produce "losers," and most domestic financial firms were perceived to be among these "losers." Thus, we equate "public interest" with both the improvement of the welfare of the unorganized consumer public and an improvement in the condition of the national economy. Whether the reforms are good or bad is a function of the situation that Japan faces. Judging from the challenges Japan faced in the 1990s, the Big Bang was a positive development for the Japanese public—at least in the economic sense. Consumers would become better able to benefit from more efficient financial services—a fact particularly important given the rapidly graying society—and the financial sector would be invigorated, increasing the chances for higher levels of national economic growth.

In Chapter 4, we start from the assumption that "public interest" is closely related to "public support," as we rely heavily on forecasts by economists to construct an image of the distributional effects and the impact on the national economy that the Big Bang is expected to have. This stance is maintained in Chapters 5 and 6, which discuss how actors reacted to the loss of public support and how economic reforms shifted from "interest group politics" to "public interest politics." How the public interest relates to public support is then explored in Chapter 8, where we provide an explanation for the rise of the public in financial politics, as seen in the events covered by Chapters 5–7. Only with this type of concrete analysis of what has been taking place since 1995 in Japanese financial politics can we offer, with confidence, a view on the relationship between public interest and public support.

Institutions in Japanese Financial Politics (1)—Bureaupluralism in Public Policymaking

Now that we have our theoretical frameworks as well as a basic image of the actors, we turn to the task of identifying the prevailing institutions (or "status quo") in Japanese financial politics. Two institutions are of interest here: bureaupluralism in public policymaking, and the convoy system of financial regulation.

These two institutions were continuously reproduced in the postwar era. While they evolved over time, their basic characteristics as described later remained constant.[45] Although the institutions were only partially

[45] According to Aoki (2001), the development of bureaupluralism in the postwar era can be characterized as the Japanese state has moved from a collusive system ("developmental state") to a more inclusive arrangement, incorporating more and more societal interests (e.g. environment, retired citizens) in the process. See Okimoto (1989) and Calder (1988) for the way the Japanese state evolved where the LDP constantly enlarged its supporting coalition. As for the continuity of the Convoy system in finance, in the postwar era, see Noguchi (1995).

supported by formal rules, actors nevertheless acted according to the strategies prescribed by these institutions, forming shared expectations about how the world works. Our goal is to obtain an image of the dynamics surrounding financial politics prior to 1995, which is the year from which we start our analysis in Part II. Who are the actors in financial politics? What are the formal rules that constrain them? What are their patterns of interaction? What are the shared expectations underlying all of these? In the following section, we deal with bureaupluralism, turning thereafter to the "financial convoy."

Bureaupluralism, as developed by Aoki (1988), is a concept aimed to capture the pluralistic bargaining that takes place within the LDP—bureaucratic alliance of postwar Japan.[46] Based on the arbitration of labor and business interests taking place at the firm level under enterprise unionism (or "micro-corporatism," according to Aoki (2001)), the bargaining within an industry is mediated by a "bureau" (or an agency) with almost exclusive jurisdiction over that industry. The bureaus also engage in bargaining within the ministry or among ministries, competing to promote the interests of the industries under their jurisdiction. The "tribesmen" (*zokugiin*) within the LDP—those legislators with special expertise on a specific policy area—intervene on behalf of the industry vis-à-vis the bureau, and promote the interests of that particular bureau-industry coalition over other bureau-industry coalitions. Bargaining in this process is carried out in arenas such as deliberative councils and the LDP's PARC, as well as through negotiations behind closed doors, involving the bureaucrats, the industries (via their industrial associations), and, often times, LDP politicians as well.

We turn now to examine the two types of policy tools available for the government to influence the private sector: laws, passed by the legislature—but usually also requiring the aid of the bureaucracy in their formulation; and, administrative tools, such as administrative orders, administrative legislation, authorizations, and administrative guidance. The latter are policy tools primarily utilized by the bureaucracy. Later we will see how each type of tool was enacted and executed in bureaupluralism. As

---

[46] Aoki's concept focuses on the interplay of bureaucratic agencies regarding budgetary politics: bureaucrats maximize two sets of interests, that of "public" and "jurisdictional constituents." In our view, this holds true not only for bureaucratic agencies but also for political parties in the pursuit of their organizational survival. Also, the competition among "bureaus" that Aoki (1988) describes is focusing on budgetary politics, but a similar mechanism is at work in public policymaking in general, including regulatory policymaking. Thus, we expand the concept to refer to an "institution" in public policymaking in general, in which bureaucratic agencies as well as political parties interact with interest groups and the public.

part of this examination, we introduce two policymaking bodies that play a critical role in this process: the deliberative councils and the LDP's PARC. We will then show how the interaction among actors may be understood, given the tools used by the government to influence the private sector.

Policy Tools

Laws are legislated by lawmakers in the Diet, as stipulated in the Japanese Constitution. In Japan's parliamentary democracy, the following observations hold. First, the ruling party (including the ruling coalition in this section's discussion) dominated both Houses of the Diet and therefore could enact their proposals as laws, given the strong party discipline present. One-party dominance prevailed between 1955 and 1993, where the LDP controlled both Houses for most of the time. The government also proposed roughly 90 percent of the bills submitted to the Diet in this period.[47] Second, the government (the executive branch), under the control of the ruling party, sometimes proposed legislation in cooperation with the legislators. Third, politicians from the ruling party typically led bureaucratic agencies, although the number of parliamentary leaders in any given agency was limited until January 2001 to two or three individuals (including the cabinet minister) under legal statutes.[48]

Under the shared expectations of continued LDP rule, and given the dominant role of government-proposed legislation, the following policy-making process became the norm. First, when a need for legislation emerged, the issue was deliberated within the government; bureaus organized the discussion via deliberative councils, with the involvement of the affected industries, the LDP "tribesmen," and experts. Second, a final report was produced, which, although not legally binding, almost always became the outline for the policy proposal. Third, the proposal was made into legislation, processed through the LDP decision-making body and then submitted to the Diet. Fourth, in the case of particularly politicized issues, the opposition might successfully oppose or force the

[47] See Haley (1995). Also see Sakakibara (1993: 57) for a table showing the high ratio of cabinet-proposed legislation to all legislation between 1975 and 1987. This trend has persisted. As of 1995, ninety percent of all bills submitted were government-proposed.

[48] The framework laid down under the basic law on administrative set-up, the National Administration Organization Act (*kokka gyosei soshiki ho*), did not go through a major revision until 1996. The cabinet minister and the parliamentary vice-minister (later called parliamentary secretary) (two in some ministries), were the only politicians in a bureaucratic agency; however, the resulting reforms would, starting from 2001, upgrade the parliamentary secretary (*seimujikan*) to deputy minister (*fukudaijin*) and would introduce a junior rank political position (*seimukan*), increasing the total numbers of politicians in the government.

legislation into revision. The opposition was sometimes able to do this, despite its minority status, by condemning the "brutality of the majority" and engaging in such strategies as boycotting the Diet deliberation. For most bills, however, the ruling party did not yield at all, and the opposition satisfied itself by attaching a morally-binding resolution to the enacted laws.[49]

Through this process, two policymaking bodies emerged—one within the government, and another within the LDP. During the second stage of this process, the issue was discussed within the deliberative councils, or advisory panels, reporting to the minister (or prime minister). The deliberative councils included representatives from the industries within and outside the jurisdiction of the bureau in charge, as well as outside experts such as academics, think tank analysts, and the like. The potential functions of these councils included "increasing the fairness of policy decisions," the "coordination of various interests," "absorbing expertise and new ideas," and "giving authority to administrative decisions."[50] Because the selection of council members, as well as the contents of the final report, were heavily influenced by the bureau that acted as the council's secretariat, the conclusion of the final report often reflected the bureaus' own conclusions (Muramatsu 1981; Vogel 1996).[51]

The second important policymaking body under bureaupluralism, operating at the third stage of the process, was the LDP's internal decision-making body (hereafter referred to as the LDP PARC). At the bottom of this body were the sub-divisions of the LDP PARC, which were organized into policy areas, often over-lapping with each ministry (e.g. commerce and industry sub-division and MITI; transportation sub-division and the Ministry of Transport). The sub-divisions were staffed with many lawmakers

[49] For more on the process surrounding the passage of legislative bills, see Haley (1995: 90–1) and Muramatsu, Ito, and Tsujinaka (1992).

[50] See the survey by Muramatsu (1981) of bureaucrats and politicians' views of deliberative councils.

[51] We may add another policymaking body operating within the bureaucracy: the Cabinet Legislation Bureau (CLB). In the third stage, the CLB, headed by a bureaucrat with a rank of just below a cabinet minister and staffed by bureaucrats from various ministries, operates to ensure that legal technicality accompanies policy proposals. This organization commands high prestige over the interpretation of statutes concerning public administration, including the constitution: the interpretation by the CLB is usually considered to be authoritative (unless cases go to courts), as can be seen in the fact that the government interpretation by the CLB over the controversial Article 9 of the constitution (ban on the armed forces) is highly influential in the political process. See Haley (1995) for the role of the CLB. From the critics' viewpoint, the CLB operates so as to maintain an entry point for the bureaucrats into the policy process: see Mabuchi (1997), where the CLB, heavily penetrated by MOF officials, raised a constitutional argument against the proposed independence of the BOJ from MOF. See also Amyx (1998 [and 2004]) for the relationship between MOF and the CLB.

who, by virtue of their lengthy engagement with particular policy areas, came to be equipped with expertise that often exceeded the expertise of the bureaucrats in charge of the particular policy area. Such lawmakers were dubbed policy "tribesmen" (*zokugiin*) and clustered around particular policy areas such as agriculture or transportation. The next organizational layer was the PARC, followed by the more senior Executive Council. Membership in the latter often included party bosses and other senior party leaders. Policy proposals submitted by the bureaucratic agencies usually passed in these fora; however, in the case of particularly politicized issues, such party organs might veto or significantly alter proposals prepared by the bureaucracy.[52]

While these two policymaking bodies of the deliberative councils and the PARC provided formal structures around which bargaining involving bureaucrats, politicians, and industries took place, it should be noted that much of the bargaining occurred informally, behind closed doors. Coordination within and between industries took place inside and outside of the deliberative councils, and coordination involving politicians took place both inside and outside of the LDP PARC. The formal structures, however, guaranteed the existence of entry points for industry actors and politicians, strongly influencing the informal bargaining process. Thus, bureaucrats typically consulted the industry actors and politicians in a stage prior to negotiations within these formal structures. *Nemawashi*, or pre-consultation was carried out on an informal basis to garner support for an initiative and ensure that the formal process proceeded smoothly.[53] Consensus was to be reached before a policy proposal emerged. Thus, decision-making tended to be incremental and time-consuming. This was especially true if a bitter conflict involving two or more industries was concerned. In such cases, it was often hard to find a solution all parties could accept. As we will see in Chapter 6, it took six years (1985–91) for MOF and its deliberative councils to produce a final report that led to the financial reforms of 1991–93. The "hundred-year-war" between the banking and securities industries over cross-entry into financial business areas made it hard to form a consensus about what should be done.

Note that politicians in the LDP could bypass part of the process involving the bureaucracy by choosing to submit the legislation themselves. However, the relatively scarce resources commanded by legislators and their respective staffs in terms of manpower, legal knowledge or policy

---

[52] See Muramatsu, Ito, and Tsujinaka (1992: Chapter 8).

[53] For *nemawashi* and the deliberative councils, see for example, Kumon (1992).

expertise meant that such occurrences were rare in the postwar period. When legislators themselves submitted legislation, it typically related to new issues that did not fall neatly into a single agency's jurisdiction.[54]

We now turn to administrative policy tools. Laws enacted through this process were executed by the bureaucratic agencies and several policy tools were available to these agencies. First, laws stipulated administrative orders. Regulators such as MOF were given the legal mandate to issue legally binding orders compelling private sector actors to engage in some way. However, under bureaupluralism, or what Okuno-Fujiwara (1997) calls relation-based governance (as opposed to rule-based governance), it was rare to see the actual issuance of such legal orders. Both regulators and the regulated industries would rather avoid such formal sanctions (which would surely lead to scandals), preferring instead an informal solution to keep things quiet.

Second, the bureaucracy was delegated by law to enact administrative legislation, or cabinet and ministerial ordinances.[55] As legal statutes tended to be worded in general terms (as in other Continental law systems) and to be very costly to change (since a policy initiative had to go through the aforementioned process to become law), many critical aspects of regulation tended to be delegated to lower echelons in the legal hierarchy. Cabinet ordinances, one rank below the laws, were worked out by the ministry in charge and the Cabinet Legislation Bureau (CLB),[56] and required cabinet meetings involving other ministries. Thus, the ministry in charge needed to enlist the support of all affected ministries before a cabinet ordinance could be issued. Ministerial ordinances, one rank below the cabinet ordinances, were issued by the bureau in charge, within the ministry in charge, and in cooperation with the ministry's Secretariat. Administrative legislation was considered part of the legal statute and parties violating its provisions faced legal sanctions.

Third, authorizations, licensing, and other legal stipulations (referred to hereafter as "authorization") permitted private actors to engage in particular activities if they met certain conditions. For example, to engage in the banking business, firms had to fulfill prescribed requirements. Again, while legal provisions established the authorization framework itself, authorization criteria were often defined by administrative legislation.

A fourth policy tool was administrative guidance, a non-binding persuasion of private actors by the government. According to Pempel and

---

[54] One such example may be the environmental issues before the creation of the Environment Protection Agency in the late 1960s to early 1970s.

[55] Independent administrative legislation is considered unconstitutional. See Shiono (1991).   [56] See the previous note on the CLB.

Muramatsu (1995), administrative guidance was typically a series of recommendations issued by the government to specific firms or to an industry, containing advice that the government believed to be in the recipient's best interests. Since administrative guidance was not legally binding, its successful use required cooperation on both sides.[57] Administrative guidance also appeared in the forms of *tsutatsu*, administrative rules establishing the procedures and interpretation of laws and administrative legislation. *Tsutatsu* only bound the lower organizational bodies within the public administration; however, this binding of the regulators might be seen as having a *de facto* binding effect on the regulated as well. This was once the case for the *tsutatsu* issued by MOF's Banking and Securities Bureau.[58] Administrative guidance, though not legally binding, was often accompanied by an implicit promise of reward or punishment, such as the granting or withholding of bank branch licensing, effectively increasing the likelihood of compliance by the private sector with such moral suasion. Administrative guidance was particularly useful for the government, as it allowed for greater flexibility to the changing environment than other means such as legal rules. Administrative guidance was an effective policy tool, provided that the process was closed to those outside the inner circle of the regulated and regulators, such as foreign firms, competing industries or the consumer public. Because of its informality, however, administrative guidance also made unclear the locus of responsibility for government actions.[59]

Relationship of Interdependence Among Actors

All of these policy tools allowed bureaucrats opportunities for the bureaucrats to wield influence through their discretionary authority.[60] Through the

[57] See Muramatsu and Pempel (1995: 69–70). On administrative guidance, also see Johnson (1982) and Okimoto (1989). See Mabuchi (1995) for administrative guidance in finance.

[58] *Tsutatsu* does not bind court decisions, however. See Shiono (1991: 78–9).

[59] Recognizing the prevalence of this administrative practice off the legal statutes, "administrative guidance" was incorporated in the Administrative Procedure Act of 1993, allowing the private parties to ask for the documentation of administrative guidance. Also, MOF, in response to criticism against the "opaque" nature of *tsutatsu*, drastically reduced their number from 1997.

[60] Administrative discretion has been an established tradition in the Japanese public administration since pre-World War I days: although such administrative discretion can be challenged in court, the court precedents adopt a standard that requires an existence of "overstepping/misuse" (*itsudatsu ran'yo*) of the discretionary power on the part of the public administration, which makes such challenges quite hard in practice (Shiono 1991). In the Japanese context, that the public administration is given considerable discretionary power was rather a given, and how to curb administrative discretion has rather been at the center of policy debates concerning public administration. This trend has been reinforced by recent

process of enacting laws, the bureaucrats themselves influenced the content of laws (primarily via the deliberative councils) as well as the form of legal statutes (particularly through the drafting process). Thus, bureaucratic actors virtually held administrative legislation in their own hands, as they did authorizations and administrative guidance. For example, how and when to provide authorization and how to enact administrative legislation were decisions basically left up to the bureaucrats. Of course, this did not automatically translate into bureaucratic dominance, as disgruntled interest groups could run to the politicians (thus, sounding the "fire-alarm").[61] Sounding the "fire-alarm" could have costs for industry actors, however. Since they were engaged in repeated interaction with the same bureaucratic actors, industry actors ran the risk of facing "punishment" by regulators in future rounds of interaction.

Similarly, while the bureaucrats may have had the policy tools to intervene in the private sector, they also needed the support of the industries under their jurisdiction to be effective. Bureaucrats did not possess sufficient amounts of information about the state of the regulated industries and thus depended heavily on private sector actors for information related to the areas under regulation. Similarly, bureaucrats depended on industry actors for cooperation regarding the implementation of their policy proposals, and for retirement positions (*amakudari*). Having relatively little legally coercive power, the bureaucracy exercised most of its administrative powers through persuasion rather than coercion (Okimoto 1989; Haley 1995). As noted previously, *amakudari* also worked as part of the incentive structure of individual bureaucratic officials, and thus the goodwill of industry actors needed to be secured if the bureaucracy wished such channels for personnel management to remain open.

An interdependent relationship also existed between the politicians and the bureaucrats. LDP politicians could influence policy tools, especially laws, and the LDP PARC guaranteed their point of entry into this process. PARC, in turn, provided opportunities for their influence over policy substance in the pre-consultation process. The bureaucrats needed the cooperation of the LDP politicians within the policymaking process, especially at the stage of discussion in the LDP PARC and in Diet deliberation. The worst-case scenario for the bureaucracy was for the politicians to line up with the industries against one of their policy proposals, as was what happened with the banking reforms of 1979–82, detailed in Chapter 6.

arguments that administrative discretion leads to inefficiency and that a shift towards a rule-based system with greater involvement of the judiciary is necessary. See Okuno-Fujiwara (1997) and Muramatsu (1994).

[61] See McCubbins and Noble (1995).

Bureaucrats also needed to be on good terms with politicians, since the latter maintained influence over high-level appointments within the bureaucracy and in public corporations (another frequent destination for retired bureaucrats, in addition to private sector firms). Bureaucratic agencies also needed to borrow the power of LDP politicians in the engaging in competition with one another. For example, the support of the "tribesmen" for postal services was essential in permitting the Ministry of Post and Telecommunications to fend off MOF's Banking Bureau on the issue of dismantling the postal savings system.[62]

LDP politicians also had reasons to be on good terms with bureaucrats. The scarcity of their policymaking resources, as reflected, for example, in the small number of individual or party-level staff, made it essential that they rely on the bureaucracy for policy expertise, particularly regarding legal and technical matters. This made the bureaucracy the most important source of information. Wielding their influence over the bureaucracy and its more particular administrative decisions was also important to the politicians, as a means of demonstrating their worth to their support constituencies and thereby justifying their requests for financial contributions and blocks of votes. For example, an LDP politician might exercise influence over a mostly administrative process such as government authorization or licensing by making a phone call to a bureaucrat, who, given the promise of repeated interaction with this politician in the future, would be pressured to accept the politician's recommendation. A bureaucrat might also use this favor as a trump card to obtain cooperation from that politician at a later time regarding another matter.

We can now summarize the relationship of interdependence among actors in the policymaking mechanism of bureaupluralism. Politicians, in their pursuit of electoral victory, depend on:

- The "constituencies," firms and interest groups, for money and/or block of votes;
- The "public" for "generalized voter support"; and
- The bureaucrats for policy expertise (legality/technicality) and "favor" toward important industry actors.

The bureaucrats, in their pursuit of organizational survival, depend on:

- The "constituencies" for retirement positions, information, and cooperation;

---

[62] Public works such as agriculture, transportation, and construction, in budget politics are also good examples of the importance of tribesmen in bureaucratic competition.

- The "public" for its support of policy and a high social status for the bureaucracy; and
- The politicians for cooperation in the PARC and the Diet, approval over some personnel matters (high-level appointments/retirements), and bargaining power to utilize in battles with other ministries.

The constituencies work to influence both politicians and bureaucrats to obtain policy outcomes that enhance their interests, through providing money and block of votes to the politicians, and through providing retirement positions, information, and cooperation to the bureaucrats. Favorable outcomes may be obtained through inducing the politicians to wield influence over the bureaucracy. Or, favorable treatment by the bureaucracy may by a byproduct of building up a personal relationship through informal meetings (including wining and dining). While the firms and interest groups do not have many direct channels of political exchange of goods and services with the public, they have reasons to fear becoming a "public enemy." Boycotts, mass protests, and widespread social criticism hurt the corporate image, and ultimately corporate profits. "Public enemy" firms may have trouble securing funding from banks or capital markets, or they may experience difficulties in expanding their businesses with other firms—which would have to consider the way in which their own corporate image might be tainted by such business tie-ups. The loss of public support also hurts the political influence of the regulatory constituencies as well. Politicians and bureaucrats are more reluctant to listen to such industry actors, because doing so will surely weaken their own level of public support.[63]

The public, along with other "outsiders," was left out of the policymaking process as described previously. In this way, the policymaking bodies of bureaupluralism were heavily biased toward the regulatory constituencies. Nevertheless, the public voted for political parties in elections and, in doing so, retained a means of conveying approval or disapproval of policies. The public also had the option of organizing mass protests or boycotts against any set of actors (politicians, bureaucrats, firms, or interest groups). Clearly, the public was an important parameter for political behavior—a fact reflected in the way in which key actors worked to maintain or enhance public support—or, at the very least, worked to avoid losing public support or being labeled as a "public enemy."

[63] To see this point, we may observe how the business and political influence of polluting companies (e.g. Chisso in Minamata Scandal) or pharmaceutical companies with contaminated products (e.g. Midori Juji in the HIV Scandal) deteriorated, following their becoming "public enemies," attracting widespread public criticism.

*Bureaupluralism as an Institution: Informality, Repeated Interaction, a
Fixed Set of Actors, and Shared Expectations of Continuity*

What emerged in postwar Japanese politics was the institution of bureaupluralism. This was a stable interaction pattern of politicians, bureaucrats,
and industry actors and based on the informal interaction of the same
actors over time, guaranteed and reinforced by formal rules, as well as by
the shared expectations of continuity.[64] Four important aspects of bureaupluralism reinforced each other: informal interaction; a fixed set of actors;
repeated interaction; and, shared expectations of continuity in this policymaking process.

First, as we saw before, much of the interaction among politicians,
bureaucrats, and interest groups takes place informally. Coercion on legal
grounds is a less preferred option than reliance on cooperation, persuasion, and consensus-building. One necessary condition for the effectiveness of such informal arrangements is that the consequences of one's
strategy (e.g. "go along" or "defy") are well understood among all actors.
This leads us to two other traits of bureaupluralism. The second nature of
bureaupluralism is that it is a system with the same actors; the third is that
it is constantly reproduced over time, or it is a repeated interaction with
similar results being produced over and over again. If the actors remain the
same over time, and the present arrangement is to continue in the future,
then the informal interaction pattern of bureaupluralism is likely to be
effective as a "rule of thumb" for actors. Each can clearly understand
the consequences of their actions within the tacit arrangements, and the
"shadow of the future" prevents the actors from deviating from the
prescribed strategies. In bureaupluralism, the political party in power is
always the LDP; the bureaucratic agency in charge is always the agency
given the jurisdiction under the statutes (assumed not to change often,
given its basic status in the legal order); the firms in a regulated industry
were, for the most part, fixed over time. Here, we may see that formal rules
operate to reinforce the stable reproduction of bureaupluralism. Laws on
public administration guaranteeing the continuity of one agency's quasi-
exclusive jurisdiction over an industry, and regulatory statutes limiting
entry and exit in an industry, contributed to the phenomenon of the same
actors interacting in a similar manner over time.

---

[64] This is what Okuno-Fujiwara (1997) calls relation-based, as opposed to rule-based government. This also corresponds to what many works on Japanese politics have described with
such concepts as "network state" (Okimoto 1989) and "reciprocal consent" (Samuels 1987).
See the summary by Curtis (1999: 59–60) on this point.

However, formal rules are only part of the picture. After all, actors can always legislate different formal rules. For this reason, the fourth characteristic of bureaupluralism is particularly important. This characteristic is the expectation of continuity, shared among actors and reinforced by the stable reproduction of the past informal interaction patterns with the same actors under the prevailing formal rules. Although nothing in the formal structures (e.g. laws or constitutions) guaranteed that the current system would be reproduced, the actors operated under implicit and shared assumptions of continuity. First and foremost, bureaupluralism was based upon the assumption of the continued dominance of the LDP. Once the LDP was out, the LDP PARC would quit being the stronghold of political influence over the bureaucracy, and the exchange mechanism between politicians, bureaucrats, and interest groups would have to undergo a significant shift. The bureaucracy could also undergo organization reform, as happened in the administrative reforms from 1996; the formal structures did not prevent any of the agencies from being stripped of their privileged positions over public policy as it related to certain industries

Informal patterns of interaction work best when actors are fixed over time. This is because new entrants to the market may fail to respect the prevailing informal practice for such reasons as lack of understanding, different priorities (profit or continued employment of core workers), and so on. Thus, if by exogenous reasons (e.g. internationalization), newcomers in the industries (e.g. foreign firms) are brought in, this arrangement cannot but be significantly affected.

All these three interrelated features of bureaupluralism, "informal interaction," "same actors," and "repeated interaction with similar results," cannot be sustained unless the shared expectations of continuity hold. Suppose one critical aspect of bureaupluralism, "repeated dominance of the LDP" collapses (as it did in 1993): what happens? The actors involved would be different as the non-LDP parties come in. The shared expectations of "continuity" will have to go: as "change of government" would emerge as a plausible possible scenario in addition to "continued LDP rule", the interdependence relationship among actors has to change. "Repeated interaction with similar results," and thus "informal interaction," would hold less in the new world, undermining the shared expectations of "continuity" in turn. In this way, by introducing an exogenous change, "change of government," which undermines the shared expectations of continuity, we may see a start of institutional change in public policy-making, or a shift away from bureaupluralism. We will pursue this further in Chapter 8.

Institutions in Japanese Financial Politics (2)—The Financial "Convoy"

We now turn to the second "institution," the Convoy System in Finance (hereafter "the Convoy"). The Convoy in postwar Japan was the institution that arose in finance amidst the interaction of the financial industries (e.g. banking, securities, and insurance) and state actors (e.g. the LDP and MOF). This was a system in which the whole convoy (i.e. financial institutions) sets its speed along that of its slowest ship (i.e. the weakest financial institution). The label "Convoy" is often used to denote the system of financial administration. However, we do not limit our "Convoy" to the observable interaction between the private sector actors and the state regulators in financial administration. In line with our views on institutions, we not only look at formal and informal transactions involving the government and actors in the private sector, but also at the institutional environments in which such interaction took place, delving into the shared expectations held by the actors in financial politics on "how finance works." We must note that the public administration component of the Convoy was an important sub-component of bureaupluralism in general as described previously.

The Convoy was a complex system of interrelated features.[65] Essentially, as the Convoy analogy suggests, no financial institutions were allowed to fail, and the state provided an implicit guarantee to sustain the "myth of no failure." The larger and more competitive firms were deterred from materializing their advantage; their compliance was secured by the regulatory rent and sanctions, or reward and punishment by the regulator. The actors were always the same, as the LDP had a consistent hold on power, MOF was the exclusive "organizer" of the bargaining process according to legal statutes, and entry and exit were *de facto* restricted, if not eliminated, by the formal rules and other informal constraints providing for the segmentation of finance. Their interaction patterns were largely informal, supported by such features of bureaupluralism as "informal administrative tools," "wining and dining", and *amakudari*: the policymaking bodies were the deliberative councils under MOF, and the LDP PARC (in particular, its financial sub-divisions). The system was based on segmentation of finance as well as surrounding institutions such as the main bank system, the

---

[65] On the Financial Convoy, see Pempel and Muramatsu (1995), Aoki and Patrick (1994), Rosenbluth (1989), and Vogel (1996); see also Ikeo (1995) and Horiuchi (1998 and 1999). For an insiders' account of the Convoy, see Nishimura (1999).

financial *keiretsu*, and cross-shareholding. "Continuity" was key to the sound functioning of the Convoy: when there were future rounds to play, actors would be strongly deterred from deviating from the prescribed strategies under the Convoy.

With our discussion of the definition of institutions in mind, we dissect the Convoy into four levels of analysis, focusing on (1) the players, (2) the formal rules, (3) patterns of interaction among actors, and (4) shared expectations.

Players

As interaction took place in the context of bureaupluralism, the state actors involved were the LDP and MOF. The LDP's continued rule was a given, and so was MOF's role as the exclusive organizer under the basic administrative legal framework. As for the actors who engage in business transactions in the financial market ("financial actors" hereafter), finance was segmented into separate industries (e.g. banking and securities) as well as within industries (e.g. within banking, city banks and long-term credit banks).

The major lines that segmented finance were those between banking, securities, and insurance. Banking and securities were divided by Article 65 of the Securities Exchange Law, enacted in emulation of the US Glass-Steagall Act in the United States as a product of the US postwar occupation (Vogel 1996). The law prohibited securities and insurance firms from engaging in other businesses (financial or non-financial) to prevent the risk of other businesses influencing their main licensed business.

Within banking and insurance, there were further lines of segmentation. Within banking, there were the divisions between the specialized banks (long-term credit and trust) and the ordinary banks. Long-term credit banks, created in the early postwar era of scarce capital, specialized in channeling long-term loans (e.g. equipment investment) to sectors that were deemed to contribute to national economic development, as did the governmental financial institutions (Hosoda 1998). The three long-term credit banks were allowed to issue long-term bonds of five-year maturity, or financial debentures to raise capital.[66] Banks were only permitted to open a limited number of branches, as they were expected to operate mainly in the wholesale market. On the other hand, the ordinary banks concentrated on short-term deposits and loans: bond issuance was prohibited, and longer-term deposits have been basically restricted.[67] Trust banks,

---

[66] Two-year maturity bonds were also introduced in 1991.

[67] See Packer (1994) for more on the long-term credit banks.

although being ordinary banks approved to operate in trust banking in theory, were in fact another type of specialized banks. Their branch numbers were kept low, while trust banking businesses were, again, protected from the intrusion of other ordinary banks in return. Within the insurance industry, legal statues strictly separated the areas of casualty and life insurance. Thus, protected by segmentation walls set up by the administration, private financial institutions engaged in segmented competition against rivals, pursuing the maximization of size rather than profits (Yoshino, Asano, and Kawakita 1999).[68]

Within each segmented industry, there was a division between the large firms, which dominated the industry, and the smaller, weaker firms. For example, within banking, there was the division between the strong, or the large ordinary banks (the city banks) and the three large long-term credit banks, and the rest, or the weaker, smaller regional financial institutions (regional banks, mutual banks (the later second-tier regional banks), and credit-cooperative type banks). The limitations on the number of branches for the strong banks were to ensure that they would not overrun the weaker financial institutions. The regulatory system was set up so that no firms would fail within the industry (e.g. the control of the deposit and lending rates): the more efficient large firms were able to accrue rents, while they were expected to rescue smaller firms within the industry through merger under the authorities' request.

To sum up, the "insiders"—or MOF; LDP; domestic financial industries (banking; securities; and insurance)—were the significant players in the Convoy, while the "outsiders"—households; non-financial firms; newcomers to financial business (foreign financial firms, non-bank financial institutions, and non-financial firms entering the financial market)—were largely kept outside of public policymaking in financial politics. Under the Convoy, financial politics was, first and foremost, about distributional conflicts between the domestic financial industries, rather than conflicts between the providers and the consumers of the financial services, as we will see in Chapter 6.

Formal Rules

This includes the regulatory rules that provided for the segmentation of finance and some of the important policy tools (e.g. entry control and

---

[68] See Aoki and Patrick (1994) and Amyx (1998 [and 2004]) for more on the segmentation of the banking sector.

product control) that MOF could wield. Since laws governing each type of business (e.g. the Banking Law; the Long-Term Credit Bank Law; the Securities Exchange Law; and the Insurance Business Law) dictated the segmentation of the financial sector, costly legal revision would be needed to break down the walls prohibiting cross-entry. Such laws also provided for important policy tools for MOF: entry control as well as product control was set up, with the criteria for such administrative actions left to administrative legislation and other policy tools that gave much discretionary power to the regulator.[69]

Patterns of Interaction Among Actors

Formal rules were but one part of the Convoy: we may be missing a large part of this institution if we do not also pay attention to the ongoing informal interaction. First, we look at the interaction between the government and the private sector, dividing it into three parts: policymaking process, policy tools, and policy substance. Then, we will turn to the private sector practice in finance.

In the policymaking process, the financial industries would group themselves into industrial associations (e.g. the National Bankers' Associations), which were typically dominated by the large firms within the industry: such industrial associations were given almost exclusive access to the bureaucracy in charge of their industries vis-à-vis the "outsiders." The interaction between the bureaucracy and the industries would mostly take place through an informal basis, through such channels as informal "hearing" (interviewing) and wining and dining.

Regarding policy tools, the law provided important ones (e.g. licensing and authorization). However, the implementation process was largely within the bureaucracy's hands (see before). A distinctive feature of financial administration was that it was an *ad hoc* system where decisions were often made on a case-by-case basis under a "flexible interpretation" (i.e. discretionary interpretation) of the rules by the regulators. The focus was on preventive (i.e. regulating the private sector *ex ante* so as to avoid possible troubles) measures as opposed to *ex post* regulation through rule-based administrative actions. Even when troubles (e.g. scandals involving financial institutions) would occur, the preferred way was to keep matters within the inner circle of the "insiders." For example, the regulators would

[69] As the Convoy is also part of bureaupluralism in public policymaking, we may add the legal statutes guaranteeing MOF the exclusive jurisdiction over financial regulation to our list of formal rules.

sanction the regulated industries informally (e.g. administrative guidance to force the retirement of management): the industries could still avoid the scandals from becoming public, and the regulators could avoid being held responsible.

As was true for bureaupluralism in general, most policy tools available to the government were not coercive: the effectiveness of administration often depended on the cooperation of the regulated.[70] Informal interaction between the regulators and the regulated, based on the exchange of information, cooperation, and retirement positions against administrative favor (e.g. information on regulatory policy and other policies; smoother licensing) would often involve the personal ties that would be forged through such arrangements as *MOF-tan* (person in charge of maintaining personal relations with MOF officials), or a practice in which the large financial institutions in banking, securities, or insurance, would choose some middle-level officials with similar backgrounds (especially in terms of education) with MOF officials to engage in day-to-day transactions with them. Such ties would often be reinforced by such means as "wining and dining" at night, off-the-record, where each party would be expected to bring out their true thoughts and feelings (*honne*). In this way, personal ties further strengthened the material ties between regulators and the regulated. As a result, the following observation by Pempel and Muramatsu (1995: 72) certainly held for MOF's sections overseeing banking, securities, or insurance: "Because Japanese government agencies and bureaus are often closely tied to the social groups they oversee, they frequently become their protectors despite any consequent economic irrationality."

Lastly, what resulted from the regulation was a fierce competition within the segmented walls, without exit or entry. While the formal rules did not necessarily prohibit entry, they certainly made it difficult; the administrative practice by the regulator, reflecting the wishes of the industries, was by no means encouraging, if not hostile.[71] The financial institutions, when in financial trouble, would be rescued through a system of *hokacho* (literally, a notebook for contribution pledges), where financially sound financial firms would provide rescue financing under the leadership of the regulator.

Turning to the practice in private sector finance, we may point to several interrelated institutions that complemented those previously cited: "the main bank system," "cross-shareholding," "financial keiretsu," and "bank

---

[70] See Okimoto (1989), Samuels (1987), and Pempel and Muramatsu (1995).

[71] For example, see Fuchita (1997) for how the formal rules and the administrative practice would hinder new entry into securities.

dominance." Under the main bank system, the "main banks" would perform delegated monitoring of the corporate borrowers; when such borrowing firms would be in distress, the banks would rescue them, while replacing the management with managers sent from the banks. Under this system, the main banks would rather pursue long-term relational financing than operations with emphasis on short-term profit or capital base. The main bank system, along with the cross-shareholding system and financial *keiretsu*, reinforced the dominance of banking (especially the large six city banks around which financial *keiretsu* group themselves) over the financial industries (i.e. the dominance of large city banks), and the economy as a whole (i.e. the dominance of indirect finance).[72]

Shared Expectations

The shared expectations are, at the bottom of the Convoy, at a time reinforcing and reinforced by, the players, the formal rules, and the interaction patterns. We may see two sets of shared expectations about "how the world works in financial politics": one in politics (institutional environment), and the other within finance (institution).

First, there were two basic shared expectations regarding the political system: "continued LDP rule" and "MOF as the organizer of bureaupluralism in finance." The continued rule of the LDP was a "given" for a long time, giving rise to a stable reproduction of policymaking process through such established procedures as the one described before. For instance, that the policymaking process would go through the LDP PARC was not guaranteed in any legal statutes; yet, this was considered to be a "given" for those involved in the process. The great confusion among the bureaucrats and politicians shortly after the change of government (the first time in more than three decades) testifies to the extent to which this regularity transformed itself into an assumed continuity of the LDP rule. The other "given" in the Convoy was MOF's standing as the organizer of bargaining among actors: that MOF would take the initiative in financial policymaking was not disputed by the actors. MOF did not necessarily dominate financial policymaking: the financial industries have successfully challenged MOF with the LDP intervening on their behalf (as in the 1979–82 banking reforms), or have induced MOF's bureaus to fiercely champion the causes of their industries (as in the 1991–93 financial reforms). However,

---

[72] For the main bank system, see Aoki and Patrick (1994). For financial *keiretsu*, see Okimoto (1989).

that MOF was responsible for planning and executing the plans for regulatory reforms was not disputed in either case (see Chapter 6).[73]

As for the shared expectations within finance, an implicit state guarantee was assumed to be present over the financial institutions. While the deposit insurance system had been established by legal statutes since 1971, guaranteeing deposits of up to ten million yen since 1986, not many seriously thought that such a system would need to be activated in the future: as a result, the legal framework for the implementation of the pay-offs of deposits as well as the administrative organization (set up within the BOJ, the central bank) remained largely underdeveloped; the same was true for the framework to provide for the failure of securities firms. As for insurance, no such safety net existed until the major revision of the Insurance Law in 1994. That an implicit state guarantee was thought to have existed is supported by the fact that the government had to promise that all bank deposits would be guaranteed for five years (until 2001), and then postponed the payoffs for another year (until 2002): that the legal statutes for the payoffs had existed since 1971 did not matter in preparing the Japanese depositors for the payoffs.

The "implicit state guarantee" was accompanied by a "too big to fail" principle: this became apparent when the bubble burst and the bad debt problem arose in banking in the 1990s. Because of the sheer size of the top twenty or so largest banks (called "money-center banks"), the banks would be regarded as "too big to fail" (as in the Continental Illinois case in the United States in the 1980s). As we will see later, the authorities promised that such banks would not be allowed to fail; yet, one would fail in November 1997, destroying the faith of actors in the Convoy.

Again, no formal rules provided for the state guarantee beyond the limited guarantee by such systems as deposit insurance, but it was commonly believed that the banks and other financial institutions would not be allowed by the government to fail. For example, a major economic newspaper declared in 1993: "Banks would not fail and, would not be allowed to fail—this was the common sense of postwar Japanese economy" (Nihon Keizai Shimbun 1993).[74]

In this way, a myth of no failure was supported by an implicit state guarantee. The formal regulatory rules as well as the interaction patterns gave

---

[73] See Rosenbluth (1989) for the 1979–82 banking reforms, and Vogel (1996) for the 1991–93 financial reforms. The former argues that the industries dominated the process, while the latter sees more bureaucratic initiative in the reforms.

[74] This book, collecting revised newspaper articles, pursues "the precursors of the collapse of the myth of no bank failures" while observing that, "Of course, the failure of banks have not surfaced as of now." (Nihon Keizai Shimbun 1993: 1–2)

rise to a segmented competition with no entry and exit, where regulatory protection guarantees that the strong (mostly, large city banks at the center of financial *keiretsu*) do not dominate the weak (other financial institutions). As this practice of financial segmentation was constantly reproduced over time, a shared expectation of symbiosis (*sumiwake*) arose, assuming a normative content as in the case of lifetime employment. The right for survival of the weak financial institutions would come to be openly advocated against the harsh reality of market forces.[75] In this system, the same players or the "insiders" would interact over and again in informal manners, excluding the "outsiders" such as new entrants, non-financial firms, and the consumers: this was a "collusive" system as opposed to an "anonymous" system in a liberal democracy, to refer to the typology of government-private sector transactions developed by Aoki (2001).[76]

Overall, the policymaking process was one of consensus building: it worked through cooperation and consensus rather than through confrontation and coercion, in finance as well as in the political economy in general.[77] In one retired MOF official's view, bureaucratic administration and deliberative councils represented "coordination by reason and consensus." On the other hand, he also acknowledged that MOF bureaucrats found it very hard to coerce financial institutions, often run by local notables with influence over political and economic leaders, into accepting closure, or "death sentences" (Nishimura 1999: 170 and 110).

To sum up, the "organizing principles" (the fundamental principles recognized by all actors as objective characteristics as well as normative values of the institution) of the Convoy were "cooperation and stability." This may not have been peculiar to finance. Cooperation between the private sector and the government through the mechanism of bureaupluralism as described previously was once characterized as the strength of the Japanese political system.[78] Financial stability, or the stability of the financial order, was the goal of financial administration as well as of the financial industries: recovery of "financial system stability" (*kin'yu shisutemu no antei*) was repeatedly stressed by MOF, the LDP, and financial industry actors as a policy goal in the 1990s, within the context of the bad debt problem.[79] We

[75] See Chapter 4, where the reaction to the Big Bang by the "weak" is discussed. See also Nishimura (1999), which delves into this concern for the weak from the regulators' viewpoint.

[76] See his discussion of the "state" domain in Aoki (2001).

[77] See Kumon (1992), Okimoto (1989), and Samuels (1987) for the role of consensus in government policy. [78] See, for example, Okimoto (1989).

[79] Even the Big Bang plan of June 1997 included a section on "financial stability," which was not necessarily compatible with the measures enhancing competition. See Chapter 4.

must note that this objective also served the interests of the non-financial firms that had the capacity to make loans: during the high growth era, repressed interest rates guaranteed cheap capital even with an underdeveloped capital market. As long as bureaupluralism obtained across all sectors and the household (consumer public) was systematically excluded from the policymaking process, stability in the financial order was reinforcing, and reinforced by, the producer-oriented economy of postwar Japan.

Scenarios of Financial Reform

Drawing on the preceding discussions, we now turn to identifying the actors and their strategies regarding financial reform. These actors, assumed to be constant over time, are organizations—political parties, bureaucratic agencies, and firms—and each seeks survival. We distinguish state actors—that is, the politicians and bureaucrats from the remaining actors because the former have direct access to governmental decision-making whereas the latter do not. Included in the non-state actor category are the financial actors who engage in market transactions in finance and who exert an indirect influence on public policymaking.

The state actors—namely, the LDP and MOF—seek to satisfy two sets of interests, the "public interest" and "constituency interests." The LDP pursues organizational survival through winning elections. The party held power from 1955 through 1993, and regained power in 1994 after a very short period out of power in 1993–94. The LDP's top priority in 1995 was to stay in power, as its ability to command governmental resources, a valuable asset to maintaining its organizational strength, would be otherwise jeopardized. In the financial sector, the party maintains ties with the banking, securities, and insurance industries, which contributed heavily to the party through 1993. The LDP PARC and its financial sub-divisions, the policymaking bodies in charge of financial matters under bureaupluralism, closely work with the financial industry actors as well as with MOF in managing financial politics. Many of the members of these financial sub-divisions, the so-called "tribesmen" in finance, are former MOF officials, and have strong personal ties with financial industry actors. The LDP's stance toward financial reforms, then, could be expected to be closely aligned with what the financial industries or MOF's financial bureaus would choose, as long as the LDP PARC remains in control within the party. Financial policy has hardly been at the center of political debates, and financial policymaking tends not to translate into generalized voter support. Accordingly, politicians pay more attention to financial industry actors when dealing with financial issues than they do to the public.

MOF officials seek organizational survival, or keeping and enhancing the organization's political influence and social status. The MOF's Banking Bureau, Securities Bureau, and Insurance Division each represent the industry actors under their respective jurisdictions in competition with one another. These bureaus depend heavily on financial industry actors for information, cooperation, and the provision of retirement positions. This, in turn, results in greater attention by the bureaucrats to industry interests over those of the public. Under bureaupluralism, the financial industries are better represented in the public policymaking process centering on the deliberative councils and the LDP PARC than are other "outsiders." Because of difficulty encountered in reconciling conflicting interests of financial industry actors, financial reform was a gradual process. Japan's consensual style of public policymaking translated into lengthy negotiations and generous compensation to the "losers" in the reform process, to avoid the elimination of any industry actor. MOF bureaucrats depended on the cooperation of private sector actors to carry out their initiatives, and any reforms that drastically altered the financial landscape, leading to the emergence of "losers," were less preferred.

We may group financial actors into two sets, depending on whether reform outcomes were expected to make the financial firm a "winner" or "loser." The winners would be expected to press for reforms that were wider in scope, deeper in degree, and faster in pace, while the losers would be expected to forestall reforms—if not oppose them outright. However, the winners may not know that they will emerge the post-reform winners, due to uncertainty. Thus, unless actors are well aware of their potential gains, they are unlikely to actively pursue financial reforms by lobbying state actors. Private firms—both financial as well as non-financial—pursue organizational survival. To do this, they engage in profitmaking activities, but their even more important priority lies with the continued employment of core workers.[80] The non-financial firms, as well as new entrants into finance, have fewer stakes involved in financial reforms than do those "losers" among the domestic financial industries; the former has more to gain in terms of profit, while the survival prospects of the latter may be put

[80] This assumption applies to domestic firms only: foreign (especially American) financial firms are known to have higher priority placed on profit than continued employment, reflecting the difference in corporate governance. See previously given note on different views on corporate governance.

in jeopardy. We thus expect the voice of the latter to be more vocal in opposition. The public may hope for increased choices and efficiency for financial services, while security may be another concern, which may or may not interfere with increased competition within finance.

We distinguish the "insiders" from the "outsiders" in line with our discussion of the policymaking mechanism of bureaupluralism and the Convoy. The insiders, with privileged positions within the Convoy, include the LDP, MOF, and domestic financial institutions. From this, we can see that the relationship between the financial industries and the state actors (the LDP tribesmen and the financial bureaus in MOF)—or more specifically, the dependence of the latter on the former for votes, money, information, cooperation, and retirement positions—gives state actors the incentives to pursue the interests of domestic financial institutions over the interests of "outsiders," which consist of non-LDP parties, non-MOF agencies, new entrants to the market such as foreign financial firms, non-financial firms, and the consumer public.

How can financial reforms occur in this situation, given the fast pace of change in the environment surrounding finance, reflected in technological innovation and the international integration of financial markets? We suggest two criteria under which "change" can occur. These criteria relate to the evolution of specific coalition patterns, and to the emergence of specific patterns of interaction between state and societal actors. A four-by-two typology of financial reforms posits that coalition patterns defined by "who wins and who loses" correspond to possible reform outcomes, in terms of scope and depth of reform—as well as to the issues of timing and pace of reforms.

First, we may posit a continuum of how coalition patterns change, building on our discussion of "counter-coalition" and "defection" in the framework of institutional change. At one extreme lies the "status quo" (S), where there is no shift in coalitions. The same actors with privileged positions in the prevailing institutions, or the "insiders," will go on to manage financial reforms relying on the policymaking process of bureaupluralism. We may expect reforms to take place over a long time, after a careful consensus-making process with compensation to the losers. This corresponds to financial politics as characterized by Vogel (1996) and Rosenbluth (1989). Next, we may proceed to "inclusion" (C), where some "outsiders" who are left out of bureaupluralism are brought into the public policymaking process, while this process itself is left intact. This corresponds to the mechanism of the continuous expansion of the supporting coalition of the LDP as recorded by Calder (1988).

These two patterns represent evolution within the institution of bureau-pluralism. However, it may be that the coalition patterns change, bringing about an institutional change in public policymaking. Defection (D) is the next category in which some "insiders" shift their strategies and bring about the demise of the old institution in which they previously enjoyed privileged status. In such cases, the "insiders" switch sides, circumvent established procedure, and create alternative policymaking mechanisms. At the extreme, replacement (R) is a situation in which "outsiders" displace the "insiders," eliminating the prevailing public policymaking process.

The second criterion looks at what drives the state actors' behavior in initiating reforms, reflecting the two sets of interests that state actors seek to enhance: "interest group politics" (I) and "public interest politics" (P). In the first category, the exchange of goods and services between organized economic interests (such as interest groups and firms) and political actors drives politics. Here, the flow of goods and services from the economic "winners" to the political actors would induce the latter to shape, propose, and carry out economic reforms, reflecting the public interest. While this pattern does not exclude the possibility that the economic winners still influence the political process based on their provision of goods and services, it may also happen that political actors see benefits in advocating economic reforms independent of such transfer of resources. For example, if economic reforms are expected to benefit the national economy as a whole or the unorganized households, reform measures may be politically attractive for politicians as well as bureaucrats, even though no economic actors may be inducing politicians to act in such a way through the exchange of goods and services. Political parties can boost public support, increasing their chances of winning seats in the next election. Or, bureaucratic agencies may expect wider acceptance for their policy measures by the public and thereby hope to solidify their reputation within society and enhance the chance of organizational survival.

Combining "status quo," "inclusion," "defection," and "replacement" with "interest group politics" and "public interest politics," we obtain a four-by-two typology of reforms (Figure 3.2). In the context of financial reforms, we ask the question "Who brought about the Big Bang?" once again. By making use of a counterfactual, we suggest the possible actors who might have brought about the Big Bang. This, in turn, enables us to obtain the following scenarios of financial reform.

(S,I): Domestic financial firms (e.g. banking, securities, and insurance) dominate the financial reforms. Gradual reforms—in terms of timing, scope, pace, and depth—are likely to emerge, after a lengthy consensus-making

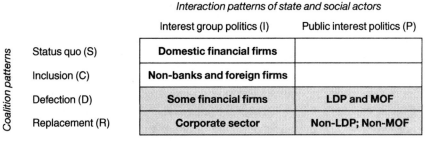

		Interaction patterns of state and social actors	
		Interest group politics (I)	Public interest politics (P)
Coalition patterns	Status quo (S)	**Domestic financial firms**	
	Inclusion (C)	**Non-banks and foreign firms**	
	Defection (D)	**Some financial firms**	**LDP and MOF**
	Replacement (R)	**Corporate sector**	**Non-LDP; Non-MOF**

Note:

Shaded: Institutional change (departure from bureaupluralism)

S: same policymaking process, insiders only
C: same policymaking process, inclusion of outsiders
D: different process, led by insiders switching strategies
R: different process, outsiders displacing insiders

I: state actors act as a result of interest group pressure
P: state actors act independently of interest group pressure

Figure 3.2 Typology of financial reforms: who brought about the Big Bang?

process with compensation made to the losers. No visible change in bureaupluralism, as the deliberative councils and the LDP PARC are the central bodies through which the reform initiative passes, and MOF organizes the policymaking process.

(C,I): Some outsiders, such as non-bank financial institutions and foreign financial firms, are integrated into the policymaking process of bureaupluralism. Reforms emerge from this process, but the "outsiders" may be allowed to have an equal standing with the established domestic financial firms, under the policymaking bargaining organized by MOF. The outcome is gradual reforms; yet, the interests of the outsiders may be more reflected more in this outcome than in the (S,I) pattern, in forms of larger scope of reforms and more liberalization, possibly combined with compensatory measures to the losers among the insiders.

(D,I): some among the domestic financial firms (e.g. large city banks) switch strategies and decide that regulatory reforms further their own interests, inducing the state actors to bring about reforms through the exchange of goods and services. In order to avoid a clash with the rest of the domestic financial firms, the reforms emerge from outside the policy-making mechanism of bureaupluralism. A drastic regulation in favor of those with competitive strength is likely to result, while the scope of the reforms may be concentrated in the areas of interest to the particular "defectors" (e.g. areas that allow the large banks to benefit) more than other areas.

(R,I): outsiders (e.g. corporate sector) choose to induce state actors through exchange of goods and services to bring about drastic reforms in finance, bringing down the policymaking of bureaupluralism in finance. The reforms would be far-reaching, encompassing various areas of finance beyond what is under MOF's jurisdiction, such as postal savings and pension funds. They are likely to be carried out as quickly as possible, reflecting the desperate need of outsiders to have an efficient financial sector.

(S,P) and (C,P): these scenarios are unlikely to result, as the state actors are unlikely to be able to effectively pursue "public interest" over "constituencies interest," if we take the existence of bureaupluralism as given. If bureaucrats and/or LDP politicians seek to achieve such goals as drastic financial reforms at the expense of the financial industries, they are likely to face tough resistance from industry actors in the deliberative councils. The consensual style of policymaking would prohibit the state actors from arriving at reforms that contradict the industries' well-being.

(D,P): some state actors (e.g. LDP and/or MOF) alter their strategies, and move to pursue "public interest" over "constituencies interest" by bringing

Coalition patterns \ *Interaction patterns of state and social actors*	Interest group politics (I)	Public interest politics (P)
Status quo (S)	**Gradual as usual: non-change** *(Domestic financial firms)*	
Inclusion (C)	**Gradual, more than in the past** *(Non-banks and foreign firms)*	
Defection (D)	**Drastic, benefiting the powerful** *(Some large banks)*	**Drastic, emphasis on finance** *(LDP and MOF)*
Replacement (R)	**Drastic, overall reforms** *(Corporate sector)*	**Drastic, overall reforms** *(Non-LDP Parties: MITI)*

Note:

In parentheses: actors who could have brought about the Big Bang
Shaded: institutional change (departure from bureaupluralism)
Gradual / drastic: concepts regarding scope, depth; timing and pace
More than in the past: measures benefiting the "outsiders" with compensation to the losers among "insiders"
Benefiting the powerful: e.g. liberalization of entry into other areas of finance
Emphasis on finance: private finance (banking, securities, insurance, and foreign exchange) under MOF jurisdiction
Overall reforms: scope including areas outside MOF jurisdiction (e.g. postal savings, pension funds)

Figure 3.3 Possible scenarios of financial reform

about drastic financial reforms. Expecting the policymaking process of bureaupluralism to function as obstacles, the state actors "go around" the process, instead of choosing alternative paths to policymaking. Financial reforms may be produced from policymaking bodies other than deliberative councils and the LDP PARC: the resulting reforms may be of earlier timing, faster pace, larger scope, and deeper extent, in favor of the unorganized public.

(R,P): state actors that are outsiders (e.g. non-LDP parties; non-MOF agencies), in pursuit of "public interest" over "constituencies interest" displace the insiders in financial policymaking. Drastic financial reforms, reaching beyond the jurisdiction of MOF, are likely to result from a totally different policymaking process than bureaupluralism.

4

Expected Economic Implications of the Big Bang

This chapter examines the economic consequences that the Big Bang reforms were predicted to have for a range of actors in the financial market, in an attempt to identify the perceived "winners" and "losers" from the reforms. The chapter begins by providing an overview of the developments leading up to the reform initiative, focusing on the period from November 1996 through June 1997. The chapter next summarizes the content of the initiative and the accompanying financial reforms. A discussion of expected economic consequences for the financial market in general follows.

Background to the Big Bang Plan

The fundamental concern that appeared in the Big Bang plan announced by MOF in June 1997 (referred to hereafter as "the plan") was Japan's aging society. Japanese society was projected to age rapidly, with serious consequences. While the population over age sixty-five occupied 14.5 percent of the population in 1995, the ratio was projected to rise drastically to 27.4 percent by 2025 (Ishi 1996, 271).[1] Given the underfunded state of the social security system, the ministry expected the aging population to rely increasingly on savings to cover living expenses. Efficiency in financial services would thus matter significantly in the long run.

The June 1997 announcement also noted the existence of 1200 trillion yen in financial assets held by individuals in Japan, while flagging a number of

[1] Corresponding figures for the United States were 12.6 percent in 1995 and 18.1 percent in 2025.

additional concerns. The ministry highlighted, for example, the need to provide smooth funding for growing businesses in the economy, acknowledged the need to deal with the forces of international competition and the "hollowing-out" of domestic industry, acknowledged the impact to date of liberalization and deregulation of the financial sector, and noted the link between the bubble years and the bad debt problem. Finally, the announcement placed the spotlight on another important development taking place in finance: the wave of scandals that had emerged surrounding the MOF and the financial sector, and the change in financial administration these scandals prompted.

We turn now to explore each of the aforementioned observations and concerns in more detail, as they provide important background to the analysis in the chapters that follow.

1200 Trillion Yen in Individual Financial Assets

The plan stated that the rapidly aging nature of society made it imperative that the 1200 trillion yen in individual financial assets be managed efficiently. Japanese citizens have long been known to save at rates higher than most of the rest of the world. Even as late as 1996, the nation's savings rate stood at 13.8 percent, compared to 4.4 percent in the United States (BOJ 1998). A persistently high savings rate over a long period had resulted by 1997 in an accumulated 1230 trillion yen in individual financial assets.[2] These assets were held primarily in the form of bank deposits, in contrast to the form in which individual assets are typically held in the United States and many other advanced industrial countries. More specifically, 58.8 percent of individual assets were held in deposit accounts, 25.6 percent in the form of insurance policies, 5.9 percent in trust funds, 2.5 percent in bonds, 2.3 percent in investment funds, and 4.8 percent in stocks. In the United States, which had $22.78 trillion of household financial assets in 1997, the corresponding figures were 14 percent held in deposits, 4.2 percent in the form of insurance policies, 32.6 percent in pension funds, 4.8 percent in trust fund accounts, 8.1 percent in bonds, 11.6 percent in investment funds, and 24.9 percent held in stocks. Thus, 90.3 percent of individual financial assets in Japan were funneled into indirect finance, while the corresponding figure was 55.5 percent in the United States.[3]

---

[2] However, Komine (1997) points out that there is nothing unusual for the Japanese household to have this amount of financial assets, however large the figure seems to be. Indeed, the comparative figure for the United States, presented below, is roughly twice as much proportionate to the relative size of the GDP.   [3] Source: MOF.

Funding for Businesses: The Shift from Indirect to Direct Financing

The plan stated that the situation of a rapidly aging society raised the imperative for emerging businesses to serve as locomotives for economic growth. In other words, the plan pointed to the need for the financial system to become more efficient so as to effectively funnel resources to growing sectors of the economy. A key related issue was the need to shift corporate financing away from primary reliance on indirect financing and toward greater reliance on direct financing—that is, to shift away from relying primarily on bank loans towards relying more heavily on the capital markets for fund procurement.

Traditionally, Japanese firms relied heavily on indirect financing. Japan's postwar financial system was built upon a set of financial policies which Hellman, Murdoch, and Stiglitz (1995) call "financial restraint." In this system, government control of interest rates paid on deposits and of entry into the sector generated rents captured by the financial institutions. These rents, in turn, induced such institutions to provide goods and services that would have been underprovided in markets of perfect competition, which require greater monitoring of investments. Additional controls on lending rates generated rents for the borrowing firms, which enjoyed lower interest rates than they could have obtained at the market-clearing level. As a result, rents were transferred from households to financial intermediaries (the banks), and then to firms.

This system was significantly undermined due to financial liberalization carried out beginning in the mid-1980s, however. Most importantly, corporate borrowers developed an alternative means of financing their investments through the capital market, from the 1980s, as a result of deregulation. Competition from the capital market undermined the banks' rents under the "financial restraint" framework. Moreover, while the gradual liberalization of deposit rates (completed in 1994) did not lead to a significant decrease in bank deposits as a percentage of household portfolios, this rate of liberalization did make it impossible to sustain the systematic transfer of rents from households to banks that had been in place under conditions of "financial restraint."

The shift from indirect to direct financing was seen as desirable because of the way in which it was expected to increase the national economy's ability to respond flexibly to macroeconomic shocks. According to US Federal Reserve Chairman Alan Greenspan, "multiple alternatives to transform an economy's savings into capital investment act as back up facilities should the primary form of intermediation fail." In his view, the development of capital markets (or channels for indirect financing) increase the economy's capability to weather macroeconomic shocks, as demonstrated by the stark contrast between the mild US recession in 1991 and the long-lasting problems of Japan in the 1990s.[4]

International Competition and "hollowing-out"

Hashimoto's initiative of November 1996 clearly stated that one of its goals was to revitalize Tokyo as a financial market, bringing it up to par with New York and London in five years—that is, by 2001. Tokyo was weak as a market for securities trading and foreign exchange transactions, compared to New York and London (Figure 4.1 and 4.2). The restriction on bond issuance, which once guaranteed banks' dominance in corporate financing, had driven yen-denominated bond issuances largely over to the London offshore market (Kaizuka 1996). When measured against international standards, Japan's financial sector lagged behind in terms of competitiveness in the development of financial products and in terms of

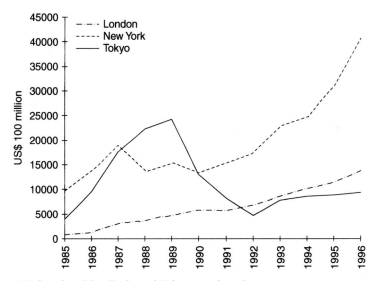

Figure 4.1 London, New York, and Tokyo: stock exchange turnover
Source: BOJ (1998)

---

[4] "Do efficient financial markets mitigate financial crises?" Remarks made before the 1999 Financial Markets Conference of the Federal Reserve Bank of Atlanta, Sea Island, Georgia in October 19, 1999. Accessed on March 8, 2000 at http://www.federalreserve.gov/boarddocs/speeches/1999/1991019.htm

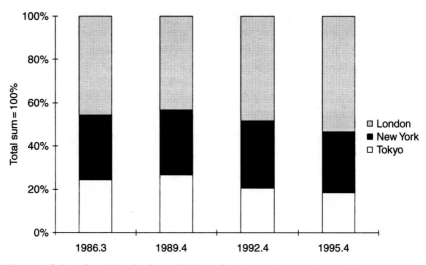

Figure 4.2 London, New York, and Tokyo: foreign exchange transactions
Source: Kaizuka (1996: 160)

efficiency. This situation came about as a result of restricted competition under the "convoy system" of financial administration. Japanese financial institutions, hampered by government regulations that included restrictions on market entry, lagged behind their Western counterparts in the areas of derivatives trading and asset-backed securities (ABS). In terms of efficiency, Japan's banks reported only a 0.5 percent return on assets (ROA) for 1985–94, compared to the approximately 1.7 percent reported by Canadian, UK, and US banks (Dekle 1997; IMF 1997).

While the plan mentioned only New York and London as financial rivals to Tokyo, intra-regional competitive dynamics in Asia were also clearly present. In the 1990s, Hong Kong and Singapore developed their markets into possible alternatives to Tokyo. Because of the difference in time zones, Asian financial centers could operate while the major international financial centers in the United States and Europe were closed. Accordingly, there was significant competition among Asian financial centers, in addition to competition with the American and European markets (Ueda 1996). At this time, Hong Kong and Singapore were steadily closing the gap between Tokyo and themselves in the foreign exchange market, in particular (Figure 4.3).

Tokyo's relative decline as a financial market vis-à-vis its rivals raised alarms within Japanese policy circles in the mid-1990s concerning the "hollowing-out" (*kudoka*) effect in finance. Having an international

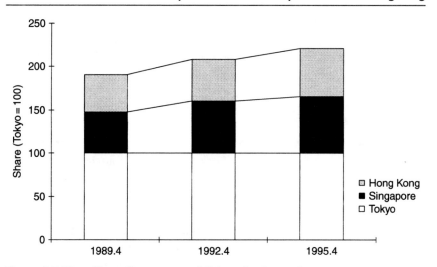

Figure 4.3 Hong Kong, Singapore, and Tokyo: foreign exchange transactions
Source: Kaizuka (1996: 160)

financial center was not only beneficial but also vital to the country.[5] Globally, the financial industry was growing rapidly within the service sector, and still had the potential to maintain high levels of employment in countries where the manufacturing sector was in decline. The situation in Japan was worrisome, as financial centers tend to disappear when the demand for financial services falls below a certain threshold, due to economies of scale and fixed costs. Even if demand later recovers to its prior level, the financial center is unlikely to be revived. And, the loss of a financial center not only results in a loss of income, but may also trigger an increase in the cost of financial intermediation and thus higher capital costs for investors, ultimately lowering economic growth (Ito 1996; Ueda 1996).

Another implication of the "hollowing-out" effect was that having Tokyo as a financial market did not necessarily mean that Japanese financial institutions would flourish. Benefits of having an international financial center might be achieved by fostering market participation by the most efficient financial institutions, whether Japanese or not. Thus, the sustenance of the Tokyo market as an industrial policy to promote the

---

[5] A financial center is a city or a market exchange where there is an accumulation of financial institutions trading many financial products in the money market, the capital market, and the foreign exchange market. An international financial center is a financial center that deals in international products and has many foreign participants (Ito 1996: 187).

competitiveness of Japanese financial firms was not necessarily compatible with promoting Tokyo as an international financial center, since such a center needed to be indifferent to the nationality of the actors (Kaizuka 1996).

Accumulation of Past Liberalization and Deregulation in the Financial Sector

It is commonly observed that MOF failed to carry out reforms of consequence over the ten years starting from 1984, when financial liberalization commenced. According to one account, although reforms were introduced, the pace was very slow, as MOF "guided the process in a gradual and orderly manner, managed liberalization to protect domestic financial institutions, and designed the reforms to maintain its own authority over these financial institutions" (Vogel 1996: 192). In the plan of June 1997, however, MOF claimed the Big Bang to be a continuation of the reform "progress" made prior to the bubble. How much liberalization has been achieved by November 1996, the time of the announcement?

Financial liberalization in Japan has its origins in the massive deficit spending of the Japanese government in the post-oil shock, low-growth era after 1975. The large-scale issuance of government bonds that financed this deficit spending forced MOF to move away from a system in which banks purchased such bonds with artificially low coupon rates and then sold them to the BOJ. MOF established a secondary market for government bonds in 1977 and introduced a public auction system for bond sales in 1978. This resulted in a government bond market where bonds were traded at market price. Hereafter the savers and the borrowers were able to bypass regulated markets and directly access the government bond market. As a result, interest rates, an important feature of "financial restraint," were liberalized by the mid-1980s—with the exception of deposit rates, which remained regulated. Deregulation "took off" in 1984, as a result of US pressure for deregulation, following the issuance of a report by the US–Japan Yen–Dollar Committee (Osugi 1990; Hoshi and Kashyap 1999).

The Financial Reforms of 1991–93 commenced the breakdown of the segmentation in finance, in which banks and securities were allowed cross-entry as well as entry into trust banking through financial subsidiaries. However, this breakdown was not complete because of tight business restrictions on financial subsidiaries. Implementation of reforms was meticulously supervised by MOF so as not to disturb the status quo.[6]

---

[6] However, it must be noted that, at that time, the 1991–93 reforms were perceived as a great leap forward, at least by MOF and the financial industries. See Nishimura (1999).

Subsidiaries were all established according to the rules of "compensation" where "losers" from the reform process, such as long-term credit banks and securities firms, were allowed by MOF to set up subsidiaries earlier than city banks (Vogel 1999: 15).

The process can be reconstructed from the perspectives of three actors in finance: firms, households, and financial intermediaries, following in the vein of Hoshi and Kashyap (1999).[7] For firms, deregulation greatly expanded financing choices because it led to the emergence of vibrant bonds markets both at home and abroad. The manufacturing sector, where the effect was clearest, saw its ratio of bank debt to assets drop from 29.5 percent in 1983 to 16.5 percent in 1989.[8] Liberalized areas in the international markets included international banking, such as Euro–yen lending; international bond issues such as the issuance of Samurai and Shogun bonds;[9] foreign exchange transactions such as the abolition of the "real demand principle";[10] and the establishment of the offshore market.[11] In the domestic market, tight control on bond issuance by banks—another feature of the "financial restraint" system of the postwar era—was increasingly relaxed, largely due to the access gained by firms to the international bond market. This development allowed firms to bypass the Bond Issuance Committee controlled by the banks. In 1993, a ratings system was introduced to substitute for the bond issuance criteria, which was finally abolished in 1996. The domestic commercial paper (CP) market, an alternative to bank borrowing, was established in 1987.

For households, the liberalization of deposit rates, which had begun in 1985 with large-scale time deposits, was completed in 1994. However, the deregulation of other saving options that would allow households to directly participate in capital markets (such as stock trading or investment trusts) were slow to be carried out. Accordingly, households saw little expansion in options for managing their savings.

For financial intermediaries, deregulation also proceeded slowly. Banks were not allowed to pursue new business areas outside traditional banking when they faced the loss of their traditional customer base, the large

---

[7] The discussion below largely draws on Hoshi and Kashyap (1999: 10), where they divide their discussion into "the responses of the borrowers, savers, and lenders" to the deregulation.

[8] Based on Table 6 of Hoshi and Kashyap (1999), which shows the ratio of bank debt to assets for publicly traded Japanese Firms over 120 billion yen at 1990 prices.

[9] Samurai bonds are Euro-yen bonds; Shogun bonds are yen bonds issued by non-residents in the Japanese market.

[10] This required the matching of trade flows for foreign exchange transactions.

[11] See Osugi (1990). Other measures include: purchase of foreign bonds by Japanese residents and widening of foreign financial institutions' access.

firms—and, most notably—those in the manufacturing sector. The government was slow to authorize new financial products, and virtually prohibited entry into other financial businesses until 1993. As a result, they committed themselves increasingly to property-related lending to smaller firms.

We can summarize the characteristics of the financial liberalization that preceded the Big Bang as follows. First, the liberalization of finance was carried out steadily since the 1980s, so the claim by MOF that the Big Bang was a continuation of the past liberalization efforts was not entirely misplaced. Second, even so, the pace of liberalization was uneven within finance. The liberalizing trend was most significant in the markets of corporate finance, where market forces outside government control (such as the Euro-market) served as impetus to greatly accelerate the pace. While the massive issuance of government bonds eventually led to the liberalization of interest rates, this was achieved at a much more gradual pace. The diversification of financial products for households as well as the diversification of permitted business areas for financial intermediaries was similarly slow. In these areas, where regulations such as foreign exchange controls could mitigate the pressures of globalization, considerations about the "stability of the financial order,"[12] the organizing principle of the convoy system of financial regulation, prevailed and reforms were indeed very gradual.

Bubble Years and the Bad Debt Problem

The Japanese economy saw a dramatic boost in economic performance in the bubble years of the late 1980s. By 1991, the bubble, characterized foremost by asset inflation (real estate and stock inflation, in particular) and a massive expansion in private investment under conditions of record-low interest rates, had collapsed. Domestic demand stalled due to a decline in private investment rates, reversing the trend of over-investment during the bubble period, and falling stock and real estate prices dampened consumption (IMF 1998: 6). Economic stagnation resulted: economic growth for the period of 1992–95 averaged a dismal 0.85 percent (Figure 4.4).

Among the various reasons for the collapse of the bubble (which a return to economic rationality would have brought about eventually, in any case[13]) and the ensuing economic stagnation, two factors appear to have

[12] See Chapter 3.
[13] See Noguchi (1993) and Yoshitomi (1998) for a discussion of the economics of the bubble, and the mechanism by which the bubble bursts.

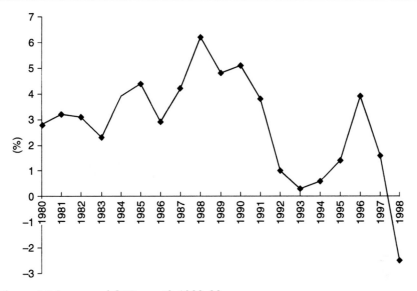

Figure 4.4 Japan: real GDP growth 1980–98
Source: Keizai Kikaku Cho (2000: 420)

been the most important. The first one was the massive interest rate hike, introduced by the BOJ (possibly under pressure from MOF). The second factor was that of over-investment during the bubble years. After over-investing amid record-low interest rates in the late 1980s, private firms entered a period of stock adjustment. As a result, private investment soared in the years 1986–90, peaked in 1991, and then dropped sharply in 1992 (Figure 4.5).

To cope with the post-bubble economic stagnation, fiscal policy was geared to providing stimulus to the economy via a series of economic stimulus packages (IMF 1998). In addition, starting in 1995, the government introduced a series of temporary income tax cuts. As a result, although the fiscal situation worsened considerably in the first half of the 1990s, the economy itself seemed to regain vitality, as the growth rate rebounded to 3.9 percent in 1996.

With signs of economic recovery in 1996, the government's policy emphasis shifted toward fiscal consolidation with the introduction of a contractionary budget for fiscal year (FY[14]) 1997, the revocation of temporary income tax cuts introduced in 1995, an increase in the consumption tax rate from 3 to 5 percent, and an increase in the national

[14] Fiscal year for the Japanese government: April–March.

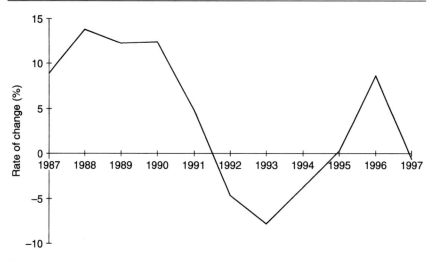

Figure 4.5 Japan: private sector investment 1987–97
Source: BOJ (1998)

medical insurance co-payment. These fiscal developments and other factors, such as banking sector instability and the Asian crisis, which reduced external demand, helped to bring the Japanese economy into recession from the second quarter of 1997 (IMF 1998).

We must bear in mind, however, that the recession that lasted until the second quarter of 1999 was not yet apparent when the Big Bang was conceived in 1996–97. While the recession was partly brought about by the changes in fiscal and health care policy, these changes were important parts of the political agenda of the second administration of Prime Minister Hashimoto, and followed on the heels of a victory in the October 1996 Lower House election. More specifically, these changes were part of Hashimoto's "Six Large Reforms," which had as their objective structural reforms simultaneously in six policy areas. The Big Bang was one of these reforms, alongside "Fiscal Structural Reforms," "Social Security Structural Reforms," and "Administrative Reforms"—which included MOF reforms.[15] Thus, the Big Bang, especially at the time of its genesis, ought to be thought of apart from the later recession caused partly by the other Hashimoto reforms. While the financial system became increasingly destabilized, there were reasons for policymakers to believe that the economic situation had come out of its worst stage. In hindsight, of course, we know this belief was mistaken.

[15] The two other reforms were education reforms and economic structural reforms.

Intimately related to the economic stagnation was the bad debt problem. As a result of the asset deflation following the bursting of the bubble and the macroeconomic stagnation of the 1990s, banks and other financial institutions amassed large amounts of bad loans. While the large manufacturing firms had shifted from the mid-1980s to the capital markets following the financial liberalization at that time, loans made by banks had been increasingly directed towards real estate projects and small- and medium-sized enterprises, often using real estate as collateral (IMF 1998: 101). The plunge in land prices thus hurt the banks. But, the plunge in stock prices similarly damaged the balance sheet of banks, as the market value of their stockholding declined.[16] Because accounting standards employed during the bubble years relied on acquired values of assets instead of on market values of assets, banks saw their off-balance sheet assets increase in size during the bubble years. Their asset holding provided them with "unrealized gains" or hidden assets. After the bubble, however, they faced the opposite situation and had to cope with serious hidden losses.[17]

What were the deeper causes of the bad debt problem? Some blame the lack of adequate monitoring of banks, due to the lack of competition and inadequate financial regulation (Horiuchi 1998). Others point to the lopsided nature of the deregulation process: deregulation in the capital markets proceeded more rapidly than did deregulation in financial products for households or deregulation in the banking business. Thus, firms borrowed less from the banks, savers continued to pour money into the banking sector, and the banks—unable to start new businesses because of regulatory restrictions—had to stick to traditional lending, chasing riskier business opportunities, and endangering their financial health (Hoshi and Kashyap 1999).

The amount of bad debts in the Japanese banking sector was often a source of confusion, as definitions of problem loans varied over time; amount also varied according to macroeconomic conditions. With these caveats in mind, Hoshi and Kashyap (1999) estimate that in September 1996: the twenty-one major banks had 18,846 billion yen of bad loans and

---

[16] Japanese banks have traditionally held a large portfolio of stocks; they were allowed to hold up to 5 percent ownership under the Anti-Monopoly Law. Banks' stockholdings represented more than 25 percent of market capitalization by 1988 (IMF 1998: 101), reflecting the practice of cross-shareholding among financial and non-financial firms.

[17] As the capital requirements under the Basle accords allowed Japanese banks to include 45 percent of these hidden assets as Tier II capital, the hidden losses caused by later asset deflation eventually resulted in a credit crunch.

9,508 billion yen of loan losses, while the figures for all banks were 24,383 and 12,035 billion yen, respectively.[18]

The banking industry and the government were slow to react in the first half of the 1990s, believing that economic recovery would resolve the bad debt problems (IMF 1998). Restructuring was slow to come in the banking industry, and loan write-offs did not happen until 1996.[19] According to Horiuchi (1998), what the government introduced as "emergency measures" were *ad hoc* measures that merely postponed a fundamental resolution of the problem. The government measures can be classified into four categories: (1) those promoting the write-offs of bad loans, (2) those promoting the liquidation of bad loans, (3) those supporting the strengthening of banks' capital bases, and (4) those strengthening the deposit insurance system (in 1996). What the measures lacked was a mechanism that would motivate banks to recover their capital bases, such as so-called "prompt corrective action" measures or public funds injection schemes.[20]

As the 1990s progressed, the instability of the financial system became a major concern for the nation, as increasing numbers of financial institutions began to collapse. Some smaller financial institutions, credit cooperatives and small banks experienced failure first. In 1994, two credit cooperatives in Tokyo made the newspaper headlines for questionable loans and operational difficulties. In July 1995, Cosmo Credit Cooperative in Tokyo went under, triggering a chain of failures centered on smaller financial institutions such as credit cooperatives and regional banks.[21]

In the winter of 1995, a problem with housing loan companies became the focus of national attention.[22] Housing loan companies (*Jusen*) were financial firms originally set up by financial institutions (primarily banks) to provide housing loans to individual households in the 1970s. When banks were later allowed to enter into this market, the housing loan companies shifted their business to loans to the real estate sector. The

---

[18] At new, more stringent standards "intended to be broadly in line with the U.S.," non-performing loans totalled 35 trillion yen (approximately 7 percent of GDP) for all deposit-taking institutions as of the end of March 1998. Based on asset quality self-assessments undertaken by all deposit institutions, which resulted in 88 trillion yen of "problem loans" (the aggregate of loans in categories II, III, and IV) in the same period, the IMF estimated that the uncovered losses could amount to 19 trillion yen, or around 4 percent of GDP (IMF 1998: 111–112).

[19] See, for example, Yutani and Tsujihiro (1996).   [20] See Horiuchi (1998: 169–79).

[21] Later on, in 1997, Hokkaido Takushoku Bank, one of the twenty largest money-center banks, which the government earlier committed not to permit to fail, collapsed. In 1998, the Long-Term Credit Bank of Japan (LTCB), and in 1999, the Nippon Credit Bank (NCB) failed, bringing the long-term credit banks' number down to one, the Industrial Bank of Japan (IBJ). See Chapter 7.

[22] See Mabuchi (1997), Nishimura (1999), and Yutani and Tsujihiro (1996) on the Housing Loan Problem. Also, see Chapters 5 and 6.

housing loan companies would borrow funds from the banks, lending these funds with an added premium. This business trend strengthened in the early 1990s, as administrative guidance issued by the Banking Bureau of MOF in 1990 instructed the banks to curb the funds available to the real estate sector but the housing loan companies were exempt from this regulation and therefore were used by their parent banks to bypass the regulation. Not only banks, but also the financial arms of agricultural cooperatives provided the funds used by the housing loan companies to make loans—loans which were increasingly channeled into risky projects.

Because of the economic downturn and asset deflation following the bursting of the bubble, housing loan companies amassed a large amount of bad loans. While there were proposals from some banks to liquidate the Jusen in 1993, MOF instead chose to prepare a rescue package that lowered the interest payment to the lenders, which were mostly banks and agricultural cooperatives. In 1995, as asset deflation worsened, it became clear that the seven housing loan companies could not survive. The loss resulting from reckless loans amounted to 6.4 trillion yen. The problem was how to liquidate the housing loan companies, as liquidation would deal a severe blow to the banking sector, as well as to agricultural cooperatives—both of whom were already suffering from bad debt problems. A tug of war between the banks and the agricultural cooperatives ensued over the issue of how to split the losses. The MOF led the banks while the Ministry of Agriculture, Forestry, and Fisheries (MAFF) and the LDP agriculture "tribesmen" backed the agricultural cooperatives. The agricultural sector emerged as the winner, as it successfully refused a burden-sharing scheme proposed by MOF. This part of the loss, which amounted to 685 billion yen, had to be drawn from the national coffers. The decision within MOF and the government was made in December 1995; the measures became law by June 1996.

The *jusen* affair stirred up a public uproar, initiating a heated political debate between the LDP and the opposition in the Diet. Not only did the inept handling of the *jusen* problem hurt MOF and the banking industry, as addressed later, but it also made the injection of public funds into the financial system very unpopular, and hence an unattractive option for policymakers thereafter. The housing loan problem was one of the turning points for the relationship between the LDP, MOF, the financial industry, and the public, as we will see in the later chapters.

Following the submission of the bill on the housing loan companies in February 1996, the government introduced three bills to the Parliament in April 1996 to cope with the situation of financial instability. The "three financial laws" of 1996 included four important measures. First, prompt correction (early warning) measures[23] would be introduced from 1998 to strengthen prudential regulation. Second, special legislation amended the corporate bankruptcy laws to cope with the failure of financial institutions.[24] Third, measures concerning the procedure utilized in the deposit insurance system for coping with bank failures were improved.[25]

Fourth, and most importantly, a number of temporary measures were introduced. These were to be effective for five years, lasting until 2001. Among these measures, the most relevant for the financial reforms was the decision to guarantee the full value of all deposits in the case of bank failures, thereby ignoring the deposit insurance limit of 10 million yen specified in the Deposit Insurance Law. As noted in Chapter 5, this measure had a large impact on the Big Bang reforms by influencing their timing, or in setting a deadline for the completion of financial reforms.

The three bills became law in June 1996, and the government declared that the worst was over for the financial system. In hindsight, of course, this view was overly optimistic. As Horiuchi (1998) charges, these government measures—including the strengthening of the deposit insurance system in 1996—turned out to be mere "patchwork" efforts that simply postponed a final resolution of the bad debt problems.

Nevertheless, it must be noted that measures necessary to stall the financial instability caused by the Housing Loan Affair and by the chain of failures of small financial institutions appeared to be in place by the summer of 1996, even though the bad debt problem and related doubts about the reliability of disclosure by financial institutions loomed in the background. Not a single major bank or securities firm comprising the core of the financial system had yet failed when the Big Bang initiative was launched (November 1996–June 1997)—even though rumors circulated about the financial troubles of some particular large-scale financial institutions at this time.

---

[23] Under this law, regulators would take action, which could include bank shutdown, if a bank's capital to asset ratio fell below a prescribed level.

[24] This would enable the Deposit Insurance Corporation to represent the depositors in a "Chapter 11" situation.

[25] A new quasi-public bank owned by the Deposit Insurance Corporation, the Resolution and Trust Bank (*Seiri kaishu ginko*), was set up to purchase the businesses of the failed credit cooperatives. A special account was temporarily created in the Deposit Insurance Corporation as well to deal with failed credit cooperatives. In accordance with the legislation, the deposit insurance corporation decided to raise the deposit insurance rate fourfold from 0.012 percent to 0.048 percent, while charging an extra 0.036 percent for five years for funding.

Wave of Scandals Hitting MOF and the Financial Sector

In the 1990s, a wave of scandals involving MOF and the financial industry were uncovered one after another, leading public outrage to increase exponentially by the middle of this decade. In 1991, a scandal broke out over loss compensation by securities firms, which were secretly favoring corporate clients over ordinary individual customers by promising compensation in the case of losses. This revelation led to public criticism of the securities industry, and also to the creation of the Securities Exchange Surveillance Commission (SESC) within MOF. This marked the first time that criticism of MOF's financial administration actually forced a change in its organization.[26]

On top of the failures of financial institutions, which began in the summer of 1995, policy failures and scandals brought further instability to the financial system. Three incidents, in particular, were critical. First, in the fall of 1995, a scandal surrounding Daiwa Bank came to light. This scandal emerged when a Daiwa Bank bond dealer in New York incurred huge losses and the bond dealer's improper business activities were not promptly reported to US authorities, even though the bank conferred with MOF officials concerning the problem. MOF was furthermore portrayed as inadequately regulating the overseas branches of Japanese banks. The incident resulted in the eviction of Daiwa from the US market, and in the emergence of the "Japan Premium," a practice of charging an interest premium on all transactions with Japanese banks in the inter-bank call market.

Second, as mentioned earlier, the Housing Loan Affair became the center of political debate in the winter of 1995–96. A decision to use public money to resolve the financial mess created by the housing loan companies, the banks, and the agricultural cooperatives evoked a public uproar against MOF, the LDP, and the banking industry. The Housing Loan Affair was a scandal for MOF as well as a policy failure. This was because many retired MOF officials were involved in the management of the seven housing loan companies and losses grew larger over time in the face of inaction by MOF officials. Moreover, MOF and MAFF bureaucrats, unknown to their respective ministers, secretly exchanged memoranda that appeared to guarantee that the financial arms of agricultural cooperatives would be given special treatment. As noted earlier, large city banks originally founded the housing loan companies and then used them to bypass

[26] It must be noted that Ryutaro Hashimoto, the prime minister in 1996, had to resign from his post of minister of finance, taking responsibility for this scandal.

regulations and supply funds to shady businesses, making a huge profit during the bubble years. They were now seen as dodging responsibility when their affiliated housing loan companies were in trouble. The actions by MOF and the banking industry came to be publicly known, as policy measures to deal with the situation were debated in the Diet. The result was heavy criticism from politicians, the media, and the public in general.

Third, so-called "wining and dining scandals" caused a public uproar in 1994–96. Here MOF bureaucrats were perceived as having engaged in a questionable relationship with rogue financiers. The result was the dismissal of two of the ministry's most senior and influential officials in 1995.[27]

Together, these scandals raised the following concerns about financial administration. First, the housing loan and Daiwa Bank scandals in particular raised questions about MOF's regulatory competence, altering the prior image of MOF as a powerful and competent agency. Second, the integrity and ethics of bureaucrats came to be highly questioned by the wining and dining and housing loan scandals, which brought to light the nexus between the government and private sector woven through *amakudari*. The scandals moreover damaged the banking sector's reputation vis-à-vis the public. We will return to this issue in later chapters.

Basic Concepts of the Financial Big Bang Plan: Principles, Pace, and Sequence

The Big Bang initiative rested on four basic concepts, according to the June 1997 plan. First, the initiative of November 1996 made it clear that the Big Bang was to be carried out according to the three principles of "free, fair, and global." "Free" referred to the overarching liberalization and deregulation measures to ensure that market principles governed the financial market. "Fair" referred to the revision of old regulations and introduction of new ones that aimed to make the market transparent and reliable. "Global" stood for the measures to harmonize Japan's standards and supervisory regimes with international standards and supervisory regimes, with the aim being to render Tokyo as an international and advanced market.

Second, the plan spelled out the timing for each measure to be enacted so that the reforms could be executed all at once. This created a self-imposed deadline, making it harder to slow down the reforms later on. Third,

---

[27] Later on, several MOF officials were arrested on bribery charges, mostly based on wining and dining. MOF sanctioned 112 officials in 1998, forcing two of its top officials into retirement. See Chapter 7.

the importance of the "stability"[28] of the financial system was stressed in the initiative. The bad debt problem needed to be resolved quickly, and the stability of the financial system—as well as the confidence from home and abroad in it—had to be secured. Reflecting this concern for financial system stability, the plan set up a five-year period during which some areas such as insurance would be gradually reformed. In this way, the Japanese Big Bang plan differed from the UK Big Bang reforms, which seemed to lack such concerns for existing firms.[29] Curiously enough, however, the Japanese Big Bang initiative was reticent on its expected effects on existing financial institutions. If the Big Bang would have negative effects on their prospects for survival, then the package and the basic principle of financial stability could very well come into conflict with each other. Lastly, the reforms were to benefit "users." Unlike past reforms, where industry interests were central to the policy debate, the users of the financial services were professed to be the main beneficiaries of the Big Bang reforms.

Each of the measures in the plan could be seen as promoting at least one of two major objectives. The first was the promotion of liberalization and deregulation through the enhancement of competition and reduction of government control.[30] The second objective was the enhancement of market infrastructure through the acceleration of market development and the introduction or strengthening of principles of fairness and transparency. Table 4.1 provides a summary of the important measures in the package, as well as of parallel measures that lay outside of the package but are often associated with the Big Bang.[31]

[28] Stability and stabilization (*antei, anteika*) are terms frequently used by MOF in the context of the bad debt problem, distinct from such reforms that are forward-looking and have vitalization (*kasseika*) as a goal.

[29] I owe this point to Steven Vogel.

[30] We classify liberalization and deregulation in the same category because most measures bear characteristics of both competition promotion and reduction of government control, making it useless to distinguish between the two criteria. For example, the de-segmentation of finance is a measure seeking to increase competition, but it also reduces governmental control on business restrictions on financial firms. In another example, which appears at first to be "deregulation," the reduction of entry control on security businesses is actually introduced in part to encourage competition. Thus, we chose to group such cases and differentiate them from cases where the development of market infrastructure (mostly through tighter regulations regarding transparency and solvency) is in question.

[31] See Dekle (1997), IMF (1997), and OECD (1997) for a summary of the Big Bang package. Discerning precisely what the Big Bang plan includes is difficult for two reasons. First, some observers include measures clearly outside the package announced by the government. For example, Dekle (1997) includes the creation of Financial Supervisory Agency (FSA) in the initiative. Second, the government's announced plan includes past developments, such as the prompt correction measures already legislated by June 1996, in the initiative, blurring the content of the Big Bang plan proper. Reflecting the problematique of the analysis, this table and the analysis below exclude such measures as international economic sanctions, which, although important, have little relevance to political conflicts over financial reforms.

Table 4.1 Big Bang initiative: principal measures

Liberalization and deregulation *Enhanced competition and reduced government control*	Enhancement of market infrastructure *Market development, fairness, and transparency*	Reforms paralleling the Big Bang
• Liberalization of initial capital transactions • Product liberalization (securities, investment trust, derivatives, loan securitization, ABS) • Complete deregulation of cross-entry into banking, trust banking, securities, and insurance sectors • Liberalization of bond issuance for commercial banks and non-bank financial institutions • Removal of the ban on financial holding companies • Deregulation of controls on entry into the securities business • Liberalization of fixed brokerage commissions • Abolition of legalized cartel in casualty insurance • Liberalization of the foreign exchange business	• Abolition of the monopoly of securities exchanges in securities transactions • Strengthening of the registered markets • Harmonization of accounting standards with international practices • Stricter disclosure rules for banks and securities firms • Creation of safety net for securities and insurance industries	• Creation of the FSA (MOF break-up) • Full revision of the BOJ Law (increased central bank independence) • Change in the style of financial administration: towards a rule-based system

While we regard the decisions to launch the initiative at this timing (1996–97) and with this scope (proposing reforms spanning across the entire financial sector) as the most important choices made, there were two additional important choices involved. These were the choices about the pace and sequence of reforms. The reforms as a whole were to be carried out by 2001; however, the pace of each of the measures was not delineated in the Hashimoto initiative of November 1996. The precise timetable emerged in June 1997, only after considerable deliberation within MOF's deliberative councils. The interplay of the industries and MOF, which determined the pace of the implementation of the measures, is examined in Chapter 6.

Another policy choice was the sequence of the reforms. The Big Bang had two phases. The first phase commenced with the liberalization of foreign exchange controls in April 1998, while the bulk of the Big Bang reforms took effect in December 1998 (major exceptions to this implementation date reflected the aforementioned issue about the pace of reforms).

The choice to pursue foreign exchange reforms first was controversial. A BOJ economist who later became a lawmaker representing the Shinshinto Party, Yoshio Suzuki, saw a major dilemma here. If the financial deregulation was carried out gradually, then foreign exchange liberalization could actually lead to the "hollowing-out" of the financial market; however, if the reforms were carried out all at once, the result could be the destabilization of the Japanese financial system. In short, there was a dilemma between efficiency and security (Suzuki 1997).

Likewise, Seiichiro Saito, another economist and veteran of the BOJ, predicted a dark future brought about by the Big Bang, precisely because of sequencing problems. Specifically, he feared that domestic financial panic could be spurred by large capital outflows if foreign exchange liberalization materialized before the domestic system was prepared. Needed preparations included the secure establishment of the payoff system of deposit insurance, the liberalization of control over market entry, price, and products, and the establishment of a safety net in the case of transitory crisis. Saito believed that the liberalization of capital transfers ought to be the last measure implemented, after these other measures were secured (Saito 1997). Why, then, was this sequence adopted? We answer this question and tell the political story behind this choice in Chapter 5.

Concrete Policies Included in the Financial Big Bang

This section provides a brief explanation of measures included in the Big Bang, which prove highly relevant to our later analysis. We focus here on how such measures were expected to affect the actors in the financial market and begin first with liberalization and deregulation measures that aimed to promote competition and reduce governmental controls. We then follow with measures focused on strengthening the market infrastructure by increasing the utility of the securities market for users, augmenting financial institution transparency, and establishing means to deal with financial institution failures.

Liberalization and Deregulation Measures

LIBERALIZATION OF INTERNATIONAL CAPITAL TRANSACTIONS

Starting in April 1998, Japanese residents would be allowed to hold deposit and brokerage accounts overseas, and overseas remittance would not require prior notification. As this measure would take effect earlier than the bulk of the deregulation measures, users of financial services would have the option of "exit," if they found investment options abroad to be more attractive.

PRODUCT LIBERALIZATION

Product liberalization in such areas as securities, investment trusts, derivatives, and asset-backed securities, would bring wider opportunities for some businesses selling the liberalized products, while hurting other businesses by bringing new competitors into their domain. For example, the introduction of money market fund accounts with settlement functions (the equivalent of asset management accounts) would benefit the securities industry, but break the monopoly of deposit-taking institutions over the lucrative business of managing the settlement accounts of households.

PERMITTING BUSINESS CROSS-ENTRY

A measure permitting business cross-entry by banks, trust banks, securities firms, and insurance firms would serve to break down the compartmentalization of finance. While the financial reforms of 1991–93 took a first step towards eliminating the segmentation in finance, those reforms strictly restricted what types of new lines of business the subsidiaries of financial institutions could engage in.[32] Such restrictions were to be abolished by the Big Bang, leaving the financial firms free to enter other financial businesses through their subsidiaries. However, the pace of permitted cross-entry would vary, reflecting consideration of the concerns by the "weak" in the financial sector. Subsidiaries of the city banks that would engage in the trust banking and securities businesses would be allowed entry into the markets in the latter half of FY1999, while the insurance industry would be guarded from intrusion from other businesses until the deadline for full implementation of the Big Bang reforms in the year 2001.

LIBERALIZATION OF BOND ISSUANCE FOR COMMERCIAL BANKS AND NON-BANK FINANCIAL INSTITUTIONS

A measure liberalizing bond issuance for commercial banks and non-bank financial institutions would break down additional lines of segmentation within banking. The first was the line that divided long-term credit banks

---

[32] There were two important exceptions to this rule, granted to banks taking over failing institutions: Daiwa Bank assuming control of Cosmo Securities in 1993 and Mitsubishi Bank (the later Bank of Tokyo-Mitsubishi) taking over Nippon Trust Bank. In these cases, the need to rescue failing "ships" was given priority over the maintenance of segmentation in finance under the Convoy System (Mitsubishi [Soken] 1997: 86).

and ordinary banks.[33] The distinction between long-term credit banks and city banks would be eliminated by abolishing the monopoly on bond issuance formerly enjoyed by the long-term credit banks.[34] Second, the line dividing banking firms from non-banks would be blurred by permitting non-bank financial institutions to issue corporate bonds and commercial paper (CP), thereby increasing their financing options.[35]

REMOVAL OF BAN ON FINANCIAL HOLDING COMPANIES

A revocation of the ban on financial holding companies would complement the deregulation of business cross-entry. The measure would be achieved through revision of the Anti-Monopoly Law that banned holding companies, and initially intended to prevent the resurrection of pre-World War II *zaibatsu*. A new law would be enacted as well, to create a legal framework for financial holding companies.

DEREGULATION OF ENTRY CONTROLS ON THE SECURITIES BUSINESS AND LIBERALIZATION OF FIXED BROKERAGE COMMISSIONS

Two measures designed to increase competition in the securities industry were also included. The first measure, the deregulation of entry controls on the securities business, would lessen the costs of entry into the securities business by downgrading the legal requirement for entry from authorization to registration. Authorization required approval by the authorities after an examination of the applicant's qualifications and therefore took time. Registration, in contrast, would be automatic, assuming that the applicant met specified requirements. A second measure involving the liberalization of hitherto fixed brokerage commissions would also drastically increase competition within the securities industry, as industry actors traditionally relied for much of their revenue on fixed commissions. The implementation of this measure was to take place in two steps: the liberalization of commissions on large transactions in April 1998, followed by liberalization of commissions on remaining transactions by the end of 1999.[36]

---

[33] Ordinary banks include city banks, regional banks, second regional banks, and trust banks.

[34] That is, long-term debentures (bonds with two- or five-year maturity) sold over-the-counter.

[35] Commercial paper is a short-term promissory note issued by a large corporation for financing purposes.

[36] In reality, taking effect in October 1999.

ABOLITION OF LEGALIZED CARTELS IN CASUALTY INSURANCE

Casualty insurance firms were compelled by law to use insurance premia calculated by an association set up by the industry. Deregulation in the casualty insurance industry was to abolish this legal obligation, thereby abolishing the quasi-cartel and introducing true competition into the industry, undermining the regulatory rents hitherto enjoyed by the industry as a whole. This measure would benefit consumers as a whole by leading to lower insurance premium rates. However, because the insured would be segmented and different premia applied, some consumers—such as young automobile drivers—would see their insurance fees go up, according to casualty insurance firms.[37] This deregulation measure reflected compliance with an agreement reached in December 1996 in the US–Japan Insurance Talks.

LIBERALIZATION OF THE FOREIGN EXCHANGE BUSINESS

Prior to the Big Bang, foreign exchange transactions could only be carried out through banking institutions authorized by MOF. This regulation, stemming from the days when Japan had to control its foreign currency transactions due to balance-of-payment concerns, increased transaction costs for non-financial firms, which saw their international business dramatically expand in the 1980s and 1990s. It also created a regulatory rent, captured by the banking sector in the form of handsome commissions. The Big Bang measure would abolish the monopoly of banks in the foreign exchange business. While this would be expected to hurt the banks, it would be expected to benefit non-financial firms, especially those heavily involved in international business, by permitting them to set up their own foreign exchange operations and bypass the banks.

Enhancement of Market Infrastructure

ABOLITION OF THE MONOPOLY OF SECURITIES EXCHANGES IN SECURITIES TRANSACTIONS

Prior to the Big Bang, securities transactions had to be made through one of eight securities exchanges, regionally distributed in Japan. This monopoly would be abolished in 1998, reducing the transaction costs for stock-issuing firms.[38]

---

[37] See Sanwa [Soken] (1999) and Nihon Keizai Shimbun (1997).

[38] Thereafter, the eight securities exchanges began to consolidate into the two Tokyo and Osaka exchanges, as an increasing number of firms became reluctant to list themselves on the smaller, regional stock exchanges.

STRENGTHENING THE REGISTERED MARKETS

The registered markets—that is, the secondary markets equivalent to the NASDAQ in the United States—were complementary to the listed firms for larger firms with tight restrictions. To facilitate the financing of start-up companies, these registered markets were to be strengthened and given a standing equal to the listed markets.

HARMONIZATION OF ACCOUNTING STANDARDS WITH INTERNATIONAL BEST PRACTICES

Corporate balance sheet disclosures were to be required on a consolidated basis. Accounting standards would be made consistent with international principles, through such measures as the introduction of market value based standards for financial derivatives and securities holding.[39] This represented a shift away from the use of acquired-value accounting standards utilized in the past, which gave rise to hidden assets or hidden losses.

STRICTER DISCLOSURE RULES FOR BANKS AND BROKERAGES

Banks and brokerages would be subject to stricter disclosure rules, designed to facilitate access to information for depositors and investors.

CREATION OF SAFETY NETS FOR THE SECURITIES AND INSURANCE INDUSTRIES

While the deposit insurance system for banks had been in existence since 1971, similar mechanisms providing for failures of securities firms or insurance companies were lacking. In the securities industry, a client protection fund was to be established,[40] covering funds received from clients but not yet invested in securities. Coverage was to be unlimited until 2001 and then limited up to ten million yen per client thereafter. While the revised Insurance Law of 1996 provided for the establishment of a fund for the protection of insurance policy holders, the scheme was an inadequate safety net for the insurance industry. This was because the fund was too small and assistance to ailing firms was to be made after problems emerged, according to the firm's market share.[41] The newly established

---

[39] For more on accounting changes, see, for example, Tanaka (1999).

[40] Established in December 1998. However, because some of the small domestic securities firms were not separately managing the clients' assets and their own accounts, the foreign securities firms decided to set up a different client protection fund, resulting in two separate client protection funds.

[41] The fund provided only up to 200 billion yen, an amount that could be exhausted by a single failure of a mid-sized insurance company. The inadequacy of this system was demonstrated in the failure of Nissan Life Insurance in April 1997.

policyholders' protection fund[42] would fully cover the policyholders' contribution plus interest until 2001, and then 90 percent thereafter (IMF 1998).

Reforms Paralleling the Big Bang

In response to public criticism, significant changes also materialized in financial administration at three levels: (1) the organizational level, leading to a transformation of the relationship between fiscal policymaking and financial regulation; (2) at the level of government—central bank interaction (or between fiscal and monetary policymaking); and (3) at the level of administrative practices, moving from the traditional style of *ex ante*, informal regulation to a more adversarial *ex post*, legalistic style of regulation. While the results of the first two measures only materialized some time down the road, it is important to note that policy discussions regarding these matters were taking place from early 1996. As we will see in Chapter 5, this mattered because it affected the calculations of political actors. Also, these three changes represent a significant part of the larger institutional change in finance involving the breakdown of the convoy system of regulation (See Chapter 8).

CREATION OF FSA IN JUNE 1998

The Securities Exchange Surveillance Commission (SESC) was created in 1992 within MOF in the aftermath of a loss compensation scandal. From 1994–95, MOF had to face increasing criticism over the amount of power concentrated in its organization. Its wide jurisdiction—encompassing budget, taxation, tariff, the Fiscal and Investment Loan Program (FILP), national property, banking, securities, and international finance—came under criticism. In particular, critics charged that fiscal policy and financial regulation ought to be overseen by separate agencies.[43]

Talk of MOF breakup picked up steam by the beginning of 1996, as the Housing Loan Package was debated in the Diet, and the policy failures by MOF (the Housing Loan Affairs, the Daiwa Bank Scandal and the ensuing Japan Premium) came to light. At the same time, reports of misbehavior by MOF officials became rampant in the media, lending force to such arguments. The ruling three-party coalition set up a committee in February

[42] Established in December 1998.
[43] See, for example, see Igarashi (1995) and Mabuchi (1997).

1996, chaired by Shigeru Ito of SDPJ. Meanwhile, the LDP had its own policy caucus on administrative reform and deregulation, the LDP Administrative Reform Promotion Headquarters (ARPH), which increasingly looked into the issues regarding the breakup of MOF and the independence of BOJ. After a heated political debate from August to December 1996, the ruling coalition decided to create the FSA in December 1996, granting it authority over financial supervision, while keeping policy planning authority on financial matters with MOF (See Chapter 5).[44]

WHOLESALE REVISION OF THE BOJ LAW, EFFECTIVE IN APRIL 1998

The relationship between MOF and the central bank, the BOJ, was transformed to allow increased independence to the latter. Enacted in 1942, the old BOJ Law reflected the militaristic regime of the time, according strong governmental control over the central bank by such means as the power of removal of BOJ President from office. This governmental influence was of more *de facto* significance, as monetary policy decisions were made not by the *de jure* policymaking body of the Bank, the Policy Committee (sometimes chided as the "sleeping board"), but by the BOJ Executive Board in consultation with MOF. MOF's strong influence over the BOJ consistently attracted widespread criticism, as the lack of central bank independence was suspected to be one of the causes of the bubble economy, in which fiscal policy considerations skewed monetary policy into keeping interest rates too low for too long.[45] After a heated political debate within the ruling coalition, as well as in two governmental advisory panels, the BOJ was granted increased independence through a major revision of the BOJ Law, effective in April 1998.

CHANGE IN THE STYLE OF FINANCIAL ADMINISTRATION SINCE 1995

In December 1995, in the wake of the Daiwa Bank Scandal and the Housing Loan Affair, and in reaction to the criticism of MOF's past relationship with the financial sector as "cozy" and "collusive," the ministry

[44] The FSA came into existence in June 1998. In the fall of 1998, an overarching authority with a cabinet minister, was created in the form of the Financial Revitalization Commission (FRC) (see Chapter 7).

[45] For examples of such a criticism, see Mabuchi (1997) and Shiozaki (1996). Shusei Tanaka of the Sakigake Party also expresses this view in an interview with Asahi Shimbun (November 26, 1996).

announced a departure from its past, *ex ante*, informal administration, and shift toward a more transparent, *ex post*, legalistic regulation of financial institutions. As a further response to the discussion of its organizational breakup, MOF issued a report on the "new image of financial administration" in September 1996, (Nihon Keizai Shimbun 1997).[46]

Expected Economic Consequences of the Big Bang

The Big Bang initiative was expected to bring about the following four economic consequences.

First, the Big Bang was expected to benefit the Japanese national economy, stimulating economic growth as well as the performance of the financial sector. According to an estimate by MITI, it could potentially raise GDP growth by 0.3 percent (Tsusho [Tsusansho] 1997). It was projected to put a halt to Tokyo's decline as an international financial center. A survey by the Organisation of Economic Cooperation and Development observes that "the planned reforms should lead to greater integration of Japanese markets and companies into the global arena, while keeping some transactions, which would have otherwise moved overseas, in Japan" (OECD 1997: 86–7). The Big Bang was expected to bring innovation in financial product development, as the underdeveloped derivatives market as well as the market in ABS products were expected to take off, thanks to the entry of more experienced foreign financial institutions (Dekle 1997).

Second, the result of increased competition was expected to be a drastic change in the Japanese financial landscape, with the emergence of takeovers, mergers, and strategic alliances in an unprecedented number and scale. On one hand, greater competition would likely make the weaker financial firms more vulnerable to bankruptcies and restructuring (Dekle 1997). On the other hand, as the entry barrier would be significantly lowered, greater participation by foreign financial firms in the Japanese financial market was also expected. As financial firms in the US and European markets boosted their efficiency through fierce competition in contrast to the protected Japanese firms, the most efficient among them were expected to establish their presence in Japan.[47]

---

[46] The FSA and the FRC (see previous note) rigorously promoted this change thereafter: this was an important part of the "institutional change" in finance. See Chapter 8.

[47] As a result of the increased competition, many anticipated that Japan might experience the Wimbeldon effect. Just as the Wimbledon tennis tournament in the United Kingdom seldom features British players, the British Big Bang drove most of the major local brokerage houses out of the market, while the City (the Wimbledon tournament itself) thrives as the

Many events under way by 2000 demonstrated the effect of increased competition. A large number of mergers and acquisition (M&A) and strategic alliances emerged in expectation of further deregulation and increased competition, linking domestic firms to other domestic firms as well as foreign firms.

Four types of alliances and takeovers emerged, in particular: within *keiretsu*, between *keiretsu*, with firms outside the financial sector, and across borders.[48] Alliances within *keiretsu* were significant for the Mitsubishi group: the four banking institutions within the group would be consolidated into the Bank of Tokyo—Mitsubishi, the core "main bank" for the Mitsubishi *keiretsu*, adding to the loose alliance with two major financial firms within the group, Tokio Fire and Marine Insurance and Meiji Life Insurance. Inter-*keiretsu* alliances also took place *en masse*: the most important of all were perhaps the mergers across *keiretsu* lines of mega banks, a development that had to have significant effect on the economic landscape by altering the grouping of firms around the six major *keiretsu*. The mega merger of Daiichi Kangyo Bank (DKB), Fuji Bank, and the Industrial Bank of Japan (IBJ) created the largest bank in the world by 2001. The merger of Sumitomo Bank and Sakura Bank meant not only the creation of another financial giant but also a merger of the main banks of the Sumitomo and Mitsui *keiretsu*: in line with this development, the merger of Sumitomo and Mitsui Life Insurance was also announced. With the merger of Sanwa Bank, another one of the six largest city banks, with Tokai Bank and Asahi Bank, announced in March 2000, meant a reduction in the number of large banks from about twenty in 1995 into four major groups: the Mitsubishi group, the Mizuho group (DKB–Fuji–IBJ), the Mitsui–Sumitomo group, and the Sanwa–Tokai–Asahi group. Alliances outside the financial sector were also significant: Nippon Credit Bank (NCB), which was temporarily nationalized in 1998, was sold to a group of firms headed by Softbank, a software company known for its investment in the high-tech sector.

Lastly, international alliances and takeovers mushroomed, as noted before. As of this writing (May 2000), the banking, securities, and insurance industries have all seen the takeover of domestic firms by foreign counter parts. Foreign financial firms have already increased their presence in the

main financial center in Europe. Likewise, the Big Bang was expected to bring about a situation in which Tokyo prospered as a financial center while a large number of Japanese financial firms suffered a fate similar to their counterparts in the United Kingdom. However, there was little agreement on the likely extent of this effect.

[48] For more on *keiretsu*, or the six large financial groups in Japan, see, for example, Okimoto (1989).

Table 4.2 Examples of announced M&As and alliances (November 1996–May 2000)

1) Within *Keiretsu*
- Consolidation within the Mitsubishi Group: Mitsubishi Trust Bank, Nippon Trust Bank, and Tokyo Trust Bank merging with the Bank of Tokyo—Mitsubishi
- Alliance across banking, securities, and insurance within the Sanwa Group: Sanwa Bank organizes "Financial One" with six other financial firms in trust banking, life insurance, casualty insurance, and securities

2) Across *Keiretsu*
- Merger of Sumitomo Bank and Mitsui Bank: the Mitsui-Sumitomo Bank groups together two large banks that historically functioned as the core bank for the Sumitomo and Mitsui *keiretsu*.
- Merger of Mitsui and Sumitomo Life Insurance: this follows the above merger in the banking sector.
- Merger of the DKB, Fuji Bank, and the IBJ: the newly created Mizuho Bank would be the largest bank in the world in terms of asset size.
- Merger of Sanwa, Tokai, and Asahi Banks: the new bank would be the second largest in Japan, and the third largest in the world in terms of asset size.

3) Entry into the Financial Sector by Non-financial Firms
- Takeover of the NCB by a three-company alliance led by Softbank: Softbank (software and high-tech investment), with Orix (non-bank financial company) and Tokyo Marine and Fire Insurance, enter into the banking sector

4) Across Borders
- Takeover of LTCB by a consortium of US and European companies led by Ripplewood Holdings (US)
- Takeover of Yamaichi Securities by Merrill Lynch (US)
- Takeover of Heiwa Life Insurance by Aetna (US)
- Strategic partnership (including management participation and stock ownership) between Nikko Securities and Travelers Group (later Citigroup) (US)

Source: Nihon Keizai Shimbun, Asahi Shimbun, and Yomiuri Shimbun

Tokyo market, through M&A operations, often taking over troubled Japanese financial institutions, and through strategic alliances.[49] Compared to the virtual nonexistence of foreign takeovers of Japanese financial institutions prior to 1995, the change is stark: the Long-Term Credit Bank of Japan (LTCB), once a prestigious long-term credit bank, was taken over by a consortium of US and European investing firms led by Ripplewood Holdings; mid-sized life insurance companies were bought up by foreign entities; Merrill-Lynch took over the businesses of the bankrupt Yamaichi Securities—the fourth largest and once the leader among the Big Four of the securities industry. Table 4.2 shows some examples of important M&A and strategic alliances put in place after the Big Bang was announced in November 1996.[50]

[49] An IMF report observes: "foreign financial institutions have already won a substantial share in securities trading and asset management business." (IMF 1998: 129, fn. 4)

[50] See *Nihon Keizai Shimbun* (August 19, 1999), *Asahi Shimbun* (May 31, and June 1, 1998; October 21, 1999; March 28, April 19, and April 30, 2000), and *Yomiuri Shimbun* (April 20, 2000). Note that the table reflects the information available as of writing, May 2000.

The third expected outcome of the Big Bang was *an acceleration in the shift from indirect finance to direct finance, as non-financial firms and households see their options increase and the banking sector shrinks in size.* As for the corporate sector, Hoshi and Kashyap (1999) estimated that the banking loan demand would shrink at least 20 percent under the most conservative scenario.[51] If a scenario of 30 percent shrinkage in bank loans were to materialize, the share of deposits in personal financial wealth were anticipated to decrease from 59 percent to 48 percent. A corresponding contraction in size appeared inevitable in the banking sector, which dominated Japanese finance throughout the postwar era. This, in turn, implies a great reduction in the number of banks, as well. Under this estimate by Hoshi and Kashyap, the fourty-five weakest among the 142 major banks might have to go out of business in order to accommodate the 20 percent loan shrinkage.[52]

Fourth, the second and third points as well as the change in financial administration suggested the following: *the dominance of the banking sector in the economy and the postwar main bank system would face increased pressures for change.* For the banking sector, the Big Bang meant increased competition within the sector, resulting in a decrease in demand for loans and a decrease in the number of banks. Moreover, an important part of the main bank system was the government's regulatory framework, overseen by MOF and the BOJ. This framework constrained the behavior of financial firms so that their behavior remained consistent with the implicit rules of the main bank system, but at the same time provided regulatory rents for the banks so as to ensure their monitoring function over firms (Aoki, Patrick, and Sheard 1994). However, the change in administrative practices and the deregulation brought about by the Big Bang would be expected to dismantle this very regulatory framework. Consequently, the Big Bang would likely undermine the banks' incentives to act as main banks.

Through increased competition, the abolition of regulatory rents, and the disappearance of regulators who (at least were believed to) have the power to punish and reward, the reforms produce a new pressure for survival. Changed bank incentives could be most salient when firms confronted

---

[51] The most conservative scenario was one in which only the large manufacturing firms (the ones that are most likely to shift towards capital markets) were assumed to converge to the level of bank dependence seen in the United States (in terms of asset/debt ratios), while all remaining firms were assumed to move halfway towards the US level.

[52] A cautionary note must be added in that this estimate simply calculated the share of loans for each bank and estimated how many banks would need to exit so that the cumulative shrinkage in loans will be accommodated. (Hoshi and Kashyap 1999: 41–2) As there is no way to know how much each bank would adjust loan balances, it must be said that this estimate allowed for a large margin of error.

possible failure. At this point, the main banks would face three options, according to Aoki, Patrick, and Sheard (1994). The main bank could call in bad loans (thereby abandoning its position as main bank), rescue the firm by supplying refinancing, or take the case to court and pursue a court-led bankruptcy procedure. The concern for short-term profitability, due to increased competition, combined with the disappearance of positive inducements such as regulatory rents and of sanctions such as intervention by regulators, could override the perceived benefits of long-term relationships with firms that accrued through relational financing. Thus, main banks might be expected to increasingly opt for the first and third options rather than the second. As a result, we were likely to see fewer instances of troubled firms being rescued by their main banks.

"Winners" and "Losers" of the Big Bang

We now turn to the task of identifying what the initiative implies to the financial actors so that we may anticipate their strategy in the political process. If the actors stand to "win," or see gains, they would have the incentives to push for the Big Bang; in contrast, if they expect to "lose," or expect their interests to be hurt, they would have the incentives to forestall the initiative. To this goal, we will reassess the Big Bang measures from the standpoint of each financial actor. Our chief task is to separate the likely "winners" from the "losers" of the Big Bang reforms.

The financial actors—those who engage in business transactions in the financial market—comprise the following: the households; non-financial firms; newcomers to financial business (foreign financial firms, non-bank financial institutions, and non-financial firms entering the financial market); the banking sector (large city banks and weaker banking institutions—smaller city banks, long-term credit banks, trust banks, regional financial institutions); securities firms; and insurance companies.

Households

The Big Bang may imply two potentially conflicting concerns for households: profitability and security. Concerning profitability, the households stand to benefit from the competition promoting measures of the Big Bang initiative, as the returns on their financial assets are expected to increase. Greater options for their asset management will materialize thanks to foreign exchange liberalization (through the new "exit" option) and product liberalization. Greater competition among financial firms will enhance the efficiency of the financial services provided to households. The liberalization of entry control (i.e. introduction of cross-entry among banking, securities, and insurance; reduction of entry control in securities; liberalization of foreign exchange business) will bring newcomers to financial services, increasing the likelihood that consumers will be able to enjoy better services. Likewise, the abolition of price controls (e.g. fixed brokerage commissions and quasi-cartelized casualty insurance premia) was likely to result in lower prices for financial services in general.

On the other hand, the Big Bang potentially raised concerns for security among consumers. The introduction of these reforms meant that the security of their deposits under the Convoy System would disappear, and the depositors would held accountable for their own choices from 2001 onward, although market enhancing measures such as the creation of a safety net and improvement in disclosure standards would make increased information available for investment decisions.[53]

Thus, each individual faced higher risk in the post-Big Bang world. It must be noted, however, that the rise in insecurity might have materialized anyway with the deepening of financial instability from the summer of 1995. Regardless of whether the rise in risk was brought about by the Big Bang or not (at the objective level), this concern for security must have been salient at the time of the Big Bang initiative, especially in the environment of financial instability.

How did the consumer public balance these concerns of profitability and security? How did they perceive the Big Bang? Although these are tough questions to answer, we may be able to benefit from a survey of the households run by a non-profit organization affiliated with the BOJ in June 1997, seven months after the announcement by Prime Minister Hashimoto and two weeks after the MOF package.[54] First of all, only 33.9 percent knew about the Big Bang, while 65.8 percent did not. Among those who knew, when asked what its consequences were likely to be, 33.4 percent saw positive effects and 35.9 percent gave negative forecasts, while 13.2 percent saw little influence on their lives. Asked about the criteria for choosing their means of savings, "safety" came on top at 49.3 percent, followed by "liquidity" at 30.9 percent and "profitability" at its record low at 15.3 percent. Regarding self-responsibility (*jiko sekinin*), or the investors' responsibility

---

[53] Whether this is enough is another issue, given the asymmetry of expertise between service providers and consumers. Supplementary legislation on financial services specifically designed to protect consumers was later introduced.

[54] This was a survey of 6000 households (71.4 percent response rate). The survey data is available from the web site of this non-profit organization, the Central Council for Savings Information (http://www.saveinfo.or.jp).

for their own choices, 52.1 percent thought that investors ought to be held accountable for their stock investment, while the figures were 29.2 percent for investment trust (in bonds), 25.6 percent for deposits, and 19.5 percent for insurance. The share of people who "would be at a loss if told to take responsibility" (*jibun de sekinin wo mote to iwaretemo komaru*) were 13.2 percent for stocks, 20.7 percent for investment trust in bonds, 46.5 percent for deposit, and 47.5 percent for insurance (Hirasawa 1997). In another survey on dwellers in the Tokyo metropolitan area performed by the think tank, Dentsu Soken (affiliated with the top advertisement agency, Dentsu) in July–August 1997, 76 percent responded that they did not know the content of the Big Bang.[55]

These surveys strongly suggest that the consumer public was largely unaware of the Big Bang at least during the main time frame of our analysis, 1996–97. In the first survey, among the one-third who knew about the initiative, those who saw negative outcomes were slightly more than those who saw positive results; only one-third among those who knew about the Big Bang, that is, one-ninth of the surveyed households, saw beneficial results from the Big Bang. As regards the choice between profitability and security, the latter was clearly important for most of them, as can be seen by the survey on the criteria for selecting means of savings ("safety" was valued more than three times greater than "profitability"). Thus, while they might be expected to benefit from the increasing returns on their financial assets in the long run "objectively," the consumer public was largely unaware of the issues at the time, and only a small share among them saw the Big Bang to be beneficial.

Non-Financial Firms

Non-financial firms stood to benefit from the "user-friendly" reforms, while the resulting shift towards indirect finance and the downsizing of the banking sector could be expected to bring about the loss of protection provided by their main banks and all the other benefits associated with the main bank system.[56]

The pro-competition reforms would likely be beneficial to the corporate sector in that they would increase efficiency in the financial services

[55] This was a survey of 854 people over the age of eighteen (580 answers obtained). Among those who responded, 28 percent said that they did not know of the Big Bang, 48 percent replied that they had heard about the term, "the Big Bang"; 21 percent answered that they had a fair idea of what it was, and only 3 percent said that they knew the contents quite well. The survey results are available from Dentsu's web site at http://www.dentsu.co.jp (accessed on April 24, 2000).The headline of *Yomiuri Shimbun* ((Osaka), November 23, 1997) that reports this survey said, "80 per cent do not know the contents of the Big Bang."

[56] For a comprehensive account of the main bank system, see Aoki and Patrick (1994).

provided to the firms. The liberalization of international capital transactions and products would increase the firms' financing options. The liberalization of foreign exchange business could mean less transaction costs for international businesses. In addition, the measures enhancing market infrastructure would benefit the corporate sector. The smaller firms would have better access to the "registered markets"; the consolidation of securities exchanges as well as the abolition of their monopoly on securities transactions could mean a decrease in stock issuance costs.

While these changes imply better financial services and financial market access for the firms, the Big Bang could have negative implications for the firms as well. As mentioned earlier, the Big Bang weakened incentives for the main banks to act as such. This issue was especially crucial to the firms whose dependence on the main banks was high. Even in the case of financially healthy firms, the banks, conscious of their capital requirements, were highly likely to curtail their loans. When corporate borrowers experienced financial difficulties, the main banks would likely be especially reluctant to provide refinancing and would increasingly choose to abandon their main bank responsibilities for court-led bankruptcy procedures.

Thus, the Big Bang implied mixed results for the corporate sector, with the relative impact depending on the reliance by particular firms and industries on the banking sector. The corporate sector can be divided into two segments: large manufacturers with relatively low dependence on loans, and small manufacturers and other sectors—with high dependence on bank loans. According to Hoshi and Kashyap (1999), as of 1995, the former had a 17.56 percent ratio of bank debt to assets, while the figure was 29.95 percent for the large firms in wholesale and large retail and over 30 percent for the rest.[57] Large manufacturing firms were likely to see the benefits brought about by the Big Bang, as their less dependence on the main banks would insulate them from the change in the main bank system. However, for the smaller firms and those in industries with tougher prospects (e.g. debt-ridden construction firms), the Big Bang would makes their banks survival-conscious, possibly leading them to adopt harsher standards for their loans and become less willing to provide protection in case of financial hardship.

In sum, the large, manufacturing firms were the clear "winners." The rest—small firms and firms in other industries—likely faced a situation similar to that of consumers. In the long run, they might be able to gain

[57] Table 5 of Hoshi and Kashyap (1999). This is based on the *hojin kigyo tokei* (statistics of incorporated firms) released by MOF. Large firms are defined to have book value of equity greater than 1 billion yen.

advantage from the "user reforms" in terms of profitability; however, in the short-term, and in the context of economic stagnation, they were likely to worry about the likelihood of tighter credit and less protection from their banks.

Newcomers to Financial Markets: Foreign, Non-bank, and Domestic Firms

Three entities—foreign financial firms, non-bank financial firms, and non-financial firms setting up a financial business—would qualify as "newcomers" to the financial markets, traditionally dominated by the established, domestic banking, securities, and insurance industries.

First, foreign financial firms clearly stood to gain from the Big Bang reforms. The liberalization of international capital transactions and product control meant that foreign firms would be able to make use of their efficient services developed abroad and gain a competitive edge over domestic competitors. The liberalization of entry control as well as price control was also likely to benefit the foreign firms that would try to build up a presence through market niches. For example, the abolition of a legalized cartel in casualty insurance was expected to benefit the foreign insurance firms with expertise in products with segmented customers, such as car insurance.

Indeed, the foreign financial firms strongly supported the Big Bang measures. For example, Tadao Ishihara, board chairman of the Japanese subsidiary of an American investment bank (Goldman Sachs, Japan), gave a full endorsement of Hashimoto's initiative in an interview. He suggested that globalization and information technology drove the transactions to the most efficient, low-cost market; in general, the Japanese "corporate capitalism"—based on such features as lifetime employment, enterprise unionism, *keiretsu*, and cross-shareholding that built long-term trust relationships—needed to give way to the US style market, based on the belief in market efficiency. He strongly advocated the liberalization measures included in the Big Bang initiative: cross-entry deregulation, brokerage fee liberalization, and so on. He summed up his views by saying,

it is important to build a market in which the real worth (of financial institutions) will be taken at face value without the constraints of such relationships as main banks or main underwriter. It will take time to untie the bureaucratic interests and the egotism of the (financial) industry. However, nothing gets done if we allow "support in principle, oppose in particular" (*souron sansei kakuron hantai*).[58] . . . I

[58] This is a common saying describing the response to deregulation: everybody is for deregulation in principle, as long as it does not affect oneself.

strongly hope for policies that make it possible to have a real feel of the positive aspects of deregulation such as "what could not be done can be done" and "what used to be expensive becomes cheap" (Nihon Keizai Shimbun 1997: 79–80).

Second, non-bank financial firms might have greater opportunities to start new businesses with the decrease in entry control. Moreover, they would obtain an important means to finance their operation with the deregulation of bond issuance. President Yoshihiko Miyauchi of Orix Corporation, a major lease firm, had been a vocal advocate of deregulation, as an "outsider" trying to enter the financial market dominated by the banking industry.[59] In an interview, he stated that the Japanese Big Bang deserved positive evaluation to a certain extent in that it furthered reforms with deadlines, although he added that much more was needed to make the Tokyo market internationally competitive. He revealed his past frustration with regulation in saying:

in the past, there was a thought current in Japan that there was no need for other financial institutions than the established ones such as the banks. Commercial paper (CP) originated in such financial service industries as the U.S. lease business, as a means of financing. However, in Japan, there was a regulation keeping us from using it. I feel that this prohibition has been without just cause. In the Big Bang, our existence (in the financial sector) will be rightly situated.

In this interview, Miyauchi expressed his expectation that non-bank financial firms would be able to lend money financed through CP and corporate bonds, and revealed his strong sense of rivalry with the banks (*Asahi Shimbun*, June 28, 1997). Miyauchi's comments endorsed the view that non-bank financial firms would benefit from the Big Bang reforms. The non-bank financial firms would have better alternative means of financing to bank loans, and would be able to better compete with the banks.

Third and last, non-financial firms entering the financial market would benefit from the Big Bang measures that drastically lowered the entry barriers. To see this, we may refer to an interview with the founder of a non-financial firm that had started operating in the insurance business. The top firm in the security guard industry, Secom, entered the casualty insurance market in September 1998; its founder, Ryo Iida, states that he had been hoping for entry for the past twenty years, but was unable to do so by any means although he consulted MOF and other casualty insurance firms. However, with the Big Bang breaking down financial segmentation and materializing

---

[59] Miyauchi's drive for deregulation led him to be involved in governmental advisory panels on deregulation: he had been heading a subcommittee on deregulation of the advisory panel on administrative reforms since April 1996.

liberalization, his firm was able to enter into the business with such environmental change (*Kin'yu Zaisei Jijo*, January 4, 1999).

In sum, the newcomers to financial businesses—the foreign financial firms, the non-bank financial firms, and new entrants to financial industries— shared strong support for the Big Bang initiative, which included liberalization measures that advanced their business interests. The sentiment revealed in the interviews presented here differ notably from the ones with domestic financial actors (see later) in that interviewees are supportive, without reservation, of the benefits of the Big Bang reforms, and in fact advocate for greater reform. These actors were the clear perceived "winners" of the Big Bang.

Banking Sector

The Big Bang initiative contained measures that reflected the banks' long-held wishes to break into other financial markets by bringing down the wall of segmentation between banking, securities, and insurance. However, it also included measures expected to hurt the banking sector in general. Banks might suffer from the liberalization of international capital transactions and product liberalization, as these measures decrease the importance of bank deposits and loans for their customers. The liberalization of foreign exchange business eliminates their lucrative monopoly in this domain. The increase of competition in the banking sector may potentially result in forcing the less competitive banking institutions to exit the market.

Thus, we see a fissure between two segments of the banking sector. Large city banks may be the few that stand to gain from the reforms, while their prospect for survival itself is uncertain. The others, that is, the weaker deposit-taking financial institutions, including the smaller city banks, long-term credit banks, and trust banks as well as regional financial institutions (regional banks and credit cooperatives), would not gain much from the Big Bang reforms, as they were heavily constrained in their ability to benefit from the reforms by aggressively entering into new financial territories.

STRONGER BANKS: LARGE CITY BANKS

While the increased competition from foreign financial firms threatened domestic banks' prospects for survival, the liberalization of cross-entry and the removal of the ban on financial holding companies could mean a new line of business, and the issuance of bonds a new means of financing, for powerful city banks with large capital base. However, the bad debt problem damaged the banks' balance sheets, while the extent of damage differed from one bank to another. The relatively unscathed banks, with their more secure capital base, are in a better position to exploit the benefits from the reforms than the others with damaged balance sheets.

The powerful city banks have the potential to benefit from the Big Bang, while their prospects for survival are uncertain. Two interviews of large city banks' managers, recorded by a journalist, Soichiro Tahara, exemplify this ambiguity that the Big Bang initiative implies for the large city banks: one shows confidence while the other shows ambiguity. President Yoshifumi Nishikawa of Sumitomo Bank, the second largest city bank, welcomed the Big Bang, stating that their bank had not been able to adequately provide new products to their customers because of heavy regulation by MOF: the result was their bank being eventually shut out of the world of corporate finance. While the competition with foreign financial institutions might be tough, he showed confidence for the prospect of winning the competition through their customer base in wholesale and personal banking. On the other hand, a board member of Sanwa Bank, the third largest city bank, Takayo Mochizuki, told Tahara that the Big Bang had both positive and negative sides, and that, to be honest, there were no Japanese banks which would be able to compete with foreign financial firms on a par. He said that his bank would rather "survive than win" in the post-Big Bang world, where the probability of foreign banks winning would be one half (Tahara 1998: 212–17).

Thus, some large city banks with large and sound capital base may be the few ones to benefit from the Big Bang reforms. However, they also face a high degree of uncertainty as to their prospects for survival.

WEAKER BANKING INSTITUTIONS: SMALLER CITY BANKS, LONG-TERM CREDIT BANKS, TRUST BANKS, AND REGIONAL FINANCIAL INSTITUTIONS

Later, we will see how the Big Bang affects the weaker institutions within the banking sector. First, the less powerful city banks may have trouble surviving the increased competition unless they drastically restructure their operations.[60] Reflecting their low capital base and profitability, they would need to concentrate their available resources to the retail businesses, in which they may have the competitive edge vis-à-vis the larger city banks or

---

[60] These banks began to curtail their overseas businesses; some of them (e.g. Tokai and Daiwa) started to aim to become "super-regional banks," meaning that they would concentrate on the retail market.

foreign financial firms. If the restructuring proves insufficient, consolidations of their businesses or mergers may be needed to benefit from economies of scale and generate the necessary funds for the investment needed in information systems.

Journalist Soichiro Tahara records an anonymous interview with a president of a smaller city bank (*kai togin*).[61] Asked why the smaller city banks did not oppose the Big Bang, the banker answered, "it reflects the nature of Japanese banks, nourished over a long period of time, to accept the intentions of MOF without being able to oppose them". The president also said that they were unable to come up with a rationale that oppose the Big Bang's "right cause" (*taigi meibun*), which claimed that the Japanese financial industry might be left out of the world and the Japanese customers would flee to New York and London, if they would stick to the outdated Japanese style of business (Tahara 1998: 216–17). This interview supports the view that the smaller city banks were far from pushing for the Big Bang.

Second, the long-term credit banks expected to be negatively affected by the Big Bang. True, the powerful among the three, the IBJ, could benefit from cross-entry measures by fully entering into securities and trust businesses, where the subsidiary of the IBJ had already proven its strength even under strict restriction.[62] In contrast, the two other long-term credit banks, hard hit by the bad debt, lacked the capital necessary to benefit from the Big Bang.[63]

Still, even for the IBJ, the Big Bang reforms would hurt its vital interests: the wall that protected them from the powerful city banks would be torn down by the liberalization of bond issuance, or the abolition of the monopoly on long-term bonds enjoyed by the long-term credit banks. The long-term credit banks would be left with a small number of branches, making it impossible to compete with the city banks in the retail market. The wholesale market would be their strategic focus, in which they must face tough competition with the more competitive foreign financial firms.

The IBJ played a prominent role in forestalling financial reforms in the 1990s. Any efforts to liberalize the bond market immediately elicited staunch opposition from the IBJ, according to government officials in

---

[61] There were only four of them, Tokai, Asahi, Daiwa, and Hokkaido Takushoku. Hokkaido Takushoku went under in 1997. In 1999, Tokai and Asahi announced a plan for merger under a financial shareholding company.

[62] For example, the securities subsidiary of IBJ was at the top among the banks' securities subsidiaries in underwriting corporate bonds as of FY1995 (until end of February 1996). The banks' securities subsidiaries occupied one-half of the total amount, although this area was only liberalized in 1993 (Mainichi Shimbun 1997: 21).

[63] Both of them later collapsed the LTCB in 1998 and the NCB in 1999.

charge of the issue.[64] IBJ President Masao Nishimura stated his views in an interview with *Nihon Keizai Shimbun*, a leading economic daily. Basically he agreed with the "Free," "Fair," "Global," reform plans by Prime Minister Hashimoto. He thought that liberalization measures such as the abolition of financial segmentation needed not to be discussed all at once, but would be better discussed in order of priority. While he was not against the bond issuance by ordinary banks, he felt that these measures ought not to be dealt with at the same level as other measures, given that the groundwork had not been laid for these matters through discussions. He did not think that the liberalization of bond issuance would result in the vitalization of the Tokyo financial market, the goal of the Big Bang; he believed that other measures such as financial holding companies, taxation, and accounting standards, were of much greater urgency (Nihon Keizai Shimbun 1997: 105–6).

These views expressed by IBJ President Nishimura provide us with insight on the expected positions taken by the long-term credit banks. While they basically favored the reforms, they were also interested in slowing down the measures that hurt their vital interests—in particular, the bond issuance by city banks—by mentioning other issues of "greater urgency" and trying to question the benefits of such measures.

Third, the picture looks bleak for trust banks as well. The powerful city banks would be able to fully encroach on their territory, while the trust banks already engage in the banking business with much fewer branches compared to their rivals. The trust banks also saw their assets severely damaged during the bubble years, because of their heavy reliance on the real estate sector: their average ratio of non-performing loans to outstanding loans was twice as much as that of city banks as of September 1996.[65] The resulting weak capital base decreased the likelihood of trust banks going into other financial sectors. On top of this, the increased competition from the foreign financial firms must be added: trust banking had been authorized since the mid-1980s for them, and they had steadily gained ground in the Japanese market since.

Chuo Trust Bank President, Shozo Endo stated in an interview that he did not have any objections to the goal of revitalizing the Tokyo financial market, but he believed that the "hollowing-out" came mainly from

---

[64] Personal interviews with a MITI official who was in charge of industrial finance in the past, and Eisuke Sakakibara, a retired MOF official who had a large role in the Big Bang (Chapter 5) on January 27, 2000. According to the MITI official, this was often expressed in an angry phone call from its top management.

[65] For the period ending in September 1996, the seven Trust Banks (all trust banks except Daiwa) averaged 9.5 percent as the ratio of non-performing loans to outstanding loans; the figure was 4.8 percent for the ten city banks (Mitsubishi [Soken] 1997: 75–6).

tax issues, cumbersome procedures, and high costs. He thought that the cross-entry for financial institutions would have little direct link to this problem. He also mentioned that nine foreign firms were allowed to open up their branches in 1985–86 and to operate without restrictions on their businesses. According to him, the trust banks had historically been kept from freely opening branches while engaging in the loan trust business.[66] The introduction of "fair" and "free" in a formalistic manner in the market reality—where such peculiarities as public finance,[67] cross-shareholding, and the influence of the main banks exist—could lead to unforeseen problems and to oligopoly in the financial market. The priority in financial reforms was to secure political and social stability, as the case differed from experimenting in a laboratory and irreparable loss could result. Accordingly, there is a need to maintain "fair terms of competition" without being overwhelmed by the prevailing "mood" (Nihon Keizai Shimbun 1997: 55–6).

This interview by a president of a trust bank matches the expected stance of the trust banks. While supporting the Big Bang in principle, Endo raised other concerns (e.g. taxation) than those which hurt the vital interests of his bank (the wall keeping the powerful city banks at bay from trust banking), endorsing the view that they prefered to slow down such measures. That they perceived threats from the city banks and the foreign firms, and that the trust banks did not welcome the Big Bang measures on the whole are clear from his comments.

Fourth and last, regional financial institutions would be hurt by the Big Bang and liberalization measures in general. Regional banks and smaller financial institutions (e.g. credit cooperatives) would be hurt by the enhanced competition brought by liberalization measures[68] (which would enable the city banks and securities firms to encroach their customer base), while the liberalization of cross-entry would be of little benefit to them, as most institutions would lack the capital needed to aggressively engage in new financial businesses.[69]

---

[66] This was one of the core businesses for trust banking that city banks' trust banking subsidiaries were prohibited from engaging in under the reforms of 1991–93.

[67] He refers here to the Postal Savings System.

[68] Not only measures contained in the Big Bang (e.g. liberalization of foreign exchange business hurting the regional banks), but also paralleling liberalization measures regarding the interest control and branch control would increase the opportunities for large city banks and securities to encroach their customer base.

[69] Only Yokohama Bank, the largest regional bank, set up a securities subsidiary, which required 10 billion yen capitalization. As trust banking was allowed for regional banks proper under the 1991–93 reforms, many regional banks were starting this business; however, it must be also noted that such growing areas of trust banking as pension fund trusts would necessitate a large investment (Mitsubishi [Soken] 1997: 98–100).

Nagoya Bank President, Senmaro Kato, a former chief of one of the sector's industry associations,[70] stated his view in an interview. To him the Japanese Big Bang Initiative was "unavoidable" (*yamu wo enai*) as a countermeasure, considering the gap between Tokyo and the overseas market. However, it created problems for regional financial institutions; bringing down the walls between securities (and banking) could mean hardship for smaller financial institutions, if they were unable to respond. In finance, if the "symbiosis" (*sumiwake*) disappears, the large banks will come attacking smaller financial institutions' business base, while foreign firms will come in as well. There will be situations in which smaller financial firms will be phased out of the market. However, Kato asked, is this good for Japanese finance? While he did not oppose deregulation, he hoped for measures that would keep in place the lifeline for smaller, regional financial institutions. For example, he asked, would it not be necessary to have a system that prevents "useless competition" (*muda na kyoso*)? In his words, "it is important that the profit margin is secured" (Nihon Keizai Shimbun 1997: 80–1). President Takashi Tamaki of Chiba Bank, a major regional bank, expressed a similar view. While he felt the reforms aimed for stopping the "hollowing-out" of Tokyo ought to be carried out as quickly as possible, the cross-entry issue affected the entire financial structure of Japan; mere liberalization would bring unnecessary "confusion" (*konran*), and he thought considerable time should be spent on thinking carefully through such a "grand design" (Nihon Keizai Shimbun 1997: 91–2).

These two interviews by heads of regional banks clearly show the regional financial institutions' stance towards the Big Bang. While they did not openly oppose the Big Bang initiative as a whole, seeing it as unavoidable, they at the same time perceived that liberalization would force them to fight a losing war against the large banks and the foreign firms, and thus feared that the measures enhancing competition might threaten their prospects for survival. Thus, they would opt to slow down the pace of measures regarding cross-entry, arguing that the "grand design needs [to be formulated over] time" and try to stall the extent of enhanced competition brought about by the measures. They would argue that "useless competition" and "unnecessary confusion" should be avoided and that "the lifeline for smaller financial institutions" and their "profit margin" ought to be preserved.

---

[70] The Second Regional Banks' Association.

Securities Firms

The Big Bang could deal a severe blow to the securities firms by abolishing the price control on brokerage commissions and bringing the powerful banking sector into the securities business.[71] Those developments as well as the liberalization of entry controls increased the likelihood that the more efficient foreign investment banks would present themselves as formidable rivals. The liberalization of international capital transactions could result in the loss of business to overseas markets.

However, the Big Bang might bring positive benefits to the securities business as a whole: the pie itself could become bigger. The liberalization of product control as well as the strengthening of the stock markets might be expected to accelerate the shift from indirect to direct finance for both depositors and corporate borrowers. For example, investment trusts were expected to attract a larger portion of households' assets; bond issuance, of which the securities firms would underwrite, was expected to increase as means of corporate finance.

President Hideo Sakamaki of Nomura Securities, the top firm in the industry, claimed in an interview that he supported the Big Bang. Moreover, provided that taxation issues would be resolved and restrictions on securities firms' businesses lifted, he willingly accepted the liberalization of brokerage commissions. According to Sakamaki, Nomura would "still be able to fight" (*mada tatakaeru*), as it still had a net asset three times larger than Merrill-Lynch, despite recent losses due to affiliated non-bank financial institutions. He shows his sense of rivalry with the banks by scoffing at the idea of banks aiming to become universal banks by integrating securities businesses as "nonsense" (Nihon Keizai Shimbun 1997: 162–3).

Despite the potential benefit of the Big Bang, the sense of insecurity seemed to be quite high even for the top firm, Nomura, which would be the most likely candidate to survive the race, (as the comment that they would "still be able to fight" suggests). For the vast majority of securities firms, the Big Bang might not be beneficial at all: their prospects for survival would be directly threatened.[72] Because the new opportunities for profit were largely to be found in wholesale businesses, an oligopolistic situation by large securities, foreign securities firms, and large banks' securities subsidiaries could

---

[71] See previous note on the remarkable achievement of securities subsidiaries of banks since 1993.

[72] Despite the existence of a few mavericks among the securities business, such as Matsui Securities (a small-size firm), whose president looked forward to the liberalized securities market, evidence overwhelmingly suggests that most firms in the business worried about their survival.

be the result (Mitsubishi [Soken] 1997). As mentioned earlier, the increase in competition was expected to drive many smaller firms out of business through exit or takeover. Thus, the securities industry as a whole would not actively promote the Big Bang measures, which could jeopardize the prospect for survival for many firms in the industry. Indeed, the securities industry's strong opposition was part of the reason why the revision towards further deregulation of cross-entry initiated in 1993 and originally scheduled to take place by the end of FY (March) 1996, was put off until the end of 1997 (*Asahi Shimbun*, March 26, 1996).

Insurance Companies

The Big Bang measures would bring about the liberalization of cross-entry between insurance and other financial businesses, hurting the industry by allowing the large banks to sell insurance products, while few insurance companies would deem it beneficial to be deeply involved in the banking business, where over-banking was already a concern. The insurance reforms of 1992–94 had already been bringing about changes, prior to the Big Bang: the cross-entry between life and casualty insurances through sub-sidiaries had started in October 1996. The industry also has to compete with foreign insurance companies, whose domestic presence had histori-cally been limited to the "third sector," or niche markets that fall in between life and casualty insurances (such as cancer insurance), but whose pressures for liberalization were intensified by the US–Japan insurance talks that held from 1993 (See Chapter 6). Thus, the increased competition within the insurance industry, among domestic life and casualty insurance firms as well as among foreign insurance companies, might be of more urgency to firms' survival than the distant threats of banks' intrusion into the insurance business. Nevertheless, however distant such threats might be, the insurance companies would seek to curtail threats from the outside as much as possible.

The life insurance industry had attracted a large amount of capital dur-ing the bubble years of the late 1980s, thanks to the high guaranteed rates on the products compared to the low long-term interest rates. However, the burst of the bubble and the following years of low interest rates hurt this industry by creating a wide gap between its high guaranteed rates to the insured and the low returns on their investment. Thus, with short-term survival in doubt for many firms, life insurance companies were not in a mood to welcome any increase in competition that would threaten their survival.

The casualty insurance industry did not suffer from this problem, and except for a few firms, their balance sheets looked healthy as a result of amassed regulatory rents. However, the industry would be strongly affected not only by the liberalization of cross-entry, but also, more importantly, by the abolition of the legalized cartel on the insurance premia. This legalized cartel enabled rents that enabled the insurance industry to sustain its high costs. The industry would face tougher competition with the entry of foreign insurance firms, and this would drastically cut insurance premia on products such as car insurance (Sanwa [Soken] 1999).

Accordingly, the insurance industry in general might have been expected to be reluctant to accept the Big Bang measures, if not oppose them outright. Two statements by industry actors—one from the life insurance sector and the other from the casualty insurance sector—enable us to confirm our hypothesis about insurance industry preferences (Nihon Keizai Shimbun 1997: 183–4 and 197–8). President Sukenari Ito of Nippon Life Insurance, the nation's largest life insurance company, claimed in 1997 that the financial reforms needed to be carried out quickly. However, specifically regarding life insurance companies, he stated:

the roles of life insurance companies which manage and preserve personal financial assets long-term are increasing in importance with the aging population. [However,] if competition becomes extremely intense (*kyokutan ni gekika*), the stability of the management (*keiei no antei*) of the life insurance companies may be lost, making it harder for them to fulfill their given roles.

Speaking of cross-entry, he further stated:

it is important that each financial institution secures profitability in its own core business. To enter into other fields because the core business is not doing well is an expansion without profit, and reflects a failure to learn a lesson from the bubble. The discussion on cross-entry should be made after introducing the holding company system.

Speaking of his company, in particular, which was the most likely candidate to enter into other financial fields because of its fiscal health and size, he stated, "the core business will be insurance, and if we are to engage in banking and securities, it will be to the minimum degree necessary."

President Kimihiro Higuchi of Tokio Marine and Fire Insurance, the top firm in casualty insurance, in 1997 welcomed the beginning of reform discussions under the leadership of the prime minister. However, while the point of the reforms lay in the vitalization of market functions, he doubted whether cross-entry between banking and insurance would have this result. While he feels the walls of business segmentation must come down, he also believes a "soft-landing" is necessary. He cites the example of insurance products sold in banks, and calls attention to the danger of the banks' possible misuse of their large power. "While the insurance industries may go into banking and securities in the future, the casualty insurance has just entered life insurance in October 1996" and such prospects are distant. Speaking of the reforms on the premia calculation association (the quasi-cartel), he stated:

that system applies to the areas of individual insurance that highly affect the public (*takai kokyosei*) such as fire and car insurance. With liberalization, on the one hand, competition to discount will take place, while on the other hand, premia on high risk products will drastically increase and there may be cases in which people may not be able to receive insurance coverage.

Thus, the insurance industry would prefer to curtail increased competition in their industry and slow down cross-entry liberalization. Ito's comments such as "expansion without profit is not learning from the lesson of the bubble," as well as Higuchi's skepticism of the link between cross-entry and market vitalization, and his alarm against bank dominance endorses this view. The casualty insurance firms would also hope to curtail the liberalization of price control, as Higuchi's alarm about the danger that drastic competition could bring demonstrates. That they are not likely to be the ones to promote the introduction of the Big Bang seems to be obvious from the comments of the presidents of the two most powerful firms in the insurance industry.

Conclusion

A number of factors provided background pressures for large-scale financial reforms in Japan. These included the aging population, the 1200 trillion yen of financial assets largely held in deposits, the shift away from indirect to direct financing, international competition, the danger of "hollowing-out" or Tokyo losing its position as a main international financial center, incremental liberalization from the mid-1980s, the bubble economy and resulting bad loan problem; and scandals engulfing MOF and the financial sector. The Big Bang package that emerged dealt both with liberalization and deregulation, promoting competition and reducing government control, while also enhancing the market infrastructure and increasing transparency and fairness in the market. The package was expected to have far-reaching effects. These included stimulating economic growth in Japan

Table 4.3 Distributional effects of the Big Bang: "Winners," "Potential Winners," and "Losers"

Financial actors:

1) Households
2) Non-financial firms
3) Newcomers to financial markets (foreign financial firms, non-bank financial firms, and non-financial firms entering the markets)
4) Banking sector
   a) stronger banks—large city banks
   b) weaker banking institutions—smaller city banks, long-term credit banks, trust banks, and regional financial institutions
5) Securities firms
6) Insurance companies

1. "Winners": supporters or potential initiators of the reforms
The Big Bang reforms clearly benefit the actors, and they are aware of this fact.

- Newcomers to financial markets (foreign financial firms, non-bank financial firms, and non-financial firms entering the markets)
- Non-financial firms with little dependence on banks (e.g. large manufacturing firms)

2. "Potential Winners": potential supporters of the reforms
The Big Bang reforms may benefit these actors, but the benefits are unclear.

- Households
- Non-financial firms with dependence on banks (e.g. small and medium, troubled sectors)
- Stronger banks (large city banks)

3. "Losers": opposition to the reforms
The Big Bang reforms hurt the actors; the actors are aware of this fact.

- Most banking institutions except large city banks
- Securities firms
- Insurance companies

---

and enhancing performance of the nation's financial sector; drastically changing the Japanese financial landscape by promoting takeovers, mergers, and alliances in unprecedented numbers and on an unprecedented scale; accelerating the shift from indirect finance to direct finance; weakening the hitherto dominance of the banking sector in the economy; and placing heavy pressures for change on the main bank system. In the process, the Big Bang was projected to produce "winners," "potential winners," and "losers." Table 4.3 summarizes the distinction among the three categories of actors. Most firms in the domestic financial industries— with only a few exceptions—stood to lose from the Big Bang. This is important to note because the content of previous financial reforms—such as the 1981 banking reforms and the 1991–93 financial reforms—reflected the dominant concerns of financial industry actors.

In the next chapter, we will turn our attention to the political process of the Big Bang initiative. The analysis of the interplay of state actors, political parties and the bureaucracy, will lead us to distinguish the "economic winners" ("winners" and "potential winners" in this chapter) that we found through this chapters' analysis, from "political winners" who would see political benefits to be reaped from the reforms. The focus of our attention will be on whether "economic winners" or "political winners" propelled the reforms forward.

Part II

Analysis of Financial Politics

5

A Political Analysis of the Emergence of the Big Bang Initiative

This chapter examines the politics surrounding the emergence of the Big Bang Initiative, seeking to determine who brought it about and why. The analysis focuses in particular on developments between the fall of 1995 and November 1996, when then Prime Minister Hashimoto announced the initiative. The Hashimoto initiative (hereafter the "Initiative") laid out the overall framework of the reforms, including their timing, scope, sequence, and implementation deadline. Details of the reform plan were subsequently worked out in the MOF's deliberative councils, and were announced as the Big Bang Plan in June 1997. This plan was later legislated by the Diet in June 1998. Importantly, the overall framework of the November 1996 Initiative was not modified significantly in either the MOF Plan of June 1997 (hereafter "the Plan"), or by the laws enacted to implement the measures.

The chapter argues that the political economy of the Big Bang can be best explained according to the logic of actor behavior detailed in Chapter 3. This logic focuses on the maintenance of organization survival and holds across political parties, organizations, and firms. To make this argument, the chapter first reflects on two sets of interests that political actors need to ensure survival and uses this to lead into a brief overview of the chapter's main argument. The chapter then provides an in-depth narrative of events in the political process through November 1996. This narrative delves into developments at the suborganizational level. The chapter then turns to provide an organizational level evaluation of the facts presented in the narrative. Finally, the chapter tests our argument against competing explanations and concludes with a review of the chapter's main arguments.

Balancing the Interests of Support Constituencies and the General Public

State actors, political parties, and bureaucracies must cater to two sets of interests in their quest for organizational survival.[1] One set is that of the constituencies which provide goods and services to political actors. Interest groups provide votes and money to political parties for their electoral campaigns. Regulated industries provide information, cooperation with administrative measures, and positions in the private sector for retiring bureaucrats from government agencies. At the same time, political actors must satisfy a second set of interests: that of the general public. Public support is vital for political parties that face regular elections. Public support also provides bureaucratic agencies with better acceptance of their policy measures, thus securing survival by demonstrating their positive contribution to the nation.

How do political actors strike a balance between the two sets of interest? As Aoki (1988) notes for the bureaucracy, these two sets of interests may or may not be compatible. If the two coincide, we observe little contention. If the constituencies desire one thing and the public seeks another, however, how will the political actors react? The short answer is that it depends on how important the support of the constituencies or of the public is to the actors' survival. How is this degree of importance determined?

Here, we offer the following hypothesis:

In a democracy where all political actors must respond to both constituency interests and the public interest, the degree of public support for the organization in question determines its behavior when the two sets of interests diverge because a loss of public support adversely affects the organization's prospects for survival. More specifically, a loss of public support leads the organization to adjust its behavior in an attempt to regain this support.

In a situation in which public support is high, the organization will choose to pursue the constituents' interests, as it can afford to risk some loss in public support without putting its own organizational survival at risk. If public support is lost for some reason, however, the organization cannot risk further loss of public support by catering to jurisdictional

---

[1] In the language of Aoki (1988), these two factors determine the political stock that the bureaus command. While Aoki's discussion centers on the "bureaus," or bureaucratic agencies, we expand the scope of discussion to include the political parties, as these two factors also seem to determine the "political stock" of the parties as well.

interests. This is because other political actors are likely to seize the opportunity to respond to the desires of the public, as a means to boost their own public support, and in doing so may intervene on behalf of the public in a way that threatens the existence of the organization.

Consider the alternative scenario in which public support for a particular organization is high and constituency support is low. Assuming that the situation occurs in an industrial democracy where there are mechanisms such as elections, mass protests, and boycotts for translating popular discontent into policy outcomes, constituents face significant risk in challenging the organization, since their opposition has the potential to elicit accusations from the public that their behavior works against the public interest. Because the loss of public support has a relatively greater impact on a given organization's prospects for survival than does the loss of constituency support, we focus on the former in the analysis that follows.

Our story of financial reforms is one in which constituency interests and public interest come into conflict. The constituents of financial administration under bureaupluralism—the domestic financial industries—wanted gradual reforms on the whole. The public interest, however, seemed to lie in "drastic reforms" which would stop the "hollowing-out" of the Tokyo financial market, but undermine the prospect of survival for most financial firms. The Big Bang Initiative would emerge out of LDP and MOF concerns for survival, and each actor would strike a balance between these two sets of interests, depending on the relative importance of constituent or public support to the actor's survival.

For the LDP, the new dynamics of party competition mattered most. Table 5.1 shows the seat distribution before and after the 1996 Lower House elections. In 1995–96, a major controversy erupted over the use of taxpayer money to liquidate seven housing loan corporations called *jusen*. This Housing Loan affair reduced public support for the LDP. At that time, the ruling LDP was seeking electoral victory over its rival parties, Shinshinto (the New Frontier Party formed in 1940 and the newly formed Democratic Party of Japan (DPJ)), both of which advocated fundamental reforms (including administrative reforms) and deregulation. The LDP was also in a three-party coalition with the Social Democratic Party of Japan (SDPJ) and the Sakigake Party. The LDP thus faced competition from within and outside the ruling coalition. This was an unprecedented situation. Prior to the breakdown of its one-party dominance in 1993, the LDP had never faced a credible threat of replacement from its opponents. A concern for survival ultimately drove the LDP's behavior: the LDP incorporated the issues of its rivals into its own party agenda (Otake 1999). In the

Table 5.1 Seat distribution before and after the October 1996 Lower House elections

	Before	After
LDP	211	239
SDPJ	30	15
Sakigake	9	2
Others	34	10
CPJ	15	26
DPJ	52	52
Shinshinto	160	156
Total	511	500

Notes: Before: 511 seats (multi-member districts) including 18 vacant seats
After: 500 seats (300 seats from single-member districts and 200 seats from Proportional Representation)
Parties in Bold: The Ruling Three-Party Coalition

LDP: Liberal Democratic Party
SDPJ: Social Democratic Party of Japan (the former Socialist Party of Japan)
Others: includes other parties and non-partisans
CPJ: Communist Party of Japan
DPJ: Democratic Party of Japan (newly formed in September 1996)
Shinshinto: New Frontier Party (formed in 1994)

Source: Asahi Shimbun, October 21, 1996

absence of fierce electoral competition, the LDP may have preferred different options, reflecting its privileged status within bureaupluralism; however, the electoral dynamics at the time motivated the LDP to follow its rivals' positions.

The MOF suffered an even more severe loss of public support in the wake of the Housing Loan affair and other policy failures and scandals in this period. It too acted according to the dictates of organizational survival: arduously opposing any efforts to break up its organization, while pushing for drastic financial reforms that might increase its chances of survival. Since drastic financial reforms would decrease the ministry's regulatory power and weaken its ties with financial institutions, the MOF would likely have preferred a more gradualist approach. However, the ministry's behavior in 1994–95 consistently reflected that organizational survival was its top priority.

Who Brought about the Big Bang?

Many credit Prime Minister Hashimoto for the Big Bang Initiative, emphasizing his political leadership. Yet, there seems to be little consensus about the causal dynamics beyond this fact. The newspaper *Nihon Keizai*

Shimbun claimed that the Big Bang was strategic "reform [carried out] from above" by MOF, which made selective use of a report issued by a government panel and called the Ikeo Report (see below) (Nihon Keizai Shimbun 1997). Some say it came about when MITI saw opportunities to encroach upon MOF territory (Saito 1997); others identify two top officials at MOF, including Eisuke Sakakibara (whose flamboyant personality later earned him the nickname of "Mr. Yen") (Tahara 1998).

Given this confusion, we focus first on providing an accurate account of who brought about the Big Bang. Our objective, however, is not to merely identify those who advocated the reforms but also to uncover why these reforms materialized at this particular time, why they were so wide in scope, rapid in pace, and sequenced as they were. To do this, we examine the incentives of those actors who brought about the reforms, and identify the logic that dictated their behavior.

The process surrounding the emergence of the Big Bang Initiative was complex. In an attempt to simplify, we have broken down this process into ten interrelated groups of events:

(1) foreign Exchange reforms (Fall 1995–)

(2) financial instability, the Housing Loan affair and scandals (Fall 1995–)

(3) the Housing Loan Diet (January–June 1996)

(4) BOJ and MOF reforms: a response to criticism (February–August 1996)

(5) political debate on MOF reforms: the Ito Plan and possible options (August–September 1996)

(6) critical juncture for MOF reforms: the LDP Group of Eight on September 18, 1996

(7) Lower House Elections of October 1996, Hashimoto's Six Major Reforms, and the conclusion of debate on MOF reforms

(8) Ikeo Report

(9) developments within the MOF on the Big Bang

(10) developments within the LDP on the Big Bang

Foreign Exchange Reforms (Fall 1995–)

The Council on Foreign Exchange and Other Transactions, a MOF advisory panel, began its deliberations on the reform of foreign exchange regulations in November 1995. The council issued the final report in June 1996; a task force to draft the legislation based on this report was set up within the MOF; and the legislation was submitted to the Diet in March 1997.[2] In March 1998, a Project Team (PT) on administrative reforms within the three-party ruling coalition of the LDP, the Social Democrats, and Sakigake issued a proposal for a drastic revision of foreign exchange regulations. Importantly, this report set the pace for later deliberations on foreign exchange reforms by the MOF panel.

Two sets of actors played a significant role in this event. First, two lawmakers from the LDP's Administrative Reforms Promotion Headquarters (ARPH) were behind the PT's proposal advocating drastic liberalization: its head, Kiyoshi Mizuno (who also chaired the PT), and Yasuhisa Shiozaki, an LDP lawmaker from the Upper House (Tahara 1998). Mizuno had long been a vocal advocate of deregulation. As a former cabinet member and a senior member of the LDP, he wielded considerable influence within the party on issues of administrative reform and deregulation. His organization, the ARPH, was independent from PARC, the policymaking body, and only had to report to the LDP's Executive Council, and to LDP President and Prime Minister Hashimoto. Shiozaki, as a former official at the BOJ, was a junior Diet member whose expertise in finance attracted the attention of Mizuno, who assigned him to financial matters in the ARPH.[3] Shiozaki had been a strong advocate of financial liberalization: he authored an article as early as February 1995, stressing the need for financial liberalization to halt financial "hollowing-out" (Shiozaki 1995). While the ARPH played pivotal roles in various financial matters such as the BOJ reforms, the MOF breakup, and other aspects of the Big Bang (discussed later), the role of the ARPH in foreign exchange reforms would be particularly crucial. The ARPH decided the content of the reforms by accelerating and deepening revisions, according to Tomotaka Kojima, the MOF official in charge of foreign exchange reforms (Tahara 1998).

The second actor was a senior MOF official in charge of foreign exchange control, Eisuke Sakakibara. Sakakibara pushed for foreign exchange deregulation, convinced that the revolution in information and communication technology meant Japan would have to alter its strategy and open up its closed financial system to remain competitive with Europe and America (Sakakibara 2000, chapter 9). He was unable to successfully carry out this deregulation because of opposition from within the MOF. He, therefore,

---

[2] It became law in May 1997 and took effect on April 1, 1998.
[3] Author interview with Kiyoshi Mizuno, July 19, 1999.

came to Mizuno, implicitly asking him to take up the issue at the ruling coalition's PT and pressuring him to decide in favor of drastic deregulation. According to Mizuno, Sakakibara wrote the scenario and played the title role while Mizuno directed it; Shiozaki confirms this story (Tahara 1998).

While Sakakibara appeared to be the main actor here, the role played by elected officials was also important: without their involvement, Sakakibara would have been unable to surmount the formidable opposition from within the MOF. Opposition stemmed, in particular, from those "veterans"[4] in the International Financial Bureau (IFB). The abolition of the foreign exchange law meant complete abandonment of regulatory power by this bureau, thus threatening the reemployment prospects of these officials in the private sector (Tahara 1998: 143–5). Sakakibara (2000, chapter 9) also recalls that there was a sharp division of opinions in the IFB over the abolition of the monopoly over foreign exchange business enjoyed by the banking industry. Only a minority pushed for the abolition, while most of the bureau's senior officials opposed the idea because the reforms were seen as too drastic and because the banks vehemently opposed them. The involvement by the ARPH was thus essential in surmounting opposition within the MOF.[5]

That the foreign exchange reforms were decided and implemented first, had a great effect on the course of financial reforms thereafter. Because foreign exchange deregulation gave an exit option to Japanese asset holders, the deregulation of the domestic financial market became inevitable. Accordingly, the deregulation of foreign exchange became the forerunner to the Big Bang reforms. Sakakibara was aware of the implications of the reforms, as the sequencing was a conscious choice. In his memoirs, he argues that he was aware that changes in international finance were likely to trigger a drastic change in domestic finance. This had been the case with US financial deregulation of the 1970s and 1980s, which was triggered by the emergence of the Euro–dollar market.[6] Sakakibara explained that while he had previously been opposed to "deregulation without principles," he now believed that Japan would have to alter its strategy toward opening up

---

[4] Within the MOF, there are "career" officials with potential for promotion up to the Administrative Vice-Minister, and there are "veteran" officials with lesser potential for promotion. See Amyx (1998 [and 2004]) for a detailed discussion of these two sets of bureaucrats.

[5] Author interview with Kiyoshi Mizuno, July 19, 1999.

[6] Tahara (1998) confirms this point: he records that Kiichi Miyazawa, the former prime minister with expertise on finance (and serving as finance minister under the Obuchi and Mori Cabinets), told him in the beginning of July 1997 that what Sakakibara did (i.e. the foreign exchange reforms) would have a large impact, even though most lawmakers passed the law without realizing it.

its closed system of finance and information if it was to stay in competition with Europe and America. He attributed the heightened imperative for openness to the revolution in information and communication technology that occurred over the decade and rapidly brought about the cyber-market and globalization (Sakakibara 2000, chapter 9).

Financial Instability, the Housing Loan Affair, and Scandals (Fall 1995–)

Financial instability started with the failure of a small financial institution in Tokyo in July 1995, and intensified with the failure of other financial institutions in the fall of 1995. The Daiwa Bank Scandal in this year also brought down public trust in the MOF's ability to handle financial matters. This, in turn, gave rise to a Japan Premium in the international inter-bank market—a surcharge on borrowing by Japanese banks that revealed a similar loss of trust in the Japanese financial system. Coming on top of this development, the ministry proposed to use taxpayer money to solve the Housing Loan affair, thus stirring up fierce public anger toward the MOF. Public trust in the ministry's competence was lost, and wining and dining scandals involving some of MOF's top officials further shattered public confidence in the ethics of these officials. Agriculture emerged victorious in negotiations over how to split the losses of the housing loan companies between the agricultural sector and the banking sector, thus symbolizing a defeat for MOF, which oversaw the negotiations. The budget proposal including a request for the use of public funds was finally submitted to the Diet in December 1995, as the losses that neither the banks nor the agricultural financial institutions were willing to bear had to be covered by public money.

During this process, MOF's political influence steadily decreased over time. One downfall seemed to lead to later problems. According to the head of the Banking Bureau at that time, Yoshimasa Nishimura, MOF did not have the power to change the course of the policy discussion in the Housing Loan Affair because the incident increasingly became an agricultural issue more than a financial matter. He recalls, "The fact that I lost credibility because of the Daiwa Bank incident and lost the initiative in the resolution of the Housing Loan Problem was critical [to outcomes]." He overestimated MOF's ability to deal with the issue and the degree to which the ministry's lost credibility would translate into lost policymaking influence (Nishimura 1999: 144–5).

The Housing Loan Diet (January–June 1996)

The regular Diet session that began in January 1996 was called the "Housing Loan Diet" (*jusen kokkai*). At the center of the debate was a legislative package proposing the use of taxpayer money to liquidate the seven *jusen* housing loan corporations.[7] As Diet deliberations proceeded, public anger reached a feverish pitch. Public opinion surveys indicated that the Housing Loan package was wildly unpopular. According to an *Asahi Shimbun* poll in February 1996, 87 percent of the Japanese public opposed the package, and most held the bureaucracy responsible for the fiasco (*Asahi Shimbun*, February 28, 1996).[8] To the question, "Who do you think is the most responsible for this Housing Loan Affair?", the most frequent response at 27 percent of respondents was the bureaucrats at MOF and MAFF (responsible for agriculture), while the large banks which set up the housing loan companies[9] followed in second, cited by 20 percent of respondents, ahead of the housing loan companies (19 percent), and the politicians (15 percent). Those who responded that the agricultural cooperatives were primarily responsible comprised a mere 3 percent. Public trust in politics was also shown to be unusually low: 73 percent responded that they did not trust today's politics. However, the LDP's support was 46 percent, up 3 points from December 1995), while the support rate for its rival, Shinshinto, dropped 3 percentage points in the same period to 16 percent (*Asahi Shimbun* February 28, 1996). In a different poll published two weeks later, the *Asahi Shimbun* reported that Prime Minister Hashimoto's approval rate had dropped to 36 percent from the 61 percent[10] recorded when he took office in January 1996. This time public support for the LDP was also down considerably, falling from 36 to 24 percent (*Asahi Shimbun* March 12, 1996).

Meanwhile, support for the main opposition party, Shinshinto, had risen from 9 to 14 percent (*Asahi Shimbun* March 12, 1996).[11] Shinshinto

[7] For the Housing Loan affair, see Yutani and Tsujihiro (1996), Amyx (1998 [and 2004]), and Nishimura (1999).

[8] Note the wording of the question: "The Government included 685 billion yen in the budget proposal to cover the bad debt of housing loan companies. Do you support or oppose using the taxpayers' money to deal with the bad debt?" It is rather surprising that as many as 7 percent answered that they supported this action.   [9] Called the "mother banks" (*botai ko*).

[10] The last poll with the same methods was in January 1996.

[11] Note that this poll was carried out by telephone interview (2000 questioned, 1143 responses). It is still puzzling why the newspaper alternated between two polling methods. It acknowledged that because of the difference in methods, telephone interviews tend to have a lower support rate than face-to-face interviews. Thus, one may raise the possibility that the newspaper sought to consciously interpret public opinion in one way over another to support its cause: it repeatedly published editorials in strong opposition to the package (*Asahi Shimbun*, February 28, 1996 and March 4, 1996).

heavily criticized the government's *jusen* resolution package, pushing instead for a more transparent solution that utilized legal bankruptcy schemes—an alternative also supported by the media. In March, Shinshinto lawmakers picketed the Lower House's Budget Committee for over three weeks to prevent the passing of the budget proposal containing the allocation of funds for *jusen* liquidation.[12]

BOJ and MOF Reforms: A Response to Criticism (February–August 1996)

As a response to the heated public and political opposition to the budget proposal in the Housing Loan Diet, the LDP and the ruling coalition began to pursue the MOF's responsibility as a means to smoothly pass the package as well as deflect public criticism. The first call for MOF reforms came from Koichi Kato, Secretary General of the LDP, in February 1996, and the ruling three-party coalition of the LDP, the SDPJ, and Sakigake set up a PT on MOF reforms in the same month. The media mistook Kato's televised comments, in which he proposed moving the BOJ and the section of MOF overseeing financial administration to Osaka, for a call for the breakup of MOF. While MOF's top career official requested that Kato follow up and clarify his comments, Kato consciously chose not to revise his misinterpreted comments and let the media turn up the heat on the ministry (Tahara 1998).

Shigeru Ito from the SDPJ headed the PT, and it included LDP ARPH members such as Mizuno and Shiozaki.[13] While Sakigake vocally advocated the breaking up of the MOF, the SDPJ's position was yet unclear. Views ranged widely within the LDP: some, such as Shiozaki, who represented the BOJ, strongly pushed for the breakup of the ministry, while others, such as Hakuo Yanagisawa, a former MOF official, adopted a more cautious stance (Mabuchi 1997).

In addition to formulating plans to reform the MOF, the LDP's ARPH also came up with a proposal to revise the BOJ Law. Although this plan to reform the central bank did not originate with the MOF, ministry officials were willing to concede a loss of influence over the central bank, as long as its authority over financial administration was not revoked. By this time,

---

[12] This strategy backfired on the party, as the public largely disapproved. As a result of the diplomatic success such as the agreement with the United States to have a base in Okinawa returned, in May 1996, the public support for the LDP was up to 47 percent while support for Shinshinto was down to 14 percent.

[13] For an analysis of the political process leading to the breakup of the MOF, see Mabuchi (1997). The account provided here owes much to Mabuchi's detailed research on this process.

there was a clear awareness within the ministry that some loss of authority might be necessary, given the degree of criticism of the MOF (Tahara 1998).

The ruling party's PT thus proceeded from March 1996 to work on BOJ reform. Within the LDP, there was still resistance from Yanagisawa and other Diet members who were skeptical of the idea of giving independence to a central bank, which was legally a private bank and devoid of outside checks. However, Shiozaki and those who wished to see increased independence got the upper hand within the PT, and voices of dissent were ignored. Shiozaki recalls: "This was possible only because it was a three-party coalition. It would not have been possible if it was an LDP-only government" (Tahara 1998: 36–9).

It was thus decided that the BOJ would be given independence. The PT issued a "basic document" outlining the course of MOF reforms in June, in which it stated that bills revising the BOJ Law and the MOF organization would be submitted jointly to the next regular session of the Diet.

In the meantime, heated discussion of MOF reforms was ongoing and involved MOF officials, politicians, and the media. In its early stage, the debate centered on the issue of whether the financial inspection and supervision departments ought to be kept under MOF's aegis given the ministry's policy failures. Between February and June 1996, a tug-of-war ensued between the PT on the one hand, and the MOF and particular LDP Diet members on the other. The PT, led by Ito, Sakigake members, and some LDP members such as Secretary General Kato and Shiozaki, pressed for the breakup of the MOF. Meanwhile, the LDP Diet members allying with the MOF sought to limit the extent of change to the ministry. Once the budget proposal containing the Housing Loan package passed the Diet in April 1996, the LDP became less interested in the reforms of the MOF, and the group that sought to limit change seemed to gain the upper hand. Ito, however, came under heavy pressure from the media to advance the MOF breakup, spurring him to assemble a PT "basic document" in June. This document specified that the bill for MOF reforms would be submitted to the Diet in January 1997, the issue of splitting up of the financial supervision/inspection functions would be examined, and the specific contents of the bill would be determined by September 1996 (Tahara 1998).

Political Debate over MOF Reforms: The Ito Plan and other Options (August–September 1996)

In August 1996, Ito came up with his own plan which would (1) integrate the Banking, Securities, and International Finance Bureaus into one

Financial Bureau, and (2) break up the MOF and set up an independent commission to oversee financial inspection and supervision. Because Ito made sure that the plan went through the ruling party coalition by leaking it to the media before he showed it to the other parties, the LDP's Kaoru Yosano refused to accept the draft plan, calling foul play. Although Yosano was a member of the PT, he was known to be close to the MOF, and an advocate of separating off the financial inspection (but not supervision) function. There were many within the LDP who supported Yosano. Yet, LDP Secretary General Kato was not among them. Kato was in charge of the party's election campaign and feared the negative impact on the party of being portrayed by the media as close to the MOF, in light of the upcoming Lower House elections (Tahara 1998).

This incident highlighted the emergence of a clear split within the LDP during the debate over dismantling the MOF. One group of lawmakers with past close ties with the MOF adopted pro-MOF positions. In the discussion leading up to the June 1996 "basic document," many finance "tribesmen" (*zoku giin*)[14] in the financial sub-divisions of PARC also vehemently expressed their disapproval of the fact that MOF reforms were being discussed at the ruling party's PT outside its control (Tahara 1998). On the other hand, another set of lawmakers chose to adopt positions in conflict with MOF wishes. Some lawmakers at the ARPH, the LDP's spearhead for administrative reforms, pressed for MOF reforms. These included Mizuno and Shiozaki. Kato's reaction to Yosano's refusal clearly shows that this group's reach extended into the party's top echelon.

To sum up this complex issue, there were two dimensions of contention: first, whether to split only the function(s) of inspection, or inspection and supervision altogether from MOF; and second, the legal form the new organization would take.[15] Regarding the first issue, MOF sought to limit its loss to inspection, while Ito and others pressed for inspection and supervision. Regarding the second issue, there were other issues to be decided as well: under which agency the new organization would be

---

[14] See Inoguchi and Iwai (1987). Tribesmen are the LDP lawmakers who are highly specialized in one policy area (e.g. construction, agriculture, transportation), grouping around the sub-divisions of PARC. Their groups, highly influential in the policymaking of bureaupluralism, came to be called "tribes" and its members "tribesmen".

[15] Under the National Administrative Organization Law (*kokka gyosei soshiki ho*), three broad categories of administrative organizations were available for such a new organization: (1) "Article 3 organizations," such as Ministries, Agencies, and Independent Commissions, which can engage in independent administrative activities; (2) "Article 8 organizations," such as Deliberative Councils and Commissions, which are organizations which report to the Ministries and other Article 3 organizations; (3) "Article 8–3 organizations," which were special agencies with semi-independent functions.

Table 5.2 Available options for MOF reform

1) Article 8. Under MOF (Securities Exchange Surveillance Commission [SESC])
2) Article 8–3. Under MOF (National Prosecution Agency[i])
3) Article 3. Agency under MOF without Minister (National Tax Agency)
4) Article 3. Agency under Economic Planning Agency without Minister
   (Defense Equipment Agency[ii])
5) Article 3. Agency under Prime Minister's Office (PMO) with Minister
   (Environment Protection Agency)
6) Article 3. Agency under PMO without Minister (Imperial Household Agency)
7) Article 3. Independent Commission under PMO (Fair Trade Commission [FTC])

Note: In parentheses are existing agencies under equivalent legal status
[i] To insulate public prosecution from political influence, the National Prosecution Agency has a special legal status: it is under the Minister of Justice's direction, yet the Prime Minister appoints its chief and the Justice Minister does not intervene in specific cases. (Mabuchi 1997)
[ii] This agency is headed by a career bureaucrat, and is under the Defense Agency, which is, like the Economic Planning Agency, an agency under the Prime Minister's Office with a Cabinet Minister.
Source: Based on Mabuchi (1997: 194–9)

placed; whether the organization would have a cabinet minister or not for Article 3 organization; and whether it would be a commission with a steering board or an agency with a single head. As shown in Table 5.2, there were seven options available altogether, even though all the options were not clearly observable at that time (Mabuchi 1997).[16]

Critical Juncture for MOF: The LDP Group of Eight (September 18, 1996)

On September 18, 1996, a critical event happened to set the course of future events. The LDP's Group of Eight, a gathering of its top officials, decided to take the inspection and supervision functions away from the MOF and transfer them to a newly established independent commission under the Prime Minister's Office. Of all the arrangements under consideration, this was the one most opposed by the MOF. Thus, despite its earlier internal split on this issue, the LDP had finally decided to adopt the "toughest" option.

At the meeting, Executive Council Chairman Shojuro Shiokawa argued that both financial inspection and supervision ought to be separated from the MOF and reorganized as a commission similar in status to the Fair Trade Commission (FTC). Doing otherwise would endanger the LDP's chances in the Lower House elections. Other members supported this view. Clearly, the upcoming Lower House elections on October 20, 1996 were the key factor in their decision: the LDP had to compete against

[16] The list slightly modifies Mabuchi's chart 4.1, by distinguishing between Article 8 and Article 8–3 organizations (Mabuchi 1997: 195).

opposition parties that strongly advocated the MOF breakup. MOF was shocked by the LDP's unexpected decision: one of its top officials visited Kato the following day and threatened to quit his job, to no avail (Mabuchi 1997; Tahara 1998). Following the LDP's decision, the ruling coalition's PT adopted the same decision a week later (*Asahi Shimbun* September 25, 1996).

This episode was a clear turning point in the LDP–MOF alliance. When the LDP was faced with a credible threat to its continued rule, the party did not choose to protect the MOF on an issue that was of the greatest importance to the ministry: organizational survival. This event would influence MOF's later behavior vis-à-vis the Big Bang.

Lower House Elections of October 1996, Hashimoto's Six Major Reforms, and the Conclusion of Debate over MOF Reforms[17]

The Lower House election was held on October 20, 1996 and administrative reform comprised the main agenda for all party electoral platforms (*Asahi Shimbun* September 29, 1996). The LDP won 239 seats, 12 short of majority, and once again formed a coalition with the Social Democrats and Sakigake—although the latter parties did not receive cabinet portfolios. Shinshinto came in second with 156 seats, while the newly formed DPJ obtained only 52 seats.

Prime Minister Hashimoto formed his Second Cabinet on November 7 and designated structural reforms as the main item on the political agenda. Administrative reforms in particular—including the MOF reforms—topped his priority list. On November 11, 1996 he announced the Big Bang Initiative, proposing drastic financial reforms. Eventually, his agenda would include six areas: administrative reforms, fiscal reforms, financial reforms, social security reforms, economic structural reforms,[18] and educational reforms.

Following the October 1996 elections, some LDP members and MOF officials sought to reverse the decisions reached prior to the elections on MOF reform. During late November to early December 1996, however, Hashimoto made it clear that the financial inspection and supervision functions would be altogether separated from MOF, settling the issue. As the final say, the ruling three-party coalition decided on December 24, 1996 to give the new organization Article 3 agency status under the Prime Minister's Office without a cabinet minister. This organization was later established in June 1998 as the FSA.

---

[17] This section relies heavily on Mabuchi (1997).

[18] Economic structural reforms were basically MITI's program to promote corporate-friendly reforms such as deregulation, taxation reforms, and labor market reforms.

The Ikeo Report[19]

A report authored in 1996 by a group of experts likely influenced the debate on what was necessary for financial reforms. Kazuhito Ikeo, an economist, chaired this three-person working group (WG). The WG had its origin in a request made in early 1996 to Prime Minister Hashimoto by Shusei Tanaka to speed up deregulation. Tanaka was Chief of the Economic Planning Agency (EPA) and a Sakigake party member. Hashimoto requested that Tanaka make his proposal concrete, and it was decided that the Economic Council, administered by Tanaka's agency, would be in charge of the task of coming up with action plans to speed up deregulation in six major policy areas, including finance. Ikeo headed the WG on finance. It was agreed that the group would be small in size, have no representatives from the financial industry and was not required to go through *nemawashi*.[20] This way, the group would be free to speak openly concerning the needs of Japanese finance. The WG, with the help of EPA officials, spent the summer of 1996 working on the proposal. On October 17, 1996, days before the Lower House election, they published a report (the Ikeo Report) containing a proposal for financial reforms.

The Ikeo Report attracted little attention, being virtually ignored by the media. Nevertheless, it is relevant to our discussion because the content, timing, and scope of the reforms proposed within it closely resembled the Big Bang Initiative put forward by Hashimoto in the following month. That a proposal so similar emerged from a committee of experts comprising an advisory panel to the prime minister likely increased the receptivity of elected officials to the Big Bang measures, whose benefits to the economy this report endorsed. Importantly, the report also increased the burden of proof on those who would have preferred to forestall the Initiative.

Developments within MOF Related to the "Big Bang"

Financial reforms implemented from 1991 to 1993 brought down the wall that long segmented the world of Japanese finance. However, in order to "alleviate the drastic change," the MOF placed severe limitations on business that the newly established financial subsidiaries could engage in.

---

[19] This section, unless otherwise noted, is based on a personal interview with Kazuhito Ikeo (July 9, 1999).

[20] *Nemawashi* is a practice to seek prior informal approval from all those concerned before proposing a plan, a widely observed practice in Japanese organizations in general.

According to the MOF, a revision was to be made within two or three years after the law took effect (April 1993), and the ministry initially planned to revise the business restrictions on financial subsidiaries by the end of FY1995, or March 1996. This was postponed for one year for a number of reasons. First, the securities and trust banking sectors were opposed to the idea, as they feared that the powerful banks would further increase their presence in their markets. Second, the banks had to face the more imminent bad debt problem and thus were incapable of more forcefully taking up their cause. And, third, the MOF's Banking Bureau, which was supporting the banks' position, was overburdened with the Housing Loan affair and therefore unable to manage the reform discussions (*Asahi Shimbun* March 26, 1996).

Thus, financial reforms seemed on the surface to be stalled. According to the *Asahi Shimbun*, "work on financial reforms aimed at changing the economic structure were not proceeding" as the June 1996 Diet session focusing on the Housing Loan affair came to a close (*Asahi Shimbun* June 16, 1996). In hindsight, this observation was true only if one looked solely at the traditional policymaking channels of bureaupluralism. Underneath the surface, three separate streams of financial reforms were under way: (1) the Securities Bureau's "Petit Bang"; (2) the International Finance Bureau's foreign exchange reforms; and (3) the Working Team (WT). The work of each was later integrated into one Big Bang proposal endorsed by the ministry as a whole.

The Securities Bureau's "Petit Bang"

In June 1996, MOF's Securities Bureau, under the leadership of its chief Atsushi Nagano, created a new sub-division under its advisory panel, the Securities and Exchange Council (SEC). Its goal was to discuss the drastic reforms necessary to reshape the securities market for the twenty-first century. Although this initiative did not attract much attention in the media, Nagano personally started a wide campaign from the summer of 1996, paying "visits to five hundred people" in the worlds of business, academia, and media. He referred to his plan for securities reforms as the "Petit Bang", rather than the "Big Bang" (Tahara 1998). As the head of the Securities Bureau, the scope of his proposed reforms was limited to the securities sector, excluding banking and other fields in finance.

The reforms were clearly intended to address the problem of "hollowing-out" of the Tokyo market, wherein transactions in the capital market flowed out to freer overseas markets such as New York, London, and

Singapore. According to Nagano, the priority targets for the financial reforms were first, those who manage assets or raise money, second, the Tokyo market, and third, financial intermediaries (Nagano 1997). This represented a shift from prioritizing "providers" to prioritizing the "market" and "users," and was an important development: policymaking under bureaupluralism had been biased toward providers—that is, toward financial intermediaries.

The International Finance Bureau's Foreign Exchange Reforms

Earlier we saw how Sakakibara, the head of the MOF's IFB, collaborated with the LDP ARPH (Mizuno and Shiozaki) to push for foreign exchange deregulation, despite internal resistance. While it appeared on the surface that the LDP was pressuring the MOF, we know from this episode, revealed by Mizuno himself, that the MOF was not pushed into accepting these reforms. Rather, there was an internal rift within the MOF: Sakakibara, the top MOF official in charge of such matters, advocated deregulation, and this measure became MOF policy.

How does Sakakibara account for this action, which would shrink his organization's scope of regulatory authority? Here is his reply:

The largest problem of MOF's financial administration, including the handling of the Housing Loan [Affair], was that its responsibility was disproportionate to its too regulatory power. Thus, we took the plunge and abandoned regulatory power. For example, the regulatory power of the IFB could be easily by-passed through the backdoor [by private actors]. . . . While the world thinks that MOF has strong regulatory power, in reality it is not so strong. . . . [In the Housing Loan affair,] there was a myth that MOF was strong and ultimately in charge, and the world, the media, and even MOF itself believed this. That is why there was an absurd mistake made. The IFB's regulatory power was *de facto*, becoming just power in name, and it is ridiculous to reign with such regulatory power. . . . Times have changed. As in Europe and America, the financial industry acts freely, and we abandon regulatory power as much as possible. Because we (the bureaucrats) know this best, we ought to be the first to speak out.[21] (Tahara 1998: 150–51)

Working Team on Financial Reforms

A WT on financial reforms was established within the MOF in February 1996. Comprised of middle-level officials from various bureaus, and

[21] The parentheses in the preceding paragraph are added by Tahara; brackets are added by the author.

headed by a division director in the IFB, the WT engaged in the discussion of drastic, overarching reforms that would bring the long process of financial deregulation to completion (H. Noguchi 1997). Although the Banking Bureau was officially in charge of the financial reforms, it was preoccupied with the Housing Loan Diet. Realizing the opportunity to move reform forward, the WT discreetly formed a strategy for comprehensive reform that covered banking, securities, and foreign exchange. The WT's reform study incorporated parallel developments in the areas of securities and foreign exchange reforms. Sakakibara (2000: 143) suggests that inter-bureau coordination of the Big Bang reforms was taking place within the MOF. His main agenda of foreign exchange reform had the support and understanding of the Securities and Taxation bureaus through his close relationship with these bureau heads. According to Sakakibara, an elaborate plan was ready by October 1996.[22]

The plan was not presented immediately to the outside world, as there was an initial internal split between those supporting and those opposing the plan.[23] Immediately after the election of October 1996, however, Prime Minister Hashimoto and his staff began to ensure that the agenda for all-out structural reforms would materialize. When his aides suggested finance as one of the prime minister's reform pillars, the MOF supplied its plan and Hashimoto promptly adopted it (Otake 1999).

In summarizing the MOF's role in the Big Bang, it is important to note that the MOF did not go through the usual policymaking mechanism of bureaupluralism. While Sakakibara talked with the chiefs of the related MOF bureaus regarding foreign exchange reforms, he did not consult beforehand with the related industries (Sakakibara and Tahara 1999). Sakakibara (2000: chapter 9) recalls how he passed his proposal through the deliberative council on foreign exchange control, whose important members included the banking industry, which stood in clear opposition to the proposal. Anticipating opposition from financial industry actors, Sakakibara tried to enlist the support of the mass media, the trading companies, and the manufacturing firms (Sakakibara 2000: 148–51). In the same way, Nagano bypassed the affected industries in formulating the securities reforms in the discreet operations that took place in the WT.

[22] Personal interview with Eisuke Sakakibara, January 27, 2000.

[23] According to Sakakibara, at the senior level of the decision-making process within the MOF, the Banking Bureau was not keen on pressing the reforms, while the Securities Bureau led by Nagano and the International Finance Bureau under him were advocating the reforms.

Why did the MOF distance itself from the regulated industries, its partners under bureaupluralism? Sakakibara recalls,

Had we consulted the industries, they would have opposed us. We knew that public opinion would be on our side, and we decided that if we launched it with a lot of noise, industry could not oppose us....It was obvious that deregulated businesses would be in trouble. Thus, we could not consult those industries that would have faced trouble due to deregulation. (Sakakibara and Tahara 1999: 135–6)

In short, MOF officials began to bypass the traditional policymaking mechanisms of bureaupluralism to escape the influence of regulated industries. They adopted a new priority, giving the "users" of financial services or the market greater priority than the financial intermediaries, whose interests had largely dominated financial politics in the past. MOF bureaucrats were aware of the negative aspects of the drastic reforms, including the way in which they would require the ministry to forfeit some regulatory power, and there was an internal rift between those who supported the drastic reforms and those who opposed them. However, the former groups gained the upper hand and their views became the MOF's policies: MOF, through its three suborganizations, proceeded toward drastic, overreaching reforms.

We will now inquire into the mechanism that led the pro-reform views to prevail over opposing views that stressed the negative by-products of these reforms. These included the loss of regulatory power, weakening of ties with regulated industries, and the potentially dangerous consequences of not resolving the bad debt problem first. Was it, as Sakakibara's comments imply, a rational behavior by enlightened bureaucrats? Or, do we have a better explanation? We will return to this issue in the next section but first, let us examine developments within the LDP regarding the Big Bang, for these internal party developments reveal another bypassing of the traditional mechanisms of bureaupluralism.

Developments within the LDP Related to the Big Bang

Two sets of actors within the LDP were actively involved in the Big Bang: (1) the LDP ARPH, and (2) the Prime Minister and LDP President, Ryutaro Hashimoto.

Administrative Reform Promotion Headquarters[24]

The earlier discussion of foreign exchange reforms already pointed to the ARPH's peculiar standing within the LDP, as a body independent from the LDP's main policymaking organ, PARC. The discussion also revealed the cooperative role played by the ARPH in working closely with an MOF official to introduce drastic foreign exchange reforms. At the same time, we saw that the ARPH was also actively involved in the ruling coalition's PT on MOF Reforms established in February 1996. In June 1996, for example, the ARPH drafted what was made public as the "Hashimoto Vision" on administrative reforms, which set the basic framework for later policy discussions. Let us now examine more closely the ARPH's role in promoting the drastic deregulation of the financial sector.

Mizuno, the head of the ARPH, explains that because LDP Diet members were busy savoring their return to power, PARC hardly intervened in the activities at the ARPH on financial deregulation. The ARPH also enjoyed a close working relationship with Hashimoto: Mizuno and other core members of the ARPH met with him on a weekly basis in the fall of 1996 to discuss administrative reforms and deregulation. Shiozaki also attests that the PARC finance divisions were uninterested in reforms. He points out the critical role that coalition rule played in providing the ARPH with an opportunity to exercise particular influence at this juncture. The power-sharing arrangement temporarily shifted decision-making power away from the PARC divisions and into the hands of the ruling coalition's PTs.

The ARPH, with Mizuno as its head, Yanagisawa as the chief secretariat, and Shiozaki as his deputy and in charge of finance, took up the issue of deregulation beginning December 1995. The group worked thereafter to put together the government's annual deregulation action plans. In the summer of 1996, Mizuno asked Shiozaki to work on his own plan for radical financial reforms. His request was motivated by a realization that a piecemeal approach was doomed to failure.

Shiozaki's draft plan shared the time frame with the Initiative: it was to be carried out over five years through 2001, when deposit insurance payoffs were to commence, when necessary. Shiozaki's draft contained measures for the deregulation and de-segmentation of banking, securities, and foreign exchange. In this way, his draft plan overlapped with the Big Bang. An important difference, however, was that his plan was even more comprehensive than the Big Bang. It included measures related to

[24] Unless otherwise noted, this section relies on personal interviews with Kiyoshi Mizuno (July 19, 1999) and Yasuhisa Shiozaki (July 6, 1999).

taxation, public finance (including the consolidation of public financial institutions), and pension fund regulation.[25] The plan was drafted with little prior consultation with the MOF or financial industry actors, and he presented the draft to the ruling coalition's PT on Administrative Reforms in August 1996.

In the following month, the ARPH held hearings with MOF and the affected industries based on this draft plan.[26] The industries agreed to the need for reforms in general, yet once discussions came down to specific measures, they asked the ARPH to "spare" them. A high-ranking Banking Bureau official from MOF stated that the ministry supported the idea in principle, but because the bad debt problem was not resolved, the reforms were impossible.

The ARPH's draft plan seems to have stopped here, in terms of its impact on the Initiative announced in November 1996. That the Initiative mainly dealt with MOF's jurisdiction over finance, excluding public finance and social security issues that were included in Shiozaki's plan, seemed to suggest that the ambitious ARPH plan was not the one adopted as the Big Bang. However, the ARPH made sure that its agenda became party policy by including it in the party electoral platform prepared in September 1996 for the October elections. Yanagisawa drafted the first part of the platform, which laid out the basic party goals, including administrative reforms. The platform also included a section on deregulation, in which it stated that the party would aim for deregulation and financial market development, working toward a Japanese version of the Big Bang (Jiyu Minshu Tou 1996). In this sense, Shiozaki may be credited for being the first to publicly use the label "Big Bang," although it apparently did not attract much public notice at the time.[27]

In sum, the LDP ARPH, in close cooperation with Hashimoto, pushed through the foreign exchange reforms, drafted a comprehensive plan on financial reforms, and made their cause for deregulation and administrative reforms an important part of the party platform. An interesting issue here is the relationship between the ARPH and the MOF. The two worked together on the financial reforms, while the ARPH went after the MOF regarding its breakup. In particular, the ARPH worked closely with MOF

---

[25] The "Free, Fair, and Global" principles of the Big Bang Initiative also did not appear in Shiozaki's plan.

[26] Shiozaki claims to be the first to come up with the label "Big Bang," as the draft plan presented in September was titled, "Aiming for the Big Bang Japanese Version."

[27] For example, the term "Big Bang" did not appear in *Asahi Shimbun*, a major newspaper, until the day Hashimoto announced the Initiative (based on the author's search through the *Asahi Shimbun* database).

officials on foreign exchange reforms. In the case of financial reforms, it competed with the MOF in drafting its own plans. While the ARPH did not cooperate or coordinate in planning, the substance of its plans overlapped significantly with the MOF's draft, which included matters primarily under its jurisdiction (thus, areas outside its jurisdiction such as public finance, which included the Postal Saving system, were left out). Later, the ARPH would also be actively involved in carrying out the Big Bang, once it emerged as the prime minister's Initiative. At the same time, however, the LDP ARPH was the most ardent advocate of the breakup of the MOF. As mentioned earlier, a division of views existed in the ARPH regarding the MOF reforms but the reformers gained the upper hand largely due to the dynamics of a three-party coalition.

Prime Minister and LDP President Hashimoto

Ryutaro Hashimoto was elected as the LDP President for a two-year term in September 1995. He took office as prime minister in January 1996, after the resignation of Tomiichi Murayama, a Social Democrat. Murayama resigned immediately after submitting to the Diet a budget proposal that included the Housing Loan package. The top priority of Hashimoto's administration was to make it through the tumultuous session of the "Housing Loan Diet," which began days after his Cabinet was inaugurated. He successfully managed to pass the Housing Loan and other financial packages by June 1996. The Lower House election was then held on October 20, 1996. Although victorious, the LDP reaffirmed its three-party coalition with the Social Democrats and Sakigake. Hashimoto formed his second Cabinet in early November 1996.

The dynamics of LDP competition with rivals and coalition partners drove the party's position on administrative reform issues (Hashimoto's top priority item) both before and after the elections. Shinshinto, under its head, Ichiro Ozawa, advocated fundamental reforms of the Japanese system from a neoliberal viewpoint.[28] Meanwhile, the newly formed DPJ advocated a challenge to the "bureaucracy" (*kan*) by the "people" (*min*), cashing in on the wild popularity of Naoto Kan, its leader. Kan had successfully fought off the bureaucracy while serving as Minister of Health and Welfare under Murayama.[29] Sakigake, the LDP's coalition partner, was

---

[28] This paragraph draws largely on Otake (1999).

[29] He successfully uncovered the hidden documents in his ministry that showed the involvement of Health and Welfare officials in the scandal concerning the HIV-contaminated blood products.

trying to avoid being submerged in the three-party coalition. Seeing that its efforts for the reforms of government corporations were not working, Sakigake pushed for even more reforms. Given this party configuration, Hashimoto had to appeal to public opinion by packaging his administrative reforms so as to compete with those of Ozawa and Kan. Thus, he situated the reforms within a larger reorganization of the state, economy and society, basically embracing Ozawa's program, while also engaging embracing Kan's agenda of challenging bureaucracy-led politics with the reorganization of all central government agencies (Otake 1999).

With the October 1996 elections, Hashimoto finally had a cabinet earned through electoral victory, and he began accordingly to implement his own agenda of reforms as part of larger structural reforms of the Japanese "system." The reforms, launched one after another, would eventually grow into his "Six Major Reforms." Hashimoto appeared to have developed this agenda after serving as MITI Minister under Murayama, at which time he engaged in numerous policy discussions with MITI officials on the need for structural reforms.[30]

MITI had a large impact on Hashimoto's agenda of structural reforms as a whole, and on the economic and administrative reforms, in particular.[31] The ministry's role in the Big Bang reforms was less central, however. The initiative to start financial reforms originated with Hashimoto, and it was he who decided to launch financial reforms at this time. Furthermore, the content of the Big Bang plan originated with the MOF. Hashimoto's personal secretary on special duty from MOF was deeply involved in the development of Hashimoto's November 1996 initiative. In fact, this individual was the main drafter of the document outlining the "Free, Fair, Global" principles (Otake 1999).[32] While MITI had been working since 1992 on financial reforms through its advisory panel—and, in particular, on the liberalization of corporate finance[33]—the Initiative was the MOF's brainchild and would later be implemented by MOF through its deliberation councils. A former senior MITI official casually observed that the MOF, which had been unwilling to carry out financial reforms in the past, in this case usurped the issue from MITI, which had been working diligently on these issues for quite some time.[34]

---

[30] Hashimoto's strong ties with MITI were evident when, upon taking office in January 1996, he took the unusual step of appointing a MITI official as secretary in charge of political affairs, a position usually filled by the prime minister's own personal staff.

[31] Author interviews with MITI officials.

[32] This was also supported by personal interviews with officials from MOF and MITI.

[33] MITI's Industrial Structure Council's sub-division on industrial finance had been working on this issue since 1992 (Author interview with a MITI official).   [34] Author interview.

Summary: Who Brought about the Big Bang?

In summary, the following observations can be made about the roles of various actors in bringing about the Big Bang. The reforms were carried out in two stages and the sequencing decision to begin with the deregulation of foreign exchange arose largely out of a strategic move by Sakakibara at the MOF. Yet, it also reflected a number of coincidences. These included the fact that "mavericks" such as Sakakibara and Shiozaki were in control of particular areas (Sakakibara in charge of foreign exchange control and Shiozaki in charge of deregulation). The unclear causal relationship between foreign exchange controls and domestic finance also helped enable this potentially explosive issue to sail smoothly through the Diet (Otake 1999). The first sequence of foreign exchange reforms was thus largely a product of cooperation between the LDP ARPH and some MOF officials. This approval of reforms in the summer of 1996 made drastic reform of the domestic financial market (the second stage of reforms) inevitable thereafter. In the absence of such domestic reforms, the threat of a massive capital outflow was very real. Hashimoto, however, clearly decided the timing (November 1996), scope (encompassing private finance), and pace (until 2001) of the bulk of these financial reforms. He gave the directions, seeking to enhance public support of the LDP and his administration.

The other actors' influences on Hashimoto's decisions can be seen at two levels. The first level involves placing the financial reform agenda in the list of priorities adopted by Hashimoto's Second Cabinet, and thus influencing the timing of the reforms. The second level involves coming up with the actual plan and later implementing it, thus setting the scope and pace of the reforms. The LDP's ARPH was the major influence at the first level, while the MOF wielded considerable influence at the second. The LDP ARPH carried administrative and other reforms through the ruling three-party coalition; it drafted its plan of financial reforms and made their later implementation a campaign promise. While not determining the actual content of the reforms (such as their "scope"), the LDP ARPH made sure that the Hashimoto government would carry out overreaching, drastic financial reforms. Under bureaupluralism, financial administration was under the jurisdiction of the LDP's PARC and its sub-divisions. The jurisdiction of the LDP ARPH, however, extended further, and the ARPH pushed for reforms that would affect jurisdictions overseen by ministries other than the MOF (such as social security and public finance).

At the second level, the MOF came up with the actual plan almost exclusively, and was later active in implementing it, even though it had to compete with the LDP ARPH, MITI, and the Ikeo group to do so. Those in Hashimoto's staff who were on special duty from the MOF were the primary drafters of the Initiative. The actual plan, which then served as the starting point for policy discussion later carried out in MOF's deliberation councils, was the one already prepared—though not yet presented—by the MOF. Until the political initiative of the prime minister, an internal split in the ministry between those who advocated the reforms and those who opposed them, or preferred a more cautious approach, was not resolved.

Organizational Level Evaluation

We now turn to an organizational level evaluation of the facts to show that the logic of organizational survival is what drove the actors' behavior and how the logic of organizational survival operates to integrate suborganizational behavior into an organizational strategy.

Why was the MOF Willing to Propose and Implement the Big Bang?

Sakakibara's statements clearly showed that the MOF was willing to part with regulatory power. The positions advocated by Nagano and others in the ministry furthermore promoted a departure from the relational networks (based on regulatory power) that characterized the policymaking style of bureaupluralism. These networks helped ensure a constant flow of valuable information, enhanced cooperation between the ministry and its regulatory constituents, and provided post-retirement positions for officials. Why would the MOF willingly abandon such benefits? After all, the opposition these actors faced from within the ministry was not unexpected, since it was derived from conventional bureaucratic behavior, which relied on such tokens of power as regulatory control, discretionary authority, or the size of the budget. How could such abandonment of regulatory power and the benefits associated with bureaupluralism gain the upper hand in MOF policies?

It is only by putting it in context that we can answer the question. This was a time when the MOF was under attack from all political parties, the media, and the general public—largely because of policy failures and scandals. The threat to break up the ministry was real enough for the MOF to place organizational survival above all other concerns.

We saw earlier that political actors ensure their survival by gratifying constituency and public interests. When public support is lost, and the organization is in jeopardy because of its ties with regulated industries, its priority quite naturally shifts from constituency interests toward public interest.

This is what happened in the case of the Big Bang reforms. MOF had strong incentives to shift its focus from securing the benefits inherent in bureaupluralism to securing public support to prevent its organizational breakup. The ministry chose to recoup lost public trust by advocating measures beneficial to the economy as a whole, but which had negative repercussions on its own organization: by hurting its constituency interests it cut itself off from private sector support. It appears that those within the MOF who advocated the reforms were well aware of the potentially beneficial impact of the reform initiative on the discussion of the MOF breakup. Indeed, such concerns were raised following the LDP's Group of Eight meeting in September 1996, where it was decided to dismantle the organization.[35]

The Hashimoto administration's political leadership, by deciding to launch the reforms at that particular time, put to rest the internal differences of opinion within the MOF. While openly resisting the prime minister may not have been an option, the ministry could certainly have stalled the process. In effect, the MOF had two choices: "forestall" or "seize the moment." The former option corresponded to constituency interests. The MOF could have reasonably argued, for example, that a cautious approach was required, pointing to the need to first resolve the bad debt problem.[36] The latter option corresponded to public interests. The MOF could hop on board with Hashimoto's Initiative to launch drastic reforms that had previously been impossible due to industry resistance.

Without an overpowering concern for organizational survival, "forestall" may well have been chosen by the MOF, as seemingly legitimate concerns such as financial "stability" would likely have weighed heavier than the prime minister's political will. In this case, the bureaucracy could have negotiated or attempted to persuade the prime minister of the possible negative consequences of his Initiative. After all, given the future uncertainties, it would have been difficult to definitively reject the contention that the bad debt problem needed to be resolved first.

[35] Author interview with Eisuke Sakakibara, January 27, 2000.

[36] This may have been the Banking Bureau's stance, judging from the way in which the re-examination of the 1993 financial reforms was postponed for one year in the spring of 1996 as mentioned earlier. Also see Nishimura (1999) on this point.

However, with survival as the paramount concern, the rationale behind the MOF's actual decision to "seize the moment" becomes obvious. Hashimoto's top agenda was administrative reform. And, he wanted the Big Bang in place. In the wake of severe political and public criticism, it made sense for the ministry to cooperate with the prime minister, and to seek his support. Even under conditions of high uncertainty, it was clear that ministry support for Hashimoto's drastic deregulation would gain higher marks with the public than would the adoption of a cautious approach that would preserve the MOF's ties with the financial industry— the focus of public criticism. Furthermore, policy discussion surrounding the financial reforms was not wholly reliant on bureaucratic expertise. The findings of the Ikeo Report supported Hashimoto's position and incorporated the analysis of private sector actors. Thus, it was apparent that the public's perception of their interest would reside with the "seize the moment" option.

While Hashimoto's political leadership certainly shaped the MOF's behavior, this was not a case of mere political dominance over the bureaucracy. The MOF was preparing to launch major financial reforms from early 1996, when it first faced the threat of organizational breakup, well before Hashimoto's Initiative. This fact supports our interpretation that there was a shift in bureaucratic strategy—away from constituency interests to public interests—when organizational survival was threatened by declining public support. Behind the scenes, MOF strategies to recoup public trust were already being actively pursued at the suborganizational level at this point of time.

In hindsight, the MOF's calculations were erroneous, as organizational breakup occurred despite the ministry's support for the Big Bang.[37] Let us now turn to the LDP's behavior before we integrate the developments at the suborganizational and organizational levels.

What Drove the LDP's Behavior?

Why did the LDP drastically undermine the MOF presence in finance? What happened to the stable LDP–MOF alliance of the postwar era?

Let us reinterpret the above narrative from the LDP's point of view. While the LDP had to take responsibility as the main ruling party in the highly unpopular Housing Loan bailout package, it also faced tough

[37] The bureaucracy faced a dilemma: in order to ensure the program's success, it had to emphasize political leadership and minimize its role, which made its aim to recoup public support unattainable.

179

competition from rivals Shinshinto and the DPJ, as well as from coalition partners Sakigake and the Social Democrats. Electoral competition with its rivals led the LDP to follow these rivals' programs of administrative and systemic reforms. Sakigake and the Social Democrats pushed the ruling coalition's position more toward administrative reforms (or MOF reforms) by appealing to public opinion. Thus, the LDP faced a threat to its own organizational survival and its position as a ruling party. The two were related. The LDP's time out of power from 1993 to 1994 left many LDP lawmakers bitter and resolved that such a thing would never happen again.[38] The elections of 1993 had effectively transformed the collective perspective: the scope of possible scenarios was drastically widened to include the LDP's loss of power, something that was never considered prior to 1993.

The LDP, therefore, sought to recoup public support, even if it meant that doing so would jeopardize its constituents in financial politics: financial industries through the financial reforms, and the MOF through the administrative reforms. The ARPH and Party President Hashimoto were the two main suborganizational actors who carried out this agenda.

First, let us examine the ARPH's role. The LDP let the ARPH carry out the financial reforms, bypassing the PARC, an important pillar of bureaupluralism where the regulated industries were known to be influential. The financial sector's monetary contributions were important to the party.[39] Realizing that the reforms would improve the party's public image even if they hurt most of the industry, the ARPH—supported by party leaders but not by the PARC—took the initiative on financial reforms. The same thing can be said about administrative reforms. Again, the ARPH acted as the spearhead for the MOF's breakup, bypassing the PARC, which grouped politicians in support of the MOF. The MOF, the LDP ally in the pre-1993 world, did not fare well when the LDP faced the specter of electoral defeat. It is true that the LDP had developed a grudge against the MOF while it was in the Opposition in 1993–94 (Mabuchi 1997). However, the party was attempting to pass the Housing Loan package through the Diet at the same time as it was discussing the breakup of the MOF. Besides, MOF's influence upon public works and its other abilities to assist LDP lawmakers with their

---

[38] Personal interview with Kiyoshi Mizuno, July 19, 1999.

[39] One must note that the importance of such financial support has been relatively reduced by the introduction of public financing of electoral campaigns in 1994. Since 1994, public money has been given to political parties meeting certain criteria. Also note the empirical observation by Otake (1997b) that the electoral reforms of 1994 reduced the amounts of campaign funds involved in elections.

individual constituencies were left intact from the pre-1993 era. Not surprisingly, the MOF had its allies within the LDP. Yosano and others tried to stall the breakup. However, electoral concerns led the ARPH's position to be adopted as the LDP's party platform.

Next, how can Hashimoto's role be interpreted? As LDP President, he incorporated issues developed by rival parties—issues related to administrative reforms and other structural reforms—into his political agenda. Once he won the October 1996 elections, he was constantly under pressure from the rival parties and the media to deliver on his electoral promises. Moreover, Hashimoto's support base within the LDP was weak: if he was to maintain political viability, he had to rely on public support by carrying out the administrative reforms (Tahara 1998).

A seemingly puzzling relationship between the LDP and the MOF emerges through this process. As mentioned earlier, the ARPH worked closely with the MOF's Sakakibara to establish the first sequence of the Big Bang, the foreign exchange reforms, while it drove the LDP into breaking up the MOF. Both agencies independently developed financial reform plans.[40] Once the MOF's plan was accepted, both agencies worked to support it. Hashimoto worked closely with the MOF on the Housing Loan affair and launched the Big Bang with the ministry's help. Yet, he dealt the final blow to the MOF reforms by deciding its breakup in December 1996. How can we understand these seemingly contradictory developments?

Our claim—that the LDP sought to recoup public support in face of tough electoral competition that threatened the party's continued rule and survival—enables us to make sense of these developments. The LDP cooperated with the MOF to bring about the Big Bang, defying financial industry actors, because deregulation attracted public support and its rivals campaigned for it. However, the same logic led the LDP to go against the MOF on administrative reforms: the issue was popular and its rivals were pushing it. The LDP's behavior was driven by efforts to recoup public support lost in the Housing Loan affair in the face of party competition. What emerged was a mixture of cooperation, competition, and conflict between the MOF and the LDP as each organization acted according to the logic of organizational survival.

---

[40] Shiozaki emphasizes that his plan was drawn up independently from the MOF and the LDP financial "tribesmen" (Personal interview, July 6, 1999). On MOF's side, Sakakibara confirms that there was no prior consultation with the LDP ARPH on the Big Bang Initiative (Personal interview, January 27, 2000).

Integrating the Suborganizational and Organizational Levels of Analysis

While the preceding analysis centered on such organizations as the MOF and the LDP, the narrative of events also necessarily involved significant individuals and groups of individuals such as Hashimoto, Shiozaki, Sakakibara, and the ARPH. Delving into the mechanism of how the logic of organizational survival operates will enable us to link the organizational and suborganizational levels of analysis.

In reality, as the narrative suggested, there were internal fissures in the MOF and the LDP, reflecting the two sets of interests that the political actors sought to enhance. When asked in a February 1996 poll if they thought that organizational reforms such as the breakup of MOF should be carried out, 65 percent of the public responded in the affirmative (*Asahi Shimbun* February 28, 1996). Newspaper editorials urging the breakup of the MOF appeared one after another. The *Asahi Shimbun*, a leading daily newspaper, campaigned for this goal with sensational headlines such as "The laughter of the MOF can be heard," and "Are you prostrating yourself to the MOF?" In 1996 alone, the newspaper issued at least nine editorials aiming specifically to pressure the political actors to break up the ministry.[41] Given this situation, it is quite understandable that the individuals within the organization who tried to shift the emphasis away from constituency interests and toward public support won the "policy contest" within the organization.

This process of integration of different views into one strategy reveals how the logic of organizational survival operates, enabling our analysis to proceed from the suborganizational level up to the organizational level. The split within the MOF reflected the two concerns of political actors, public support and the constituencies' well-being, as did the differences within the LDP. While the ARPH and Kato sought to increase public support for both financial and administrative reforms, there were lawmakers who promoted other sets of interests that the LDP had to consider, such as the financial industries and/or MOF who had been the LDP's partners in policymaking during bureaupluralism. At the end, the strategy to pursue public support through drastic administrative reforms won out over the more cautious alternative of preserving the LDP's ties with the MOF.

---

[41] The headlines are from the titles of the editorials of June 6, 1996 and November 23, 1996 of *Asahi Shimbun*. The nine editorials appeared in addition to other more numerous editorials, which mentioned in passing the need of MOF breakup. They appeared on February 8, June 6, June 17, August 8, September 25, October 5, November 20, November 23, and December 4 of 1996. See Otake (1999) for the role of *Asahi Shimbun* in the breakup of MOF.

The logic of organizational survival decided the winner in the internal split over possible options in both the LDP and the MOF, integrating different positions within the organization into one organizational strategy.

Assessment against Competing Explanations

We turn next to test the strength of our organizational survival hypothesis against five alternative explanations drawn from depictions of policymaking commonly found in the literature. These explanations claim that the Big Bang was one of the following:

(1) a predesigned and coordinated initiative by a single bureaucracy (MOF or MITI);

(2) the result of domination in the policymaking process by financial institutions;

(3) the result of politicians overriding bureaucrats;

(4) the result of non-financial firms and MITI gaining the upper hand over financial industries and the MOF;

(5) an achievement by LDP backbenchers promoting consumerism as a result of the 1994 electoral reforms that introduced single-member districts (SMDs).

Bureaucratic or Legislative Dominance (1, 3)

The preceding account suggests that the Big Bang initiative was not a pre-designed and coordinated movement by any single bureaucrat. Despite the MOF's wide influence, the ministry's plan would not have emerged without Hashimoto's decision to launch the Initiative, and the time and scope of the reforms. It would have been difficult for the ministry to overcome the regulated industries' objections to the Big Bang without Hashimoto's political leadership. On the other hand, if we look at the role played by the MOF in the preparation and implementation of the Big Bang, there is no way that this can be understood as MITI's scheme. Thus, we reject the alternative explanation "1".

Was the Big Bang, then, the result of the dominance of elected officials over bureaucrats? Hashimoto's political leadership certainly mattered. Yet, the MOF was willing to carry out the reform plan that it had been discreetly preparing for quite some time. Thus, in the absence of MOF resistance, we also reject explanation "3". Instead, we characterize the process as an outcome of a strategic interaction of the MOF and the LDP, involving cooperation, competition, and conflict, decided on an issue-by-issue basis.

Dominance of Financial Institutions (2)

What about the possibility that the Big Bang was brought about as a result of the domination of financial politics by financial industry actors? Most financial institutions had reasons to oppose the Big Bang, as the heightened competition it would introduce into Japanese finance would jeopardize their prospects for survival. The powerful city banks were the few candidates who might have had incentives for pushing for such financial reforms. Indeed, they worked hard through the MOF's Banking Bureau to pursue their cause vis-à-vis the long-term credit banks as well as the securities industry. They also strove to pursue liberalization of the bond market through MITI.[42] However, in 1995–96 the powerful city banks were unable to campaign for drastic financial reforms from which they would benefit. Due to the Housing Loan Affair, the city banks, along with the MOF, attracted a great deal of criticism from the public and politicians at this time. In this situation, there was little possibility that the powerful city banks could successfully lobby state actors to launch the Big Bang reforms. Newcomers to finance, such as non-bank financial institutions, would also have had a hard time campaigning for the Big Bang, as they were similarly constrained by the negative publicity surrounding the Housing Loan Affair. In fact, the *jusen* housing loan companies were non-bank financial institutions themselves.

Then, might foreign financial institutions have dominated financial politics? Foreign pressure, especially by the United States, had increased the presence of foreign financial firms in Japan since liberalization in the 1980s. However, there is little evidence of any foreign pressure leading up to the Big Bang. While bilateral insurance talks were ongoing prior to the Big Bang announcement, there was little in the discussions to spur Japanese political actors to launch drastic financial reforms at this time.

Bureaucratic Turf-war between MITI and MOF; or, MITI and the Corporate Sector Prevailing over MOF and the Financial Sector (4)

We now turn to explanation "4", which would claim the dominance of the corporate sector and MITI in financial politics. As the representative of

---

[42] Personal interviews with MITI officials.

the corporate sector under bureaupluralism, MITI had been involved in financial politics through its deliberative council on industrial finance, and had been working on the issue of financial liberalization for some time. Corporate bond issuance, securities commissions, and asset management of pension funds were among the issues discussed at the LDP's ARPH as well as at the government's panel on deregulation in 1995–96, and MITI was very much involved in this process. Large non-financial firms, as well as large city banks, urged MITI to speed up the liberalization process.

In these ways, MITI advanced the cause of financial reforms. However, there would be a large gap between the topics of financial reforms addressed by MITI and those addressed in the Big Bang Initiative, suggesting that the Initiative was not a true reflection of MITI preferences. The MOF's efforts to launch drastic financial reforms seem to have been carried out independently from MITI until the very end. There is little evidence of negotiation over these issues between the two ministries. MITI's role was one of laying the groundwork for financial reforms. According to a MITI official, the efforts for financial reforms within MITI did not involve its top echelon, being limited to *nemawashi* among politicians and scholars on the necessity of such reforms.

Without MITI, we are left with the corporate sector as the possible candidate to campaign for drastic reforms. However, we find little evidence of industrial organizations lobbying effectively for such goals. According to a senior *Keidanren* official, financial institutions pushed the Federation to qualify its support for the Big Bang reforms (Vogel 1999).

Consumers' Victory Achieved by LDP Backbenchers as a Result of 1994 Electoral Reforms (5)

Finally, we need to test our explanation against an alternative that is increasingly influential in the study of Japanese politics: the rational choice explanation focusing on the effect of electoral systems. This explanation would hold that the electoral reforms of 1994, introducing the SMD system, altered the incentives of the individual LDP lawmakers, so that they became more representative of consumer interests and pushed their party leaders toward consumer-friendly reforms. The bureaucracy, if involved at all, would correctly anticipate its political master's wishes and change direction toward this goal accordingly.

According to Rosenbluth and Thies (1999), this would imply that a turn toward old regulatory practice, based on close business–government ties, would come under more frequent and successful attacks from consumer groups, and parties associated with such policies would be punished at the polls. As we saw earlier, the Big Bang is an outcome consistent with this explanation: it brings benefits to the consumers by increasing their chance to manage their financial assets better. However, this interpretation is problematic.

First, the effect of the 1994 electoral reforms was not yet clear in 1996, when the first Lower House election under the new system took place. Otake suggests that the basic characteristics of Japanese elections under the multiple-member district system (MMD), in which contests among individual candidates are based on personal support networks, were largely intact despite the introduction of the SMD. He concludes that while the 1994 electoral reforms succeeded in reducing the flow of campaign funds, they largely failed in achieving the more fundamental goal of rendering elections more party- and issue-oriented (Otake 1997b). That the 1996 elections were not issue-oriented may follow from our earlier point: all parties had administrative reforms as part of their party platforms. Given the uniformity of the party platforms, the elections could not become anything but contests among individual candidates.

Second, electoral reforms were not a necessary condition but merely an accelerating factor behind the LDP's observed behavior. The LDP's preference to avoid an election loss at all costs was evidenced by the party's discussions at the Group of Eight Meeting. LDP lawmakers were resolved not to repeat their experience of being in the Opposition in 1993–94.

The possibility of being toppled from power due to party realignment or the dynamics of party competition, rather than a change in electoral rules, drove the LDP to match the other rival parties' platforms for reforms. It is doubtful that an exchange of votes and favors took place between consumers and the LDP in the period surrounding the 1996 elections. Although the explanation "5" would hold that the implications of the 1994 electoral reforms to regulatory policy would be a turn toward consumer-based regulation, only one-ninth of the public was aware of the benefits of the Big Bang reforms as of July 1997 (well after the November 1996 Initiative). And, administrative reform—hardly a consumer-friendly issue—was much more central to the election campaign.

In contrast, our explanation can account for both the consumer-friendly Big Bang reforms and those reforms only remotely related to consumer interests, such as administrative reforms. In our explanation, public support is what matters and affects the dynamics of party competition. Public support can be obtained for a program perceived to be a "good" program, regardless of whether it objectively benefits consumers or not. As long as the rival parties' platforms attracted public support, regardless of their link to the public's day-to-day life, the LDP matched the other parties' platforms to avert loss of power. The financial reforms were just one part of the larger agenda of administrative reforms and structural reorganization of Japan; the LDP pushed for reforms to increase the public support of the party.

Finally, the rational choice explanation cannot adequately account for the bureaucracy's role. In particular, it faces an insurmountable empirical anomaly when we consider the Big Bang financial reforms as part of the bigger picture that includes administrative reforms and the MOF breakup. The LDP's decision to break up the MOF shocked MOF bureaucrats and demonstrated that the MOF was unable to correctly anticipate its masters' wishes after all. The same point may be made about financial reforms. Was the MOF adopting this strategy of gradualism on the surface and preparing for drastic reforms in the background in response to the LDP's wishes? Our explanation that attributes the two different strategies to the internal fissure within MOF, reflecting the two sets of interests that MOF caters to, better explains why MOF behaved this way.

Conclusion

Japan's Big Bang emerged from strategic interaction between the MOF and the LDP, wherein each acted according to the logic of organizational survival. Both the LDP and the MOF saw political gains in obtaining public support. With the loss of public trust, due to scandals and performance failures—and most notably, the Housing Loan affair—both organizations faced a threat to their survival. And, both organizations sought to regain public trust by prioritizing the public interest over particular constituent interests.

Japan's Big Bang financial reforms represent a shift within the MOF and the LDP away from constituency interests and toward public interest. For many years, analysis of Japanese politics has emphasized "stability" over "change." Yet, the Big Bang Initiative did not emerge out of the normal decision-making procedure in Japanese politics. The LDP ARPH bypassed the LDP's PARC and its sub-divisions—key policymaking organs under bureaupluralism that prioritized constituency interests. The MOF prepared drastic financial reforms without consulting the affected industries through deliberative councils, as had long been the norm.

In summary, we argue that former Prime Minister Hashimoto deserves credit for the timing, pace (setting the deadline), and scope of the Initiative. We also argue that the LDP's ARPH deserves to share some of the credit with Hashimoto for the timing and that the MOF and the LPD's ARPH might share the credit for the sequencing of reforms. We turn next to consider the influence of financial industry actors on outcomes. We know that the influence of financial institutions on the policymaking process has been strong in particular instances in the past, sometimes even surpassing the MOF's might. Why then were financial firms unable to forestall or even reverse the Big Bang? This examination will take us into the second phase of the Big Bang reforms under analysis: the period after November 1996.

6

The Financial Industry and the Big Bang

This chapter examines the political dynamics surrounding phase II of the passage of the Big Bang financial reforms, focusing on the process after November 1996, when Prime Minister Hashimoto announced the Initiative. The chapter analyzes the process in which the Initiative, laid out in a three-page announcement, was navigated through the deliberative councils and the Diet to become the eventual reform plan.[1] In the last chapter, we saw that the process up to November 1996 was not dominated by those who might have benefited most from the planned reforms but, rather, was dominated by state actors—the LDP and MOF in particular— who sought political gains of their own. We now turn our attention to the roles played by those who might be expected to experience material losses due to financial reforms. In Chapter 4, we determined that most financial institutions, with the exception of a limited number of large city banks, would suffer losses in the Big Bang reforms because these reforms would take away the regulatory protection they had for so long enjoyed. Since financial institutions had exercised strong influence over the course of past financial reforms (Rosenbluth 1989; Vogel 1996), it is natural to wonder why they were unable to shape reforms to their liking this time.

To address this puzzle, the chapter begins by reflecting on two ways economic reforms may come about, in order to give a sense of what types of economic reform patterns one would expect to see under bureaupluralism. The chapter next provides a narrative of the events in the period after November 1996, to document the degree of influence exercised by financial

---

[1] Legislation containing the Big Bang reforms was submitted in two stages. The first component of reforms related to change in foreign exchange regulations. Here relevant legislation was submitted to the Diet in March 1997 and became law in May 1997. The second set of legislation, submitted to the Diet in March 1998 and passed in June 1998, covered the bulk of the Big Bang reform measures. The latter set of legislation was preceded by a MOF announcement in June 1997 of a detailed reform plan that reflected proposals from the ministry's three deliberative councils.

industry actors. The chapter then provides a brief overview of three cases of financial reform in the recent past: the 1991–93 financial system reforms, the 1992–94 insurance reforms, and the 1979–82 banking reforms. Comparing our case of the Big Bang reforms with these earlier cases helps highlight why the influence of financial industry actors was weak in the Big Bang case relative to the past.

Two Political Paths to Economic Reform

As in the last chapter, we begin our discussion with two sets of interests, the "public interest" and "constituency interests." To ensure their survival, political actors must keep both in mind when formulating policies. In this section, we see how these sets of interests give rise to two types of economic reforms. By "economic reforms," we refer loosely to changes in economic regulations implemented by the government, including the rules that serve to empower and constrain economic regulators themselves (as these may be expected to impact economic regulations in various ways).

Economic reforms may be driven by one of two forces: interest group politics or public interest politics. The former corresponds to constituency interests. Here the exchange of goods and services between organized economic interests and political actors drives politics. More specifically, the flow of goods and services from economic "winners" to political actors induces the latter to propose, shape, and implement economic reforms.

Alternatively, economic reforms may be launched in pursuit of the public interest. In other words, they may be motivated by a desire to raise the level of welfare in the economy as a whole. This does not exclude the possibility that organized interests benefiting from reforms also influence the political process through their provision of goods and services. However, it is possible that political actors perceive that there are benefits to advocating economic reforms that are independent of such a transfer of resources. For example, if economic reforms are expected to benefit the national economy or unorganized households, politicians—as well as bureaucrats—may find the pursuit of such measures politically attractive, even if economic actors are not inducing them to act in such a way through the exchange of goods or services. Economic reforms might benefit political parties by boosting their levels of public support, thereby increasing their chance of winning seats in the next election. Similarly, such reforms might lead to wider acceptance by the public of policy measures put forward by bureaucratic agencies, thereby solidifying the reputation of these agencies within society and heightening their chances of organizational survival. In such cases, elected officials and bureaucratic actors might be considered "political winners."

In Chapter 3, we saw that bureaupluralism was a system in which regulated industries prevailed in cases when the two aforementioned sets of interests collided. The victory of the regulated industries was largely due to the policy-making mechanism in which policy proposals passed through deliberative councils and the LDP PARC. Thus, if bureaupluralism remained intact, we would expect economic reforms to be driven by interest group politics.

However, in the last chapter, we saw that public interest politics prevailed in Phase I, which centered on the emergence of the Big Bang: the LDP and MOF sought to recoup public support through the promotion of "good" economic reforms, acting independently from industry influence. Toward this goal, those within the LDP and MOF bypassed the channels of bureau-pluralism, such as the deliberation councils and the LDP PARC, and thereby also bypassed their respective constituencies: financial industry actors. However, we must examine developments in Phase II before declaring the death of bureaupluralism. In this phase, the Initiative went through the normal channels of bureaupluralism and the financial industry exercised its influence, as expected. It is by observing how the Initiative was affected as it went through this process that we obtain an accurate understanding of what happened to bureaupluralism. The next section provides a narrative of the events in Phase II, and then contrasts the developments here with political dynamics surrounding past cases of financial reform, in which bureaupluralism represented the normal pattern of policymaking interaction.

Developments Following the Prime Minister's Initiative

In this section, we provide a narrative of the events during Phase II of the Big Bang—that is, in the period after November 1996. Within this narrative, we focus on three arenas from which developments pertinent to the Big Bang reforms emerged: deliberative councils, the larger political economy context, and the legislative process.

Deliberative Councils (November 1996–June 1997)

The Big Bang Initiative, announced in November 1996, was contained in a brief, three-page paper. This paper explained why the Big Bang was necessary, referring to the aging population, the need for increased efficiency, and global competition. It also established the goal of completing the reforms and revitalizing Tokyo as an international market so that it might compete on par with the New York and London markets by 2001. The paper further outlined the three basic principles underlying reforms—to make Japanese finance "free," "fair," and "gobal"—while stressing the need to resolve the bad debt problem in the banking sector and stabilize the financial system. Finally, the paper presented a simple list of agenda items related to deregulation and liberalization for consideration.[2] Hashimoto and his Finance Minister, Hiroshi Mitsuzuka, asked the relevant deliberative councils to commence work on putting together more detailed plans. The councils were also instructed to commence deliberation on the measures immediately in their sub-divisions (*Asahi Shimbun* November 15, 1996).

The deliberations primarily involved five MOF councils: the Financial System Research Council (FSRC), in charge of banking; the Securities and Exchange Council (SEC); the Insurance Council (IC); the Business Accounting Council; and the Council on Foreign Exchange and Other Transactions.[3] Reflecting our main research interest in the politics of "winners and losers," we focus below on the politics within the first three councils, where the conflict between banking, securities, and insurance industry actors was most prominent.[4] These three councils issued reports in June 1997, which, along with other reports, were integrated into the official announcement made by MOF on the financial reforms. As each issue contained in the Big Bang Plan was discussed in Chapter 4, we do not

[2] This list included nine, very broadly defined examples, such as cross-entry of business, product liberalization, price liberalization, foreign exchange deregulation, improved disclosure, and the harmonization of accounting standards. For details about particular items, see Chapter 4.

[3] Hashimoto initially asked the Minister of Justice and the Minister of Finance to carry out the Big Bang, and charged the Justice Ministry's Judicial Council with clarifying the penal code prohibiting gambling, in the context of promoting derivative products. The Judiciary Council is excluded from analysis here, however, as its role was largely secondary to that of the MOF councils.

[4] It is important here to note the rationale for excluding from analysis here a number of additional councils. The Council on Foreign Exchange and Other Transactions, which carried out the forerunner reforms in foreign exchange regulations, issued a June 1996 report advocating drastic deregulation. The process through which MOF and the LDP successfully preempted potential objections by the banking industry to this report has already been discussed in Chapter 5. The Business Accounting Council, whose discussions included matters important to the corporate sector—most notably, the move toward consolidated accounting standards—only issued its interim report in June 1998. Moreover, the deliberative process in this council was largely devoid of distributional conflicts among economic actors. Thus, despite this council's importance, we do not examine it in detail here. Finally, a panel also existed that reported on nonblank financial institutions to the head of the MOF's Banking Bureau and which discussed issues surrounding the issuance of corporate bonds and commercial paper. Again, however, this panel played a relatively minor role in the process of the Big Bang reforms.

repeat its significance in detail here but instead provide a summary of the main agenda item, the related industry's position on this action, and the outcome of the reform proposal. This information is drawn primarily from summaries of council proceedings made available by MOF and from journalistic sources. (MOF web page; *Asahi Shimbun*[5]; *Kin'yu Zaisei Jijo*[6])

FINANCIAL SYSTEM RESEARCH COUNCIL

The MOF's Banking Bureau managed the FSRC. Five main items were under consideration by the FSRC:[7] the liberalization of restrictions on financial holding companies, the relaxation of business restrictions on financial subsidiaries and sister companies operated by banks under financial holding companies, entry by banks into other areas of financial services through the sale of financial products such as investment trusts or insurance, the liberalization of conditions imposed on commercial banks in their issuance of corporate bonds, and the liberalization of conditions imposed on non-banks in the issuance of corporate bonds.

The banking industry's position was to accept, on the whole, each of the five items. The rationale for acceptance varied across items, however. The first three items represented aggressive steps toward liberalization and the industry's acceptance of these reforms reflected the greater chance of industry actors to "win" or economically benefit from these reforms. Industry actors also accepted the final item regarding liberalization of corporate bond issuance by non-banks because this setback to their business monopoly was offset by the simultaneous proposal for the liberalization of securities products, thereby providing a means of defense for banks against other industries.[8] Finally, the banking industry as a whole accepted the liberalization of corporate bond issuance by commercial banks (as well as the entry of city banks into the trust business), although industry actors were divided on these measures. In these ways, the banking industry's

[5] Issues from the following dates: November 16, 1996, December 4, 1996, December 27, 1996, January 31, 1997, February 14, 1997, March 4, 1997, March 21, 1997, April 12, 1997, April 15, 1997, April 22, 1997, May 17, 1997, May 23, 1997, May 31, 1997, June 7, 1997, June 14, 1997, and June 15, 1997.

[6] Issues from the following dates: March 24, 1997, April 7, 1997, May 26, 1997, June 23, 1997, July 7, 1997, July 14, 1997, July 21, 1997, July 28, 1997, November 24, 1997, January 19, 1998, and March 19, 1998.

[7] Deliberation took place primarily within the Financial Function Revitalization Sub-Committee of the FSRC; similar delegation of responsibility was seen in the SEC and in the IC. Here we simplify our narrative by referring to the main council body, since the main councils adopted the reports issued by their sub-divisions as their official reports.

[8] The banking industry was also united in its denouncement of the system of government-backed financial institutions—most notably, the national postal saving system. The latter, they argued, was a behemoth enjoying an unfair competitive advantage over private sector banks.

accepted reform measures that represented a combination of outright victory, setback, and victory of the city banks over other "losers" within banking.

The result was that liberalization moved forward in all of the main agenda item areas. The pace of liberalization was often delayed, however, by resistance of the "losers," who resented the entry of the powerful large banks into their business areas. While the banking sector was able to increase its presence in the securities business from 1997 to 1999, it would not be permitted entry into the insurance business until the end of the Big Bang—that is, until 2001.[9] Bond issuance by ordinary banks was also to be liberalized in the second half of 1999, whereas such liberalization would take place in FY1998 for non-bank institutions.[10]

SECURITIES AND EXCHANGE COUNCIL

The MOF's Securities Bureau managed the SEC. The council's discussions focused primarily on three areas: expanding the objects of investment through liberalization of investment trust and asset management account products; enhancing the functioning of the market through abolishing mandatory use of the securities exchange, imposing stricter disclosure requirements, and tightening supervision; and, reducing the role of financial intermediaries through a two-step liberalization of brokerage commissions, permitting diversification of securities firms and the establishment of financial holding companies, downgrading administrative control of market entry control, a two-step relaxation of restrictions on business carried out by the securities subsidiaries of banks.

The securities industry's position, on the whole, was to "acquiesce" to these measures. Specifically, it pushed for product liberalization. At the same time, it demanded that a "one-set principle" be adopted, wherein liberalization perceived as damaging to the sector—such as liberalization of brokerage fees—would be accepted as long as other measures to develop market infrastructure—such as abolishing mandatory use of the securities exchange, liberalization of diversification, and a review of securities

---

[9] In FY1997, investment trust sales were permitted in rented space at branches; by 1999, banks were permitted to engage in direct sales. The business restrictions on banks' subsidiaries in securities and in trust would be lifted in the second half of FY1999. See below for the timetable of banks' entry into the insurance business.

[10] This measure encountered strong opposition from the LDP at a later stage, however: the housing loan companies, the principal actors in the Housing Loan Affair, were also non-bank financial institutions.

taxation—as introduced simultaneously. The industry also requested a soft-landing, or delay of the competition-enhancing measures to allow adjustment for the smaller firms in the business. Finally, it opposed the entry of banks into the securities business as well as the concept of "universal banks," out of concerns for banks' abuse of their business positions.

The securities industry was granted most of its wishes as a result of its "acquiescence" in these ways. Product liberalization took place and the "one-set principle" was observed, as the liberalization of brokerage commissions was coupled with permitting securities firms to diversify their business areas and the abolition of requirements that they trade through securities exchanges. Meanwhile, the council, lacking jurisdiction itself over taxation matters, put in a "request" with the relevant authorities that policies surrounding the taxation of securities be revised. Opposition by the securities industry to the banking industry's encroachment on their business area had mixed results: it did not stop the banks from entering but at the same time, the securities industry was able to obtain liberalization on some products that competed with those of banks—such as asset management accounts, which have settlement functions. The request for a soft-landing was likewise granted. The brokerage commission would be liberalized in two steps, with the first stage implemented from April 1998 and covering large transactions of over fifty million yen. This would then be followed by complete liberalization by the end of 1999. Bank entry into the securities business would also be permitted in two steps: securities subsidiaries of banks would have most of their business restrictions lifted in FY1997, but entry into the core of the securities business—that related to stocks—would only be allowed in the second half of FY1999.

INSURANCE COUNCIL

The Insurance Department of the MOF's Banking Bureau administered the IC, and two sets of actors within the insurance industry, casualty and life insurance firms, dominated the council. The council had four main agenda items: breaking up the legalized cartel on casualty insurance premiums; permitting a wider spectrum of companies to serve as shareholders for insurance firms, permitting cross-entry into and from insurance through subsidiaries, and permitting entry for banks into the insurance business through the sale of insurance products. The industry's position on these proposals was very simple. Motivated by the desire to protect its own industry's benefits, it opposed, on the whole, all of the proposed measures.[11] That is, the industry opposed price liberalization and bank entry into the insurance business, while at the same time pushed for financial holding companies and insurance companies to be permitted entry into other areas of financial services.

In the end, the insurance industry did not get all of its wishes. While granted permission to enter other financial business areas, insurance companies did not get their wish when the government permitted the establishment of financial holding companies by corporations, but not for mutual companies (the legal form adopted by many life insurance companies). Price liberalization, fiercely opposed by casualty insurance firms, also materialized. Here, we must note that the US–Japan Insurance Talks were taking place in the background and an agreement was reached in December 1996, whereby the Japanese government promised to liberalize the premium rates for casualty insurance (*Asahi Shimbun* December 15, 1996).[12]

Although the best scenario for the insurance industry would have been to keep the banks entirely out of their business areas, this was not possible.[13]

---

[11] The industry cited the following in defending its position:

(1) skepticism over the benefit to consumers of increasing the choice of products for consumers;
(2) concern for the survival of insurance firms and the possible negative impact of the proposed reforms on employment in the industry;
(3) concern over the domination by banks over the corporate sector, as reflected in the main bank system of the past;
(4) the need to alleviate "drastic change";
(5) the need to distinguish insurance from the rest of finance, since insurance products not only function as investments but also provide life security; and
(6) conclusions emerging out of past reform debates (i.e. the reports issued by the council in 1994 and 1996) that the cross-entry from other financial businesses ought to be carried out only after the cross-entry between life and casualty insurance had solidified.

[12] In the US–Japan insurance talks, ongoing since 1993, the US government sought to thwart the entry of Japanese life and casualty insurance firms into the "third sector" of insurance business. This area included such niche products as cancer insurance, where American firms dominated the market, and the US government viewed the prohibition of cross-entry as a trade-off for the restricted entry into the "first" and "second" fields of insurance, the life and casualty insurance markets. In 1994, the two countries reached an agreement wherein Japanese insurance firms would be allowed to enter into the third sector of the market, following deregulation of the life and casualty insurance markets. Afterwards, however, differences emerged over the interpretation of the agreement, with Japanese firms seeking to enter into the third field through their new subsidiaries, and the US industry crying foul play. The dispute between the two countries was in progress as the Big Bang was being announced. Finally, in December 1996, an agreement was reached: the Japanese would liberalize the casualty insurance price controls by July 1998 (this was included in the Big Bang Initiative), while the Japanese firms' subsidiaries would be allowed into the third insurance sector from 1997, with restrictions attached (Asahi Shimbun 1997: 65–72; Nihon Keizai Shimbun 1997: 64–71).

[13] In the earlier debates in the council, some members sought to keep banks out of the insurance business, arguing that insurance differed from finance and its liberalization need not be completed by 2001. They further argued that the process of past reforms dictated that the entry of banking into insurance should be permitted only well after the cross-entry of casualty and life insurance, effective in 1996, was solidly established.

Nonetheless, the insurance industry was successful in minimizing the degree of intrusion by banks into the insurance sector. The banks were able to enter through subsidiaries only in 2001, while entry into insurance by other financial industry actors and entry by insurance firms into other fields would be allowed earlier. The banks would not be able to sell insurance products, except for a small set of insurance products related to bank loans and issued by a sister or parent company. Moreover, despite this very tight restriction, bank entry into the insurance business would not be permitted until 2001.

Related Developments

Three developments in the wider political economy provided a critical context for the policy debate of the Big Bang in Phase II. These included two sets of scandals in the financial sector and the onset of financial and economic crisis.

RACKETEERING SCANDALS INVOLVING BANKS AND SECURITIES FIRMS (SPRING 1997–)

A series of racketeering scandals shook the business world from 1997 and the banking and securities industries suffered a severe blow due to their deep involvement. Racketeers, called *sokaiya* and specializing in intimidation at shareholders' meetings, have long been known to be influential in the Japanese corporate world. Corporate leaders, fearing the disruption of shareholders' meetings by such racketeers, allowed themselves to be extorted by paying such individuals off. Such payoffs were made punishable in 1982 under the Corporate Law in an attempt to preserve equity among shareholders. The practice, however, did not die away. According to one survey, 64 percent of corporations admitted to providing some kind of financial benefit to racketeers. (*Asahi Shimbun* November 29, 1997)

Although a number of large firms in various fields (including manufacturing and department stores) were discovered to have engaged in unlawful conduct, the blow to firms in the financial industry was particularly heavy. In the spring of 1997, as a result of an investigation by the public prosecutors, the top management of Nomura and other top securities firms, as well as the top management of Daiichi Kangyo Bank (DKB), one of the top city banks, were arrested and indicted for succumbing to racketeers' demands. The MOF also issued administrative orders banning the implicated firms from engaging in certain businesses for a period of time starting from July 1997. In the case of Nomura Securities, the administrative measures were expected to negatively affect the firms' businesses by undermining the services that could be provided to institutional investors; in the case of DKB, they were intended to constrain the ability of the bank to move forward with the Big Bang process of cross-entry and strategic alliances for a year (*Kin'yu Zaisei Jijo* August 18, 1997).

The racketeering scandals also more directly affected the businesses of the firms involved: governments as well as customers let their discontent known through their choice of firms. Many branches of the national and local governments excluded the involved securities firms from underwriting their bonds or chose to reduce transactions with the DKB. The consumer public dealt a visible blow to the firms involved in the scandals by their choices. Most corporate employees in Japan receive a bonus in the month of June, thereby leading to an increase in the balance of individual deposits across banks. Yet, in June 1997, the amount of deposits made by individuals into the DKB rose by only 7 billion yen, while amounts deposited into other top banks increased by 300–500 billion yen. Moreover, the figure for the DKB decreased by 200 billion yen in July 1997 and continued to decrease through August 1997. The trend of individual depositors punishing the DKB only stopped in the fall of 1997, when a financial crisis (see Financial and Economic Crisis and Hashimoto's resignation) triggered a flow of deposits back to the larger banks, deemed to be safer than the smaller and more troubled banks. Similarly, the top three securities' firms saw their profits shrink in FY1997, and a loss of business due to the racketeering scandals was cited as one of the major reasons for this poor showing (*Asahi Shimbun* September 4, 1997; *Kin'yu Zaisei Jijo* August 18, 1997 and May 4, 1998).

The timing of this racketeering scandal had an important impact on Phase II of the Big Bang. It meant that the securities industry, in particular, was heavily constrained in its ability to forcibly defend its turf against the encroachment of the banking industry. With its top management resigning in disgrace and being arrested, the securities industry—usually led by Nomura and other top firms—was in no position to wield significant political influence.

FINANCIAL AND ECONOMIC CRISIS AND HASHIMOTO'S RESIGNATION (NOVEMBER 1997–JULY 1998)

The financial crisis, which was once thought to be under control with the passage of the Housing Loan and other financial packages in June 1996, returned with greater intensity in the fall of 1997. In April 1997, Nissan

Life went under, becoming the first life insurance company to fail in the postwar era. A rescue operation for Nippon Credit Bank, the weakest among the three long-term credit banks, was introduced after tumultuous negotiation between MOF and financial firms in April 1997. As part of this negotiation, financial institutions ranging from banks to life insurance companies were asked by MOF officials to provide a contribution to "save the financial system." Then, in the fall of the same year, a full-blown financial crisis hit. First, in early November 1997, San'yo Securities, the ninth largest securities firm, announced its failure. Next, in the middle of the month, one of the major money center banks that the government had promised was too big to fail, Hokkaido Takushoku Bank, went under. Yamaichi Securities, one of the Big Four securities firms soon followed, with its business folding a week later.

In the midst of this crisis, the LDP decided in mid-December 1997 to inject a total of 10 trillion yen in public funds into the financial system through the Deposit Insurance Corporation.[14] However, because these developments coincided with an economic downturn, partly due to the fiscal contraction starting from April 1997, the situation turned into a credit crunch. The banks, conscious of capital requirements, were now reluctant to make loans. Accordingly, small firms in the economy suffered from a tighter cash flow and encountered trouble financing day-to-day needs. On December 22, 1997, the Nikkei Stock Price Index plummeted to below 15,000, for the first time in two years and five months. MOF and the LDP came up with a second set of plans on December 24: MOF would allow banks to choose between two accounting standards (based on market value or acquisition value), so as to facilitate the banks' ability to meet the BIS capital/asset ratio.[15] The LDP also came up with a scheme that would put a maximum of thirty trillion yen—comprised of ten trillion yen in government bonds and twenty trillion yen in government-guaranteed loans—toward the resolution of bank failure and toward the operation of banks in order to encourage them to make loans. (Nihon Keizai Shimbun 1998)

The injection of public funds (in forms of a government guarantee) became law in February 1998, and by March 1998, 1.81 trillion yen had been injected into twenty-one banks, including each of the eighteen

[14] The government financed this public fund injection through the issuance of government bonds.

[15] They would also delay the implementation of the capital requirements for up to one year beyond their scheduled April 1998 introduction for banks that only engaged in domestic businesses (and to which BIS standards did not apply).

largest banks (Kin'yu Zaisei Jijo March 23, 1998).[16] While the conditions of repayment differed from one bank to another according to a bank's financial health and banks were forced to submit restructuring plans, most banks requested the same amount of public funds (approximately 100 billion yen). This behavior reflected concerns that if some banks with damaged balance sheets were the only ones to ask for public money, the capital injection plan itself might cause other banks to go under by stirring up public anxiety.

However, the market did not react as expected and the financial crisis persisted, with the economy sliding into negative growth. Between May and July 1998, the ruling coalition and the government went on to draw up a "total plan" for financial revitalization to resolve the bad debt problem. Schemes to facilitate the transactions of bad loans and real estate were discussed, and a public bridge bank was set up by drawing on public money to assume the businesses of failed banks (Kin'yu Zaisei Jijo July 13, 1998). The Long-Term Credit Bank of Japan (LTCB) faced a tough speculative attack from foreign investors from June 1998 (Takeuchi 1999). Upper House elections, held once every three years, came in July 1998, amidst the economic and financial crisis. The LDP lost its majority, resulting in Prime Minister Hashimoto's resignation.[17]

MOF WINING AND DINING SCANDALS RESULTING IN ARRESTS AND RESIGNATIONS (SPRING 1998)

The racketeering scandals involving banks and securities firms, mentioned above, exposed the spending habits of banks and led public prosecutors to target MOF officials next for investigation. Documents obtained by prosecutors provided evidence of the wining and dining of MOF officials by financial institutions. This resulted in the arrest of five officials in March 1998, and the resignation of the finance minister and MOF Administrative Vice-Minister, the top permanent ministry official. In an unprecedented

[16] The injection took the forms of preferred stocks and subordinate debt and loans so that the government would not actively take over the management rights of the firms. In contrast, in the later Financial Diet of the fall of 1998, it was decided that the newly created FRC would also purchase common stock, enabling it to possibly intervene in the management of the financial institutions. See Chapter 7.

[17] Despite the fact that the Lower House, where the LDP retained a majority, had the decisive vote on the identity of the prime minister, the prevailing norm in the LDP and the broader political world dictated that Hashimoto take responsibility for the electoral defeat, considered to be the public's demonstration of non-confidence.

move, MOF announced in April 1998 internal sanctions on 112 officials, including the retirement of 2 of its senior officials.[18]

This incident dealt a final blow to MOF's political influence before its breakup and the creation of the Financial Supervisory Agency (FSA) in June 1998. Public trust in the bureaucracy hit a low. Not only was the competence of officials now in question but also the ethics of officials were now in doubt. In a public survey by Asahi Shimbun given in March 1998 in the aftermath of this scandal, 71 percent responded that they did not trust the bureaucrats, up from 65 percent in the midst of the MOF reforms in 1996 and 51 percent in 1994 as the Housing Loan Affair began to unfold (*Asahi Shimbun* May 15, 1994, December 12, 1996, and March 4, 1998).[19]

Legislative Process (March–June 1998)

Most of the policy proposals adopted by the deliberative councils in June 1997 were written into legislation by March 1998 and became law in June 1998, while the foreign exchange reforms, the "forerunner," became law one year earlier in May 1997. The legislative process of the Big Bang was not a very exciting one. In fact, one lawmaker, upon observing developments surrounding the foreign exchange reforms, noted that most lawmakers who passed the law did not understand the significance of the Big Bang (Kaieda 1997).

The Big Bang was not welcomed unanimously by the political world, especially from 1997, as Japan crept into economic and financial crisis. For example, Seiroku Kajiyama, an influential LDP lawmaker, argued at the time that US-style free marketization, such as that reflected in the Big Bang, would only benefit foreign firms to the detriment of Japanese firms. Views toward postponing the Big Bang gained ground among politicians, critics, and journalists, as well as within the financial world, at this time (Tahara 1998). Nevertheless, the Big Bang legislation sailed through the Diet with little opposition. Despite the financial crisis, the package had public support: newspaper editorials claimed that "the current crisis should not be made into a pretext to postpone or water down the financial reforms" (*Asahi Shimbun* January 21, 1998).

---

[18] One of the two forced to resign was the Securities Bureau Chief Nagano, the leader of the securities reforms in the Big Bang. The public prosecutors also uncovered a similar wining and dining scandal involving the Bank of Japan. A BOJ official was arrested, and numerous BOJ officials were sanctioned in a similar manner.

[19] Based on this author's research into the Asahi Shimbun's web-based database, containing data from 1984 onwards, 1994 is the first year in which a question concerning public trust in the bureaucracy appears in such surveys.

The scandals help to explain the nature of the situation. As the legislation was being submitted to the Diet in March 1998, the MOF Wining and Dining Scandals reached its peak with the arrests of its officials. The charges were that the officials gave favor to particular financial firms in their authorization of new products and in revealing the schedule of financial inspections, in exchange for being the beneficiaries of wining and dining.[20] (*Asahi Shimbun* March 6, 1998) This incident gave a final endorsement to an already popular view that the Convoy System (see Chapter 3), involving close cooperation between the financial industries and MOF, needed to be reformed into a rule-based system, modeled after the United States, in which the regulators and the regulated maintain a distance from each other. As the wining and dining scandals were seen as representing the pathology of the old system of financial administration, the Big Bang came to be perceived as a measure whose introduction was desired as early as possible. This trend was symbolized in an event in which MOF officials in charge of financial administration uniformly expressed their remorse for their involvement in the wining and dining scandal to the Diet Committee deliberating on the Big Bang legislation, stressing that the proposed legislation would change the nature of financial administration (*Asahi Shimbun* April 29, 1998). Under such circumstances, the cost of canceling or postponing the Big Bang would have been prohibitively high for any political actor.

Summarizing the Narrative

Let us briefly summarize the narrative of the events given above before proceeding to the next stage of analysis. Big Bang reform objectives centered on liberalization and deregulation, and on the enhancement of market infrastructure. Although financial industry actors invariably pushed for the liberalization of restrictions on financial shareholding companies, there were at the same time numerous distributional conflicts surrounding this issue. Such conflicts can be characterized as occurring between the

---

[20] While the provision of financial benefits to government officials with specific regulatory power had been prosecuted repeatedly to this point, this was the first time that mere wining and dining was prosecuted in a corruption case. This shift reflected a change in prosecutorial standards as well as a possible change in social norms that determine what is acceptable behavior. Contrast the wide criticism in 1998 against the *MOF-tan* system (i.e. financial industry's representatives who build close relationships with MOF officials to get information on MOF policy) and the way the system was treated five years earlier in the Nihon Keizai Shimbun (1992). Also, Tahara (1998) recalls how the standards about wining and dining differed in the 1980s from that observed in the 1990s.

perceived "winners" emerging from such reforms, seeking to maximize their gains, and the inevitable "losers" forestalling such developments. Specifically, the large city banks—the likely winners emerging from the reforms—lined up against all the rest, even though attitudes on specific issues did differ across these city banks.[21]

Conflict took place along two dimensions. First, positions adopted by large banks clashed with those of securities and insurance firms in the battle of the industries. Second, within industries, the more powerful city banks butted heads with the long-term credit banks and trust banks. Meanwhile, larger firms won out over smaller ones in the securities and insurance sectors. Within the FSRC, the first conflict was resolved in favor of the banks when banks were permitted entry into the securities and insurance businesses; the second conflict occurred when long-term credit banks opposed bond issuance by city banks, and trust banks sought to limit the business conditions for trust bank subsidiaries of city banks. At the SEC, the securities firms sought to limit the intrusion of banks into their business fields; the insurance industry's primary concern at the IC was the fear of the banks' dominance of the whole economy based on the main bank system, which would translate into a dominance in their fields if their activities were allowed unfettered.

While the perceived losers in the reform process united in their opposition against the encroachment of the banking sector into other business areas, attitudes differed across industry actors: securities firms acquiesced to liberalization but sought compensation, while insurance firms opposed the measures. In the SEC, liberalization of brokerage fees was seen as inevitable, but securities firms sought at the same time to gain acceptance of other reforms they viewed as beneficial and were successful in obtaining government support for the principle of reforms being put forward in one set. However, in the IC, liberalization was not given and industry actors frequently argued that insurance was different from finance and appealed to past deliberative decisions that bank entry into insurance should come only well after cross-entry by life and casualty insurance firms into each others' businesses had been well established. In doing so, industry actors tried to justify why the 2001 deadline for reform implementation given by the prime minister should not apply in the case of insurance, and why bank entry into insurance should come only after 2001 (MOF web page).

The financial reforms were wide in scope, covering not only the banking and securities fields, but also foreign exchange and accounting

---

[21] For example, some banks acquiesced on securities but opposed reforms on insurance.

standards. Even so, most measures included in the Initiative fell under the administrative jurisdiction of the MOF's financial bureaus. Importantly, however, critical related issues such as financial taxation and public finance (i.e. the national postal savings system) were left outside the scope of the Big Bang.[22] Accordingly, the measures debated in Phase II came neatly under the jurisdiction of the MOF's three financial bureaus and five councils, but excluded deliberative organs such as the MOF's Taxation Bureau or the Ministry of Post and Telecommunications (which oversaw postal savings).

The involvement of politicians on behalf of the regulated industries in the whole process was relatively insignificant. Admittedly, there was some intervention in fields such as life insurance by the LDP and other parties, when industry actors sought to forestall the intrusion by banks into their business areas (Asahi Shimbun June 14, 1997).[23] While such interventions meant a great deal to the affected industries, their efforts did not impact the larger picture of the reforms. In the case of life insurance, for example, political pressure did not keep the banks out of the insurance market or result in the exclusion altogether of insurance from the 2001 deadline for reform implementation; rather, political intervention was successful in gaining limitations on the number and types of insurance products banks could sell and in postponing bank entry into the insurance business until the end of the five-year reform period. In this way, the situation was not one of open defiance by the regulated industries or their political allies against Prime Minister Hashimoto or MOF on these matters.

Nevertheless, bureaupluralism as a policymaking process had not yet died away. During Phase II, the Big Bang Initiative sailed smoothly through negotiations involving the regulated industries and experts in the deliberative councils. Moreover, the LDP's financial zoku formally had their say when the Initiative went through the LDP PARC and its financial sub-divisions on the way to becoming legislation, and were able to informally provide input through applying pressure on the bureaucracy. Throughout Phase II, the MOF's three financial bureaus (Banking,

[22] This observation again endorses our view that stresses the role of MOF over that of MITI in the Big Bang political process. Although the deliberative council under MITI presented a report that was intended to reflect the "true image" of the Big Bang in May 1997 (Tsusansho 1997), this report's proposals were wider in scope than the Big Bang reforms actually enacted, and included matters outside MOF's jurisdiction, such as the postal savings system and the pension fund system.

[23] The life insurance industry sought to influence the process by making use of its massive sales force (400,000) as well: some tens of thousands of letters opposing the sale by banks of insurance products were sent to MOF's Banking Bureau, according to a leader of the life insurance labor union (*Kin'yu Zaisei Jijo* June 23, 1997).

Securities, and International Finance) presided over the bargaining process. The content of the package as well as the policymaking process—involving deliberative councils and the LDP sub-divisions of the PARC—matched up well with the jurisdictional interest of the MOF's three financial bureaus.

The perceived industry losers from reforms wielded their influence most in setting the pace of the reforms. Specifically, they were able to influence conclusions on when and under what forms the specific measures of liberalization and deregulation would apply to their businesses. The securities firms were able to have their "soft landing" priority translated into two-step liberalization for such matters as brokerage commissions and business restrictions placed on the securities' subsidiaries established by banks. The complete liberalization of brokerage commissions would only materialize in 1998, and the banks' subsidiaries would have to wait until 1999 to engage in the securities business in full strength. While securities firms had to swallow price liberalization and deregulation of business cross-entry, they were more or less successful in ensuring that other desired reforms became bundled into the same reform package, with the exception of tax reforms on financial products—an issue that lay outside the purvey of the three financial bureaus. In this way, securities firms swallowed "bitter pills" along with "sweeteners," such as an abolition of the mandatory use of securities exchanges and the lifting of the ban on business diversification by securities firms. The insurance industry was even more successful in having future bank entry into insurance postponed. For bank subsidiaries, this would only happen by 2001, and banks themselves would only be able to sell a very small set of products by this year. Accordingly, the media characterized the "hole" being drilled into the insurance business as very small.

Yet, we must note that there was no reversal in Hashimoto's master plan. The basic plan laid out in the Initiative announced in November 1996 survived the deliberative councils and the LDP PARC. The timing (beginning immediately, with completion by 2001), also survived. Likewise, the basic principles of "free, fair, and global," and each sub-category of measures under these headings, including liberalization of cross-entry restrictions, deregulation of product control, liberalization of commissions, foreign exchange deregulation, stricter disclosure rules, tighter supervision, and accounting standards, were maintained. Importantly, many of these reforms had distributional effects. Despite opposition by regulated industries—and by the insurance industry, in particular—the Big Bang laws in the end included reforms pertaining to banking, securities, insurance, foreign exchange, and accounting standards—just as had the November 1996 Initiative.[24] In this way, industry opposition failed to spur the elimination of any important component of reforms.

In sum, the regulated industries, most of which stood to "lose" from the reforms, were able to wield influence in affecting the pace of the reforms by delaying specific measures perceived to be hurtful or by limiting the scope of particular measures. Because state actors (i.e. MOF and the LDP) developed the Initiative with little involvement from regulated industry actors during Phase I, the industries' influence was concentrated in Phase II through the process of bureaupluralism. However, the Big Bang Initiative itself was not reversed, and neither was any important part of the Initiative dropped. Conceived by MOF and the LDP through a process of cooperation, competition, and conflict during Phase I, the Initiative was carried through the process of bureaupluralism in Phase II. While financial industry actors affected the pace of the reforms, they had little effect on the basic framework of reforms, or on their timing, scope, or sequence.

A question nonetheless remains: why were the reforms not reversed? After all, financial industry actors have been known in the past to wield strong political influence over regulatory reforms. What kept them from doing so this time? In order to answer this question, we turn now to briefly survey three cases of financial reforms that preceded the Big Bang, in the hope of highlighting important differences in political–economic dynamics between the former and latter.

Three Previous Cases of Financial Reform

Our analysis focuses on the politics of regulatory reform in finance, with a particular focus on the distributional effects of these reforms. Thus, we are interested in past cases of financial reforms that shared many similarities with the Big Bang but produced different results. With this in mind, we examine three previous cases of financial reform: the financial system reforms of 1991–93, the insurance reforms of 1992–94, and the banking reforms of 1979–82.[25] These three cases share with the Big Bang the same

[24] The conflict among the banking, securities, and insurance industries played out via the Banking Bureau, the Securities Bureau, and the Insurance Division of the Banking Bureau, which organized bargains at the inter- and intra-industries levels.

[25] In dating these cases, the beginning years (1991, 1992, and 1979) refer to the time when the respective deliberative councils issued their final reports on the reforms, and the end years (1993, 1994, 1982) refer to the time when the reform laws took effect.

set of actors, political and economic settings, and fields targeted for reform. Although we have claimed that the Big Bang reforms were drastic and wide in scope, these previous forms represent outcomes that might be depicted as gradual and piecemeal reform.

The first and second cases from the early 1990s represent the most recent major reform efforts under bureaupluralism with distributional effects in the fields of banking, securities, and insurance—areas also under contention in the Big Bang. The Big Bang was likewise a case in which many industry actors were expected to be hurt by reforms, and thus was one in which we might expect industry actors to seek political remedies. The third case selected for comparison represents a rare occasion of political conflict between the banking industry and the MOF that led to the intervention of the LDP. As such, it might be expected to provide clues as to the nature of political influence of financial industry actors under bureaupluralism. By contrasting the case of the Big Bang with these three, we hope to obtain a clearer view of the changes affecting the policy-making process of bureaupluralism.

Financial Reforms of 1991–93

The Big Bang was an effort to complete the de-segmentation of the financial system that began with the financial reforms of 1991–93. Thus, the issues involved overlapped, despite an exclusive focus on banking and securities in the latter. In the 1991–93 reforms, attention focused on cross-entry into the banking and securities businesses, as well as on cross-entry within banking and the breaking down of barriers between trust and long-term credit banking.

Following the 1984 Yen-Dollar Committee report, the MOF's deliberation council on banking, the FSRC, commenced discussion on financial system reforms—specifically on the de-segmentation of finance. The MOF's deliberation council on securities, the SEC, was brought into the reform discussions from 1988, after the FSRC issued an interim report pressing for de-segmentation. This development reflected the Banking Bureau's recognition that successful reforms could not be obtained without the participation of the Securities Bureau. Intense discussion followed between 1988 and 1991 within and between the two councils. Final reports were issued in June 1991 and the measures were legislated in the spring of 1992, taking effect in April 1993.

The outcome of bargaining between the industries was that the core business of the industry facing competition with a new entrant would be protected while cross-entry would be allowed at the margins. Specifically, cross-entry was to be allowed under the form of a single-business subsidiary (e.g. city banks would set up separate subsidiaries for the trust and securities businesses), but the new entrants would be allowed to enter the market only gradually and with strict business restrictions. The losers in this process would be the trust banks, the long-term credit banks, and the securities firms; the winners would be the city banks, as the more resourceful city banks would be able to enter various financial business areas. While all sides had something to gain, the nature of gains differed. While the losers' gains were temporary (e.g. delay in new entry and strict business restrictions attached to the newly established subsidiaries), the banks' victory—permission to enter into the securities business—was permanent (Vogel 1996; Nishimura 1999).

This case typifies the policymaking dynamics of "bureaupluralism": the MOF's Banking and Securities Bureaus clearly worked out the bargain among the regulated industries. The respective councils functioned as the arena where the interests of the regulated industry were expressed and mediated under MOF initiative. The principle, if any, was that of gradualism: a high-ranking official in the Banking Bureau at that time confirms that, whatever the reasoning attached, the essence of the 1991–93 reforms—the introduction of the subsidiaries system—was "the alleviation of drastic change" and "protection of the weak" (Nishimura 1999: 64). Largely through the affiliated deliberative council (FSRC for banking; SEC for securities), each industry presented a "heroic" (Vogel) lobbying effort to influence the outcome of "how and when" cross-entry would occur so as to maximize gains or minimize losses. Some "losers" wielded great political influence: the long-term credit banks, led by the powerful Industrial Bank of Japan (IBJ), and the securities firms, led by Nomura Securities, largely determined the course of discussion at the deliberation councils through their influence over MOF (Nihon Keizai Shimbun 1992).[26]

As in the case of the Big Bang, the 1991–93 reform outcomes were also influenced by wider events affecting the political–economic environment by the time the legislation reached the Diet in spring 1992. These events included the fall of the stock market, scandals involving banks and securities firms, and the resulting organizational reforms of the MOF.

The demise of the stock market weakened banks and securities firms alike, making it easier for the MOF to coerce these private sector actors into

[26] In the case of the IBJ, that its concerns were reflected in the policy debate stemmed from the fact that the IBJ had been very much involved in the past decision making in financial administration (Nihon Keizai Shimbun 1992; Mainichi Shimbun 1997).

cooperation with the reform plan. At the same time, however, it made financial industry actors less interested in pursuing cross-entry in the first place (Vogel 1996). Numerous scandals also emerged involving large banks (such as the IBJ, Sanwa Bank, and Sumitomo Bank). These related to the shady transactions made during the excesses of the bubble economy in the latter 1980s.

Securities forms were shrouded in an even larger scandal, referred to as the "Loss Compensation Scandal." In June 1991, it was reported that the top four securities firms were engaging in practices of compensating the losses suffered by their large corporate clients. While the practice itself was not illegal, strictly speaking,[27] it nonetheless triggered public outrage because of the way in which it exposed inequity in the treatment of large corporations and individual investors. The latter, of course, were not compensated for their losses. The loss compensation scandal ended up muting the "most powerful group opposing meaningful reform" (Vogel 1996: 187). However, the scandal also raised questions about the MOF's competence in financial administration and raised the possibility of organizational breakup. Following the scandal, Prime Minister Toshiki Kaifu charged an advisory panel on administrative reforms to develop a policy recommendation on reforming financial administration. Although proposals to break up the MOF through the establishment of an independent commission were among those that emerged out of this panel, MOF outmaneuvered its critics. In the end, reforms were limited to the creation of a commission in charge of securities regulation within MOF and a substantial increase in staff working on securities oversight (Vogel 1996).

Insurance Reforms of 1992–94

Reforms in the insurance industry were pursued parallel to but separate from reforms in the banking and securities industries. In 1989, the IC commenced reform discussions, spurred by the insurance industry's push to realize a long-held wish to enter into other financial businesses such as trust and securities. Large life insurance companies, in particular, spearheaded this push. The issue was largely left on the sidelines for some time,

---

[27] It was illegal for securities firms to guarantee the possible loss before engaging in securities transactions. However, unless such promises were in written forms, it was hard to prove that such engagements were in place. When the losses materialized, the securities firms would often engage in loss compensation for their best customers fearing loss of business (*Asahi Shimbun* July 28, 1991). This practice, called loss compensation, was made illegal in the aftermath of the scandals.

however, as the struggle between banks and securities firms occupied main stage. In April 1991, the council issued an interim report advocating a wider scope of cross-entry than previously considered, including the insurance business. This report's proposals were reflected in the FSRC's final June 1991 report on financial reforms. In line with the reform process surrounding the banking and securities sectors, the MOF's Insurance Division in the Banking Bureau took the lead in working out the bargaining in the policymaking process. With help from the heads of the respective industry associations, who represented the presidents of the largest firms in life and casualty insurance, the Insurance Division coordinated intra-industry discussion, skillfully moving beyond past distinctions made based on firm size, as well as overcoming the rift between life and casualty insurance (Nihon Keizai Shimbun 1992).

However, with the collapse of the bubble economy—and the plunge in stock and real estate values from 1991, in particular—the insurance industry lost its appetite for entering into new business areas. This was especially the case for the life insurance industry, whose portfolios were heavily weighted with stocks and real estate holdings. In 1992, the IC issued its final report on comprehensive reform, and the wholly revised Insurance Business Law went into effect in 1994. While entry by casualty and life insurance firms into each other's business areas via subsidiaries was introduced in October 1996, provisions for entry by insurance or other industries were not included. Entry into the insurance sector by non-insurance firms would be postponed until after cross-entry within the insurance industry was carried out.[28]

Banking Reforms of 1979–82

The Banking Law of 1982 represented a comprehensive revision of the Banking Law of 1927. According to Rosenbluth (1989), its contents reflected two important decisions: first, the decision to permit banks to engage in the dealing and retail sale of government bonds; second, the decision not to impose substantially stronger disclosure requirements on banks. The two case studies provided by Rosenbluth document bureaupluralism at work in its heyday.[29]

The decision to permit banks to engage in the dealing and retail sale of government bonds was the outcome of a fierce battle between banks and

---

[28] See Sanwa Soken (1999: 252) for the list of the measures included in the 1992–94 insurance reforms.

[29] This section largely draws on Rosenbluth (1989: chapter 4). See also Chapter 4.

securities firms. By the late 1970s, banks were increasingly concerned about their government bond holding, which had increased as a result of a ballooning government deficit and the Bank of Japan's reluctance to repurchase the government bonds as arranged,[30] due to the central bank's fear of stirring up inflation as a result. It was in this context that the debate over the retailing and dealing of government bonds emerged: banks sought to enter this area of business, to the displeasure of the securities firms, which enjoyed a monopoly here. Initially, the government responded to bank concerns through the creation of a quasi-auction market for government bonds.[31] Yet, this did little to quiet the banks, which persisted with their demands to be permitted to move beyond the traditional banking business into the securities and international finance business. Deliberative councils affiliated with each industry behaved as expected: the advisory panel on banking supported the banks, while the advisory panel on securities argued that bank entry should be avoided.

A deadlock between the two financial industries emerged, and MOF officials discreetly sought a resolution. The LDP chose not to intervene, caught in between two powerful industries that were each important supporters of the party. Finally, after much heated exchange between the industries, the Banking and Securities Bureaus struck a compromise in November 1980.[32] This compromise essentially became law in April 1981. It was decided that a neutral Committee of Three, approved by both industries and comprised entirely of retired MOF officials, would decide the timing and other details regarding the banks' entry into government bond dealing and retailing.

The second main issue discussed in the context of this package of financial reforms had to do with disclosure requirements. MOF sought to introduce tighter disclosure requirements, in spite of opposition from the banking industry, but failed due to political intervention from the LDP. The disclosure requirements proposed by MOF emerged out of the ministry's efficiency campaigns, in which it sought to foster financial system stability through the consolidation of small financial institutions

[30] The central bank would absorb about 90 percent of the government bonds held by the banks after one year from the issuance.

[31] Other measures include the following: banks were given choice over their accounting methods to cope with the book losses; the Fiscal Investment and Loan Program would increase the absorption of government bonds (Rosenbluth 1989: 104–5).

[32] Basically, the banks would be allowed to enter into the retailing and dealing of government bonds, although this would not lead to the abolition of the regulatory wall between securities and banking. Securities firms would be given, on the other hand, permission to trade short-term securities issued in the Euromarket, including certificates of deposits and commercial paper. See Rosenbluth (1989: 108–11).

via mergers. This was strongly opposed by the small financial institutions themselves, however. A 1980 proposition made by MOF to the banking sector reflected a combination of carrot and stick approach: banks would face stricter disclosure rules and would be forced to limit their loans to any single borrower to 25 percent of their total assets but, in return, they would be permitted to engage in the trading and retail sale of government bonds. Heavy lobbying by the banking industry of the LDP (dependent upon financial contributions from the sector) led the PARC sub-divisions on finance to redraft much of the legislation so that it enabled the banks to enjoy the "carrot" without the "stick."

Comparing the Financial Big Bang to Past Financial Reforms

The aforementioned three cases reveal four important differences between previous cases of financial reform and the Big Bang.

First, whereas regulated industry actors were actively involved in the planning phase in earlier reform examples, they were notably absent at this stage in the Big Bang. It was the norm in the past for reform plans to be discussed carefully and thoroughly within the deliberative councils, where the views of the industry representatives as well as experts were expressed. Thereafter, the actual reform plan was proposed and then turned into legislation by MOF. It took six years for the FSRC and three years for the SEC to come up with the final plan in the 1991–93 reforms; the IC took three years to put together the 1992–94 reforms; and, the FSRC spent more than four years on the 1979–82 reforms.[33] In contrast, MOF and the LDP bypassed industry actors and the deliberative councils in launching the Big Bang reforms. It was not until *after* the proposal of the Initiative, which set the overall framework of the reforms, that the deliberative councils were asked by the prime minister to transform the proposal into concrete terms. Moreover, deliberation lasted less than a year before the emergence of the reform proposal. The Hashimoto Initiative was announced in November 1996, and the MOF councils issued the final reports on banking, securities, and insurance in June 1997.

Second, whereas past reforms were clearly led by the bureaucracy, the political leadership provided by Hashimoto in generating the Initiative renders the Big Bang case markedly different. If political intervention

[33] For the banking reforms of 1979–82, the FSRC spent four years (1975–79) before issuing a final report on the wholesale revision of the Banking Law (Rosenbluth 1989).

existed in past reforms (as in 1991–93 and 1979–82), it was on behalf of particular regulated industries seeking to thwart or realize certain reform measures, and there was no doubt about the fact that the reform initiative was under the control of the bureaucracy. While the Big Bang reform plan came largely from within MOF, it became a component of Prime Minister Hashimoto's Six Large Reforms—the central agenda of his government—once the prime minister took it up. Thereafter, the Big Bang was perceived primarily as Hashimoto's program rather than a program belonging to MOF.

Third, the scope and pace of reforms in the previous cases were clearly smaller and slower than in the Big Bang. The Big Bang sought to address banking, securities, and insurance, as well as other financial service areas. Whereas gradualism was the norm in past reforms, with deadlines lacking much primacy, the Big Bang differed. Although the trait of gradualism was present in the initiative stage, it is not an accurate depiction of the nature of events in Phase II, when the measures contained in the Big Bang were kept in place.

Fourth, while MOF "organized" bargains in the previous reform examples, the ministry was unable to retain this role in the case of the Big Bang. Here we note an important similarity before highlighting the dissimilarity. Scandals played a large part in propelling the Big Bang reforms as well as in propelling the 1991–93 reforms. In the latter example, scandals undermined the reputation and political clout of the securities industry, forcing them to accept entry into their business field by banks. The scandals also damaged the MOF's standing to a lesser extent, spurring its organizational reforms in the form of the creation of the SESC. In the Big Bang, MOF was badly hurt by the scandals, resulting in its organizational breakup; while the banking industry suffered the greatest damage through the Housing Loan and other scandals, the standing of the securities industry was also seriously damaged by the racketeering scandals. Thus, in both the 1991–93 and Big Bang reforms, scandals served as catalysts for reform. MOF and the industries it regulated were forced to accept reforms when their political influence was undermined by scandals.

Despite this similarity, there was a major difference between the Big Bang and previous cases. In the past, no one questioned the MOF's role as the organizer of reform "bargains": it was an accepted matter of fact that MOF initiated and led reforms, mediating between the industries that supported or opposed them, and sometimes inviting the intervention of the LDP. In the Big Bang, however, the MOF's role as the organizer of reform "bargains" was clearly under question. As detailed in Chapter 5, MOF played an active role in devising the strategy for the Big Bang. Yet, the Big Bang itself was not presented as part of the MOF's campaign (unlike the ministry's earlier "efficiency" campaign and proposal to tighten disclosure rules in 1978–82); neither were the reforms processed through the deliberative councils by MOF. Instead, the reforms were presented as a prime ministerial initiative, with marked efforts by MOF to downplay its involvement in devising the reform plan.

Why was the Financial Industry Unable to Stop the Big Bang?

How do the differences in the Big Bang case highlighted above—the absence of involvement by the regulated industries in the planning stage, the existence of political leadership, the larger scope and quicker pace of action, and the loss of MOF standing as the "organizer" of bargains—help us understand why the regulated industry actors were unable to reverse the reforms?

Anticipating opposition from the "losers" in the reform process, the bureaucrats and politicians bypassed the regulated industries and the deliberative councils at the planning stage (Phase I). This, as explained in Chapter 5, came about from the efforts by the LDP and MOF to secure their own organizational survival. The LDP chose to court public opinion over the preservation of its ties with MOF in the wake of the Housing Loan Affair. It incorporated its rivals' electoral platform of structural reforms, as it faced a believable threat of replacement. MOF faced an imminent threat of organizational breakup, and sought to recoup public confidence lost by the policy failures and scandals, rather than preserving its traditional style of financial administration.

Because of this bypassing strategy by the bureaucrats and politicians, the regulated industries were only allowed to participate at Phase II. What mattered here was the Prime Minister's political leadership, as it raised the costs for industry actors to successfully challenge and reverse the course of the Big Bang reforms. The previous cases showed that the regulated industries were able to significantly alter, even reverse, the course of the reforms to suit their interests in the past. The banking industry demonstrated its ability to reverse what was decided by MOF through heavy political lobbying to the LDP in 1979–82; that the securities industry possessed powerful political resources in the Diet was shown in 1979–82 as well as in 1991–93. Likewise, in the Big Bang, it was not that the "losers" were unable to raise any objections whatsoever. Indeed, the life insurance companies—and the securities firms to a lesser extent—were able to delay the entry of bank subsidiaries into their line of business.

However, such efforts by industry actors were only made at the level of particular details aligned with their respective interests, such as with the objections to the entry of bank subsidiaries into other business areas; opposition efforts were not made at a more comprehensive level. In other words, industry actors did not pursue the goal of significantly altering the key components of the Big Bang Initiative framework through such things as trying to postpone the implementation deadline of 2001, or trying to have a particular reform measure dropped. No corporate leader of the financial sector interviewed by Nihon Keizai Shimbun (1997)—that is no head of a city bank, long-term credit bank, trust bank, regional financial institution, securities company, or insurance firm—openly opposed the prime minister's Big Bang Initiative, which professed to vitalize the Tokyo market. The "losers" merely expressed reservations regarding the specific measures included therein. This behavior warrants an explanation, as there were very few financial firms that stood to gain from the Big Bang. As Tahara (1998: 216) notes, "for the large majority of the financial world, the Big Bang was clearly an annoyance."

Why would the regulated industries' opposition be limited to particular measures? It was because the Big Bang was one of the main pillars of the prime minister's political agenda.[34] In November 1996, the financial industry actors suddenly faced a program, launched by the prime minister and embraced by the LDP. Big Bang-type reforms were part of the ruling party's electoral platforms as a result of the efforts made by the LDP ARPH. Thus, to campaign for the reversal of the Big Bang through lobbying the LDP would become too costly, in contrast to the case of 1979–82. The use of counterfactuals helps illustrate the differing cost of choosing this option in the Big Bang case: imagine a world in which MOF would take credit and full charge over the reforms as in the past as the organizer of bureauplural-ism, and contrast it to the real world, in which Prime Minister Hashimoto put his government at stake with this proposal, presenting it as his own. While MOF's political influence was considerably weakened by the Housing Loan and other financial scandals, and was thus potentially vulnerable to the industries' defiance as expressed through lobbying of the LDP, one can easily see that industry actors would have had a much

---

[34] This may be important as well in understanding why the deliberative councils were able to come up with the reform plan in less than a year in the Big Bang. It is not hard to see that the prime minister needed considerable results within a tangible amount of time.

harder chance trying to challenge a program that was a pillar of the prime minister's political agenda.[35]

To say the above is not to deny that there was important variation in how much change was brought about as a result of this political leadership. Both private industry and bureaucratic actors mattered—especially in the area of insurance, where reforms seem to have been most effectively opposed. Variation could be seen in two respects. First, the attitudes toward liberalization adopted by industry actors representing different services varied. That is, we observed a range of attitudes, from acceptance, to acquiescence, to opposition. Because the banking industry as a whole was expected to reap the most benefits from reform, it was quite natural that banks would not object to the reforms but would instead accept them. There was a large difference between the reaction by the securities and insurance industries, however. While the two industries were in agreement in their rejection of bank entry into their areas of business, the insurance industry was much more vocal in raising its opposition against the measures outlined in the Big Bang Initiative, while the securities firms sought to acquiesce to liberalization and procure maximum compensation.

Second, variation was seen in positions adopted by the bureaucratic entities in charge of the reforms, with that in charge of insurance standing out from the rest. The Banking Bureau, hit by various scandals and policy failures, vowed to depart from its traditional style of administration,[36] while the Securities Bureau was very eager to proceed with the Big Bang under its head and ardent advocate of reform, Atsushi Naganoan. Meanwhile, the Insurance Department was reluctant to initiate drastic reforms that would jeopardize the status quo in the industry. During the US–Japan Insurance Talks, there was even a scene in which Eisuke Sakakibara (the head of the International Finance Bureau and advocate of foreign exchange reforms) advised the Insurance Department to liberate itself from the insurance industry's influence.[37] Industry actors, however, under the encouragement of the Department, went on to make unsuccessful

[35] Evidence suggests that MOF was aware of this benefit of having the prime minister as the leader of the reforms. Tahara (1998) notes how Nagano emphasized Hashimoto's involvement in his interview, being reluctant to become too conspicuous as the initiator of the Big Bang.

[36] For the planning of the Big Bang in Phase I, however, the Banking Bureau appears to have been less enthusiastic than Securities and International Finance Bureaus, headed by Nagano and Sakakibara. See Chapter 5. Nevertheless, once it was decided that the Big Bang would be launched, the Bureau was much more willing to advance the deregulation, compared with the Insurance Division. Interview with Eisuke Sakakibara, January 27, 2000.

[37] This episode confirms the internal division within MOF, mentioned in Chapter 5, between those who advocated drastic reforms and those who sought to proceed as in the past, in close cooperation with the industries.

political lobbying efforts to thwart the unwanted liberalization of the insurance sector (Asahi Shimbun 1997: 65–72). This reluctance to move forward with reform may have been reflected in the nature of discussions at the IC, slowing the pace of the liberalization in the insurance sector.

Yet, even the insurance sector could not override the decision to place a 2001 deadline on implementation or the decision to permit entry of banks into the insurance sector. The fact that the Big Bang was part of the prime minister's main political agenda seems to have counted more than the concerted efforts by bureaucrats and industry actors to slow down the reforms.[38] Thus, the fact that the Initiative was not bureaucracy-led but instead led by politicians raised considerably the hurdles for the regulated industries to carry out effective opposition at a more comprehensive level.

However, it is not impossible to successfully oppose a policy proposal made by the prime minister. Coalitions internal or external to the LDP sometimes overrode prime ministerial initiatives in the past. For example, a number of prime ministers experienced failure in the 1970s and 1980s in their attempts to introduce a system of indirect taxation.

Importantly, the Initiative launched under the political leadership of Hashimoto also enjoyed widespread public support over the more gradual alternatives that followed the patterns of past reforms. Hashimoto put forward the Initiative after winning the 1996 elections with a campaign pledge for reforms. When the reform plan was criticized, the reasons given tended to be because liberalization was seen as not far-reaching or rapid enough, or because the scope of reforms was perceived as too limited; for the most part, the reform plan was not criticized for potentially jeopardizing the stability of the financial order. Efforts by the regulated industries to slow down the pace of reforms were criticized by the media as "egotistic" and as actions taken with "disregard for consumers."[39]

On top of this came the scandals. In addition to the Housing Loan and other financial scandals dragging down the banking sector's political influence in 1996, the heads of DKB and Nomura Securities were being investigated—and were eventually arrested—for the racketeering scandals from March 1997 on. This all occurred just as the deliberation over the Big Bang reforms was taking place at the MOF councils. As the involvement of the

---

[38] Several representatives of the insurance industry made arguments to postpone banks' entry until after 2001 and to drop insurance from the Big Bang reforms from the discussion topic of the Insurance Council. Asahi Shimbun (1997) reports that Sakakibara pressured the Insurance Division into accepting a full-scale liberalization, emphasizing at times that the Big Bang, including insurance, was the prime minister's directive.

[39] See the editorials in Asahi Shimbun (November 13, 1996, February 19, 1997, and June 15, 1997). Also see *Yomiuri Shimbun* (June 14, 1997).

other top three securities firms became clear, the securities industry was in no position to wield great political influence as it had in the past, even if it wished to do. In this atmosphere, it would have been impossible to build a coalition among lawmakers, within or outside the LDP.[40]

Moreover, apart from the difficulties private industry actors faced in building a political coalition in opposition to reforms, a campaign to reverse the reforms would also have posed risks to the profits (and hence the chance of survival) of those firms that dared to participate. Industry actors had good reasons to avoid being labeled a "public enemy," especially for those banks and securities firms which were hurt by the waves of scandals, as campaigning towards forestalling the reforms while the firms' directors were being arrested would inevitably have raised the ire of the public, and damaged business. The racketeering scandals of 1997–98 demonstrated that the scandals negatively impacted firm business, as the public made its discontent known through their choice of firms. DKB, Nomura Securities, and other firms involved saw their businesses severely affected.[41]

The scandals in finance reinforced the notion of inevitability—that is, the notion that there was "no going back." Thus, the scandals raised the costs of pursuing more gradual alternatives to the Big Bang—associated in the mind of the public with the reform of financial administration, including reform of the MOF. In the wake of the racketeering scandals, the "free, fair, and global" principles of the Big Bang came to be professed in newspaper editorials as the necessary conditions for the revival of the obsolete Japanese market into a transparent, efficient market on a par with its European and American rivals (Asahi Shimbun May 21, 1997). The MOF wining and dining scandals further reinforced the need for a drastic departure from the current methods of financial administration: In this way, MOF reforms and the Big Bang were seen to go hand-in-hand. The logic was that eliminating discretion in financial administration—and basing financial regulation instead on the "free, fair, and global" principles of the Big Bang—was necessary to prevent the recurrence of such scandals (*Asahi Shimbun* March 8, 1998). In this environment, it would have been very

[40] The intensity of public criticism is shown in such editorials as the ones in Asahi Shimbun. See the issues of May 21, 1997 for the DKB, and March 8, 1997 and May 31, 1997 for Nomura Securities. The Big Bang was expected to be supported by the LDP's electoral rivals such as the Liberal and Democratic parties, as these parties were strongly pushing for administrative reforms and deregulation.

[41] As noted earlier, the DKB was the only large city bank whose household deposits declined in June 1997—a month in which all the other large city banks saw their household deposits increase significantly. The top three securities suffered from a loss of business from national and local governments, as well as from individual clients.

hard for anyone to argue against the Big Bang without being characterized as an advocate for the preservation of the old financial system—one symbolized by the convoy system, which came to be discredited by the financial crisis and vilified with the eruption of scandals.

Conclusion: The Big Bang as a Reflection of Victory by the "Political Winners"

In concluding the chapter, we return to the two types of political movements that might be seen as generating economic reforms: interest group politics and public interest politics. Recall that in the former, economic actors induce political actors to pass reforms through the provision of goods and services; in the latter, reforms come about when political actors act independently of organized interests and are motivated by political gains seen to accrue through the promotion of the public interest. This chapter has shown that although the regulated industries wielded some influence over the pace of the reforms, the more important elements of the Big Bang reforms such as timing, scope, and sequence, fit the category of public interest politics. This was true not only in Phase I (the planning phase leading up to November 1996), but also in Phase II (post-November 1996).

It was not the regulated industries' wishes but the calculations of state actors such as the LDP and MOF that won out in the end. Thus, we conclude that the Big Bang as a whole was a case of economic reforms where public interest politics overrode interest group politics. In other words, the political considerations of state actors rather than the economic consideration of the regulated industries drove the Big Bang.

In the next chapter, we use the fall 1998 Financial Diet to assess whether developments observed in the Big Bang may be seen as representative of a more permanent evolution of bureaupluralism in financial politics today.

7

New Developments in Bureaupluralism: Comparing and Contrasting the Big Bang to the 1998 "Financial Diet"

In this chapter, we ask what the Big Bang case allows us to say about the policymaking process of bureaupluralism. We begin by reformulating our findings in the last two chapters on the new developments in bureaupluralism. We then consider our observations in light of what has arguably been the other most prominent reform effort in financial politics in recent years: the Financial Diet of 1998. In this session of the Diet that focused on resolution of the bad loan crisis in the banking system, legislation was enacted to provide for a massive injection of public funds into the banking system, to establish a plan utilizing a bridge bank to deal with bank failures, and to completely separate financial policymaking from fiscal policymaking. We then proceed from this case study to derive our main empirical contention regarding financial politics: in the post-1993 world of coalition governments and volatility in the governing party, the emergence of financial crisis out of performance failures and scandals provides a setting in which public support determines political behavior in financial policymaking. How our findings in financial politics can be integrated into this claim, and how the claim applies to each set of actors (politicians, bureaucrats, and regulated industry actors[1]) is then examined. Finally, we contrast our explanation with alternative explanations, focusing in particularly on the electoral rational choice explanation that contends that the voting public matters—a claim not unlike our own.

[1] In this chapter, we use "regulated industry actors" interchangeably with "firms and interest groups" (as introduced in Chapter 3).

New Developments in Bureaupluralism Emerging Out of the Financial Big Bang

In Chapter 3, we defined bureaupluralism as "an institution of public policy making in which policies are produced through the inter- and intra-industrial bargaining presided over by the ministerial bureaus in charge, which engage in intra- and inter-ministerial bargaining within the government, with the occasional intervention by the LDP lawmakers on behalf of the industries." The bargaining of bureaupluralism is carried out through arenas such as deliberative councils and the LDP PARC and through closed-door negotiations among bureaucrats, industry actors (often acting through their industrial associations), and often times LDP politicians. Bureaupluralism has been the norm of financial politics, as shown in our three cases of past reforms in Chapter 6, and is not extinct in financial politics; even the Big Bang was a product of bureaupluralism. Nonetheless, new dynamics were also clearly present in the case of the Big Bang reforms. In covering a number of sectors including banking, securities, and insurance, deregulation under the Big Bang gave rise to significant distributional conflict among industry actors. The pattern of conflict resolution that emerged differed from that seen in 1991–93 or in 1979–82, when industry actors worked through this conflict via deliberative councils, with the help of their bureaucratic and political allies, before a master plan for reform emerged. In the case of the Big Bang, reforms emerged as a political initiative of the prime minister, overriding the regulated industries' wishes in a relatively short amount of time (the relevant deliberative councils only took seven months to issue their final reports). By examining more closely the stark contrast between policymaking dynamics surrounding the Big Bang reforms and policymaking dynamics underlying earlier financial reform efforts, we find six interrelated developments that affect the previously stable policymaking mechanism of bureaupluralism.

1. *The Big Bang was a case of economic reforms carried out under the guise of "public interest politics" rather than "interest group politics."* The Big Bang was carried out as part of the drive of state actors to procure public support rather than as part of the drive of industry efforts to influence the reforms to their benefit through the exchange of goods and services with state actors.

2. *The MOF and the LDP began to develop an alternative mechanism of policy-making to bureaupluralism, bypassing the LDP PARC and deliberative councils. A rise in the roles played by LDP members in financial policymaking*

apart from the traditional PARC–MOF interactions reflected the declining role of the MOF as the "organizer" of political bargains. In devising the Big Bang and MOF reforms, suborganizational actors within MOF and the LDP bypassed the policymaking mechanism of bureaupluralism, such as the deliberative councils or the LDP PARC, relying instead on such organizations as the WT (Working Team) within MOF and the LDP ARPH. Such suborganizational actors came to command the behavior of their respective organizations, as their positions were deemed by the members of these organizations to be most conducive to organizational survival (the ultimate goal shared by all members) within the context of public animosity toward their organizations in the wake of the scandals that commenced in 1995.

In some fields, such as taxation, the LDP PARC was known to wield a large influence over the substance of reform measures; yet, even in such cases, the LDP did not come up with concrete plans but rather, left the details to be largely worked out by bureaucrats. This was true, for example, in the case of taxation, where details were left to the MOF's Tax Bureau to work out.[2] However, reflecting MOF's loss of standing as the "organizer" in the policymaking process, the LDP ARPH had been planning its version of the Big Bang independently of MOF and the LDP PARC, even utilizing a detailed time schedule. An LDP lawmaker once remarked that the reason for bypassing the PARC was that LDP PARC sub-divisions on finance were uninterested in any reforms.[3]

3. *State actors kept the involvement of regulated industry actors in the planning phase to a minimum, in anticipation of opposition from these actors.* These industry actors first had an opportunity to speak out about the reform plan when the prime minister publicly announced the plan. Consequently, special interests were prevented from crushing the plan before its presentation to the public.

4. *The reform package was presented as one of the pillars of the prime minister's policy platform and attracted more public support than the gradual reform alternatives, thus raising the costs to industry of opposition, particularly since these industries were ridden with scandals themselves.* The Big Bang was a plan not only supported, but also led, by the prime minister. Consequently, industry actors faced difficulty in raising effective and comprehensive opposition through forming a coalition within the LDP, as they had in past reforms. The cost of opposition was raised further by the fact that the Big

[2] See Kato (1994).   [3] Author interview.

Bang proposal was more popular than its more gradual reform alternatives. Financial scandals and financial crisis had discredited the former convoy system of financial regulation, making it clear that a break from the past was necessary.

5. *MOF lost its standing as the organizer of policymaking bargains, due to its regulatory failures and scandals. An important factor that differentiated the Big Bang reform from the 1991 to 1993 reforms was that MOF was unable to claim any credit for the reforms if the reform proposals were to be supported by the public.* MOF increasingly lost political influence from 1995 on because of the Housing Loan scandal, Daiwa bond trading scandal, and other regulatory failures and scandals. MOF did not lose its standing entirely, however. The deliberative councils in Phase II were organized by MOF as in the past; besides, our earlier discussion showed that MOF was very much involved on the whole in developing the Hashimoto Initiative. However, from a comparative perspective, the contrast between policymaking dynamics in the early 1990s and in the latter 1990s is stark. *As late as 1991–93, MOF was clearly the initiator and manager of reforms and this fact was taken for granted under the stable system of bureaupluralism. If bureaupluralism remained intact in the period leading up to the Big Bang, then we would have similarly assumed a prominent role for MOF in formulating the Initiative.*

MOF officials faced a dilemma at this time. While the financial reforms were launched to re-coup public trust, the ministry could claim little credit for the reforms. The scandal-ridden ministry's support of the reforms would only have raised the public's scrutiny of the reforms and jeopardized their viability by leaving them vulnerable to political objection. Thus, MOF officials repeatedly disavowed ownership of the reforms, and instead sought to credit Hashimoto with their inception.[4] That MOF tried to efface itself behind the political initiative marked an important departure from the past and symbolized a lack of consensus that MOF was the appropriate planner and organizer of financial reforms.

6. *MOF and the LDP were cooperating, competing, and coming into conflict in the process of financial policy. This contrasted with the past, when an LDP–MOF alliance was the prevailing norm. The LDP was willing to sacrifice its ties with MOF to cope with the electoral threats in the post-1993 world.* In the Housing Loan Affair, the LDP cooperated with MOF as it had in the past, as one of the ruling parties responsible for the policy proposals planned by the bureaucracy. This reflected a pattern of continuity with the pre-1993 days

---

[4] See the Nagano interview in Tahara (1998) mentioned in Chapter 5.

of one-party dominance. Yet, in the Big Bang, the LDP ARPH competed with MOF in the planning of financial reforms. After LDP President Hashimoto launched the plan, the LDP cooperated with MOF on the issue. In the MOF reforms, the LDP ARPH pursued MOF's breakup, in the face of opposition by the MOF and its LDP allies. This confusion may be explained by the LDP's pursuit of survival in the post-1993 world, in which coalition governments and constant threats of electoral replacement were the new reality. The LDP chose to ally with MOF in many policy areas as it had in the past. Yet, the party's coalition with the Social Democrats and Sakigake pushed the LDP to favor MOF breakup. When the rival parties were campaigning for the popular agenda of reforms in the face of the October 1996 elections, the LDP chose to incorporate its rivals' platforms to pursue survival. In doing so, it sacrificed MOF's organizational integrity for this goal and thereby potentially jeopardized its ties with MOF—long nurtured through close cooperation in such fields as public works. This strategy worked, as the LDP was rewarded with electoral victory in October 1996.

Comparing and Contrasting the Big Bang with the Fall 1998 "Financial Diet"

Were the aforementioned developments unique to the Big Bang? And, is the disruption of the previous stability in bureaupluralism an ephemeral phenomenon or something more permanent? It is too early to tell with certainty. The Big Bang is the most recent case we have that involves financial reforms with distributive effects among industries. For the purpose of speculation, however, we turn now to extend our scope of analysis to another case, holding as many factors constant as possible to preserve the effectiveness of our comparative analysis.

An examination of policymaking dynamics surrounding the so-called Financial Diet, which took place in the fall of 1998 and focused on addressing the bad debt problems in the banking sector, allows us to verify whether our findings are valid in financial politics after 1995. Not only is the bad debt problem in banking closely connected to the Big Bang (and reforms in the MOF as well) but this case also enables us to contrast our observations from the case study of the Big Bang with regard to the relationship among MOF, LDP, and financial industry actors in the post-1993 world. This interplay of actors was made even more complex in the case of the Financial Diet because of the emergence of new opposition parties—most notably, the Democratic, Heiwa-Kaikaku, and Liberal parties. With the LDP's loss of its majority in the Upper House in July 1998, a reform bill could only pass in the Diet through cooperation between these parties.[5]

In 1998, the government formulated successive measures to cope with deepening financial crisis. In February 1998, the government enacted legislation to inject up to 30 trillion yen of public funds into the banking system.[6] In March 1998, approximately 1.8 trillion yen was injected into the large banks to strengthen their capital bases. The ruling coalition at this time, comprised of the LDP, the SDPJ and the Sakigake Party, worked with the government to set up the Committee for the Promotion of the Revitalization of Finance. Under this committee, the government and the LDP worked on a "total plan" to resolve the bad debt problem. The plan included measures to address the slumping real estate market through the accelerated disposal of real estate held as collateral for bad debt, since the decline of the real estate market was perceived to be at the root of the bad debt problem. The total plan[7] also included a bridge bank plan.[8] Although details of the plan were made public in June and July 1998, the financial crisis persisted through the summer of 1998. The LDP lost the Upper House elections in July 1998, Hashimoto resigned, and Keizo Obuchi was elected LDP President in a three-way race, succeeding Hashimoto as prime minister.

The extraordinary Diet session[9] in the fall of 1998 has often been referred to since as the "Financial Diet," since much of the session centered on legislative measures to resolve the financial crisis, which erupted in late 1997 and lasted through this time. Based on the "total plan" devised over the summer, the government submitted six bills to the Diet in August 1998. Among these were bills intended to accelerate the disposal of real estate, the most important source of the bad loans, and bills to introduce a bridge bank plan.

In this section, we give a narrative of the politics surrounding the Financial Diet, dividing developments into two stages and focusing on measures occupying the center stage of policy discussions. First, we

[5] See also Amyx (2000 [and 2004]) for a discussion of the Financial Diet.

[6] Thirteen trillion yen was for strengthening the capital base of operating banks, and seventeen trillion yen was for resolving the failed banks' bad debts. These were "ceilings" for government guarantee on loans: the actual expenditure was initially 1.8 trillion yen, as stated below. See Chapter 6.

[7] For the content of the Total Plan, see *Kin'yu Zaisei Jijo*, July 13, 1998.

[8] A bridge bank is a quasi-public bank which would take up the performing loans of a failed banking institution. Bridge banks are set up so as to prevent massive bankruptcies of borrowing firms who relied on loans of failed banks.

[9] Regular Diet sessions are held from January to June, with session extensions possible. Other sessions are called Temporary Sessions, except for the Special Sessions, which are convened immediately following an election following the dissolution of the Lower House.

examine the August–September 1996 period, when debate focused on revitalization of the banking sector. Second, we turn to the October 1996 period, when the focus of debate was on recapitalization of the banking sector. We then compare our observations from the past two chapters against our findings about the policymaking dynamics surrounding the Financial Diet.

Revitalization of the Banking Sector (August–September 1998)

The opposition, consisting of the Democrats, the Liberals, and the Heiwa-Kaikaku Party,[10] joined together with the LDP Young Turks (see below), to dominate the political debate in this stage. The central issue at hand was a policy proposal to replace the February 1996 recapitalization scheme (a scheme that injected public funds into operating banks) with a "revitalization" scheme (a scheme to inject public funds into banks near failure by first forcing their closure).

The opposition jointly submitted a counter-proposal in September 1996. The bills submitted by the opposition included the following measures[11]:

1. The finalization of MOF organizational reforms. This included the creation of the Financial Revitalization Committee (FRC) as an independent committee with a cabinet minister as its head, to assume full control over financial policymaking until 2001, when Hashimoto's administrative reforms would then be carried out and a Financial Services Agency created. The FSA, created in June 1998, was also to be subsumed, as was the MOF's financial planning powers.

2. The introduction of a scheme for the legal liquidation of failed banks, including a system of financial administrators with special power over the process, and temporary nationalization in cases in which the functioning of the financial system was endangered. Provisions also included abolishing the plan created in February 1998 for the injection of public funds into operating banks.

3. The establishment of a Resolution and Collection Corporation (RCC), a government-backed asset management corporation modeled after the Resolution and Trust Corporation established by the US government in the midst of that country's Savings and Loan Crisis in

[10] This was the Upper House arm of the Komeito party, traditionally a powerful opposition party since the 1960s: Komeito itself was merged into the Shinshinto party between 1994 and 1997.

[11] For details, see *Kin'yu Zaisei Jijo*, September 14, 1998. Also see Sakakibara (2000, chapter 4).

the 1980s. This organization would be established through the merger of the Resolution and Collection Bank and Housing Loan Administration Corporation, entities set up in 1995–96 for the resolution of bad debt held by smaller financial institutions and for the disposal of failed housing and loan companies. The newly established RCC would purchase non-performing loans from failed financial institutions.

A month of intense negotiations ensued in the Diet between the LDP and the opposition. One of the main issues was the future of the Long-Term Credit Bank of Japan (LTCB). The bank stood on the verge of failure, as its stock price approached zero as a result of a severe speculative attack.[12] The opposition sought forced nationalization of the bank, while the LDP pushed instead for recapitalization, thereby avoiding its shutdown. Another issue of contention was the creation of the FRC, which would finalize the separation of financial regulatory powers from MOF. Here the LDP was divided, as it had been in earlier stages of MOF reform (see Chapter 5), with some party members willing to accept the creation of this new entity while others opposed its creation. The LDP faced a time constraint imposed by diplomatic concerns, however: the prime minister felt he could not visit the United States without a deal, and his visit was scheduled for September 20, 1998. Although the LDP could have forced its way in the Lower House, it still would have faced difficulty getting the bills passed in the Upper House. Thus, the party needed to make a deal with at least part of the opposition (*Kin'yu Zaisei Jijo* September 21, 1998).

Intense negotiation between the LDP and the opposition—particularly with the Democrats—ensued. The MOF's involvement in the process progressively decreased after August 1998.[13] Within the LDP, a number of junior lawmakers with expertise in finance, including Yasuhisa Shiozaki and Nobuteru Ishihara,[14] began to take the initiative, handling negotiations with the Democratic Party, independently from the party decision-making bodies such as the PARC and its sub-divisions. In the heat of the debate, these "Young Turks" would even openly confront influential party leaders such as the heads of PARC and the Diet Affairs Committee.[15]

---

[12] The intensity of the speculative attack was aided by the diffusion of rumors and the fact that Japan lacked an effective regulatory framework to guard against speculative attacks. See Takeuchi (1999) and Sakakibara (2000).

[13] This did not mean that MOF abandoned its efforts to influence outcomes; such efforts continued. However, the ministry did lose control over the course of the events. Author interview with Yasuhisa Shiozaki, July 6, 1999.

[14] Ishihara headed the PARC's sub-division in finance during the Housing Loan Affairs.

[15] This paragraph draws heavily on a personal interview with Yasuhisa Shiozaki (July 6, 1999).

Shiozaki, one of the main participants in this process, later credited the loss of the LDP majority in the Upper House elections as a major factor making this situation possible.[16] On the Democratic Party's side, young lawmakers with legal and/or financial expertise (including Yukio Edano, Yoshio Sengoku, and Motohisa Ikeda) drafted their own counter-proposal without the help of the bureaucratic agencies (such as MOF and the Cabinet Legislation Bureau), resulting in a completely independent enactment process from the bureaucracy (Amyx 2000 [and 2004]).

The LDP under its leader, Prime Minister Obuchi, decided to "fully swallow" (*marunomi*), or fully accept, the opposition's plans, while some among the opposition agreed to spare the LTCB from forced nationalization.[17] A deal was made in a meeting of the heads of the LDP, the Democrats, and the Heiwa-Kaikaku Party on September 18, 1998, two days before Obuchi's scheduled US visit.

Recapitalization (October 1998)

Before Obuchi's US visit, things looked as if the opposition and the LDP Young Turks had their way over the LDP mainstream on financial issues— that is, over the "tribesmen" (*zoku*) gathered around the LDP PARC and its financial sub-divisions. The revitalization or forced nationalization scheme seemed destined to replace the recapitalization scheme of February 1998. However, the economic environment surrounding the Japanese financial system changed in two important ways during September and October 1998, significantly affecting the course of policy debate.

First, by this time the Asian financial crisis, which had broken out in 1997, had evolved into a global financial crisis. Over the summer of 1998, the crisis first spread to Russia and then to Brazil and other nations in Latin America. In the United States, a major hedge fund nearly collapsed, only to be rescued by a major package organized by the Federal Reserve Bank of New York in September 1998. Given this crisis situation, the United States shifted its stance on Japanese financial policies, abandoning its support for a "public funds injection only with strict conditions attached" for a "public funds injection at all costs to save the global financial system from collapse." US government officials conveyed this shift in policy stance to Prime Minister Obuchi during his September visit. The Group of Seven (G7) also issued a joint statement on October 4, 1998, strongly pressing for

---

[16] Yasuhisa Shiozaki, speech delivered at Stanford University on May 3, 1999.

[17] Later in October 1998, however, LTCB liabilities were found to exceed the bank's debt, and thus the LTCB was nationalized under the newly introduced plan.

an injection of public funds *prior to* bank failures. Second, on October 5, 1998, the Nikkei stock price index dived down past the 13,000 mark, and the stock price of many large city banks plunged to within the vicinity of 100 yen. The financial system was near collapse. Given this crisis situation, many people, including leading economic figures, campaigned for the introduction of a recapitalization scheme involving the pre-failure injection of public funds (Sakakibara 2000, chapter 4).[18]

These environmental changes—the shift in the US stance and the deepening of the crisis—may have had a strong impact on the political debate. The LDP financial mainstream (led by such lawmakers as Yukihiko Ikeda) regained control over the policy debate from the LDP Young Turks. Heiwa-Kaikaku switched sides in the beginning of October 1998, as did the Liberals, breaking down the unified opposition front against the LDP. In this process, MOF regained its influence, although its presence was kept invisible, due to severe public criticism lingering as a result of its wining and dining scandals.[19]

As a result, the recapitalization plan passed in the Diet on October 16, 1998, following the passage of the revitalization scheme on October 12. The following sets of bills emerged:

1. Revitalization bills, consisting primarily of the opposition's proposal (see above) with some modifications.[20] The addition of an eighteen trillion yen ceiling on the government guarantee raised the total amount of public funds available for this purpose to thirty-five trillion yen.

2. The so-called "early strengthening" bills, a bank recapitalization plan based on the LDP proposal. The plan included recapitalization of banks via the RCC's acquisition of common and preferred stocks, upon application by undercapitalized banks.[21] It also included the establishment of a government guarantee ceiling of twenty-five trillion yen for this purpose.

---

[18] This paragraph draws largely on Sakakibara (2000, chapter 4) and an author interview with Shiozaki on January 27, 2000.

[19] Sakakibara described the new approach as the "whisper" approach (Author interview, January 27, 2000). Shiozaki did not deny that there were numerous instances of contact with MOF officials throughout the process, but emphasized the independence of the policymaking process (Personal interview on July 6, 2000).

[20] For example, while the opposition sought to integrate all financial powers into the FRC, including supervisory powers residing in Agriculture and other ministries, the compromise that emerged limited to what used to be under MOF's jurisdiction (*Kin'yu Zaisei Jijo* October 5, 1998).

[21] Note that in February 1998, the acquisition of common stocks was avoided because it was thought at that time that the government's intervention into banks' management ought to be avoided. This time, government's involvement in bank management was explicitly introduced.

Assessing the Power of Alternative Explanations

We now posit our observations about the new developments in bureaupluralism against the preceding narrative. Our key contentions, again, are that the Big Bang was a case of economic reforms driven by "public interest politics" rather than by "interest group politics," and that state actors kept the involvement of regulated industry actors in the planning phase to a minimum, in anticipation of their opposition.

Very little surrounding the Financial Diet points to the effective influence of regulated industry actors. The LTCB, whose survival was in the hands of politicians, had little to say in the process—even though we might expect firms in distress to do whatever possible to prevent their ruin. The banking industry was by no means in control of the heated political debate among the opposition, the LDP Young Turks, and the LDP financial mainstream. Instead, the LDP and the opposition sought to enhance their respective standings by emerging as the ones credited with resolving the financial crisis. MOF and the LDP also began to develop an alternative mechanism of policymaking to bureaupluralism, bypassing the LDP PARC and the deliberative councils. In particular, reflecting the decline of MOF as the "organizer" of political bargains in finance, there was a rise in the prominence of policymaking in financial politics *within* the LDP, apart from policymaking interactions between the LDP PARC and MOF.

The development of an alternative policymaking mechanism to the LDP PARC and the deliberative councils was notable in this process. The newly established *ad hoc* committees in the LDP and the government gave birth to the "total plan."[22] In September 1998, the involvement of the PARC dwindled as the negotiations progressed, for the Young Turks with expertise in finance took the initiative in negotiating with the Democrats. The deliberative councils were nowhere to be seen: MOF involvement, if any, was minimized during the first stage ("revitalization"), and its presence in the second stage ("recapitalization") was low profile, unlike in the past.

The reform package was also presented as one of the pillars of the political program of the prime minister, attracting public support over its gradual alternatives, and thus highly raising the costs of opposition from the industries, ridden with scandals themselves. The financial legislation was the main program for the new Obuchi government; however, this did not prevent the opposition from raising a counter-proposal, which seemed

---

[22] The great involvement of MITI in the planning of "total plans" serves as another piece of evidence that the jurisdiction of bureaucratic agencies under bureaupluralism has become increasingly blurred.

to receive support from the public and the market. This observation points to the obvious reality that a political program presented by the prime minister may raise obstacles to intra-party opposition but does not prevent the opposition from raising objections. *What mattered more than the leadership of the prime minister in both the Big Bang and Financial Diet was public support for whatever measures were presented.*

MOF also lost its standing as the organizer of the bargains, due to its policy failures and scandals. An important difference between the 1991–93 reforms and the Big Bang reforms was that MOF could not claim credit at all if the reform proposals were to be supported by the public. MOF and the LDP were moreover cooperating, competing, and coming into conflict in financial policymaking, unlike in the past where a cooperative alliance was more the norm. The LDP was willing to sacrifice its ties with MOF in coping with the electoral threats of the post-1993 world.

Finally, MOF did not act as the organizer of financial politics during the Financial Diet of 1998. As a result of the deepening financial crisis and the wining and dining scandals in early 1998, which involved arrests of MOF officials for bribery, MOF nearly lost control over financial policymaking: discussions. In stark contrast to the process of MOF reforms in 1996, it had very little control over the establishment of the FRC, which would seal its organizational breakup.

However, MOF did not completely lose its grip over financial policymaking. As Sakakibara (2000) implies, MOF may have had a role in influencing the policy discussion at the G7 as well as a role in bringing about the shift in the US stance in the second stage of Financial Diet negotiations. In these cases, the ministry worked with the LDP finance zoku while maintaining a low profile. Nevertheless, even while retaining influence, the ministry exercised it through channels other than the traditional channels of bureaupluralism. In other words, the conduit of influence was not the Banking Bureau or its affiliated deliberative councils. Moreover, as in the Big Bang, MOF retreated from its former lead role in financial policymaking, pursuing instead a strategy of maintaining a low profile. Again, this differed sharply from the traditional policymaking dynamics of bureaupluralism seen in 1991–93 and earlier periods when MOF was assumed to be in charge.

Some members of the LDP, such as the head of the PARC at the time—Yukihiko Ikeda, an ex-MOF official—were not keen on the creation of the FRC or the definitive breakup of MOF that the FRC's creation symbolized. Yet, the Young Turks within the LDP were willing to cooperate with the Democrats, who strongly advocated the breakup. The LDP Young Turks and the Democrats clearly competed with MOF in regard to financial policymaking, and they confronted MOF on the creation of the FRC and other measures (such as the measures taken vis-à-vis the LTCB). The Democrats consciously bypassed MOF in their planning of the reform package.[23] While the Young Turks in the LDP cooperated with MOF during the summer, they became increasingly alienated from the ministry thereafter. Accordingly, MOF became increasingly excluded from the policy process during the first stage of the Financial Diet.

Prime Minister Obuchi decided to fully swallow the opposition's plans, including the creation of the FRC. This mimicked the strategy observed before the 1996 elections of incorporating the reform agenda of the Liberals and Democrats. In another instance in January 1998, a leader of Sakigake deplored the flexibility of the LDP on the issue of breaking up the MOF, which prevented his party, the junior coalition partner, from distinguishing itself from the LDP. The LDP was said to "do anything to preserve its rule," and was compared to a mollusk by its critics for its willingness to compromise policy matters so as to keep a hold on power. "How can one confront such a party?" some asked, in frustration (*Asahi Shimbun* February 28, 1998).

In the Financial Diet, the strategy of fully swallowing opposition proposals appeared to work once again. The Democrats, while having their plans successfully adopted as part of the financial revitalization scheme despite their standing as the opposition, failed to cash in on this success. This may be due, in part, to the fact that the Democrats lost control over the process in October 1998, as suggested. This loss of control was reflected in the voting behavior of the Democrats in October 1998. The Democrats voted for the first set of bills having to do with financial revitalization, but opposed the second set of bills passed in this month, which pertained to recapitalization. Later, their head, Naoto Kan, would admit that his strategy in the Financial Diet of "responsible opposition," which involved cooperating with the ruling government when the need arose, failed to boost his party's public support. Obuchi cruised into office and his approval rates rose over time as the economic and financial crisis receded. The legacy of the Financial Diet was that the LDP, seeking to avoid the embarrassment of another total concession—such as the one made in September 1998—opted thereafter to build a solid coalition. In January 1999, the party reached out to the Liberals, forming a coalition government. The coalition was enlarged to include the Komeito (known as the Heiwa-Kaikaku Party in the Upper House) later in the year.

[23] See Amyx (2000 [and 2004]).

New Patterns in Financial Policymaking

The above demonstrates that the new developments in bureaupluralism observed in the Big Bang case were also present in the case of the Financial Diet. Thus, the changes in policymaking dynamics observed in the Big Bang were neither unique nor ephemeral. Rather, they represent a new trend in financial politics, observable since 1995. Below we offer a more generalized version of the changes in bureaupluralism in financial politics, in light of the developments surrounding the 1998 Financial Diet.

1. *Public interest politics now dominates financial politics.* Political actors seek to institute reforms that equate with the public interest in their quest for public support. The influence by regulated industries on political actors and on the reform outcomes are weak compared with the past, and are increasingly peripheral in the planning of economic reforms. This fact is largely due to the availability of alternative policymaking processes (see below).

2. *Alternative policymaking processes to bureaupluralism are now in place: the LDP PARC and the deliberative councils play less important roles as forums in which the substance of the policy proposals are decided.* It is not that the organs of bureaupluralism no longer function; the LDP PARC remains a decision-making body through which all measures must pass to obtain party approval, and MOF and the FSA runs deliberative councils to devise plans regarding the future of finance. However, many *ad hoc* arrangements have sprung up to displace such institutionalized organizations and now serve as the arenas in which the substance of the reforms tends to be decided. The LDP ARPH, the three-party coalition's WP on MOF reforms, the MOF's WT on the Big Bang, the committees in the LDP and the government that worked on the "total plans," and the LDP Young Turks in the Financial Diet all testify that the policymaking process of bureaupluralism has lessened in importance in financial politics.

3. *MOF lost its standing as the organizer of bureaupluralism as a result of a series of policy failures and scandals.* MOF was involved in a variety of policy failures and scandals, losing political influence as these events unraveled. In the Big Bang and the second stage of the Financial Diet, the ministry could not claim credit for playing the role of planner. In the first stage of the Financial Diet, its involvement in the policy planning process was minimal.

4. *Political initiatives displaced bureaucratic initiatives in financial politics.* This point follows from the preceding point, as politicians filled the vacuum created by the departure of the bureaucracy. Hashimoto's political leadership and MOF's self-effacement, served as a contrast to the situation surrounding

the 1991–93 reforms organized by MOF, and provides evidence for the displacement of MOF by political leaders as the "organizers" of reform initiatives—even though MOF remained largely responsible for the content of reforms. This trend was particularly evident in the first stage of the 1998 Financial Diet, when MOF was kept on the sidelines and negotiations between the LDP and the opposition also determined the content of reforms.

5. *MOF and the LDP today interact strategically with each other, cooperating, competing, and engaging in conflict according to the dictates of organizational survival.* The LDP cooperated with MOF on some issues, as it did in the past with the Housing Loan incident. Yet, it also competed with the ministry in the planning of the Big Bang and in the first stage of the Financial Diet. And, open conflict between the two organizations was starkly evident in negotiations surrounding the MOF reforms. There is no static equilibrium relationship between the two institutional actors today, as each acts to increase its own chances of survival.

Public Support as a Determinant in Financial Politics

The observations about the new developments in bureaupluralism (Table 7.1) lead us to the following claim: *in the post-1993 world of coalition governments and changes of government, with the financial crisis involving performance failures and scandals, public support determines political behavior in financial politics.*

Below, we explain how this claim holds in two ways. First, we demonstrate how the above observations can be integrated into this empirical conclusion. Second, we will examine how it holds among three sets of political actors: the political parties, the bureaucracies, and the regulated industries. Figure 7.1 illustrates the changes in bureaupluralism in financial politics, as explored in this section.

Table 7.1 Observations about the New Developments in Financial Politics

(a) "Public interest politics" is now dominant in financial politics over "interest group politics."
(b) Alternative policymaking processes to bureaupluralism has been developed: the LDP PARC and the deliberative councils have become lessened in importance in their role of being the forums in which the substance of the policy proposals are decided.
(c) MOF lost its standing as the organizer of bureaupluralism as a result of a series of policy failures and scandals.
(d) Political initiatives displaced bureaucratic ones in financial politics.
(e) MOF and the LDP are now in a strategic relationship with each other: they cooperate, compete, and conflict, according to the dictates of the logic of organizational survival.

(1) Financial politics under bureaupluralism (until the 1991–93 reforms)

Bureaupluralism / "Interest Group Politics"

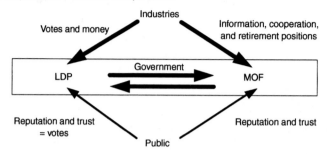

Government = LDP + MOF
Bureaupluralism/Interest Group Politics = LDP + MOF + Industries

(2) New developments in financial politics (1995–)

Changes:
(1) Post-1993 world: coalition governments and changes of government possible
(2) Failures: performance failures (financial crisis) and scandals

Bureaupluralism / "Interest Group Politics"

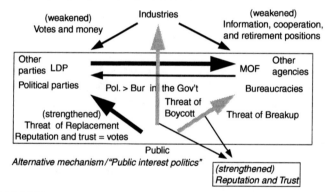

Resulting changes:
a. *political parties displace the bureaucracy*
b. *The Government (= state actors) includes more actors*

Government under Bureaupluralism = LDP + MOF
Government in the new world = LDP + Other Parties + MOF + Other Agencies

c. *Increased inclusiveness in the decision making process*
Bureaupluralism/ Interest Group Politics
$$= LDP + MOF + Industries$$

Alternative Mechanism/ Public Interest Politics
$$= LDP + Other Parties + MOF + Other Agencies + Public$$

Figure 7.1 Politics of financial reforms: before and after a diagram of political input into the government

Note: Economic reforms are produced from the Government as "output." Arrows represent political influence; thickness depicts strength.

Relating the Analytical Claim to Observed Behavior

In the post-1993 world of coalition government and change of governments, the LDP faced a believable threat of replacement by its rivals. Added to this environment was a series of performance failures (policy failures for MOF; bad performance for financial firms) and scandals in finance from 1995, which culminated in a financial crisis in 1997. The latter represented a performance failure for all actors.

MOF was discredited as the legitimate "organizer" of financial policy-making in the public's eyes. This led politicians to displace bureaucrats as the policymakers of economic reforms. The LDP acted strategically towards MOF in the post-1993 world where change of government was a reality. While having close ties with MOF still provided electoral benefits—such as the procurement of public works—the LDP had a higher priority. This priority was fending off rival parties, which sought to cash in on the negative notoriety that the LDP and MOF earned for themselves in the Housing Loan Affair. The process of weighing these two conflicting goals led to an internal rift within the LDP. However, as expected by the logic of survival, those seeking to maximize public support won out, amid an atmosphere of heavy public criticism of MOF.

The regulated industries also attracted widespread public criticism over their role in scandals and the failure of financial firms that came largely as a result of questionable conduct during the bubble period. The political influence of the financial industry thus waned, increasing the importance of other source of political support—most notably, the public.

The public's increased importance vis-à-vis financial institutions strongly influenced the decision to adopt the Big Bang for the LDP, as well as MOF. The LDP faced platforms of drastic reforms—including massive deregulation—from its electoral rivals, while financial institutions were also making important financial contributions to the party. The two conflicting goals of massive deregulation and maintenance of political donations led to an internal rift within the party. Even so, the believable threat of electoral replacement in the post-1993 world spurred the party to adopt the popular reform agenda, via the incorporation of proposals by the opposition. This trend strengthened during the Financial Diet, when the LDP fully swallowed the popular opposition platform.

Meanwhile, MOF faced the outraged public, which sought to dismantle the ministry and thereby threaten its organizational survival—MOF's ultimate priority. MOF had two sets of concerns vis-à-vis the financial institutions it regulated. These firms provided to the MOF such benefits as information, cooperation, and retirement positions. However, drastic reforms to revitalize the financial market, something that would create many "losers" among regulated industry actors, seemed necessary to improve the Japanese economy. MOF chose the latter reform path over the former concern, although the existence of these two conflicting goals did lead to an internal rift within the ministry. Again, in the environment where MOF had to fear for its survival because of heavy public criticism, considerations for the public interest won out over those for the regulated industry actors.

In this way, there were three dimensions of colliding interests: the LDP's strategy towards MOF, the LDP's strategy toward financial firms, and MOF's strategy toward financial firms. In all three cases, an internal rift appeared in the LDP and/or MOF and was resolved by the victory of those who sought to prioritize obtaining greater public support—something deemed essential for survival of the respective organizations. Thus, we see the logic of organizational survival operating in an environment wherein political actors act to re-coup an earlier loss of public support. This behavior, in turn, represents the dominance of public interest politics over constituency or interest group politics.[24]

The rise of alternative policymaking mechanisms to bureaupluralism reflects that MOF has been discredited as the "organizer" of policy deals and displaced by politicians, that the public has displaced the regulated industry actors as the source of political influence, and that the public interest has won out over the interests of the bureaucracy and the regulated industry actors in the process of intra-organization struggle. The deliberative councils were no longer the arenas where MOF presided over the bargaining between financial firms. While politicians displaced MOF in financial policymaking, the LDP PARC—so central to bureaupluralism—was not the one to assume the Initiative. In the internal LDP struggle, the PARC advocated the interests of the regulated firms (and of MOF in the battle surrounding MOF reforms). Other actors in the LDP, such as the LDP ARPH and the Young Turks, eventually gained the upper hand with a more popular agenda of reforms.

Below, we construct a simple typology illustrating the differences between bureaupluralism and the alternative policymaking mechanisms, including the various *ad hoc* arrangements that emerged in financial politics

---

[24] That is, this holds if we view MOF as "constituents" (and thus similar to "regulated industries") in that their organizational interests come into conflict with the "public interest" in MOF reforms.

from 1996. One caveat must be noted here: a single set of policymaking mechanisms has not yet emerged to replace bureaupluralism as an alternative mechanism. Therefore, for the purpose of illuminating the fact that bureaupluralism is no longer the only "rule of the game," we group together the various *ad hoc* arrangements that sprung up outside of bureaupluralism and label them as the "alternative."

Actors central to the two systems clearly differ. MOF stood at the core of bureaupluralism as the organizer of bargaining among the regulated industries; the LDP would occasionally be called in to resolve a conflict between financial firms and the bureaucracy. The public was not without influence on the bureaucracy, as reputation remained important for government agencies; similarly, the public retained influence on politicians through their votes. However, the public was not included in the policymaking process of bureaupluralism for the following reasons: the LDP faced little threat of electoral replacement, the bureaucracy's role as the "organizer" was taken for granted, and the regulated industry actors were guaranteed entry into the policymaking process through the deliberative councils and the LDP PARC, where the consumer public was not well represented. "Bureaupluralism" thus includes the LDP, MOF, and the regulated industries as the central actors, Under this system, the government which produced the economic reforms consisted of the LDP and MOF. Thus, economic reforms under bureaupluralism tended to reflect the domination of interest group politics over public interest politics.

In the alternative policymaking mechanism, the public is included while the regulated industries are excluded. The public exerts considerable influence on the LDP, which faces a credible threat of electoral replacement. MOF, which faces a threat of breakup due to loss of public trust, actively pursues public support. The regulated industries, hit with scandals and financial crisis, also face the threat of a consumer boycott, just as they experienced in the wake of the racketeering scandals. The deliberative councils and the PARC lose prominence as the policymaking forums, reducing the relative importance of the regulated industries' political influence. Politicians and bureaucrats pursue public support rather than seeking to please industry actors. The government includes non-LDP parties. Because the LDP has been removed from office once, non-LDP parties now directly affect the output of economic reforms. This was seen in the way in which Sakigake directly influenced the course of MOF reforms and in the way the Democratic Party influenced legislative outcomes in the Financial Diet. Similarly, the indirect influence of non-LDP parties was evident when the LDP incorporated or co-opted its rivals' platforms into its own, either in coalition with other parties or while remaining in opposition to them.

We may add another new phenomenon: the increased presence of non-MOF agencies in financial politics. MITI played a prominent role in the Big Bang and the formulation of the "total plans," while the FSA shared policy-making power with MOF and possessed financial supervisory power after its creation in 1998. Thus, the "alternative" policymaking mechanism now includes the LDP *and* other parties, MOF *and* other agencies, and the public. The government is now composed of the LDP, other Parties, MOF, and other government agencies. With the rise of alternative policymaking mechanisms, public interest politics rather than interest group politics now serves as the primary determinant of financial policy outcomes; meanwhile, within the government, the political parties displace bureaucratic agencies as actors taking the policymaking initiative.

We reiterate that bureaupluralism has not disappeared in the new world. After all, bureaupluralism clearly reared its head in Phase II of the Big Bang. And, as of 2004, deliberative councils and the PARC continue to function as decision-making bodies.[25] Thus, it is more appropriate to visualize this new trend as an *addition* of potential alternative mechanisms of policymaking, and *not* necessarily *as a replacement*. In other words, bureaupluralism is no longer the only rule of the game in producing economic reforms. The new world is one in which bureaupluralism and alternative policymaking mechanisms coexist or overlap.

Relating the Analytical Claim to each Set of Actors

Next, how does our claim that public support matters pertain to politicians, bureaucrats, and the regulated industry actors? To say that public support matters for politicians is not to deny the importance of political leadership. Hashimoto's leadership in the Big Bang prevented the regulated industries from building an opposing coalition within the LDP—a strategy that worked in the 1979–82 banking reforms to defeat MOF proposals. However, a proposal by the prime minister, who serves concurrently as the LDP President, would not prevent the emergence of opposition from outside of the LDP, as we saw in the case of the Financial Diet. Thus, we

[25] The FSRC, SEC, and IC were integrated into the Financial System Council, in line with the creation of the Financial Supervisory Agency and the integration of the Banking and Securities Bureaus into one Financial Planning Bureau within MOF in 1998. As of 1999, this council deliberated on legislation regulating the financial services across fields, including banking, securities, and insurance. PARC was also instrumental in the 1999 decision to delay the payoff for one year, to 2002. See, for example, *Asahi Shimbun* (December 21 and 29, 1999).

submit that the more crucial causal factor here is not so much the prime minister's presence as the popularity of the prime minister's proposal relative to other policy alternatives.

This claim is supported by the LDP's behavior, which was driven by the logic of organizational survival in 1996 and in the Financial Diet. Facing the credible threat of electoral replacement due to its loss of public support—as was the case in the wake of the 1996 Housing Loan Affair and in the wake of the Upper House defeat in 1998, the LDP chose to increase public support by two means. First, it fully swallowed its rivals' policies; second, it sacrificed its ties with MOF, as MOF became a liability with its drastic violation of the public's trust.

It may not be surprising that our claim holds for political parties. After all, they regularly face elections, where public support directly determines their organizational survival. Nevertheless, the post-1993 world is one in which coalition governments and a potential change of government have emerged, and these developments cannot be discounted as factors drastically increasing the chances (and fears) of electoral replacement.

What about the bureaucracy and the regulated industries? We contend that public support acts as a parameter for behavior for these actors as well. By "parameter," we do not suggest that the public exercises direct influence upon the behavior of these actors. The public, as an actor, does not threaten the bureaucracy or regulated industries via mass protest or other forms of direct action, although such actions remain a theoretical possibility (recall the mass demonstration of the 1960s). As is commonly observed, the Japanese public or consumers do not tend to behave in an organized manner (Vogel 1999). However, even when unorganized, they may be—under certain conditions—able to influence the behavior of other actors when the latter have good reasons to seek public support.

The political calculations of actors are affected by considerations of how the public might react to their behavior. Admittedly, the public's attention span is short and its focus of attention narrow.[26] Its effectiveness is a function of the intensity with which its attention is devoted to a particular field, such as financial politics, or to a particular actor, such as MOF or the banking industry.

In our case study of the financial politics of the late 1990s, the public was highly responsive to financial politics in the wake of the scandals, the

---

[26] See, for example, the classical study of public opinion by Lippmann (1997 [1922]) wherein he identifies brevity of attention and narrowness in range of attention as characteristics of "the will of the public" that democratic theories have difficulties dealing with ("Public Opinion," chapter 21).

performance failures, and the financial crisis that led to numerous failures of financial institutions. The bureaucracy and industry actors attracted heavy public criticism. Let us see below how the loss of public trust worked to affect the political behavior of these two sets of actors.

Public trust in MOF increasingly weakened due to doubts arising about two areas: competence and ethics. First, its competence came to be doubted in the wake of the policy failures and financial crisis, where many financial institutions failed despite the ministry's repeated promises that the worst was over and some banks were "too big to fail." Second, the scandals—and most notably the wining and dining scandals—raised questions as to the ethics and integrity of the bureaucratic agency. In this environment, where public trust in its organization was lost due both to questions of competence and ethics, the organization faced a credible threat of breakup. Once discussions were raised (in early 1996), MOF immediately began its efforts to re-coup the lost public trust through its WT, bypassing the mechanism of bureaupluralism. This effort collided with concerns for the regulated industries, the dominant consideration in past reforms under bureaupluralism, and resulting in internal conflict in the organization. However, the former side that sought to boost public support emerged as the winner under the threat of breakup, which was the least preferred scenario for both sides. This process demonstrates the way in which the logic of organizational survival operated.[27]

The regulated industries were severely affected by the scandals and financial crisis, even while they appeared to suffer little from a public backlash, as these scandals culminated in the arrests of employees and outraged the public. The financial crisis, partly a product of the scandals and the questionable conduct during the bubble years, focused the public's attention on financial politics, as financial institutions failed one after another. The behavior of the banking industry, in particular, incensed the public in at least three ways. First, the banking industry was slow until 1996 to commit itself to restructuring, continuing to pay relatively high salaries even while an economic recession negatively affected workers in other sectors.[28] Second, lower interest rates adopted as a means for

---

[27] As mentioned earlier, this effort raised a dilemma for the bureaucracy—if the unpopular MOF claimed credit for the proposal, it would jeopardize it—and thus, the Big Bang did not prevent the organizational breakup. Nevertheless, this miscalculation about the result should not concern us, as their rational calculations themselves are what brought about the Big Bang.

[28] For example, despite the massive loss due to the non-performing loans, the large banks did not opt to write out the losses from the balance sheets at a massive scale until 1996, when Sumitomo Bank became the first bank to do so, suffering losses in the fiscal year (Yutani and Tsujihiro 1996). See also Nihon Keizai Shimbun (1998) for the banking sector's slowness in restructuring and Mainichi Shimbun (1997) for an example of criticism of high salaries in the banking industry.

stimulating the lagging economy partly functioned as well to lessen the burden of the banking sector paralyzed in the bad debt problem. Yet, the years of low interest rates also meant that households received very little interest on their deposits, and thereby generated a strong sense of dissatisfaction among the general public. Third, the government utilized public funds to help resolve the Housing Loan affair, and drew on public funds as well as in the two banking plans of February and October 1998. This use of taxpayer money spurred the public to more closely scrutinize the banking sector.

In sum, the convoy system in finance came to be vilified by the scandals and discredited by the performance failures that culminated in the financial crisis, leading the public to focus their attention on financial politics. This indirectly affected the political behavior of financial industry actors in two ways. First, it made the cost of open objection to general reform of the financial system, of which the Big Bang was a part, prohibitively expensive. Second, it led the public to demonstrate their power to directly affect the businesses of those under heavy public criticism. While consumer reactions to the racketeering scandals did not prove fatal to the financial institutions involved, the incident demonstrated that the public posed a credible threat of boycott, and suggested that the costs of being perceived as a "public enemy" in the post-deregulation world may be prohibitively high, since deregulation raises concerns for survival among regulated firms. In Chapter 6, we noted a comment made by a president of a lower-tier city bank that those opposed to the Big Bang could not offer a "just cause" (*taigi meibun*) for opposition that could effectively counter the Big Bang (Tahara 1998: 217). This statement supports our claim that the public acted as a constraint on the actions of regulated industry actors. The considerations for the "just cause," an implicit reference to public support, made the financial industries refrain from boldly pursuing their own interests. In this way, the public indirectly functioned to raise the costs to the regulated industries of forestalling the economic reforms for their own benefits.

Comparison with Alternative Explanations

Our main contention about financial politics since 1995 has been that the public now matters as a determinant of financial reforms. In this section we contrast our argument with alternative explanations, focusing in particular on how our argument differs from that put forward by proponents of electoral rational choice, who also place emphasis on the public's role, but do so via a very different logic.

Among the alternative explanations for the Big Bang identified in Chapter 2, the analysis provided in Part II so far clearly rejects "bureaucratic dominance" (i.e. a coordinated scheme by MOF or MITI), "interest group dominance" (i.e. dominance of the interests of financial industries or other industries), "political dominance" (i.e. a victory of politicians over bureaucratic resistance), and the hypothesis citing reforms as a product of a counter-coalition formed by the corporate sector and MITI. The roles played by Hashimoto, the LDP ARPH, and other political actors, as well as the important role played by the internal rift in MOF over whether to emphasize the public interest or constituency interests, would all be overlooked by explanations focused on political or bureaucratic dominance. Most of the financial institutions saw their interests hurt by the Big Bang; moreover, neither financial firms nor other potential economic "winners" dominated the political process that gave rise to the reforms. Instead, interest group politics, based on the exchange of goods and services between political actors (politicians and bureaucrats) and industry actors, was subdued by public interest politics. That MOF had been discreetly planning the Initiative from early 1996 on with little coordination with MITI makes it impossible to adopt the "corporate sector–MITI coalition" hypothesis.

The electoral rational choice perspective shares our theoretical emphasis on the public. Electoral rational choice builds upon principal-agent theory and would see the public controlling LDP backbenchers via elections, while the LDP backbenchers control LDP leaders through the party caucus, and LDP leaders control the bureaucracy with their ultimate veto power (Ramseyer and Rosenbluth 1993). We agree with electoral rational choice in its dismissal of arguments that the public is unorganized, and thus immaterial. While proponents of electoral rational choice emphasize the power of the vote as a means of the public exercising control over politicians, we suggest that the public also exercises influence because the bureaucracy and private financial firms have incentives to seek public support. How, then, do we distinguish our contentions from electoral rational choice? We approach this question from two directions.

First, it is unclear whether the exchange of votes and favors between political and economic actors existed between the consumers and the LDP, as electoral rational choice proponents suggest was the case. We contend that the assumed link between the behavior by the voting public and the LDP, wherein the public selects a party according to how much party policies support consumer interests and the LDP selects consumer-friendly policies in anticipation of punishment at the polls if it does otherwise, does not hold in our case. We saw in Chapter 4 that consumers were largely unaware of the benefits of the Big Bang, and the central issues of the elections—such as administrative reforms—could hardly be characterized as consumer-friendly. How could the LDP lawmakers adopt a pro-consumer stance in 1996, anticipating consumer support, when a mere one-ninth of the public was even aware of the benefits of the Big Bang in 1997? The consumer-friendly financial reforms were merely a minor issue in the 1996 elections. These elections were fought over administrative reforms, which had very little direct relationship to consumer interests. The causal link between administrative reform and the benefits such reform generates, such as lower taxes, is less transparent than is the causal link between regulatory reforms and lower prices for services. Administrative reforms were popular, but not because their *contents* were perceived to benefit the general public. Rather, they were popular because, as part of the anti-bureaucracy agenda of the Democrats, they symbolized a blow to bureaucratic dominance and therefore to the traditional *procedures* of policymaking carried out to that point. It is therefore erroneous to interpret the LDP's advocacy for administrative—or other—reforms as an attempt to portray the party as consumer friendly in the expectation of winning the support of consumers at the polls.

Our explanation, however, can explain both consumer-friendly reforms and reforms such as administrative reforms, which have only a distant link to consumer interests. In our explanation, what matters most is public support and how the presence or lack of this support affects the dynamics of party competition. In this way, we care less about the objective benefits of reforms to the voting public; public support may be obtained for a program perceived to be "good," regardless of whether it objectively improves the welfare of consumers or not. We simply assert that as long as the rival parties' platforms attracted public support, the LDP would have matched these parties' platforms to avoid a repeat of their tragic loss of power in 1993. The financial reforms were just one part of the larger agenda of administrative reforms and structural reorganization in Japan; the LDP pushed for reforms to enhance public support for the party. Although reforms may or may not have a direct impact on the public's welfare, they clearly attracted public support. This was demonstrated in the case of the Democrats, whose leader, Naoto Kan, attracted much public support for his anti-bureaucracy agenda. As reforms (of the central government and of the larger "system") became the central issue in the 1996 elections, the

LDP attempted to prevent a loss of public support to its rivals by matching its rivals' platforms. In short, it was not that the LDP expected support from consumers in return for its consumer-friendly policies; rather, the party simply adopted these reforms because they were popular with the public and the party sought to compete with its rivals.

A second way to distinguish our explanation from that of electoral rational choice is through a comparison of the causal factors that drove policy changes in the Big Bang. In particular, we focus here on the increased emphasis in the Big Bang on promoting the interests of the consumer public, as reflected in the introduction of drastic deregulation measures. Judging from work by electoral rational choice proponents Rosenbluth and Thies (1999), this interpretive framework would view electoral reforms as the most likely factor driving the Big Bang. In contrast, our explanation identifies two changes or causal factors: the change of government in 1993 and "failures,"—that is, performance failures and scandals. Given these changes, we showed how the public's influence over the behavior of the politicians, bureaucrats, and industry actors has strengthened.

Our explanation is more robust than one focused on electoral reforms for two reasons. First, if we view the electoral reforms as producing victory for the voting public and pushing the LDP towards a pro-consumer stance, then we would have to lump the Big Bang together with the Housing Loan Affair—that is, the Housing Loan Affair would have to be interpreted as a process in which "the LDP ultimately forced the banks to absorb huge losses rather than require taxpayers to bail out their mortgage-lending subsidiaries" (Rosenbluth and Thies 1999). It is hard to believe that there was *any* person (aside from a few political scientists) in 1996 in Japan who believed that this outcome represented the public's victory at the expense of banks. Rosenbluth and Thies mischaracterize when they assert that "the banking sector was obliged to foot the entire bill," as the government used 685 billion yen in public funds to resolve the problem. This expenditure was clearly what the public was most fixated upon in 1996. Moreover, why would we expect there to be any possible alternative to banks absorbing huge losses in this type of situation?[29] Why did the LDP not accept contributions from banks in 1996? It certainly was not because the LDP was feeling financially secure and without a need for campaign contributions from banks. Let us not forget that the LDP demanded campaign contributions

[29] Legal recourse was virtually impossible in the absence until April 1996 of a legal infrastructure for addressing the major failure of financial institutions. The institutional context of Japan, where the cost of legal recourse is much higher than in the United States, seems to be neglected in the electoral rational choice approach.

again from banks in 1999, well after the electoral reforms were in place. The reason the LDP forewent contributions from banks in 1996 was clearly because of the public's severe criticism of banks at this time. In face of the numerous anomalies, we are forced to reject this explanation about the Housing Loan. Given the link between the Big Bang, MOF reforms, and the Housing Loan Affair, it follows that this explanatory framework is inadequate for the Big Bang as well. The Big Bang was conceived in early 1996 by MOF, and the MOF reforms by the LDP—each in response to public outrage arising out of the Housing Loan Affair.

Second, and more importantly, the change of government in 1993 rather than electoral reforms led LDP lawmakers to face a credible threat of electoral replacement in 1996, in the wake of the loss of public trust coming out of the Housing Loan Affair. True, the change of government took place as a result of a failed attempt to introduce electoral reforms. However, the Lower House elections of 1993 were carried out under the old electoral system of multiple-member districts (MMD), proving that a change in the rules was possible in the system. The changes in electoral rules may have a long-run effect upon legislator behavior, but the empirical evidence shows that not much had changed aside from decreased campaign spending by the 1996 elections (Otake 1997b).

A comparison of the situation surrounding the passage of the consumption tax in 1989 and the situation surrounding the Housing Loan Affair also makes it clear that the change of government experience had a greater impact on the behavior of politicians than did the shift in the electoral system. The LDP's loss of power in 1993 generated a shared sense of frustration within the party, as a result of the party being in the opposition, and heightened concerns for survival. While the electoral systems differed in 1989 and 1996, *how* this difference would affect the respective elections was far from pre-determined in 1996. Instead, the worlds of 1989 and 1996 were very different as seen from the eyes of LDP politicians. While a loss of public support was common in both election years, loss of power was not a probable scenario in 1989, given the record at the time of uninterrupted one-party dominance for over thirty years. By 1996, however, LDP politicians had learned from the 1993 experience that such a thing could happen. If we adopt our explanation—that a change in government after thirty-eight years of non-change spurs a change in the shared expectations about "how the world works"—that is, that it spurs an "institutional change" in politics—then the fear of replacement held by LDP lawmakers is much more clearly explained.

Conclusion

In this chapter, we sought to investigate the changing nature of bureaupluralism. We derived general observations from the Big Bang case, then contrasted these against the experience of the Financial Diet of the fall of 1998, the most recent reforms in financial politics. As a result, five trends—the rise of alternative policymaking mechanisms other than bureaupluralism, the rise of "public interest politics," the loss of MOF's position as the organizer of bureaupluralism, the displacement of bureaucratic initiatives by political ones, and the new strategic relationship between the LDP and MOF according to the logic of organizational survival—were identified as the new developments in bureaupluralism in financial politics. This led us to our main contention about financial politics since 1995: the public matters as a determinant of reforms in financial politics in a world characterized by possible changes in government and financial crisis.

We supported this claim in two ways. First, we highlighted the difference between the policymaking mechanisms of bureaupluralism and new alternative policymaking mechanisms that have emerged more recently. Specifically, we showed how a decision-making process which once included only the LDP, MOF, and regulated industry actors in the decision-making process shifted to a diverse and *ad hoc* arrangement in the post-1993 world of coalition governments and changes in government. Accompanying the emergence of this alternative policymaking mechanism was the emergence of public interest politics, wherein the public plays a central role to the exclusion of regulated industries (and MOF at times). Similarly, governmental actors under the new policymaking mechanism now include other parties and other agencies, as well as MOF and the LDP.

Second, we showed that public support acted as a parameter for behavior of the bureaucracy and the regulated industries and was increasingly important as well for the LDP in its pursuit of survival in the post-1993 world, where electoral replacement was the new reality. In other words, the unorganized public indirectly affected the behavior of actors by altering the costs of their actions. The bureaucracy as well as the regulated industries had good reasons to seek the public's support, even independent of reasons of political control.

We reiterate that bureaupluralism is not dead—that is, it has not been permanently replaced by new policymaking mechanisms; the case of the Big Bang and today's financial politics instead provide evidence for a new trend wherein new policymaking mechanisms sometimes *displace* bureaupluralism. In other words, bureaupluralism is no longer the only "rule of the game" in producing economic reforms. The new world is one in which bureaupluralism and alternative mechanisms coexist.

The comparison of our explanation against alternative explanatory paradigms provided evidence of the greater robustness of our explanation. Importantly, while our explanation shares a theoretical emphasis on the public with proponents of electoral rational choice, we showed that our explanation differs in important ways from this interpretive framework and the latter must be rejected for two reasons. First, the assumed link between the exchange of votes and pro-consumer policies is erroneous. Consumers were largely unaware of the benefit of the Big Bang in 1997 and the 1996 elections were hardly fought over deregulation. Our explanation focused on the dynamics of competition among political parties for public support is more accurate. To garner public support, the LDP did not necessarily need measures that would objectively improve the public's welfare; rather, the party needed reforms that were popular. It was for this reason that the LDP adopted the opposition parties' reform agenda as its own. Second, we showed that the empirical evidence overwhelmingly suggests that the change in government in 1993 and performance failures/scandals—our causal variables—rather than electoral reforms focused on by proponents of electoral rational choice brought about the Big Bang.

In the next chapter, we situate the Big Bang in the larger context and ask the following questions: What drove the changes in financial politics? And, where did our two causal factors of change—a change of government in 1993 and performance failures/scandals come from? The answers emerge out of our framework of institutional change, introduced in Chapter 3.

Part III

The Meaning of Change

8

Two Institutional Changes

Part II provided evidence of significant change in Japanese finance. The massive deregulation measures since 1996 and the resulting flood of mergers and strategic alliances in finance support this contention. However, finance in Japan has been on a path of drastic change since the 1960s. There have been numerous notable developments, including the lift of the ban on inward foreign direct investment in 1964, the creation of the government bond market in the late 1970s, the liberalization of current account capital transactions in 1980, and the liberalization of deposit rates and the corporate bond market from the mid-1980s. As economist Yukio Noguchi notes, "if you take any period of ten years, you have two totally different worlds." In his view, technological innovation fundamentally drives the changes in finance, and regulatory reforms are but random events that ought to be dealt with by a stochastic model.[1]

Indeed, things change fast in the world of finance due to technological innovation, and the Big Bang might be seen as another significant event along with many others in finance over the past thirty years. Globalization driven by technological progress has been an important trend in the world of finance, as exemplified by the drastic increase in international capital flows, largely made possible by advances in computer technology. Accordingly, one might argue that environmental changes such as technological innovation and globalization have proven crucial in triggering deregulation in domestic finance in places such as Japan. One might argue, for example, that the development of the Euro-market undermined the effectiveness of domestic regulation.

We contend that the choices about timing and the pace and scope of reform make a large difference to the Japanese nation, thus rendering

---

[1] I thank Yukio Noguchi for this point, made during an author interview with Noguchi in July 1999.

them worthy of analysis. In particular, choices made years earlier are likely to determine whether the Japanese economy will have an efficient financial sector in the 2020s—when most anticipate that Japan's demographic crisis will commence, with the retirement *en masse* of baby-boomers on top of continued decline in the birth rate. Even though technological advances may make financial reforms inevitable in the long run, when and how such reforms are carried out is largely a matter of domestic political economy.

This said, our analysis of domestic finance and public policymaking is unsatisfactory if it does not delve into the causes of the changes that we claim are in progress. Thus far, we have treated the cause of the change in government and of the performance failures and scandals as exogenously determined. We now proceed to incorporate them into our analytical framework. In this chapter, we relate our story in Part II to the larger picture—that is, to the developments in the environment in which the Big Bang and other financial reform efforts unfolded.

To link our story of domestic political economy to a story about environmental changes, such as those represented by technological innovation and globalization, we rely on the theoretical framework of institutional change developed in Chapter 3. We first summarize our earlier discussion of institutions and institutional change, and of the prevailing institutions in financial politics. We then proceed to identify the causal links between the environment, the domestic political economy, and the world of finance. Next, we relate the Big Bang to the other changes in finance. Based on the above, we identify two "institutional changes" in the Japanese political economy, showing that the convoy system in finance (hereafter the Convoy) broke down in Japan over the 1990s, while bureaupluralism in public policymaking is in decay. We close the chapter with a prediction, derived from our causal framework, on the future of bureaupluralism.

Review: Conceptualizing Institutions and Characteristics of Two Key Institutions in Japanese Finance

We have adopted the definition of institutions put forward by Aoki (2001), as "shared, stable, summarized expectations about how the world works, which may not be unique." In this definition, institutions are shared expectations about the state of the world, that come to be taken for granted due to the confirmation of these expectations over time. Institutions convey "summarized" information to subjectively rational actors engaging in strategic behavior. The phrase, "how the world works," refers to the rules that inform the actors about the consequences of actions under conditions of strategic interaction among actors. The phrase, "which may not be unique" raises the possibility of multiple equilibria. An institution arises out of feedback between the objective and subjective worlds. An institution is an equilibrium that arises from the repeated, strategic interaction of actors in the objective world, as well as a summary representation of such an equilibrium that is collectively shared by actors as subjective beliefs; a feedback mechanism between the two makes institutions self-sustaining.

Our theoretical framework of institutional change mentioned earlier addresses the politics, or distributional conflicts, involved in the process of change. Institutional change is essentially a shift in shared perceptions about how the world works. It comes about through a collective learning process based on an evolutionary selection mechanism of strategies derived from the actors' subjective beliefs about how the world works. It is caused by the gap between the faster pace of environmental changes (including the institutional environment) and the slower pace of adaptation in domestic political and economic institutions. This gap appears in the form of "failures," or, more specifically, as "performance failures" and "scandals," which lead actors to question the taken for granted aspect of the institutions. "Nature"—that is, environmental changes in technology or in the institutional environment—eventually determines the outcome of the competition among institutions by rewarding or penalizing various actor strategies. Successful strategies proliferate. Yet, a political struggle takes place between those actors who see the process as one of institutional resilience and/or have stakes in preserving the status quo, and those actors who perceive that lasting change is underway and/or see their interests enhanced by the new institutions.

The distributional concerns surrounding institutional change come into play only when the old and new institutions are not Pareto-rankable. The political struggle is facilitated by symbols derived from such sources as history, foreign practice, ideology, and leadership. In the process, "reformers" may replace "conservatives." This may happen either via the formation of a counter-coalition (from the outside), or via defection (from within). When a critical mass of the agents shifts its views about how the world works and the new institutions become taken for granted, we call the result "institutional change."

Institutional complementarity often makes institutional change in a single policy domain difficult. However, once change occurs in one institution, it is likely that actors will reassess other institutions in the environment, thus starting a chain reaction of change. Institutional "decay" is a situation in which the shared expectations about how the world works come to be increasingly questioned by "mavericks," due to the appearance of "failures." However, the process of institutional change may always be halted, as "nature" may signal a return to the status quo or "conservatives" may crush the "mavericks" in a political struggle. In such cases, we observe another form of "institutional resilience," in which the institution demonstrates its robustness against minor deviations from the status quo.

The two prevailing institutions in Japanese financial politics before 1995 were bureaupluralism in public policymaking and the convoy system of financial supervision. Bureaupluralism in the Japanese political economy was an institution of public policymaking utilized in every sector under conditions of LDP one-party dominance, which lasted from 1955 to 1993. In this institution, policies were produced through the inter- and intra-industrial bargaining presided over by the ministerial bureaus in charge, which engaged in intra- and inter-ministerial bargaining within the government, with occasional intervention by LDP lawmakers on behalf of industry actors. The bargaining was carried out in arenas such as deliberative councils and the LDP PARC, as well as through negotiations behind closed doors. Politicians, bureaucrats, and industries were intricately linked in this process by a relationship of interdependence, while the public was largely left outside the policymaking process. Bureaupluralism was a stable pattern of interaction among politicians, bureaucrats, and industry actors, emerging out the informal interaction of these same actors over time and guaranteed and reinforced by formal rules. The existence of the institution of bureaupluralism was contingent on actors' shared expectations of continuity in this process into the future.

The financial "convoy" was another institution that arose in finance amidst the interaction of financial actors and state actors. The identity of actors was fixed over time: the LDP held the reigns of power, MOF was the exclusive "organizer" in the bargaining process according to legal statutes, and entry and exit were *de facto* restricted—if not prohibited—by the formal rules and other informal constraints providing for the segmentation of finance. The interaction pattern of actors was largely informal, supported by such features of bureaupluralism as "informal administrative tools," "wining and dining," and *amakudari*. The policymaking bodies were the deliberative councils under MOF, and the LDP PARC (in particular, its financial subdivisions). The system was based on segmentation of finance as well as on the existence of supporting institutions such as the main bank system, the financial *keiretsu*, and cross-shareholding. Essentially, the state allowed no financial institutions to fail, providing an implicit guarantee so as to sustain beliefs that failure was beyond the realm of possibility. The larger and more competitive firms were deterred from materializing their advantage; their compliance was secured by the regulatory rent and sanctions, or reward and punishment by the regulator. Continuity was key to the well-functioning of the convoy: with future rounds to play, actors were strongly deterred from deviating from strategies prescribed under the convoy. The organizing principles of the convoy, the prevailing institution in finance, were cooperation and stability. Stability of the financial order was the ultimate goal of financial administrators as well as of financial industry actors. Stability also served the interests of non-financial firms, which enjoyed uninterrupted access to financing under such conditions. In the high growth period, repressed interest rates guaranteed cheap capital to these firms, even in the presence of an underdeveloped capital market. As long as bureaupluralism obtained across all sectors and the public was excluded from the policymaking process, stability in the financial order reinforced, and was reinforced by, the producer economy that prevailed in postwar Japan.

What drives "institutional change"? Reexamining the Context of Japanese Financial Politics

What drives "institutional change"? "Institutional change" is fundamentally the collective perception that "things are not going right." This consensus evolves out of the emergence of "failures," or the gap between the pace of environmental changes and the pace of institutional adaptation, and provides motivation for actors to pursue alternative strategies. We turn now to see how this framework applies to our story of financial politics.

Changes in the Environment

We can identify three types of changes in the environment applicable to our story of financial politics in Japan of the 1990s: technological innovation, internationalization, and demographic maturity. Technological innovation has been a significant source of change in finance worldwide. The development in computer and communication technology has drastically reduced the cost of financial transactions as well as contributed to the developments of new products based on financial technology. Strange (1998) summarizes technological innovation in finance under

255

three headings: computers (e.g. money settlement), chips (e.g. credit cards), and satellites (e.g. communication via satellites and the Internet). International capital flows, including short-term (e.g. portfolio investment) and long-term (e.g. foreign direct investment) investments, have increased drastically over the past twenty years. Acceleration of these capital flows was especially rapid in the 1990s with the rise of the emerging markets in the developing world.

The most important innovative change in the mid-1980s may have been the rapid development of derivative markets. The size of these markets increased vastly in the 1990s. Derivatives drastically enhanced the ability of financial actors to manage risks and reduce transaction costs, and thus increased the efficiency of the international capital market. They also provided the means of arbitrage over differences in funding costs and returns as well as over national regulations, thus increasing pressures for the global integration of capital markets (Chadha and Folkerts-Landau 1999).

Such developments in finance led to the increased global integration of capital markets. With regard to our story, this means the integration of the Japanese capital market into the overseas market. The Japanese market has increasingly become sensitive to what happens in the overseas market. As we saw in Chapter 4, Japanese stocks are now increasingly traded in London largely due to lower transaction costs (including taxation). In this way, trends in London have an immediate effect on Tokyo. Japanese banks now have increased exposure to international markets, after their extended presence of the late 1980s of the bubble economy and the increase in size of the international capital market in general in the 1990s. In this situation, the domestic banking system is increasingly influenced by developments abroad. To see evidence for this point, one need only recall the Daiwa Bank Scandal in New York in 1995 and the emergence of the Japan Premium in 1997–98, in which Japanese banks were forced to pay a surcharge in the international call market due to the weak condition of the sector.

Another environmental change is the demographic factor. As mentioned in Chapter 4, the bulk of baby-boomers will reach retirement age by 2020, while the birth rate for the younger generation whose contributions to the pension system support today's pensioners, has declined steadily. This demographic development translates to a need for increased financial sector efficiency, as an increasing number of citizens depend on their past savings to sustain their livelihood. While demographics do not represent an imminent threat and therefore do not determine when and how financial reforms materialize, demographic factors do have the effect of delineating a deadline, making such financial reforms inevitable sooner or later. This ticking time bomb of demographic maturity may be used by "reformers" as a focal point to increase support for their cause.

"Failures"

What kind of failures may emerge in financial politics? A failure in general economic performance is clearly one. We may think about four types of economic situations along a continuum, which each produce different effects: an economic boom (high growth, nearing the potential growth rate, such as experienced by the United States in the late 1990s); economic stagnation (low growth, wherein a clear discrepancy emerges between potential and actual growth rates, such as that experienced by Japan in the early 1990s); an economic slump (negative growth, such as that experienced by Japan after 1997); and, economic depression (a negative growth rate accompanied by a social catastrophe, such as that seen in the Great Depression). In our framework, we are unlikely to see true "failures" in an economic boom. At such times, performance failures and scandals by actors may arise, but they are unlikely to undermine collective beliefs regarding "how the world works."

Thus, we focus on the remaining three types of economic situations. While the economic situation may be viewed as part of the policy environment, we interpret it here as a "failure," or the result of a response by domestic political and economic institutions to the changing environment. The economic situation arises from the interaction of the actors within the domestic political economy. If one adopts a position that the economic situation is beyond the control of the actors (including of the government), then, the economic situation may be the "environment."[2] However, if the government and other economic actors have the tools to impact the economic situation, then it may alternatively be viewed more as a "failure."

The Japanese experience suggests that actors have the impact on the economic situation—at the least, this is what actors collectively believe to be true about how the world works. Consider, for example, Japan's economic stagnation in the 1990s and policies adopted by the government in response. After the collapse of the bubble, the government increased its

---

[2] The rational expectations school of thought in economics represents one example of this view.

fiscal spending through the implementation of various economic packages. In 1995 and 1996, economic growth picked up. The government's fiscal policy may or may not have been effective in materializing economic growth, objectively speaking. Nonetheless, if economic stagnation persists, it tends to be perceived as a policy "failure" by the actors—regardless of whether the government truly has the ability to bring the economy out of the stagnation or not. Thus, we adopt below the view that the economic situation is a function of the response by domestic political and economic institutions, rather than something in the environment beyond the control of actors.

The economic situation can be expected to influence actor views on how the world works. When the economy is booming, actors do not tend to doubt whether their strategies are the best possible ones. On the other hand, when the economy is in stagnation, actors have a greater tendency to doubt the worth of the prevailing institution. Similarly, when the economy is in a slump, a collective awareness that something is wrong in the prevailing institutions is likely to emerge; this would eventually culminate in a perception crisis (Aoki 2001) if the economic situation turns from stagnation to crisis, as it would if the economy fell into depression.

The second possible "failure" in financial politics relates to the performance of the financial system. As with strong economic performance, even if the financial system is working as expected, with banks booming with record profits (e.g. Japan in the 1980s), little "failures" may emerge. However, if scandals related to the financial system occur at such times, they are likely to be dismissed as exceptions. In contrast, when financial institutions encounter financial difficulties due to mismanagement and/or bad loans, and this leads to instability in the financial system—perhaps with some major financial institutions failing—the results may be different. If the financial system reaches a point of crisis in which the meltdown of the system is feared or even materializes, in the form of a massive bank run and/or a bank moratorium—such as was seen with the "bank holiday" in the United States in the 1930s or with the Japanese financial panic of 1927—then financial system performance has clearly worsened and other components of "failure" such as scandals are likely to be uncovered.[3] Examples include unlawful conduct such as embezzlement and corruption, unethical conduct involving deals carried out despite conflict of interest, and mismanagement due to erroneous diagnosis of the situation—perhaps owing to excessive optimism. Combined with "performance failures,"

---

[3] See Teranishi (2000) for the Japanese financial panic of 1927.

"scandals," if recurrent, provide the symbol or "focal point" for those doubting the worth of the prevailing institution. As a result, the notion that there is something wrong in the institution rises.

Change in the Institutional Environment

The change of government in 1993 may be the most important institutional change in the institutional environment of the financial politics of 1990s Japan. Why such a change of government happened is beyond the scope of our analysis. However, we may speculate that the above notion of "failures" can be expanded to make sense of this event to a certain extent. The change of government came out of the strategic interaction of lawmakers, who sought to respond to the growing sense among the populace that something was wrong with politics. This sentiment came to be reflected in phrases such as those referring to Japan as a country with "first rate economics but third rate politics." The cause for this growing sentiment of dissatisfaction with politics was three-fold: recurrent political scandals such as those centered on Recruit and on Tokyo Sagawa Kyubin, the inability of politicians to deal with important issues such as how Japan should "contribute" to the Gulf War or electoral reforms, and environmental changes such as the end of the Cold War.[4]

This institutional change related to the change in government is an important causal factor in our story of financial politics. Change in the governing party after thirty-eight years of continuous single-party rule brought a new awareness to political actors that such a change is possible. Under stable LDP rule, this was a distant scenario in actors' minds, as can be seen by such common expressions used by government officials as "*the party*" (*tou*), implicitly suggesting that there could only be one ruling party, the LDP.[5] Actually witnessing a change in power strongly affected the mindset of lawmakers by making the threat of electoral replacement at the party level (as opposed to the individual level) real. One of the most important strengths of the LDP was that it had dominant access to government resources, such as public works and regulatory policies. Its power was guaranteed by the decision-making process that made sure that any policy proposal or legislation proposed by the government would pass its internal

---

[4] Kohno (1997), Pempel (1998), and Curtis (1999) provide some examples of the explanations as to why the change of government took place in 1993. See Woodall (1994) for these political scandals.

[5] The arrival of coalition politics by the electoral loss of 1989 in the Upper House may have made the politicians more aware of such a possibility, although to a lesser extent than the actual change of government. I owe this point to Michael Thies.

policymaking body, the PARC. This situation was one of "equilibrium" in our usage, as the process was sustained based upon a set of common expectations rather than on a legal code. However, being thrown out of power made this policymaking channel ineffective for the LDP, and the party's lawmakers suddenly faced a loss of influence over government agencies, as the new non-LDP coalition ensured that these agencies severed ties with the LDP. When the LDP came back to power, its top priority was to stay in power at all costs. Thus, the LDP was quick to incorporate or "fully swallow" its rivals' programs through compromise or imitation, earning itself the label of "mollusk," as we saw in the previous chapters.

The change of government not only made the LDP sensitive to the increased threat of replacement but also changed actors' collective expectations about how politics works. If ruling parties are expected to change over time, then the policymaking process cannot be left unaffected. "Bureaupluralism" as a stable institution arising out of the bargaining among the LDP, the bureaucracy, and industry actors had to change in a number of ways. First, the policymaking process had to change to involve other parties' policymaking bodies. Since 1993, coalition government has been the norm and the decision-making process accordingly involves negotiation among the ruling parties.

Second, political actors now must take into account the various possibilities that arise from re-alignment of party coalitions. Since today's opposition may be tomorrow's ruling party, the opposition's political influence increases. Therefore, the bureaucracy and regulated industries must pay more attention to the opposition than in the past.

Third, since the change of government has become a possibility, political parties—and especially the LDP—are now more sensitive to the need to garner general public support. When the change of government was only a distant threat, the LDP could concentrate its efforts on cultivating support from constituents such as interest groups and industry actors. However, with change in rule a possibility, the LDP must be more sensitive to the wider public support than it was in the past, when it was able to pursue wildly unpopular policies such as the consumption tax without much fear of electoral replacement, given that it was the only pro-business catch-all party in the Cold War context. This new imperative of needing to seek wider public support may be exacerbated by the 1994 electoral reforms, which introduced a single-member district and proportional representation component into the election formula. It is not that political parties now take support groups such as interest groups lightly; the support from such groups may be even *more* critical for individual lawmakers to win re-election than they were in the past, with the new electoral rules—and, specifically, with the single-member districts. However, at the same time, the party label may become all the more important under the new electoral system, because of the single-member district wherein one party puts forward a single candidate and because of the proportional representation component in the Lower House, where the public votes for a party.[6] Thus, in cases in which the political parties have to choose between traditional organized constituencies and the general public, they have stronger incentives today to choose the latter.

In this sense, one important effect of this change in the institutional environment is that it has made actors aware that they are operating under a higher-level institution in which the public matters—that of liberal democracy. Of course, the public mattered even in pre-1993 politics, but the key point here is that relevant actors have become increasingly aware since 1993 that the public is the ultimate decision-maker in a liberal democracy. And, this new awareness comes as a result of the expanded scope of possible political scenarios. Thus, we may characterize this development as a process in which the higher-level institution of liberal democracy became increasingly incorporated into actors' calculations over strategic choices, as a result of experiencing a change in government. Theoretically speaking, we may refer to this process as one in which liberal democracy shifted from simply being part of the institutional environment, perceived to be beyond actor control and outside strategic calculations, to being an institution in and of itself.[7]

Public Interest and Public Support

Thus, with the emergence of an increased likelihood of change of government, the public matters more in politics. In the earlier chapters, we saw that the role of the public in financial politics increased drastically through the rise of alternative public policymaking channels. The emergence of "failures" made the public more aware of and focused on the issue of finance and on the actors involved—that is, on the LDP, MOF, and financial institutions. The political parties, the bureaucratic agencies, and

---

[6] I owe this point to Michael Thies.

[7] Objectively speaking, actors are interacting in a multi-layered set of institutions. However, some institutions are recognized by actors as exogenous to their interaction, due to their limited reasoning ability: such institutions compose the "institutional environment", which rather acts as a parameter to actors' strategy. Once part of the institutional environment shifts to an institution, actors start incorporating the institution into their strategy-formation process. See the sections on the synchronic linkage of institutions in Aoki (2001).

the regulated industries saw their behavior more heavily constrained by the public acting as a parameter. With the help of our framework of institutional change focusing on the feedback mechanism between the objective reality and the subjective perceptions of this reality, we are able to better understand how the public operates as a parameter of actor behavior in politics.

"Public interest" is the objective criterion regarding the economic or social welfare of the general public or the consumers. In other words, it is a function of what objectively increases the welfare of the public. However, because of the imperfect rationality of actors, including the public, what matters more in politics may be "public support," which is a function of what the public *perceives* as good for them. Theoretically, "public support" needs the reality check of "public interest." For example, populist appeals without material results are bound to fail in the long run to maintain the level of support initially commanded. However, whether such feedback really materializes is questionable; political actors as well as the public may not possess a memory long enough to assess a policy decision made, say, five years earlier. For example, did the public reward or punish the LDP in 2001 for its 1996 decision to initiate administrative reforms?

Thus, for our purpose, what drives the political calculations of actors is "public support" rather than "public interest." Chapter 6 showed that, while it was unclear how administrative reforms worked to benefit the public interest, political parties adopted the reforms nevertheless, out of belief that the policies were likely to generate "public support." In the future, it may be shown that administrative reforms have little effect on the nation's well-being. In that case, this agenda may lose its appeal among the populace. However, this agenda was at the center of the political debate in 1996 because of "failures" by the bureaucracy. Whether or not administrative reforms were objectively the best way to overcome performance failures in the national economy—that is, to bring the country out of its economic stagnation—was beside the point. It may be that someday the reality check of "public interest" will prevail. Today, however, it is the politics of "public support" that drives the strategic interaction of the actors at the center of our analysis.

Causal Mechanism of Change

Where does all this leave us? We may be able to situate our account of financial politics in the larger picture in the following manner. Changes in the environment occur: technological innovation in finance, international integration in the capital markets, and demographic maturity make financial reforms with the aim of increasing efficiency inevitable. However, domestic political and economic institutions are slow to respond. "Failures" take place in the economy accordingly, as well as in the financial world. In Japan, this comes in the form of the economic stagnation of the early 1990s, the financial instability ensuing from 1995, and the accompanying scandals that plagued the financial sector.

An important change in the institutional environment then occurs: the change of government in 1993—probably a response to "failures" in politics in the late 1980s. Now the public matters more in politics, as the higher-level institution of liberal democracy increases its presence in political calculations. This triggers decay in—or, a situation in which actors start to doubt the effectiveness of—bureaupluralism in public policymaking. Hereafter, the policymaking process must incorporate non-LDP parties in the coalition or in the opposition, as well as incorporate the public (as opposed to the traditional organized constituencies). The aforementioned "failures" in the economy and financial system undermine, in particular, the institution of bureaupluralism as it functions in financial and economic policymaking under the jurisdiction of MOF. Bureaupluralism in finance—a part of the broader pattern of bureaupluralism across public policymaking in general—starts to crumble: MOF starts to lose its standing as the organizer of deals in the financial policymaking process. Institutional change in finance thus materializes. In this way, bureaupluralism in general is affected by the decay in one of its constituent components—bureaupluralism in finance.

Recall that we identified the change of government in 1993 and performance failures/scandals as the two causal factors that drove the changes observed in financial politics in the previous chapter. We may be able to reinterpret the process of how changes are brought about in financial politics as follows. Environmental changes (technological innovation, internationalization of capital, and demographic maturity) and the slower institutional response give rise to "failures" in finance and economics. Change in the institutional environment or a change in government triggers decay in bureaupluralism in public policymaking. Decay in bureaupluralism in public policymaking and financial and economic failures, in turn, translate into decay in bureaupluralism in financial policymaking, and triggers the institutional change in finance, affecting bureaupluralism in public policymaking in general.

We now have the causal mechanism for how changes in public policymaking and finance materialize but we have yet to specify the institutional changes in public policymaking and finance. What components of the system shifted so as to change the collective expectations about how the world works, and to what extent has "institutional change" materialized in the two fields? We shall return to these points soon. First, however, we turn to identify how the Big Bang relates to other changes in finance.

Relating the Big Bang to Broader Changes in Finance

We may break down the changes in finance into four parts, with each representing various definitions of an "institution."

(1) players (actors involved in financial politics);
(2) formal rules (formal regulatory rules);
(3) interaction patterns (between the government and private sector; and, among private sector actors in finance);
(4) shared expectations (about politics and about finance).

Figure 8.1 summarizes the changes in finance. The Big Bang can be characterized as encompassing change at the level of formal regulatory rules. If we recall from Chapter 3 how each feature of the financial convoy relates to another, it is clear that the players in financial politics, the formal regulatory rules, and the parameters of interaction between the government and the private sector—including the policymaking process, policy tools, and policy substance—were intertwined with one another, each reinforcing the stable reproduction of the other components of the convoy.[8] Private sector financial practices—such as the main bank system and the *keiretsu* system—complemented such arrangements in financial administration.[9] The shared expectations about how the world of finance works—the core of the convoy as an institution—both resulted from and reproduced the stable practices observed at the levels of players, formal rules, and interaction patterns. Below we focus on how the changes that materialized in finance can be dissected at each level of the institution. It will be shown that once a change takes place in one component of the institution, it triggers change in other related components of that institution.

[8] For more on the financial "convoy," see Aoki and Patrick (1994), Pempel and Muramatsu (1995), Rosenbluth (1989), Vogel (1996), Ikeo (1995), and Horiuchi (1998; 1999). Nishimura (1999) gives an account of why "financial administration lost," from the MOF's point of view.

[9] See Aoki and Patrick (1994) for how the main bank system and the system of financial administration (the "convoy") complemented one another.

Organizing principles	"Cooperation and stability" →	"Transparency and competition"
	Convoy System	New System
(a) Players		
1. Regulatory agency	Ministry of Finance (MOF)	FSA/FRC [FSA] & MOF
2. Relevant players	LDP, MOF, domestic financial firms	Addition of [non-LDP, non-MOF, "outsiders"]
(b) Formal Rules		
3. Formal regulatory rules (= Big Bang)	Segmentation Entry control Product control	Deregulation / liberalization Transparency / fairness
(c) Interaction Patterns		
4. Between the government and the private sector (policymaking process)	Industrial association of domestic financial actors Informal consultations Wining and dining *Amakudari* MOF Councils / LDP PARC	Addition of "outsiders" Formal consultations Formal conferences / meetings Lawyers / accountants hired Rise of alternatives (MOF WT/ LDP ARPH, etc.)
(Policy tools)	Preventive / *ex ante* Discretionary / *ad hoc* Administrative guidance Licensing / authorization Informal admonition	*ex post* Legalistic / rule-based Administrative orders Legal sanctions Early warning system
(Policy substance)	Regulated competition without exit or entry Hokacho (lifeboat) Too big to fail Implicit state guarantee	Enhanced competition with exit and entry Bridge banks / nationalization Bank closures Payoffs starting in 2001 (2002)
(d) Shared Expectations		
6. About politics (Institutional environment)	Continuous rule by the LDP MOF as the "organizer"	Coalition / change of rule MOF breakup
7. About finance (institution)	Myth of no failure Implicit state guarantee Symbiosis with no losers No entry/exist: "collusive" Consensus making Cooperation / stability	Potential for failure No more guarantee (payoffs) Survival race with losers Entry/exit: "anonymous" Public support Transparency / competition

Figure 8.1 The Big Bang as part of broader institutional change

Change in Each Level of the Institution

Let us recall how changes in finance are understood in our theoretical framework. The change of government in 1993 affected bureaupluralism in public policymaking. This, and failures in finance and economics brought about change in bureaupluralism in finance—an important component of the financial convoy. Below, we will see how such changes appeared at each level of the institutions.

PLAYERS

An increasing number of players entered the financial policy realm (1 and 2).[10] Due to the breakup of MOF in 1998–99 (a direct result of "failures"), regulatory authority went from being contained wholly within the MOF to being spread across three different entities, MOF, the FSA and the FRC. In January 2001, the Financial Services Agency (FSA) was formed out of the integration of the FSA and the FRC, completing the separation of financial powers from MOF.[11] Likewise, the relevant players in financial politics under the convoy system were the LDP, MOF and the domestic financial industries. However, with the change of government in 1993, the non-LDP parties in the ruling coalition became participants in policymaking, as did the opposition parties, as attested to by the outcomes of the Financial Diet in the fall of 1998. The newly created financial agencies are now the main actors in financial administration, leaving MOF on the sidelines. In the private sector, financial politics now also involves "outsiders." These outsiders include new foreign and domestic entrants, corporate users of financial services, and consumers, as shown by the Big Bang experience.

FORMAL RULES

The Big Bang policy package essentially entails the reform of formal regulatory rules (3). As shown in Chapter 4, the important formal rules that supported the convoy—segmentation of finance, entry control, and product control—are now abolished by the Big Bang package, which includes deregulation and liberalization measures, as well as addresses transparency and fairness concerns.

INTERACTION PATTERNS

Regarding the interaction between the government and the private sector, the prevailing practice in financial regulation under the Convoy—the informal interaction in the policymaking process, and the financial regulatory policy based on *ex ante* regulation—shifted towards a more formal, rule-based system with emphasis on *ex post* regulation (4). This can be broken down into three parts: the policymaking process, policy tools, and policy substance.

First, regarding the policymaking process, the industrial associations of the domestic financial industries used to be the dominant channel of interaction between the government and the industries, as in other

---

[10] Numbers in parentheses refer to numbers used in Figure 8.1.
[11] The Financial Agency, set up in January 2001, absorbed the FRC in July 2001.

sectors.[12] The means of information exchange was heavily based on informal dialogue, often carried out through the practice of wining and dining of officials. The relationship between the government and the industries was further secured through *amakudari,* or the practice of the industries hiring retired officials.[13] Now that "outsiders" such as foreign financial firms, new entrants, and corporate users have been brought into financial politics, the exclusive policymaking position enjoyed by the industrial associations of domestic financial firms must decline. With the "failures"—and the scandals in particular—we see a departure from informal means of information exchange: bureaucrats now engage in formal meetings and conferences with financial institution representatives, and the wining and dining practice is dying away due to public criticism and the resulting tight restrictions on the practice. *Amakudari* is also under heavy public criticism with the scandals involving MOF and its retired officials. In recent years, MOF has had increasing trouble in placing its retired officials within and outside government. In response to the criticism that financial administration lacked expertise (and thus resulted in such scandals as the Daiwa Bank Scandal of 1995), the FSA has recruited lawyers and accountants, notwithstanding the prevailing practice of in-house breeding of experts under the lifetime employment system. Finally, the policymaking process under the convoy approach to regulation was centered on the MOF deliberative councils and the LDP PARC. While there was no legal basis for requiring proposals to go through this process, almost all legislation regarding finance did. The industries had guaranteed entry points, as deliberative councils well represented their views, and the "tribesmen" in the LDP under their influence would intervene on their behalf at the PARC. However, as we saw in the previous chapters, today there is a dramatic rise in alternative policymaking mechanisms: MOF's WT, the LDP ARPH, and the ruling coalition's PT are examples of new arenas for debate that make the policymaking process more complex and open to actors other than the domestic financial instititutions.

Second, regarding the policy tools utilized by the government, discretionary regulation was what characterized financial administration. MOF regulated the financial industries on an *ad hoc* basis, with the use of administrative discretion over regulatory power. This was seen in the processes of

---

[12] See, for example, Okimoto (1989) for the role of industrial associations in Japanese politics in general. See Rosenbluth (1989) for the role of the industrial associations in finance in Japan prior to "institutional change."

[13] See Amyx (1998 [and 2004]) for a discussion of informal networks that link MOF officials and financial institutions.

branch licensing and product authorization, for example. Such regulatory power enabled the use of administrative guidance, or informal "guidance" over corporate behavior without specific legal grounds. However, the system has now shifted towards a legalistic (rule-based) regulatory system. In 1993, the Administrative Procedure Law curtailed the procedural discretion commanded by the government concerning regulation. It codified the practice of administrative guidance and increased the transparency of the process in which regulatory power is exercised. In the old days, troubles— such as mismanagement or scandals—would often be dealt with in secrecy between the regulators and the regulated. MOF would impose informal sanctions, such as forcing the retirement of management, through administrative guidance. Since the Daiwa Bank Scandal of 1995, MOF and the financial agencies have been issuing administrative orders requiring, for example, the submission of reform plans or the temporary shutdown of operations. While the regulatory laws have always contained such measures, the actual activation of such measures is a very recent phenomenon. In sum, the old system sought to take a preventive approach, in which troubles were to be prevented *ex ante* by the *ad hoc*, discretionary intervention of the regulator using such informal means as administrative guidance. The new system is, on the whole, a shift towards *ex post* regulation, in which the regulator intervenes after something happens in the financial sector and through such rule-based, legalistic means as administrative orders. Even in instances where the new system maintains the preventive approach—such as with the capital requirements on banks—this preventative approach takes a legal form; informal admonition has given way to early warning activated automatically according to inspection results and pre-determined objective rules.

Third, regarding the substance of regulatory policy, we see a change in the forms of competition. In the old system, competition among firms was carried out within the segmented sectors—among city banks, for example— without entry or exit. In other words, the competitors remained essentially the same over time. In the new system, competition is enhanced by the Big Bang as well as other developments in finance, such as the financial crisis of 1997–98. Entry and exit into the financial business abounds. For example, consolidation among banking, securities, insurance, and trust businesses are taking place *en masse*, following the introduction of the cross-entry schemes by the Big Bang package. The failure of the two large long-term credit banks in 1998–99 (the LTCB and the NCB) led to the entry into the banking business of both a foreign non-bank financial firm specializing in restructuring failed financial institutions and of a Japanese software giant.

In dealing with troubled financial institutions, the previous policy was referred to as *"hokacho"* and the equivalent of the "lifeboat operations" utilized by UK regulators in the 1970s. In this process, healthy banks and other financial institutions were asked to contribute to the preservation of the stability of the financial system. The "too big to fail" principle, or the proposition that some financial firms are too big to fail without causing a financial meltdown, applied as well.[14] The regulatory rent guaranteed to large financial firms under the old system was indispensable to the success of such "lifeboat operations." However, with numerous failures during the 1990s, this mechanism eventually collapsed. Healthier firms became burdened by the recurrent requests for contributions, as they themselves were facing financial difficulties due to asset deflation and general economic slump.[15] The NCB's rescue in April 1997 may mark the last case in which the lifeboat operation was carried out. The collapse of Yamaichi Securities and Hokkaido Takushoku Bank in November 1997, as well as the collapse of the LTCB a year later, showed that both the *hokacho* and "too big to fail" principles were no more followed by financial regulators.[16] As a result, the implicit state guarantee of the past is gone, and a ceiling on deposit guarantees—known as the "payoff" system—is to be reintroduced in the near future.

We may now turn to the interaction among private sector actors in finance (5). First, the main bank system may be collapsing on various fronts. The rescue by main banks may increasingly be a less favored option for large banks which have to be concerned about survival under the increased competition and financial slump; combined with the abandon of informal regulation, exemplary cases of "main bank rescue" such as the rescue of Mazda coordinated by Sumitomo Bank (under the implicit request by MOF) in the 1970s are highly unlikely to be reproduced in the future.[17] Banks will increasingly resort to legal recourse, including

[14] For more on the "lifeboat operation" in the United Kingdom, see, for example, Hosoda (1998: 239–43). For more on the "too big to fail" approach in the United States, see the section on financial regulation in Feldstein (1994).

[15] 1993 reforms in corporate law made it easier for shareholders to bring lawsuits against management to hold them accountable for mismanagement. As a result, financial firms became increasingly reluctant to contribute to the rescue of troubled firms, since the management faced an increased risk of being sued if such rescue efforts failed.

[16] This situation contrasted with what was going on abroad at approximately the same time. The rescue of a hedge fund near collapse in fall 1998, coordinated by the New York Federal Reserve Bank in the United States, suggests that the "too big to fail" principle and "lifeboat operation" as a policy tool are not yet extinct in the international context.

[17] See Pascale and Rohlen (1988) for the rescue of Mazda by Sumitomo Bank.

bankruptcy proceedings. Second, relational financing, based on the assumption of a relatively long-term horizon over which banks may reap benefits in return for loans, may decrease in importance. This is because the new environment of increased competition as well as the regulation of banks based on their capital/asset ratio, as set forth by the Basle accords, forces banks to concentrate more on short-term profitability and capital requirements.

Third, the widespread cross-shareholding among large firms, and the financial *keiretsu* system organized around the six major banks, has eroded. Firms increasingly diminish their cross-shareholding due to altered accounting standards (now market-value-based standards); meanwhile, banks are increasingly forced to relinquish their holdings of shares once stock prices rise, as they struggle to deal with their bad debt problems and survive. Likewise, the financial *keiretsu* system is eroding fast, especially now that inter-*keiretsu* alliances are quickly taking place. Sumitomo and Sakura, as well as the DKB and Fuji—four banks among the Big Six— announced their merger plans in 1999. This, in turn, has a significant effect on the Sumitomo, Mitsui, DKB, and Fuyo groups. Moreover, international alliances make the picture even more complex. For example, Nikko Securities chose Travelers Group (later to become Citigroup) as its strategic partner, severing its traditional ties with the Bank of Tokyo-Mitsubishi of the Mitsubishi Group. Fourth and last, as we saw in Chapter 4, the dominance of banking in finance steadily erodes as the shift to direct finance continues in Japanese finance. The Big Bang, by liberalizing and deregulating a variety of new products, is expected to accelerate this trend.

SHARED EXPECTATIONS

We now reach the core of the "institution" and "institutional change": the shared expectations among actors as to how the world works. We see the shared expectations at two levels in finance: in politics (the institutional environment) (6), and in finance (the institution) (7). All the observable changes at the levels of players, formal rules, and interaction patterns generate, and are reinforced by, corresponding shared expectations. The sets of players increase, the formal regulatory rules are revised, and the patterns of interaction shift. The result is a change in the shared expectations in finance.

In the institutional environment, as we saw earlier in this chapter, the LDP's continued rule has ceased to be a "given" due to the change in government in 1993. This reality, combined with "failures" such as scandals since 1995, made MOF's taken for granted standing as the "organizer" of financial policymaking deals questionable. Now, the era of coalition government has arrived, and change in government is a feasible scenario. As we saw in the previous chapter, MOF has been stripped of its jurisdiction over finance, and the role of "organizer" in the financial policymaking process has shifted away to non-MOF agencies and political parties (1 and 2).

In finance, the myth that no financial firms could fail and the implicit state guarantee gave way to perceptions that financial firms could fail and that there were no more state guarantees—as embodied in the "payoff" system drawing on deposit insurance (4). Such unwritten laws of the postwar era, reinforced by such incidents as Yamaichi Securities' rescue by a lifeboat operation in 1965, collapsed with the failure of such financial giants as Yamaichi Securities, Hokkaido Takushoku Bank, and other banks in November 1997. As Aoki (2001) suggests, this may have caused a perception crisis, convincing the actors that the institutions in place had ceased to be an effective representation of how the world worked. Yet, this transition may not be complete. Payoffs to depositors may not commence as initially planned, but rather, be postponed due to concerns that the payoffs may lead to financial instability. The national government may also hold incorrect notions of the financial situation surrounding smaller financial institutions, whose inspection remained under the jurisdiction of local governments until 2001.

The "symbiosis with no losers" (*sumiwake*), an expectation *cum* normative value embraced by some heads of weak financial institutions, gives way to a "survival race among losers," as regulated competition within segmented sectors now gives way to enhanced competition with entry and exit, brought on by the Big Bang regulatory reforms (3 and 4). This affects the policymaking process in financial politics. Finance was once a field in which the same "insiders" interacted with one another. In other words, it was a "collusive" system, to refer to the typology of the interaction between the government and the private sector developed by Aoki (2001). However, with the inclusion of new entrants, financial politics in Japan more closely approximates the situation of "anonymous markets" (Aoki) in which the government deals with private sector actors without distinguishing financial firm A from B.

The increase in the number of players in finance—including both the new entrants, as well as the "public" in financial politics—alters the pattern of interaction between the government and private sector (4). In a collusive system where all the actors are fixed over time, an informal pattern of interaction, based on a set of implicit understandings between actors supported by long-term relationships or repeated interaction, may reduce transaction costs by allowing flexible adjustment for future contingencies that cannot be explicitly specified beforehand. However, as the actors in the private sector come and go, the implicit understanding inherent in informal transactions faces more challenges from "outsiders." The interaction pattern becomes more formal, codified to provide for the market becoming more "anonymous," which entails increased demands for transparency and public accountability.[18] For example, since 1995, MOF has repeatedly stressed its efforts to depart from the "old type of financial administration." *Tsutatsu*, once notorious for their *de facto* binding power on the regulated, have been drastically reduced in number and either formalized into administrative legislation for regulation that needs to remain binding, or downgraded into "guidelines" that only affect the regulators.[19]

The nature of public policymaking in finance has changed accordingly. The old system centered around consensus building. In the words of one MOF retired official, financial administration was carried out so that "no one drowns"; in other words, it was a system of "symbiosis." However, in his view, the new environment that surrounds Japan makes it inevitable to take away the "right to survive" from some firms. Administrative and deliberative councils, which focus on "coordination by reason and consensus," may have to give way to "bloodshed and violence," arising out of market pressures or political decisions to bring about effective reforms (Nishimura 1999: 170).

Indeed, the new way of public policymaking has less emphasis on consensus building. Based on our analysis in the previous chapters, we characterize the newly emerging system of public policymaking as one in which "public support" determines the outcome. Whoever succeeds in gaining "public support" gains the upper hand; whether this means the enhancement of "public interest" is a separate issue.

What does all of the above add up to? We observe a shift in the "organizing principles" (or, the fundamental principles recognized by all actors as

---

[18] See also Nakatani (1996: 187–95) for a discussion of the shift from "insider/developing nation" style of decision-making to "outsider/democratic nation" system of decision-making in financial administration. In the former, insiders comprise the administration and domestic financial industry actors; in the latter, outsiders are made up of market players such as consumers, investors, and depositors. He attributes the need to bring about this shift to the end of the "catch-up" stage for Japanese economic development and the international integration of its national economy. While Nakatani's argument has much in common with the argument presented here, his argument puts more emphasis on the "need" for the Japanese economy to accelerate this shift, using the US system as a "focal point" to be emulated. As discussed in the next chapter, we do not share his assumption that institutional change is an inherently positive development for the Japanese nation. [19] See *Kin'yu Zaisei Jijo* (May 25, 1998: 7).

objective characteristics as well as normative values of the institution) of the institution. Under the financial convoy, cooperation and stability were the organizing principles. This was not peculiar to the financial sector, as cooperation between private sector actors and the government through the mechanism of bureaupluralism once characterized the political economy as a whole and was labeled as one of its strengths.[20] Financial stability, or the stability of the financial order, was the goal of financial administration as well as of the financial industries, organized into industrial associations along the lines of segmentation.

Today, competition and transparency are the organizing principles of the emerging new institutional arrangement. Enhanced competition jeopardizes the stability of individual financial institutions by increasing the likelihood of forced exit. The increased threat to organizational survival as well as the addition of new entrants into the market also reduces cooperation to preserve the financial order among financial actors through the industrial associations. The demands for competition and transparency, through legalistic procedural arrangements, make the relationship between the government and financial actors adversarial rather than cooperative.

Other Changes

Let us sum up below how the Big Bang has triggered other changes in finance, and vice versa. The Big Bang, or the change in formal regulatory rules, meant the demise of financial segmentation and the liberalization of actor entry and product availability. As a result, the relevant players in the financial market increased (2). The "failures" in finance since the mid-1990s led the shift within finance away from preventive, informal regulation toward *ex post*, legalistic regulation. The increase in the number of players in finance brought about by the Big Bang reforms reinforces this trend, as the policymaking process (or the pattern of interaction between the government and the private sector) shifted from "collusive" to "anonymous" (4). Because the Big Bang increases competition within the financial sector, financial firms face increased pressure for securing profit in order to survive. This makes such policies as *hokacho* as well as such private sector practices as the rescue by the main banks, relational financing, and cross-shareholding increasingly unsustainable (5). The Big Bang thus affects the shared expectations of the actors as they increasingly realize

---

[20] See the positive assessment of government-industry relations given in Okimoto (1989), for example.

that a "survival race with losers" is a more accurate picture of how the financial world works and that transparency and competition are now the organizing principles rather than stability and cooperation (7).

On the other hand, our analysis of the political process of the Big Bang in the earlier chapters suggests that the Big Bang was a product of, and reinforced by, the other related developments in finance. The change in regulatory agency, or the breakup of MOF due to "failures," was shown to have had an important effect on the Big Bang (1). Likewise, the "failures" brought about the rise of alternatives in the policymaking process and the shift towards an *ex post* legalistic approach (4), reinforcing the changes brought about by the Big Bang. Similarly, the ongoing decline of the dominance of the banking sector in finance (5) was also an important supporting development in the Big Bang, which diversifies the channels of financing for the users of financial services. The change of government in 1993 and the breakdown of the shared expectations about the LDP's continued rule, as well as the challenge to MOF's role as the "organizer" of financial politics (6), were also important in leading MOF and the LDP to launch the Big Bang financial reforms. Clearly, the increasing demands for transparency and competition in the face of financial failures and scandals reinforced the process since 1996 in which the Big Bang package was conceived and carried out (7).

Institutional Change in Finance: Collapse of the Financial Convoy

The shift in the shared expectations as well as the players, the rules, and the interaction patterns, described above, seem to sufficiently support our case: the financial convoy has broken down, and a new institution has been on the rise since 1995. In this sense, while the various components of the financial convoy were reinforcing one another, when the environment changed through failures in finance and economics and the change of government in 1993, many components within finance began to shift, from an institution characterized by stability and cooperation into one characterized by transparency and competition. The Big Bang, being a program launched by a political leader, may have provided a focal point for "reformers": in any case, it was produced by, and is producing, various related changes in finance.

The fact that institutional change, in terms of "the shift in critical mass of the actors' collective beliefs," in finance has been achieved is further confirmed by an incident in February 2000. The cabinet minister for the FRC was forced to resign because he made comments suggesting to heads of small financial institutions that he might be able to somehow influence the inspection results and the ensuing rule-based decisions on early warning and shutdown of operations. His prompt dismissal by Prime Minister Obuchi with little political opposition from within the ruling LDP shows that the collective beliefs of actors in finance have entirely abandoned the convoy system. A consensus seemed to emerge across the ruling parties and the opposition, as well as among the media, that the minister's comments were unacceptable, as they were interpreted to suggest a return to the convoy.[21] This outcome fits the definition of "institutional change" as a shift in collective beliefs about how the world works.

We may identify some critical moments in the breakdown of the convoy system. Guided by our theoretical framework that emphasizes the shared expectations in the institution, we refer below to some events that may have marked change in the shared expectations of actors in this process.

As the start of the process of institutional change, we may point to 1991, when the loss compensation scandal broke, leading to criticism of regulation of the securities industry. This may have been the start of the "decay" of the institution, where actors began to doubt its worth. One event in the process may be of particular interest. The chairman of Nomura Securities testified at a Diet hearing that MOF had given permission for the loss compensation. By revealing the truth, he chose to jeopardize his company's relationship with MOF, the regulator (Nihon Keizai Shimbun 1992: 29). This may be, according to a retired BOJ official, the first time that financial firms dared to confront the regulator, upsetting the prevailing "order" or the relationship between the government and regulated firms.[22] If so, this event may have marked the beginning of the process in which MOF's competence as the "organizer" of financial policymaking become increasingly questioned.

The next juncture may be the end of the LDP's thirty-eight year rule in 1993. As mentioned earlier, this ushered in the era of coalition government, as well as the notion among actors that "governments change." It was shown that the LDP PARC, with its "tribesmen" may not always dominate the policymaking process. Then, in 1995–96, MOF suffered from a series of "failures" (the Daiwa Bank scandal, Housing Loan Affair, and wining and dining scandals). As a result, the political process eventually

---

[21] See *Asahi Shimbun* and *Yomiuri Shimbun*, for example, issues of 25 and 26 February 2000.
[22] Author interview with Shijuro Ogata, July 5, 1999.

led to the discussion of MOF breakup, and MOF lost its standing as the "organizer" of bureaupluralism, as it lost the public trust regarding both its competence and ethics. MOF was no longer the legitimate actor in charge of financial policymaking in the eyes of actors.

Finally, the financial crisis materializes in fall 1997 and some mega banks and securities houses collapse, dealing a final blow to the effectiveness of the "institution" (the Convoy) as a summary representation of the objective reality. Now, the expectations or the "myth of no failure" and the "implicit state guarantee" are irrevocably defied by the events in the real world. The end of the *hokacho* strategy was clear in the crisis of October 1998, in which the LTCB was nationalized. Then, the prompt firing in February 2000 of the FRC minister who suggested a return to the old system confirmed the materialization of institutional change.

Institutional Change in Public Policymaking: The Decay of Bureaupluralism

We turn to the other institutional change that we can identify from our story of financial politics: the decay of bureaupluralism in public policymaking. The policymaking process in financial politics is part of bureaupluralism in the political economy in general. Clearly, what happens in finance cannot but affect the whole mechanism, although whether finance may be seen as representing the change taking place in the larger mechanism may be another issue. In this section, we first recall how much change has materialized in bureaupluralism in finance. Then, we turn to a more general argument, offering a prediction about future developments.

How much change can we see in the policymaking process? It is not that the policymaking process of bureaupluralism has been entirely displaced, even in the world of finance. While the Big Bang policy package came out before, rather than after, the discussion at MOF's deliberative councils, the package still had to go through these councils. The policy package was then referred to the LDP PARC before submission to the Diet, in line with policymaking patterns of the past. What changed is the fact that these bodies lost their monopolies within the policymaking process, as actors found ways to circumvent such processes in which the financial industries' influence was expected to be dominant. Moreover, although MOF lost its monopoly over the role of "organizer" in the policymaking process, it continued to organize deliberative councils such as the Financial System Council until 2001. As of 2000, measures related to the follow-up of the Big

Bang and the strengthening of the financial system were being produced by this council. The same can be said about the continuing influence of the LDP PARC, as was seen in the decision to postpone the start of the payoffs from 2001 to 2002.

Thus, bureaupluralism in finance is not dead; rather, it is in decay. Referring to our frameworks of institutional change and organizational survival, we may interpret the process through which alternative policy-making mechanisms arose as one of decentralized experiments, in which actors engaged when a split appeared among the entrenched actors. The "reformers" who were the minority within their respective organizations (the LDP and MOF) have found ways to go around the policymaking mechanism of bureaupluralism. They have done so by making use of the crisis situation in finance since 1995—reflected in such developments as MOF scandals, the Housing Loan Affair, the MOF breakup, the financial crisis of November 1997, and the financial crisis of October 1998. Such decentralized experiments may have corresponded to the centralized efforts to reform the public policymaking system. Such efforts appeared in the forms of calls for administrative reforms and for political leadership over the bureaucracy. In either case, actors seem to have achieved a near consensus that something is amiss about the policymaking mechanism of bureaupluralism and the way in which it aggregates interests—in other words that "decay" has materialized in bureaupluralism. This trend is not limited to finance, and applies across policy areas.

Thus, we may be seeing a start of institutional change—or of institutional "decay"—in public policymaking. Our theoretical framework suggests that this trend is likely to continue. The shared expectations of continuity with regard to informal interaction, the composition of actors and repeated interaction producing similar results that sustained bureaupluralism, cannot be stably reproduced in the post-1995 world. This is because the new world is one in which change in government, as well as deregulation and administrative reforms, have been introduced. A change in government provides an alternative scenario to continued LDP rule for actors, affecting their hitherto steady relationship of interdependence. Clearly, the exchange of votes and money for access to governmental power cannot continue to take place between the LDP and the industry actors as it once used to, and the policymaking through the LDP PARC no longer functions when the LDP is not in power. With deregulation and administrative reforms, the following changes are likely at the levels of players, formal rules, and interaction patterns. First, the numbers of sets of actors have increased in the process of circumventing the previous process and now are not stable over time because of increased entry into and exit from the market. Second, the formal rules have changed through deregulation in general and through administrative reforms shaking up the central bureaucracy since 1996. Third, the informal interaction patterns, including such means as "wining and dining" and "administrative guidance," cannot prevail without the existence of the shared expectations of continuity in the identity of actors and repeated interactions producing similar results. Moreover, such informal means of interaction are now increasingly out of favor because of the public criticism of such practices, which gathered steam over the past decade.

Whether this trend leads to an entirely new institution to replace bureaupluralism in Japanese public policymaking is unclear as of this writing (May 2000). As our theoretical framework suggests, there is always a possibility at any stage of the process of change that things revert back to normal, confirming the resilience of the institution. It may be that the shared expectations of continuity will somehow be re-instated by developments in the objective world. Indeed, bureaupluralism has shown such resilience in the past. Consider, for example, the many attempts to reform the nature of public administration—such as those undertaken by Prime Minister Nakasone in the 1980s.

Nevertheless, we try below to suggest which scenario is likely to materialize, based on our theoretical framework. We argue that outcomes depend on two factors. First, they depend on whether such experiments to circumvent the established policymaking mechanism take root. Second, they depend on whether the conditions that make public support an important concern for political parties, bureaucratic agencies, and firms—that is, the presence of "failures" and change in the institutional environment—continue to hold.

Will Institutional Experiments take Root?

In our framework of institutional change, actors with alternative strategies increase in number as such strategies are rewarded. Yet, it is unclear whether those minority "reformers" of the financial sector have been rewarded for their strategies. The LDP "mavericks" who led the way with reforms of the MOF and with other changes, such as those who emerged in the fall 1998 Financial Diet, no longer occupy the center of the political stage. Compared to 1996–98, names of reformers such as Shiozaki and Ishihara rarely appear in newspaper headlines (with the exception of Yanagisawa, who headed the FRC in 1998–99). The LDP mavericks and the

Democratic Party failed to take credit for the fall 1998 Financial Diet.[23] And, Prime Minister Hashimoto was forced to resign from office in July 1998 after a humiliating electoral defeat. In this way, he was hardly rewarded for his reform agenda. Among the MOF "mavericks," some may have been given credit, while others were forced to resign due to their involvement in the wining and dining scandals.

Looking beyond financial politics into other policy areas, however, we see ongoing decentralized experiments challenging the policymaking process of bureaupluralism. We note below two examples at the level of local governments influencing the national politics of bureaupluralism.

First, there has been a rise of direct referenda at the local government level on issues such as nuclear power plant construction, the construction of waste disposal facilities, and the location of US military bases in Okinawa. Such local referendums, which started appearing in 1996, represent a new development.[24] A referendum lacks any legal basis and therefore is not legally binding. Nevertheless, it allows the expression of the public's views on an issue, heavily constraining the decisions of political actors, especially local politicians, from the same electorate. In one such instance, a January 2000 referendum against a public works project in Tokushima prefecture, the voters of Tokushima City (the capital and largest city of the prefecture) overwhelmingly cast votes in opposition to a project supported by the Ministry of Construction (MOC) and requested by the heads of thirty-two local governments involved. After the voters of Tokushima city cast a "no" vote, however, its mayor switched sides and announced his opposition to the project. This chain of events presents a challenge to the way bureaupluralism in public works projects formerly operated. In the past, a project typically originated in requests from local government executives and legislatures, was supported by the construction industry and the LDP, and then processed by the MOC. In the aforementioned case, however, a project that started with the request by democratically elected local governments later faced public criticism as its worth came to be questioned. With the success of Tokushima, this kind of effort to circumvent the process of bureaupluralism via local referenda may be expected to be emulated elsewhere.[25]

---

[23] See Amyx (2000 [and 2004]).

[24] The first referendum to take place was in Niigata in 1996. It concerned the construction of a nuclear power plant.

[25] For the Tokushima case and the issue of local referendum in general, see *Asahi Shimbun* and *Yomiuri Shimbun*, issues of January 24 and 25, 2000.

A second example was seen with the April 2000 introduction of a special local tax on banking revenues by the fiscally impoverished Tokyo metropolitan government. Tokyo Governor Shintaro Ishihara, elected by a landslide over candidates from the LDP and Democratic Party, announced the tax on large banks soon thereafter. These banks were paying much smaller amounts in local taxes than they had in the past, due to their spending of pre-tax profits to write-off bad debts amassed during the bubble years. Ishihara proposed adopting a new criterion that taxed pre-tax profits. This move represented another effort to go around the traditional decision-making process surrounding taxation policy, which centered on the Tax Commission (a deliberative council) in the government and on the LDP Tax Research Council.

Naturally, the banking industry vehemently opposed the new Tokyo bank tax. Although the tax was technically legal under national law, the central government opposed its introduction. The Ministry of Home Affairs, in charge of local governments, argued that the tax had the potential to create inequality among local governments. According to MOF and the FRC, the tax conflicted with the central government's policy to revitalize the damaged financial system. Lacking compulsory measures to override Ishihara's decisions, central government actors simply expressed their "concerns" and unsuccessfully tried to convince him to reconsider his plan. Ishihara's strength lay in his large popularity, as revealed by two successive landslide victories. The banking sector, on the other hand, was perceived as the "public enemy." According to public opinion polls conducted by the Asahi and Yomiuri newspapers, 59 percent supported the plan while only 15 percent opposed it. The major parties (the LDP, the Democrats, the Komeito, and the Communists) in the Tokyo legislature, no doubt taking into consideration public sentiment, expressed their support, and thus an overwhelming majority adopted the plan.[26]

Some of these experiments to circumvent the traditional policymaking process may succeed and be emulated, while others may fail.[27] The interesting thing about these developments is that they point to the increased

[26] For the Ishihara case, see *Asahi Shimbun* and *Yomiuri Shimbun*, issues of February 15, 16, 17, 21, and 22, 2000. In a TV news show, Ishihara revealed the planning process. This process was very similar to the Big Bang case: expecting strong opposition, the proposal was planned in great secrecy until its announcement. The idea originated from a senior level bureaucrat of the Tokyo government, but because a premature leak would result in the plan being crushed, preparation was done in secrecy and with the involvement of only a few of staff (http://www.zakzak.co.jp accessed on February 14, 2000 10:15 PST).

[27] Ishihara's policy innovation has already been imitated: the legislature of Osaka Prefecture introduced a similar taxation scheme in May 2000, notwithstanding vehement opposition from the banking sector (*Asahi Shimbun* May 31, 2000).

importance of the public as a determinant of political outcomes, thereby suggesting that our finding in the case of financial politics is not merely an anomaly. Those who seek to create policies that are sure to be opposed by regulatory "constituencies" (e.g. the financial institutions in the Big Bang case, construction industries and local politicians in the Tokushima case, and the banks in the Ishihara case), challenge the policy by going around the policymaking process of bureaupluralism, which revolves around government councils, the LDP PARC, and local governments, and is dominated by these "constituencies." Again, we see that "public support" rather than "public interest" is key to political decisions. Whether or not the construction of a river barrier would be better for the nation is unclear, as it may prevent floods or it may turn out to be a waste of public money. Likewise, whether or not the special tax on banks increases the public's welfare is far from clear—even if Ishihara's calculation is correct that Tokyo would be able to raise revenue as a result—given the impact of the tax on other local governments and the financial system. In these cases, as well as in our account of financial politics, what matters is the fact that the public supports the outcome. In other words, the public opposes construction, and supports a tax on banks and a reform agenda. Whether the reality check applies over the long term is questionable—that is, will the public check, some day, whether the interruption of the construction plan was truly wise, whether the taxation on banks was truly effective, or whether the reforms under the Hashimoto government were truly enhancing the public interest? If not, then we have to rely on "public support" and what the public thinks is in its interests as a determinant of political outcomes, rather than what some might attempt to objectively define as the "public interest."

Will the Public Continue to Play an Important Role?

This discussion of the role of the public leads us to our next criterion in predicting the fate of bureaupluralism. We saw that "failures" are important sources of institutional changes, as they lead the actors to question the worth of the prevailing institution that tells them which strategies to choose by showing "how the world works." We also saw in our account of financial politics that "failures" inflicted the loss of public support upon such actors as MOF and the LDP, driving them to lead the reforms. We also showed that such changes in institutional environment as the "change of government in 1993" were important in increasing the public's worth in politics.

In this regard, then, we may project that the public's new importance in determining political outcomes will continue to hold, if such conditions as "failures" or perceptions that a change in government persist. As for the latter, we are quite confident that the possibility of a change in government will continue to be the shared expectation, especially given that the electoral reforms of 1994 introduced single-member districts. As for the former, Japan is in the midst of plenty of "failures," and faces many potential "failures" in the future. For example, a fiscal crisis at both national and local governments is imminent as of writing (2000). This cannot leave issue-areas that initially seemed insulated from institutional change—such as public works, agriculture, and construction—intact forever. The pension and medical insurance systems are also in danger of collapse. The unemployment benefit system is also under pressure, with the sharp rise in unemployment. The postal savings system seems intact at the time of this writing (2000): however, little is known about its objective fiscal health or whether it truly has a future as it stands. Shifting our emphasis to long-term problems, demographic maturity leads to fiscal crisis at both national and local levels. By the year 2020, an entire overhaul of the systems of taxation and social security will be needed, probably entailing a drastic increase in the national tax burden, which today remains low compared to international standards. Thus, we know that all areas of public policy will face "judgment day" one way or another in twenty years' time.

Given the increasing pace of immutable environmental changes applying to all sectors (such as technological innovation, globalization, and demographic maturity, identified earlier), we cannot but expect a shift to a more "anonymous" system of public policymaking in general, built upon the assumption that actors change over time (instead of the old institution which assumed that actors remained the same). In such a system, as in financial politics, transparency and competition will be expected to be prized more so than stability and cooperation. As one institution (such as finance) shifts, the other institutions are likely to be pressured towards a similar shift, as the demand for transparency is difficult to resist under the higher institution of liberal democracy, whose stability seems beyond doubt for some time. Transparency, then, will be key to institutional change in many sectors. We have yet to know how and where institutional change materializes in each sector and in the political economy in general; it may take "failures" in the form of such things as performance failures and scandals. However, with the ever-increasing demand for transparency, it is not hard to imagine, in any given sector, that such "failures" will become apparent and provide the grounds for institutional change.

Thus, on both counts, we see evidence that shows the deepening of this trend. That is, we see the emergence of similar experiments to the ones we saw in financial politics, and the conditions that make the public important in politics seem to hold over time across issue-areas in the political economy. Thus, we may be confident in our prediction that the decay in bureaupluralism is an initial stage of institutional change toward an alternative policymaking process; as the shared expectations of continuity collapse, bureaupluralism will progressively erode over time.

Conclusion

In this chapter, we tackled two tasks. First, we sought to situate the Big Bang within broader financial sector developments and in the political economy in general. In doing so, we sought to link our story on domestic political economy with environmental changes such as technological innovation and globalization. Second, what delved into what causes changes to come about in our story and how exactly this change comes about.

In response, we applied our theoretical framework of institutional change, developed in Chapter 3, to the account of financial politics we offered in Part II. First, we located our analysis of financial politics in the larger picture. The gap between the faster environmental changes (technological innovation, internationalization of capital, and demographic maturity) and the slower institutional response give rise to "failures" in finance and economics. The change in institutional environment—that is, the new expectation that there could be a change in government—triggered decay in bureaupluralism in public policymaking. Decay in bureaupluralism in public policymaking and "failures" in finance and economics then translated into decay in bureaupluralism in financial policymaking, an important component of the convoy system of regulation. This, in turn, triggered the institutional change in finance and affected bureaupluralism in public policymaking in general.

Second, we related the Big Bang to other changes in finance. We broke down the changes in finance along four levels with the possible ways of defining institutions in mind: players, formal rules, interaction patterns, and shared expectations. As all levels have shifted, including the Big Bang, or the changes in formal regulatory rules, we observe a shift in the organizing principles, the fundamental principles recognized by all actors as objective characteristics as well as normative values of the institution. This shift has been one from cooperation and stability to competition and transparency. The Big Bang was triggering and triggered by, reinforcing and reinforced by, other shifts in the same direction, towards the breakdown of the convoy system in finance.

As a result, we observed institutional change in finance and public policymaking. First, in finance, the convoy system based on "cooperation and stability," has broken down, and a new institution, based on competition and transparency, has been on the rise. This process may have started in 1991, when MOF's status as "organizer" first came under doubt. Such critical moments as the change of government in 1993 and the loss of MOF's standing in 1995–96, culminating in the financial crisis of 1997–98, led a critical mass of actors to change their shared expectations about how the world works. The completion of institutional change was confirmed by an incident in February 2000, in which the head of the FRC was promptly dismissed, amidst public criticism, for his casual comment suggesting a return to the old institution.

Second, in public policymaking, bureaupluralism is in decay. Reflecting the fact that the shared expectations of continuity, the identity of players, formal rules, and interaction patterns have undergone a significant change, actors have started to question the worth of the institution. Since what supported continuity in this institution cannot be stably reproduced in the future, an institutional change is likely to occur. However, as our framework of institutional change suggests, it remains to be seen whether this will lead to full-scale institutional change or another instance of institutional resilience.

Based on our causal framework, we predict that it is likely that this decay will eventually lead to an institutional change on two counts. First, such experiments involving going around the policymaking process of bureaupluralism, as observed in financial politics since 1995, have been emerging. And, second, the conditions that make the public important in politics, such as "failures" and the perceived possibility of a change in government, are likely to continue to hold in the foreseeable future in Japanese politics. Thus, bureaupluralism will erode over time, as the shared expectations of continuity collapse.

How can we summarize the role of the Big Bang in the larger picture? The Big Bang was part of the reform of the formal rules that led to the institutional change in finance, and to the breakdown of the convoy, which culminated in the financial crisis of 1997. In this crisis, it was shown that banks could fail, and a critical mass was led to shift its shared expectations about how finance works. The Big Bang was also part of the ongoing institutional change in public policymaking involving the decay of bureaupluralism, by giving rise to the practices of circumventing bureau-pluralism. This will surely continue to be observed, given the continued existence of the possibility for a change in government and the numerous "failures" looming over the Japanese political economy of today and the future.

9

Conclusion

Japanese politics has changed since 1995. This book has provided evidence of institutional change, or a shift in the shared expectations about how the world works, in the financial realm. Stability, cooperation and continuity once prevailed in the pivotal institutions in financial politics but no longer accurately characterize the post-1995 world. The convoy system of financial regulation has broken down, and the public policymaking mechanism of bureaupluralism is in decay. Eventually, this decay in bureaupluralism is likely to affect every aspect of the political economy, for the causal factors behind change in financial politics—the government's performance failures and scandals and the emergence of the possibility for a change in government—are salient to other policy areas as well.

Chapter 5 demonstrated that the Big Bang initiative cannot be explained by conventional analytical paradigms. It was not a pre-designed or coordinated initiative by a single bureaucratic agency or the result domination of financial politics by financial institutions. Neither was the Big Bang the result of a triumph of politicians over bureaucrats, of non-financial firms joining with MITI to gain the upper hand vis-à-vis the MOF and financial industries, or of an achievement by LDP backbenchers promoting consumerism as a result of the 1994 electoral reforms, which introduced SMD.

Rather, the LDP and MOF saw political gains to be made in obtaining public support independently from the exchange of goods and services with their constituents. Their strategic interaction followed the logic of organizational survival and explains the process of financial politics in 1995–96. A loss of public trust, arising from scandals and performance failures such as the Housing Loan Affair, threatened the survival of the LDP and MOF. Therefore, these organizations sought to recoup public trust by prioritizing the public interest over the interests of their regulatory constituencies. As long as survival was the ultimate goal for the bureaucracy, the views held by suborganizational groups that appeared to increase the prospect of survival eventually won out and emerged as organizational policy.

Our framework stressing the strategic interaction of actors also enables us to understand the complexity of the relationship between the LDP and MOF in 1995–96. In this period, we saw a combination of cooperation (in resolving the Housing Loan Affair), competition (in formulating the Big Bang initiative), and conflict (in the MOF reforms). The timing of the Big Bang reform initiative reflected the priorities set out in Hashimoto's reform agenda at the beginning of his second Cabinet; the pace and the scope of the reforms reflected the fact that MOF took the lead in deciding the content of these reforms; and, the sequencing of reforms reflected the relative clout of different financial industry actors vis-à-vis MOF officials and the "mavericks" within the LDP.

As shown in Chapters 4 and 5, it is unlikely that the potential economic winners from the Big Bang—such as large city banks, the corporate sector, newcomers to finance, or consumers—were influential in bringing about the Big Bang. Large city banks were uncertain of the benefits the Big Bang would bring, since they faced competition with more efficient foreign rivals. Accordingly, the efforts by the corporate sector to lobby MITI and/or the LDP for financial deregulation failed to materialize into a large-scale financial reform package. Furthermore, newcomers to finance lacked entry points to the political process, and consumers were largely unaware of the Big Bang at the time.

We demonstrated in Chapter 6 that domestic financial institutions were, on the whole, unable to effectively oppose the reforms that potentially threatened their survival by increasing competition. The study's comparison of the Big Bang to financial reforms of the past demonstrated that industry actors played a more peripheral role in the former compared to the latter. While financial industry actors influenced the pace of the Big Bang reforms, they exercised little influence over the timing and scope of these reforms. Since those who conceived of the Big Bang bypassed financial industry actors in the planning phase, representatives of the financial industry were forced to respond to an initiative that had already been made public. This differed from past instances where industry actors exercised influence prior to proposed reforms being made public. Moreover, political leadership taken on in the reform initiative by then Prime Minister Hashimoto made it difficult for industry actors to lobby against the initiative through the LDP. In addition, public support for reforms markedly raised costs to the financial industry of assembling a counter-coalition. Financial scandals leading up to the initiative severely damaged the political power of financial firms to forestall the reforms, and the scandals that emerged thereafter propelled the Big Bang forward even further, as the initiative became symbolic of the pledged departure from the convoy system of regulation, a system discredited by the financial crisis.

Our empirical analysis in Part II of various financial reforms in the 1980s and 1990s found that the critical new development in financial politics since 1995 is that the public now matters as a determinant of financial politics because policymaking now occurs in the midst of financial crisis and on the backdrop of greater political fluidity, where changes in government may occur. Alterations in the financial landscape occurred on a number of occasions in the past but the most significant change in Japanese financial politics since 1995 has been a shift in the public policymaking process toward greater inclusiveness. A public policymaking mechanism once centered on "insiders" has evolved to increasingly allow "outsiders" to wield significant influence by drawing on public support to enable them to circumvent the traditional mechanism of bureaupluralism.

Our framework of institutional change enabled us to make sense of this new trend in financial politics wherein the public matters. Two institutions played a pivotal role in financial politics before 1995: the convoy system of financial regulation and the public policymaking mechanism of bureaupluralism. The "convoy" was a regulatory approach in which no financial institution was permitted to move any faster than the slowest firm in a naval convoy. This was secured through regulatory rules, which segmented financial business areas through the restriction of entry and exit, and through reliance on informal policy tools for governmental regulation. It was also supported by shared expectations of stability or continuity in the existing arrangements, and of mutual cooperation— particularly among such insiders as MOF, the LDP, and domestic financial firms—in maintaining these arrangements. Bureaupluralism was a steady bargaining process involving the bureaucracy, the financial industry actors, and the LDP. A stable, informal pattern of interaction among these three sets of actors evolved over time, was guaranteed and reinforced by formal rules, and was sustained by mutually shared expectation of continuity in the composition of actors across time.

Institutional change in financial politics since 1995 has been evidenced by the breakdown of the convoy and the decay of bureaupluralism. Exogenous developments, such as technological innovation and the globalization of finance, as well as change in the institutional environment, brought about institutional change. More specifically, performance failures and scandals in finance, caused by the gap between the faster exogenous developments and the slower institutional response—as well as by the 1993 change of government—brought about a new development in financial politics. This new development was the increased importance of the public in politics and it served to trigger institutional change in finance and public policymaking. Through an analysis of the evolution of the convoy at the level of individual players, formal rules, informal interaction patterns, and shared expectations, we also identified a shift in the organizing principle of this institution—that is, in the fundamental principles recognized by all actors as objective characteristics as well as normative values of the institution. The shift was from cooperation and stability to competition and transparency. The Big Bang reforms themselves moreover had the effect of reinforcing these shifts and further breaking down the viability of the convoy system of regulation.

The decay of the public policymaking mechanism of bureaupluralism reflects a collapse in the shared expectations of continuity that long sustained this policymaking process. Actors have started to question the worth of the institution; nevertheless, it remains to be seen if this decay will lead to full-scale institutional change. Our causal framework leads us to predict that full-fledged institutional change is likely to occur here for two reasons. First, experiments in circumventing the traditional policy-making process have been on the rise. Second, the conditions that increase the salience of the public's voice in politics, such as policy failures and a change in government, are likely to remain salient in the political economy in general. Thus, as shared expectations of continuity fall apart, bureau-pluralism will erode over time.

In Chapter 3, we also developed a typology of financial reforms, focusing on the evolution of coalitions and the way state actors interact with societal actors. Along a continuum depicting who can participate in public policymaking, we argued that coalitions take one of four forms: a status quo-coalition, an inclusive coalition, a defection coalition, or a replacement coalition. In "status quo" coalitions, insiders remain in charge; in "inclusive" coalitions, some outsiders see their interests incorporated while a status quo policymaking process itself remains intact; in a "defection" coalition, some insiders switch strategies and circumvent the established policymaking process; and, in a "replacement" coalition, outsiders take over, eliminating the status quo policymaking mechanism. Interaction by state actors with societal actors produces two patterns: "interest group politics," in which state actors act based on the exchange of goods and services with

Interaction patterns of state and societal actors?

		Interest group politics (I)	Public interest politics (P)
Coalition pattern?	Status quo (S)	**Past financial reforms** *(Domestic financial firms)*	
	Inclusion (C)	**Gradual, more than in the past** *(Non-banks and foreign firms)*	
	Defection (D)	**Drastic, benefiting the powerful** *(Some large banks)*	**The Big Bang** *(LDP and MOF)*
	Replacement (R)	**Drastic, overall reforms** *(Corporate sector)*	**Drastic, overall reforms** *(Non-LDP parties; MITI)*

Note:
In parentheses: actors who could bring about the financial reforms
Shaded: institutional change
(departure from bureaupluralism: alternatives to deliberative councils and LDP PARC)

Gradual / drastic: concepts regarding scope, depth, timing, and pace
More than in the past: measures benefiting the "outsiders" with compensation to some "insiders"
Benefiting the powerful: e.g. liberalization of entry into other areas of finance
The Big Bang: private finance (banking, securities, insurance, and foreign exchange) under MOF's aegis
Overall reforms: scope including areas outside MOF jurisdiction (e.g. postal savings, pension funds)

Figure 9.1 Scenarios of financial reforms: Big Bang as (D: defection, P: public interest politics)

interest groups, and "public interest politics," in which state actors act independently of interest group pressure.

Our empirical analysis in Part II helped establish that within our four-by-two typology of financial reforms, the Big Bang fits the one that combines a "defection" coalition, organized by MOF and the LDP, with "public interest politics" (Figure 9.1). Moreover, we saw that the Big Bang played an important part in the institutional changes in finance and public policymaking taking place in the wider political economy.

Insights into Regulatory Reform in Other Contexts

Figure 9.1 also offers insights into other cases of regulatory reforms. Two, in particular, stand out. First, *entrenched actors may not be as entrenched as they seem.* Our analysis showed that seemingly entrenched actors such as the LDP and MOF willingly engaged in efforts of deregulation when faced with different incentive structures, such as the need to recoup lost public support or to defend their organization against dismantlement. In other words, the image of the past may be misleading when trying to predict future behavior, since strategies may need to change to achieve the same goals of maintaining public support and organizational survival.

To make this point, we showed that establishing a hierarchy of goals wherein the struggle for survival prevails over all others leads to more realistic behavioral assumptions for the bureaucracy. This logic of organizational survival enables us to account for the seemingly puzzling behavior of MOF and the LDP in this period. This logic enables us to explain why MOF would be willing to give up some of its regulatory power and why the LDP engaged in such a complex relationship with MOF in the financial politics of 1995–96.

Second, *voting may not be the only way the public influences politics.* Elections certainly matter to political parties; the strategy adopted by the LDP on the Big Bang reforms as it faced tough competition from its rivals in the 1996 elections confirms this generally accepted view. However, bureaucrats and regulated industry actors also have incentives to cater to the general public's desires so as to boost their own public support. Failures lessen public support for the organization by undermining per- ceptions of competence and ethical behavior, and political influence tends to decrease accordingly. When organizational survival is in danger, actors must put all other preferences aside to ensure this ultimate goal. In this way, the public need not go so far as to engage in direct action through such activities as boycotts or mass protests to wield political influence. Organizations have the incentive to promote the public interest whenever failures lead such organizations to be labeled as "public enemies." This finding is important, as it enables us to question the conventional assump- tion that societal actors can only exercise significant political influence through organized groups and sheds light on the public's influence outside of the voter-legislator relationship focused on by proponents of the principal-agent approach.

Implications for Economic Reforms in Other Policy Areas

Can we generalize the findings from our study of policymaking and regula- tion in the financial sector to argue that change is taking place across the Japanese political economy as a whole? On the surface, there are many areas of non-change in the political economy, such as agriculture and construc- tion; yet, it is hard to believe that the changes in bureaupluralism and the trend toward greater inclusion of the public in the policymaking process will not spill over to politics in general to some extent.[1] In budget politics, for example, the key actors were once clearly the leaders of factions for policy areas such as bullet train construction or taxation. And, budget compilation previously proceeded smoothly by dealing with these actors. Yet, the policymaking "manual" of the old days no longer works, according to one LDP staff member interviewed. Former LDP heavyweight, Koichi Kato, has also stressed the need for politicians and bureaucrats to maintain distance. According to Kato, a new form of politics has arisen in Japan where "politicians are increasingly forced to grapple with public policy issues rather than simply rely on the bureaucracy to solve most problems."[2] There is little reason to believe that his words are meant to apply only to financial policymaking.[3] Moreover, the loss of public support for government officials and occurrence of scandals has not been limited to the financial bureaucracy.

Nevertheless, it is important to ponder how finance differs from other areas in the political economy. In the next section, we consider issues of comparability and offer some possible determinants of economic reform in general by introducing a rudimentary two-level model of economic reforms. In doing so, we hope to clarify the generalizability of our findings about financial politics to other policy areas—especially agriculture, construction, telecommunications, transportation, and postal savings— where the policymaking mechanisms of bureaupluralism were also the norm.

Issues of Comparability

Our analysis concerns the politics of economic reform and covers economic regulatory reform, or the reform of economic regulation of private actors, and reform of the economic regulators themselves. Economic regulatory reform must be distinguished from budgetary politics, where public spending is the main issue, and from social regulatory reform, where the reforms of social regulations such as those governing food, drugs, and the environment are concerned. Both policy areas lie outside the scope of our argument.

---

[1] I thank Steven Vogel for challenging me to think more deeply about the cases of non-change and the problems they pose for generalizability.

[2] See Asahi Shimbun (1997) and Kato's speech at the Center for Strategic and International Studies (Washington D.C.) given on May 18, 1998 (available, as of April 2000, through Kato's web site: http://www.katokoichi.org).

[3] See Curtis (1999) for a contrary view that discounts politicians' talks of reforms.

Areas of potential economic regulatory reform include the financial, telecommunications, transportation, and energy sectors. In these areas, the regulatory rationale derives primarily from economic concerns, including natural monopolies, scarcity of resources, excessive competition, and information asymmetry.[4] Thus, reforms tend to focus primarily on governmental controls over price, entry, and the range of business enjoyed by industry actors. The aim here is for the public—that is, the consumer—to be able to pay less while enjoying greater freedom in selecting the services they use in their daily lives.

Budget expenditures naturally affect all areas of the economy, reflecting the encompassing range and size of the national budget of an industrialized nation. However, by budgetary politics, we mean the areas of political economy whose stake in budget politics for their businesses is high. Industries with heavy dependence on public works, such as agriculture and construction, fall into this category. The rationale for reforms in budgetary politics is comparable to that for economic regulatory reforms: that the reforms would bring down the price level for the services, reduce the public expenditures, and thus result in lower taxes for the general public.

However, reforms involve many different perspectives for the areas of construction and agriculture. The construction industries on the whole do not face government economic regulations related to entry or price control. What is perceived to be the pivotal hindrance in construction, the bid-rigging system, is nothing but an illegal, *de facto* system of survival that construction firms created. It is a private sector practice; therefore, meaningful reform must rely on the stricter enforcement of anti-monopoly laws—although changes in government bidding practices may be helpful.

In agriculture, revision of the laws governing agriculture, as well as related to the introduction of foreign products, may bring down the price level of food. While this would benefit the consumer public, it would also lead to the demise of the agricultural sector. However, not all the agricultural regulations are economic regulations with economic purposes, such as guaranteeing adequate supply or protection of users. The laws governing agriculture are hostile to the commercialization of agriculture, largely due to historical and political reasons. These laws deal with such areas as land use, corporate ownership, and entry control and prevent the land ownership pattern from reverting to the one that existed prior to the introduction of land reforms after Second World War, where landlords dominated

---

[4] See Okimoto and Rohlen (1988) for a discussion of "excessive competition."

sharecroppers. Because these reforms were part of the initiative to democ-ratize the economy, the issue still has a social dimension, and this powerfully hinders reforms more rooted in economic rationale. Moreover, agriculture is an area where economic reforms such as the introduction of international competition face strong opposition for reasons such as national food security and environmental protection.

What then would "Big Bang" reforms look like in areas other than finance? Would such reforms take the form of the removal of governmental regula-tory control over price, entry, and permitted business areas? Or, would they take the form of much stricter enforcement of anti-monopoly laws and a change in government practices—such as procurement, bidding, the execution of budget expenditures, and the like—as it has in construction? Or, would they take the form of a change in agricultural laws, many of which are regulations with little economic basis?

In economic regulatory reforms, the benefits to the public of reform are easier to grasp than in many other policy areas, as reforms mean that users of services pay lower prices and enjoy more discretion over service providers. In contrast, even if the price level comes down in the construction sector due to reform, the public cannot be said to benefit as directly or frequently from this change. Reforms consist less of lifting governmental regulations than of changing the behavior of the private sector by strengthening regulatory oversight. While more efficient public works operations may lead to decreased public expenditures and lower taxes, the causal link here is precarious and thus the benefits to the public are much less tangible than the benefits of economic regulatory reforms. In agriculture, those advocating reforms by citing the benefits of increased economic efficiency may encounter strong opposition from those supporting the status quo due to reasons that have little to do with economic rationale, such as food security, environmental protection and the protection of the livelihood of small farmers. Our findings in the financial policy arena are more likely to be relevant to areas such as telecommunications, energy, and some areas related to transportation, where reforms with similar aims have been carried out since the Hashimoto administration's efforts at deregulation.[5] With this limitation in mind, we turn now to identify some possible determinants of economic reforms more generally.

[5] A transportation version of the "Big Bang" was being carried out as of this writing, virtually doing away with the regulatory control over the demand and supply of transportation ser-vices. In telecommunications, the rapid diffusion of cellular phones can be partly attributed to the deregulation over the transaction rules of the cellular phones, which were formerly consid-ered as small radio broadcasting stations. In energy, the deregulation of electricity as well as oil has steadily progressed.

Role of Political Cover

In finance, we saw how MOF and financial industry actors lost public support, rendering the LDP unwilling to provide political cover to either. Under the threat of losing power, the LDP chose to support the "public interest" over "constituency interests." In this way, the provision or withdrawal of "political cover" represents a way in which politicians balance the two sets of interests when they collide with each other in the economic reform process. The relative electoral importance of a regulatory constituency versus the relative electoral importance of public support at a particular point in time appears to determine whether political cover is provided or withdrawn by politicians.

RELATIONSHIPS BETWEEN CONSTITUENCY SUPPORT AND ELECTORAL VITALITY

We seek to differentiate among constituencies according to how these constituencies appear to politicians. To do so, we need to ask how vital, or expendable, the support of a particular group is to the political parties. Here the characteristics of ties linking the LDP and industry are important in determining the amount of political cover provided to a particular industry. Finance can be distinguished from sectors upon which the LDP relies heavily to provide votes, such as agriculture and construction. Financial industries supported the LDP mostly at the party level by supplying electoral funds without making many specific policy demands. In this way, they provided "untied financial support" (Okimoto 1989). However, the degree of influence the industries were able to obtain through this contribution was significantly lessened in the post-1993 world for the following three reasons. First, the LDP lost its monopoly over this type of contribution—of maintaining the pro-business political regime of liberal democracy—as industries fearing an LDP fall from power contributed to some of the non-LDP conservative parties. Second, the financial industries, especially banking, had to curtail contributions when their businesses began suffering in the face of mounting public criticism. Third, one certain result of the 1994 electoral reforms entailed reducing the amount of money involved in campaigning. According to a retired LDP lawmaker, "the financial industries do contribute money [to the LDP], but it matters little to election outcomes."[6]

On the other hand, in construction and agriculture, electoral support is given to individual politicians, rather than to the party, and these industries

---

[6] Author interview, July 1999.

not only supply funds but also blocs of votes. This may have a large effect on the LDP's willingness to take steps that might drastically curtail the vested interests in these areas. Politicians who only receive funds through the party and those who receive funds and votes at the individual level face different incentives when facing the call for structural reforms aimed to benefit the consumer public—the latter is much more likely to be constrained by their constituencies than the former.

Electoral vitality may be merely a reflection of the over-representation of the rural population due to the electoral system. In the rural areas, the local economies heavily depend on agriculture and construction, supported by public works. The sheer number of those directly and indirectly involved in these industries, magnified by the electoral system's over-representation of the rural areas' political influence, may be another constraint on the changes.[7]

PUBLIC ATTITUDE AND VOLUME OF ATTENTION AS DETERMINANTS OF PUBLIC SUPPORT

Another variable that determines the political cover over a constituency may be the degree of public support for the industry. In other words, how would politicians appear to the public if they spoke out in favor of or against an industry?

In our analysis of financial reforms, we saw that performance failures and scandals turned the public against a particular agency. As we discussed in Chapter 3, scandals are unlikely to take root in the absence of performance failures, being dismissed as exceptions; however, scandals provide symbols, or focal points, for public criticism against agencies with performance failures. Together, performance failures and scandals undermine the prevailing institution's effectiveness as a representation of how the world works and generate a sense that something is amiss.

However, given the public's short attention span and limited range of attention, such failures must be recurrent and long-lasting to have effects. This may be part of what determines public support for a certain industry. We should also expect the volume of attention—that is, how much the public cares—to vary across fields. After all, people may decrease their support of an industry, yet may not care enough for their decreased support to have a tangible impact. Later we delve into these two issues of public support and volume of attention, depicting public support as a function of public attitude and volume of attention.

[7] Numerous works note this electoral over-representation of rural areas in Japan. See for example, Okimoto (1989).

Performance Failures and Scandals as Determinants of Public Attitude

Our story about the Big Bang tells us how significant performance failures and scandals may be in influencing the public attitude toward the respective industries or bureaucratic agencies. Policy failures and scandals hurt public trust in MOF in two respects: the policy failures (such as the financial crisis) undermined public trust in the ministry's competence, and the scandals hurt public trust in the bureaucrats' ethics or integrity. As a result, MOF faced a credible threat of breakup; protecting the agency became a very unattractive choice for politicians as they faced a heightened threat of replacement.

How MOF's political influence was hurt after 1995 can be illustrated by invoking two historical incidents. In the first incident, in the late 1980s, MOF was wildly unpopular during the attempt to introduce the consumption tax, yet LDP leadership was able to protect MOF.[8] In addition, the Recruit Scandal at this time raised concerns about the ethics of *politicians*; while two top officials of other ministries were arrested, the ethics of bureaucrats were less a focus of scrutiny. An 1988 Asahi Shimbun editorial, for example, questioned the *morale*—rather than *morals*—of the bureaucracy. The editorial stated that, despite some defects, bureaucrats "ought to be credited for their enthusiasm for their jobs and high morale" (November 8, 1988). In the second instance, of the 1991–93 financial reforms, questions arose regarding the competence of bureaucrats, but doubts regarding their ethics remained untouched. Two collections of newspaper articles by the leading economic newspaper *Nihon Keizai Shimbun*, published in 1992 and 1998, show the difference before and after 1995. In 1992, the paper suggests the possibility of MOF's incompetence in financial administration; however, its tone is much more subdued compared to another editorial from 1998. The later deals with the financial crisis of 1997–98 and severely criticizes both the competence and ethics of MOF.

The financial industry suffered from scandals, as well as from poor performance. The banks were vilified in their involvement in the scandals, their performance was hurt by their bad debt problems, their restructuring efforts were slower in pace than those taking place in the rest of the economy, and they had to rely on public funds for recovery. These events were sufficient to turn the public against the banks. The securities industry fared no better because the scandals hurt them, while the stock market's slump severely constrained their businesses. The insurance industry was the least

---

[8] See Kato (1994) for example, on how the LDP leaders closely cooperated with MOF for the introduction of indirect taxation.

affected by the scandals, yet they suffered from damaged balance sheets due to the excesses of the bubble years and the interest rate gap that emerged out of high guaranteed rates to the insured but low asset returns to insurance firms. The financial industries in general were shaken up further by the financial crisis of 1997–98, when major banks and securities firms went under.

In this environment, public repugnance against the financial industries erupted at a number of points. Recall the uproar against the Housing Loan package and the racketeering scandals, resulting in some cases in a boycott with serious effects on the profits of the firms involved, undermining their prospects for survival.

Thus, we posit that performance failures and scandals do matter in determining the public's attitude towards these actors. Yet, agriculture, telecommunications, or transportation—which some described in the past as "pockets of inefficiencies" (Okimoto 1989)—did not suffer from scandals of similar intensity.[9]

However, the construction industry faced a wave of scandals similar in magnitude to those in finance.[10] These scandals resulted in the arrests of numerous politicians, including one influential LDP politician and many local government heads—among them governors—revealing the systematic involvement of the construction industries in politics. The scandals certainly turned the public against the construction sector. In terms of performance, the construction industry also faired poorly, as it was hit by the slump in the real estate market and, at the same time, was one of the major borrowers involved in the bad debt problem plaguing the banking industry. Yet, developments did not proceed as they did with the Big Bang in finance. In this way, performance failures and scandals may alone be insufficient for the public to act as a determinant of economic reforms.

Public Visibility as a Determinant of Volume of Attention

We now turn to the second determinant of public support. As we saw from the comparison of finance and construction, the change in attitude towards one constituency may not necessarily lead political actors to take

[9] A corruption scandal in 2000 involving the public works section of the MAFF appeared to have the potential to accelerate economic reforms in the agricultural sector, bringing the pace of reforms here closer to those observed in finance.

[10] We exclude the scandals concerning the Ministry of Health and Welfare (MHW), as these concerned areas of "social regulatory reform." The MHW was riddled with scandals and suffered a loss of public trust, but public criticism did not lead to the condemnation of the industries whose actors were involved or to condemnation of health-related industries, in general.

actions that might hurt the other sets of interests they have to consider—those of their constituency. What more then is needed to spur action?

We assert that the volume of public attention matters; even if the public forms a negative opinion about certain actors, whether this leads to material results may depend on how visible and influential this discontent becomes. How is the volume of public attention determined? "Public visibility," the degree of visibility and tangibility to the public of a particular issue area, may be crucial here. How does the issue area affect the life of the average Japanese? What is the position of the particular industry in the economy?

Finance distinguishes itself from construction in this aspect. The financial crisis, in which large banks and other financial institutions collapsed, was highly visible and directly affecting daily life, giving the public many reasons to worry. Bank deposits and loans, securities investment, and insurance products have a much deeper impact on the public's life than do the products offered by the construction industry, which include houses and condominiums. Furthermore, the fact that billions and trillions of public funds were injected in the financial system made the public more concerned. During the Housing Loan Diet, the public was strongly opposed to the idea of injecting 685 billion yen—a minor sum compared to the 30 to 60 trillion yen ceiling set three years later—of taxpayers' money. Political rhetoric such as "blood tax" (*ketsuzei*) was often invoked to turn the public opinion against the banking industry, MOF, and the LDP. For MOF, the economic slump that seriously affected the public from mid-1997 may have also had an impact, as the ministry was often charged as largely responsible for this slump, due to the fiscal contraction and tax increase it introduced in April 1997. In contrast to the MOF, the MOC has maintained a low public profile.

The role of construction in budgetary politics also differs significantly from the role of finance, in terms of visibility. While inefficient public works projects may amount to a waste of public money and thus eventually lead to higher taxes, this concern is much less tangible to the Japanese public, in that the causal connection is opaque. Hence, the result—or how much more it costs taxpayers—is far from clear. Still, concerns regarding construction do exist; some of the top firms have had financial difficulties, and numerous small firms have failed. If we compare this situation to an imminent financial crisis, in which personal deposits or lines of credit—vital lifelines for the public—are endangered or taxpayer money is injected, however, we see a clear difference. The problems in finance were much more visible to the public during the financial crisis, keeping the volume of public attention on finance consistently high compared to the volume of attention on construction.

Degree of public visibility may differentiate the behavior of the construction industry and the bureaucratic actors who oversee it from the behavior of financial institutions and their bureaucratic regulators. The financial industry faces a more direct threat of sanction from the public, such as a boycott, than does the construction industry. And, this is a function of exposure to the public. Both bureaucratic agencies face a different set of incentives as well. If the MOC does not see a threat to its survival, it may have fewer reasons to jeopardize its relations with the industries by introducing reforms in the public interest at the industry's expense.

So far, we have shown that public support is a function of public attitude towards a particular sector or bureaucratic actors and public attitude is, in turn, affected by performance failures and scandals and volume of public attention. Public attention, in turn, is affected by the public visibility of an issue. An interesting comparison to the situation faced by banks was the situation faced by the postal savings system at the same time. This system was a beneficiary of the plight of the financial industries, since it competes with them for individual savings. A loss of public support for banks was accompanied by an increase in public support for the postal savings system. Individual depositors flocked to postal savings, with its government guarantee and higher interests rates paid on deposits, even though such interest rates remained low. The post offices, located in almost all municipalities, seem to have acquired increased public support because they were seen as the small depositor's ally. In addition, the local postmasters provide bloc votes, and thus vital electoral support, to the LDP, giving the latter reasons to provide them with strong political cover.

PUBLIC SUPPORT OF THE BUREAUCRACY

Turning our attention to the bureaucracy, we may posit from our findings that the concern for organizational survival gives a strong impetus for the bureaucracy to re-coup the loss of public trust even at the expense of the interests of the industries it regulated. Naturally, political cover over the bureaucracy directly affects the bureaucracy's prospects for survival. However, this is affected by the electoral clout of the sector and the public attitude towards sector actors. Moreover, the public attitude may directly affect the bureaucracy's behavior, as the bureaucracy needs the acceptance and cooperation of the public for the policy measures it devises and enforces. While the maintenance of ties with the industries under its jurisdiction are important concerns for the bureaucracy as well, the public attitude towards these ties also determines the relative importance of the industries' concerns for the bureaucrats.

In this regard, the public attitude towards the bureaucracy in general has systematically turned negative, both at the levels of competence and ethics: and the given discussion does not only apply to MOF. We previously cited the 1988 Asahi Shimbun editorial, written in the wake of the Recruit Scandals, which portrayed bureaucrats as having strong integrity. In 1993, an influential economist, Yukio Noguchi, described the bureaucracy as "ethically clean and relatively competent" while arguing against bureaucratic rule (Noguchi 1993). At the time, such a characterization did not sound ridiculous; however, this type of positive characterization was difficult to find in the media or among opinion leaders after 1995.

Public opinion polls show a declining trend of public support towards the bureaucracy in general. Asahi Shimbun polls reveal that respondents who "do not trust bureaucrats" rose from 51 percent in 1994, before the scandals, to 65 percent in 1996 following the Ministry of Health and Welfare (MHW) scandals concerning HIV-contaminated blood products, and finally, to 71 percent in 1998 after the MOF wining and dining scandals (Asahi Shimbun March 4, 1998).[11]

PUBLIC SUPPORT AND INDUSTRY BEHAVIOR

Finally, we maintain our claim that level of public support matters indirectly in determining industry behavior, by determining the nature of political cover and of bureaucratic behavior—as well as directly—through its threat of sanctions. Such factors as the industry's electoral clout, the public visibility of an industry, and the public's attitude toward an industry all affect how the industry's concerns are translated into economic reforms.

We may add another important dimension that has been missing in our discussion of domestic politics: the economic environment. Performance failures and scandals, determinants of public attitudes, reflect poor performance by an industry. That is, if all was well, we would be much less likely to see such problems erupt in the first place. How, then, is the performance of an industry determined? To answer this, we need to turn our attention to the economic environment, in which regulatory reforms take place, in order to fully capture the dynamics within the domestic political economy. The economic environment, beyond the reach of actors, may drastically change and render the existing regulations meaningless, or may reduce

---

[11] Note, however, that the 1996 research had different methodologies (telephone) from the ones in 1994 and 1998 (interviews).

the benefit of the regulation, or the "rent" to be distributed among the regulated industries.[12]

Thus, we add to the picture the dimension of developments in the environment outside the political interplay of actors in financial politics. Such environmental factors include technological innovation, international competition, and the institutional environment. This dimension affects not only the industries—though its effect on their performance is most direct— but also other actors such as politicians, bureaucrats, and the public.

Technological innovation proceeds more rapidly in finance than it does in other fields such as construction. Under such conditions, even if the regulated industries succeed in keeping the regulations that guarantee the continuation of the status quo, the effectiveness of these regulations is undermined by rapid innovation that takes place outside of the interaction of actors within the domestic political system.

Exposure to international competition is another factor that may accelerate or impede regulatory reforms. For example, if the global integration of national markets proceeds to a large degree, as in finance, failures—or a gap between what should be achieved and the reality—are more likely to be noted by relevant actors, creating the chance for the materialization of regulatory reforms. On the other hand, if an industry is insulated from the international market, as construction is at the local level, regulatory reforms may not be implemented as rapidly, as failures are unlikely to be perceived in the absence of alternatives to what is currently available.

The institutional environment may serve as another factor. What is happening in one industry may be relevant to other industries, reflecting the existing relationship. In this regard, the spillover from finance may be significant, given the pivotal position of the financial sector in the political economy. Suppose that regulatory reforms occur in finance to increase competition and increase the presence of foreign capital, drastically altering the behavior of financial firms in that they become more survival-conscious and more interested in pursuing short-term profits than relational financing (although, given the increased future uncertainty, it may not turn out to be worth the effort), then industries with a heavy dependence on financial firms, such as construction, which is heavily dependent on banks, may be forced to alter their strategies. This development then increases the chance of regulatory reforms in those industries. Meanwhile, other industries with less dependence on private financial firms, such as agriculture, may not face a similar imperative.

---

[12] See Peltzman (1998).

TWO-LEVEL MODEL OF ECONOMIC REFORMS: DOMESTIC POLITICS AND THE ECONOMIC ENVIRONMENT

Now that we have identified some causal factors from our analysis of financial politics and explored the implications for other areas of the political economy, we proceed to build a two-level model of economic reforms. In doing so, we endeavor to use our case study for theory building purposes. We posit two levels of activity surrounding economic reforms: (1) domestic politics and (2) the economic environment.

In domestic politics (D), public support (PS) can be characterized as an increasing function of public attitude (PA); Public attitude, in turn, is an increasing function of the performance of actors, indicated by such developments as scandals and performance failures (SF), and of volume of attention (VA)—which is an increasing function of a sector's public visibility (PV). Political actors' behavior, or "political cover" (PC) over an industry or bureaucracy, will be an increasing function of public support and "electoral vitality" (EV)—that is, how crucial the support from a sector is to the election efforts. The bureaucratic behavior, driven by bureaucratic survival (BS), is an increasing function of political cover and public support, the latter in fact determining the former to a large extent. Public support and political cover affect industry survival (IS).[13]

In addition to the factors mentioned previously—factors mostly affecting the industries by determining their performance—there are factors that relate more directly to the "economic environment" (E). The economic environment can be conceptualized as an increasing function of such factors as technological innovation (TI), global integration (GI), and institutional environment (IE).

Figure 9.2 shows this. We saw from the Big Bang that the nature of public support, political cover, bureaucratic survival, and industry survival are the central causal factors. By transforming the causal factors, we may posit that scandals and performance failures, public visibility, and electoral vitality within the domestic political system, as well as the economic environmental factors, provide clues for understanding and comparing

---

[13] We do not delve into the relationship between BS and IS, as PS determines the bureaucratic strategy towards a particular industry. In the Big Bang, given the low public support for the financial industries and MOF, bureaucratic survival for MOF required severing ties with the financial industries: IS may seem to be a negative function of BS. Yet, if PS is high for a particular industry, the bureaucracy may be expected to be providing a cover in its pursuit of survival. Thus, in its pursuit of survival, the bureaucracy is expected to support an industry with high public support, while it would not do so for an industry with low public support: as long as bureaucratic survival is linked to public support, this causal factor (BS) appears to be redundant.

1. D: domestic politics
PS: public support = (PA: public attitude, VA: volume of attention)
PA: public attitude = (SF: scandals and performance failures)
VA: volume of attention = (PV: public visibility)
PC: political cover = (PS: public support, EV: electoral vitality) = (PA: public attitude,
                        VA: volume of attention, EV: electoral vitality)
BS: bureaucratic survival = (PS: public support, PC: political cover)
IS: industrial survival = (PS: public support, PC: political cover)

Economic Reforms = (PS: public support, PC: political cover, BS: bureaucratic survival,
                        IS: industrial survival)
                 = (PS: public support, PC: political cover)
                 = (PA: public attitude, VA: volume of attention, EV: electoral vitality)
                 = (SF: scandals and performance failures, PV: public visibility,
                        EV: electoral vitality)

2. E: economic environment
E: economic environment = (TI: technological innovation, GI: global integration,
                        IE: institutional environment)

→ *Economic Reforms = {D: domestic politics (SF: scandals and failures,*
   PV: public visibility, EV: electoral vitality); E: economic environment
   (TI: technological innovation, GI: global integration, IE: institutional environment)}

Notes: In X = (Y, Z): X is an increasing function of Y and Z

Figure 9.2 Two-level model of economic reforms: domestic politics and the economic environment

the economic reforms across sectors. We propose this rudimentary model in the hopes of providing a building block towards a better understanding of regulatory reforms in general. By gathering data across sectors and explaining the interaction and the relationship between each factor, we may be able to see which factors in our model contribute most to advancing or impeding economic reforms.

Policy Implications

Our study has shown that we now need to shift our emphasis from "stability" to "change" in conceptualizing Japanese politics today. This shift in emphasis ought to take place not only at the level of theory but also at the level of practice, given the fast pace of technological innovation, the deepening global integration, and change in the institutional environment. Accordingly, public administration needs to be carried out with the assumption of "change" rather than the assumption of "continuity," and the long-established emphasis on following precedents in policymaking abandoned.

Our study has also shown the importance of public support for the bureaucracy. It may be said that the dismantling of MOF resulted from its officials' lack of recognition that public support is not always guaranteed and must be earned. It is true that the "political stock" (Aoki 1988) of bureaucrats has been high as a result of accumulated credit given to it during the nation's postwar economic development. However, such past "savings" were depleted during the 1990s with performance failures and scandals. Some MOF officials liken themselves to *kobushi* (old *samurai*), who contribute to the nation while receiving little credit; what motivates them, despite the lack of recognition, is that the nation will understand or appreciate them in the long run. Nevertheless, in a world in which public support determines political outcomes, a more active attitude of reaching out to the public to cultivate public support is necessary. This is particularly true given that the implicit bonding of trust between the bureaucrats and the public weakened markedly during the 1990s.

The realization that public support is not automatically guaranteed and that performance failures and scandals are key variables that affect public support will certainly improve the bureaucracy in many ways. It will force it to continuously prove its worth to the public, as well as avoid the kind of imprudent conduct often observed during the excesses of the bubble years.

Looking back on what occurred in financial politics in the 1990s, it is notable how insiders at MOF and in the financial industries were slow to grasp developments in finance. Today's world is complex and it is impossible to predict the future; nonetheless, bureaucratic and private sector actors must each attempt to formulate strategies in anticipation of what is to come in five to ten years, if public policymaking is to benefit the nation. Here the world of academia may make a contribution. If study of real world changes is accompanied by a framework that enables policymakers to better interpret and influence the complexities of the world, the worlds of academia and policymaking can well complement each other.

It is hoped that this study has provided a focal point for institutional change by demonstrating how politics is changing and by increasing actor awareness of institutional change in public policymaking. It is our wish that this study will also accelerate the search for a new system of public policymaking. We should seriously consider alternatives to the deliberative councils and the LDP PARC by asking what kind of arrangement would better reflect the public interest in a world in which stability, cooperation, and continuity no longer prevail.

The aforementioned points suggest a number of measures for improving public policymaking. These include efforts to systematically reflect new technological innovation in policy formation; efforts to reach out to outsiders, including foreign actors and the public; and questioning those things long taken for granted in the bureaucracy, such as permanent employment and the current division of labor between politics and administration.

Better use of the Internet may have the potential to materialize some of these concerns. The recently introduced use of the Internet in the public comment system and the practice of soliciting comments on planned measures, in the mold of the US public comment system, has already resulted in an inclusion of outsider views in the policymaking process. These outsiders have included the public, foreign financial firms, and even the US government.

That politics is driven by public support leads to the recommendation to introduce into public policymaking the use of public opinion surveys and private sector strategies akin to marketing. Experiences since the Housing Loan resolution suggest that MOF's understaffed public relations department is grossly inadequate in this regard.

In-house breeding of experts who can cope with new developments may be useful in many respects; however, the government may need to procure talent from other channels than the usual recruiting process. We have already seen financial inspectors, lawyers, and accountants hired into the government. Given the increasing importance of social science research for public policymaking, the recruitment of social scientists to research divisions might also be pursued.

The Need for a Fusion of Power in Relationships Between Politicians and Bureaucrats

Our analysis shows that public interest cannot be objectively determined and that public support determines politics. This fact has implications for the relationship between politicians and bureaucrats, one of the hotly contested issues in the political debate of the 1990s. As often observed in the postwar period, when consensus exists on a single goal, such as economic catch-up, bureaucrats may have a greater role to play. Yet, when goals conflict with one another in a liberal democracy, politicians are the ones to present their views and bear responsibility through elections. If our analysis is correct and public support must substitute for public interest, which cannot be objectively determined, then politicians who reflect public support should be the ones to determine what the public interest is.

Given this and the likelihood of changes of government and failures in the future, what needs to be done? We need reform of the central government bureaucracies far beyond what was done in the 1996 administrative reforms. We must more strongly fuse the legislative and executive powers, a basic principle in a well-functioning parliamentary government according to the English political thinker, Walter Bagehot (Bagehot 1928 [1867]). Since failures will occur in the future, and tough choices—such as increased burdens for the nation or the extinction of a particular sector—cannot be avoided, it is essential that public administration increase its unity with the political leadership. In the context of changes in government, it is clear that the old-style alliance between the LDP, which was always assumed to remain in power, and the permanent bureaucracy, who is always present in accordance with lifetime employment, cannot be sustained over time. As Nishimura (1999) suggests, bureaucratic initiative works best to forge a consensus among all involved. When the "death" of a certain party or an industry is involved, however, decisions made by the political leadership become necessary.

This suggests a need for increased political presence in the bureaucracy, given the decline in the political influence of the latter in the 1990s. Traditionally, the bureaucracy has prided itself on its independence from the legislative branch. However, as Bagehot claims of parliamentary government, parliamentary ministers are the best defenders of the bureaucracy against the parliament. "The appointment of a parliamentary head, connected by close ties with the present ministry and the ruling party in Parliament" is as necessary in today's Japan as in Victorian Britain.[14] Of course, Japan already has a cabinet with ministers heading each ministry; however, given the increased tasks for the government to perform, the system of two or three politicians overseeing each ministry was inadequate. No doubt in recognition of this concern, reforms effective from 2001 increase the number of politicians in public administration, following in line with the practice in the United Kingdom.

This is one important step, but we need to remind ourselves that this is not the only way to increase political presence. The increased difficulty for political newcomers to run for Diet seats, especially salient with the introduction of SMDs, may limit the resources available for a well-functioning public administration. Provided that the labor market in the private sector becomes flexible with regard to managerial resources—with a shift in the

[14] See Bagehot (1928 [1867]: 156–93, especially 165).

institutional environment for example—a US-style appointment system that recruits experts, such as lawyers and business executives, into the government with political mandates may provide an interesting alternative.

Is Institutional Change Good or Bad for the Japanese Nation?

Our framework of institutional change suggests that while the "old" institution has been discredited by failures, there is no guarantee that the "new" institution will perform better. In the process of institutional change, such focal points as foreign practice, history, and leadership provide competing symbolic systems (Aoki 2001). Objective proof that a new system will provide a better result even if introduced in a different context or institutional environment from the original one is not a prerequisite to its introduction. More often than not, what appears to be successful in other countries—like the US financial system in the late 1990s and the German "universal bank" system in the late 1980s—is pursued by advocates of change, with little prior examination of the likely impact arising from the nature of institutional complementarity—that is, arising from the impact on other aspects of the institutional environment, such as the labor market and income distribution.

This suggests that the presence of institutional change is a separate issue from whether or not this change will benefit the Japanese nation. While the costs of maintaining the old institution have become apparent, the benefits of the new institution to the public are yet unclear. The shift from stability and cooperation towards competition and transparency may be unavoidable amid the globalization trend—which forces national systems that protect domestic industries to undergo a significant shift. Yet, the extent to which such shifts should take place should be decided based upon a cost-and-benefit consideration with institutional complementarity in mind. In this regard, those who advocate the need for institutional change tend to emphasize the benefit of the institutional change, without adequately addressing the costs that such institutional changes entail.[15] Instead, a balance sheet that honestly identifies the problems that the changes bring about ought to be provided so that solutions can be developed.

---

[15] See Nakatani (1996) for an example of such works that casually dismiss the trade-offs of institutional changes.

*Better International Economic Policy through a
Multi-Disciplinary Approach*

Our analysis suggests that entrenched interests may not be as entrenched as they initially may seem. The key is to see whether actors have different incentive structures, produced by environmental changes. This observation may suggest an alternative approach to encouraging reforms in developing nations or newly democratizing nations. On one hand, former insiders may end up being the ones better equipped to carry out economic reforms; the key factor is the incentive structures. On the other hand, the introduction of some formal institutions developed in market economies and liberal democracies may only bring about nepotism of the former insiders taking advantage of the discrepancy between such formal institutions and the social reality (Aoki 2001).

Thus, careful attention to institutions, extending beyond the conventional attention on formal rules and organizations are necessary to establish the "right" set of incentives. As our study suggests, it is necessary to identify the informal interaction patterns as well as the shared expectations of the actors to grasp the true functioning of institutions.

This aspiration to better understand institutions, including the shared expectations that support them, raises the need for an inter-disciplinary approach to public policymaking that reaches beyond the boundaries of neoclassical economics. Such an approach may help ameliorate international economic policymaking in such international organizations as the International Monetary Fund (IMF) where, due to an over-emphasis on macroeconomics under the dictates of the principles of a market economy or "market fundamentalism" (Sakakibara 2000), numerous policy failures appear to have emerged during the 1990s—such as those in Russia and Indonesia.

Further Issues

The experience of financial politics—namely, the Housing Loan Affair, the MOF reforms, and the Big Bang—suggests that the media has played a significant role in influencing the public's attitude on many issues. The institutional change in the financial convoy and bureaupluralism is highly likely to have counterparts in other countries also facing technological innovation, globalization, and other "economic propellants," as well as facing similar political impediments to financial reforms.[16] According to the US Federal Board of Reserves Chairman, Alan Greenspan, the shift from stability to competition is a global trend that comes on the backdrop of rapid technological innovation:

We are seeing the gradual breaking down of competition-inhibiting institutions from the keiretsu and chaebol of East Asia, to the *dirigisme* of some of continental Europe. The advantages to applying newer technologies are increasingly evident and undermine much of the old political wisdom of protected stability. The clash between unfettered competitive technological advance and protectionism, both domestic and international, will doubtless engage our attention for many years into this new century.[17]

In the United States, the Glass-Steagall Act of 1933, which served as a partial model for the financial segmentation in Japan, was finally reformed in a significant manner in 1999. This occurred after a long process of reforms that involved a struggle of lobbying interests opposing financial reforms, namely the securities and insurance industries. It also occurred on the backdrop of other developments in finance since the mid-1980s that eventually made such regulations largely obsolete.[18] As Greenspan's comment suggests, France and the European Union, as well as South Korea and other Asian nations, may provide interesting comparative grounds to assess how different countries have coped with similar international developments.

---

[16] See Scott and Weingast (1992) for a discussion of the "economic propellants" and "political impediments" to US banking reforms.

[17] "Technology and the Economy," remarks made before the Economic Club of New York, New York on January 13, 2000. Obtained at the FRB web site accessed on March 7, 2000 at http://www.federalreserve.gov/BoardDocs/Speeches/2000/200001132.htm

[18] See again Scott and Weingast (1992).

YEN / DOLLAR RATE (AVERAGE)

1985	238.05
1986	168.03
1987	144.52
1988	128.22
1989	138.11
1990	144.88
1991	134.59
1992	126.62
1993	111.06
1994	102.18
1995	93.97
1996	108.81
1997	120.92
1998	131.02

Source: Keizai Kikaku
Cho 2000: 415

References

Alt, James E. and Kenneth A. Shepsle. 1990. *Perspectives on Positive Political Economy*. New York: Cambridge University Press.

Amyx, Jennifer A. 1998. "Banking Policy Breakdown and the Declining Institutional Effectiveness of Japan's Ministry of Finance: Unintended Consequences of Network Relations." Ph.D. Dissertation submitted to Stanford University.

—— 2000. "The 1998 Reforms in Japanese Financial Regulation: Collapse of the Bureaucratic-Led Bargain." Unpublished manuscript.

—— 2004. *Japan's Financial Crisis: Institutional Rigidity and Reluctant Change*. Princeton, NJ: Princeton University Press.

Aoki, Masahiko. 1988. *Information, Incentives, and Bargaining in the Japanese Economy*. New York: Cambridge University Press.

—— 2001. *Towards Comparative Institutional Analysis*. Cambridge, MA: MIT Press.

Aoki, Masahiko and Hugh Patrick, eds. 1994. *The Japanese Main Bank System: Its Relevance for Developing and Transforming Economies*. New York: Oxford University Press.

Aoki, Masahiko, Hugh Patrick, and Paul Sheard. 1994. "The Japanese Main Bank System: An Introductory Overview," in *The Japanese Main Bank System: Its Relevance for Developing and Transforming Economies*. New York: Oxford University Press. pp. 1–50.

Aoki, Masahiko, Hyung-Ki Kim, and Masahiro Okuno-Fujiwara, eds. 1997. *The Role of Government in East Asian Economic Development: Comparative Institutional Analysis*. New York: Clarendon Press Oxford.

Asahi Shimbun. Various issues.

Asahi Shimbun, Keizaibu. (Economic Department) 1997. *Okura Shihai—Yuganda Kenryoku* (The Rule by Ministry of Finance—Distorted Power). Tokyo: Asahi Shimbun Sha.

Bagehot, Walter. 1928 [1867]. *The English Constitution*. London: Oxford University Press.

Bank of Japan [BOJ]. 1998. *Nihon Keizai wo Chushin to Suru Kokusai Hikaku Tokei* (Comparative Economic and Financial Statistics: Japan and Other Major Countries). Tokyo: Bank of Japan.

Bates, Robert H., Avner Greif, Margaret Levi, Jean-Laurent Rosenthal, and Barry Weingast. 1998. *Analytic Narratives*. Princeton, NJ: Princeton University Press.

Brennan, Geoffrey and James M. Buchanan. 1980. *The Power to Tax: Analytical Foundations of a Fiscal Constitution*. New York: Cambridge University Press.

Calder, Kent E. 1988. *Crisis and Compensation: Public Policy and Political Stability in Japan*. Princeton, NJ: Princeton University Press.

—— 1993. *Strategic Capitalism: Private Business and Public Purpose in Japanese Industrial Finance*. Princeton, NJ: Princeton University Press.

Calvert, Randall. 1995. "Rational Actors, Equilibrium, and Social Institutions," in Jack Knight and Itai Sened, eds., *Explaining Social Institutions*. Ann Arbor, MI: University of Michigan Press. pp. 57–94.

Chadha, Bankim and David Folkerts-Landau. 1999. "The Evolving Role of Banks in International Capital Flows," in Martin Feldstein, ed., *International Capital Flows*. NBER Conference Report. Chicago: The University of Chicago Press.

Cowhey, Peter F. and Mathew D. McCubbins, eds. 1995. *Structure and Policy in Japan and the United States*. New York: Cambridge University Press.

Curtis, Gerald L. 1999. *The Logic of Japanese Politics: Leaders, Institutions, and the Limits of Changes*. New York: Columbia University Press.

Dahl, Robert A. 1971. *Polyarchy: Participation and Opposition*. New Haven, CT: Yale University Press.

Dekle, Robert. 1997. "The Japanese 'Big Bang' Financial Reforms and Market Implications." *Journal of Asian Economics* 9(2), 237–49.

Dixit, Avinash K. 1996. *The Making of Economic Policy: A Transaction-Cost Politics Perspective*. Cambridge, MA: MIT Press.

Downs, Anthony. 1957. *An Economic Theory of Democracy*. New York: Harper Collins.

Eda, Kenji. 1999. *Dare no sei de Kaikaku wo Ushinaunoka* (By Whose Fault Are We Losing the Reforms?). Tokyo: Shinchosha.

Feldstein, Martin, ed. 1994. *American Economic Policy in the 1980s*. NBER Conference Report. Chicago: The University of Chicago Press.

Fuchita, Yasuyuki. 1997. *Shoken Biggu Ban* (Securities Big Bang). Tokyo: Nihon Keizai Shimbun Sha.

Fujimoto, Takahiro. 1997. *Seisan Shisutemu no Shinkaron* (The Evolutionary Theory of Production System). Tokyo: Yuhikaku.

Fukao, Mitsuhiro. 1999. "Nihon no Kin'yu Shisutemu Fuan to Koporeito Gabanansu Kozo no Jakuten" (The Instability of the Financial System and the Weakness of the Corporate Governance Structure in Japan), in Masahiko Aoki, Masahiro Okuno, and Tetsuji Okazaki, eds., *Shijo no Yakuwari Kokka no Yakuwari* (The Role of the Market, the Role of the State). Tokyo: Toyo Keizai Shimpo Sha. pp. 149–88.

Gibney, Frank, ed. 1998. *Unlocking the Bureaucrats' Kingdom: Deregulation and the Japanese Economy*. Washington D.C.: Brookings Institution Press.

Gilpin, Robert. 1981. *War and Change in World Politics*. New York: Cambridge University Press.

Green, Donald P. and Ian Shapiro. 1994. *Pathologies of Rational Choice: A Critique of Applications in Political Science*. New Haven, CT: Yale University Press.

References

Greif, Avner, Paul Milgrom, and Barry Weingast. 1994. "Coordination, Commitment, and Enforcement: The Case of the Merchant Guild." *Journal of Political Economy* 102, 745–76.

Grossman, Gene M. and Elhanan Helpman. 1994. "Protection for Sale." *American Economic Review* (September) 84(4), 833–50.

Haley, John O. 1995. "Japan's Postwar Civil Service: The Legal Framework," in Hyung-Ki Kim, Michio Muramatsu, T.J. Pempel, and Kozo Yamamura, eds., *The Japanese Civil Service and Economic Development: Catalysts for Change*. New York: Clarendon Press Oxford. pp. 77–101.

Hamada, Koichi and Akiyoshi Horiuchi. 1987. "The Political Economy of the Financial Market," in Kozo Yamamura and Yasukichi Yasuba, eds., *The Political Economy of Japan Vol.1: The Domestic Transformation*. Stanford, CA: Stanford University Press. pp. 223–60.

Hartcher, Peter. 1998. *The Ministry: How Japan's Most Powerful Institution Endangers World Markets*. Cambridge, MA: Harvard Business School Press.

Hellman, Thomas, Kevin Murdock, and Joseph Stiglitz. 1995. "Financial Restraint: Towards a New Paradigm." Research Paper No. 1355. Stanford, CA: Graduate School of Business, Stanford University.

Hirasawa, Mitsuhiro. 1997. "Futsu Setai no Hansu ga 'Anzensei' wo Saijushi: 97 Nen 'Chochiku to Shohi ni Kansuru Seron Chosa' kara" (Half of the Households Put Top Priority on "Security": From the Result of the '97 "Opinion Survey Concerning Saving and Consumption"). *Kin'yu Zaisei Jijo*, November 24, 1997, pp. 26–9.

Horiuchi, Akiyoshi. 1998. *Kin'yu Shisutemu no Mirai* (The Future of the Financial System). Tokyo: Iwanami Shoten.

—— 1999. *Nihon Keizai to Kin'yu Kiki* (The Japanese Economy and the Financial Crisis). Tokyo: Iwanami Shoten.

Hoshi, Takeo and Anil Kashyap. 1999. "The Japanese Banking Crisis: Where Did It Come From and How Will It End?" NBER Working Paper 7250. Cambridge, MA: National Bureau of Economic Research.

Hosoda, Takashi. 1998. *Tenkanki no Kin'yu Shisutemu* (The Financial System in a Transition Period). Tokyo: Kin'yu Zaisei Jijo Kenkyukai.

Huntington, Samuel P. 1991. *The Third Wave: Democratization in the Late Twentieth Century*. Norman, OK: University of Oklahama Press.

Igarashi, Fumihiko. 1995. *Okurasho Kaitairon* (Treatise On The Breakup of MOF). Tokyo: Toyo Keizai Shimpo Sha.

Ikeo, Kazuhito. 1995. *Kin'yu Sangyo heno Keikoku* (A Warning to the Financial Industry). Tokyo: Toyo Keizai Shimpo Sha.

Inoguchi, Takashi. 1983. *Gendai Nihon Seiji Keizai no Kozu: Seifu to Shijo* (The Scheme of Today's Japanese Political Economy: Government and Market). Tokyo: Toyo Keizai Shimpo Sha.

Inoguchi, Takashi and Tomoaki Iwai. 1987. *Zokugiin no Kenkyu* (A Study of Tribesmen in LDP). Tokyo: Nihon Keizai Shimbun Sha.

Inoki, Takenori. 1995. "Japanese Bureaucrats at Retirement: The Mobility of Human Resources from Central Government to Public Corporations," in Hyung-Ki Kim, Michio Muramatsu, T.J. Pempel, and Kozo Yamamura, eds., *The Japanese Civil Service and Economic Development: Catalysts for Change*. New York: Clarendon Press Oxford. pp. 213–34.

International Monetary Fund [IMF], 1997. *Japan—Economic and Policy Developments*. IMF Staff Country Report No. 97/91. October. Washington D.C.: International Monetary Fund.

—— 1998. *Japan: Selected Issues*. IMF Staff Country Report No. 98/113. October. Washington D.C.: International Monetary Fund.

Ishi, Hiromitsu ed. 1996. *Zaisei Kozo Kaikaku no Joken* (The Conditions for the Fiscal Structural Reforms). Tokyo: Toyo Keizai Shimpo Sha.

Ito, Takatoshi. 1996. "Kin'yu Senta kan no Kyoso to Kyocho" (Competition and Cooperation between financial centers), in Kazuo Ueda and Mitsuhiro Fukao eds., *Kin'yu Kudoka no Keizai Bunseki* (The Economic Analysis of the Economic Hollowing-Out). Tokyo: Nihon Keizai Shimbun Sha. pp. 185–212.

Jiyu Minshu Tou (LDP) 1996. *Dai 41 Kai Shugiin Sosenkyo Waga Tou no Koyaku* (Our Party's Platform for the 41st General Elections of the Lower House). Tokyo: Jiyu Minshu Tou.

Johnson, Chalmers. 1982. *MITI and the Japanese Miracle: The Growth of Industrial Policy, 1925–1975*. Stanford, CA: Stanford University Press.

Johnson, Chalmers and E.B. Keehn. 1994. "A Disaster in the Making: Rational Choice and Asian Studies." *The National Interest* Summer, 14–22.

Kabashima, Ikuo. 1986. "Masu Media to Seiji" (Mass Media and Politics). *Chuo Koron* February, 110–30.

Kaieda, Banri. 1997. *Nihon Ban Biggu Ban* (The Japanese Big Bang). Tokyo: KK Besuto Serazu.

Kaizuka, Keimei. 1996. "Kokusai Kin'yu Senta toshiteno Tokyo Shijo" (Tokyo Market as an International Financial Center), in Mitsuhiro Fukao and Kazuo Ueda, eds., *Kin'yu Kudoka no Keizai Bunseki* (The Economic Analysis of the Economic Hollowing-Out). Tokyo: Nihon Keizai Shimbun Sha. pp. 159–84.

Karl, Terry L. 1997. *The Paradox of Plenty: Oil Booms and Petro-States*. Berkeley, CA: University of California Press.

Kato, Junko. 1994. *The Problem of Bureaucratic Rationality: Tax Politics in Japan*. Princeton, NJ: Princeton University Press.

Katz, Richard. 1998. *Japan: The System That Soured*. Armonk, NY: M.E. Sharpe.

Katzenstein, Peter J. 1978. *Between Power and Plenty*. Madison, WI: University of Wisconsin Press.

Keehn, E.B. 1998. "The Myth of Regulatory Independence in Japan," in Frank Gibney, ed., *Unlocking the Bureaucrat's Kingdom: Deregulation and the Japanese Economy*. Washington D.C.: Brookings Institution.

Keizai Kikaku Cho, Chosa Kyoku (Economic Planning Agency, Research Bureau). 2000. *Nihon Keizai no Genkyo Heisei 12 Nen Ban* (The Current State of the Japanese Economy Edition 2000). Tokyo: Okurasho Insatsu Kyoku.

References

Keohane, Robert O. 1984. *After Hegemony: Cooperation and Discord in the World Political Economy*. Princeton, NJ: Princeton University Press.

Kim, Hyung-Ki, Michio Muramatsu, T.J. Pempel, and Kozo Yamamura, eds. 1995. *The Japanese Civil Service and Economic Development: Catalysts for Change*. New York: Clarendon Press Oxford.

Kin'yu Zaisei Jijo. Various issues. Tokyo: Kin'yu Zaisei Kenkyukai.

Kohno, Masaru. 1997. *Japan's Postwar Party Politics*. Princeton, NJ: Princeton University Press.

Komine, Takao. 1997. "Riyosha Riben no Kojo, Keizai no Pafomansu Kojo kosoga Honrai no Igi: Biggu Ban wo Meguru Giron no Konran wo Tadasu" (The True Purpose Is To Improve Users' Convenience and Enhance Economic Performance: Rectifying the Mess in the Debate Concerning the Big Bang), in *Kin'yu Zaisei Jijo*, July 28, 1997, 22–6.

Krasner, Stephen D. 1999. *Sovereignty: Organized Hypocrisy*. Princeton, NJ: Princeton University Press.

Kumon, Shumpei. 1992. "Japan as a Network Society," in Shumpei Kumon and Henry Rosovsky, eds., *The Political Economy of Japan Vol. 3: Cultural and Social Dynamics*. Stanford, CA: Stanford University Press. pp. 109–41.

Laffont, Jean-Jacques and Jean Tirole. 1991. "The Politics of Government and Decision-Making: A Theory of Regulatory Capture." *Quarterly Journal of Economics* 106(4), 1089–127.

Levi, Margaret. 1997. "A Model, A Method, and A Map: Rational Choice in Comparative and Historical Analysis," in Mark I. Lichbach and Alan S. Zuckerman, eds., *Comparative Politics: Rationality, Culture, and Structure*. New York: Cambridge University Press. pp. 19–41.

Lippman, Walter. 1997 [1922]. *Public Opinion*. New York: Free Press Paperbacks.

Mabuchi, Masaru. 1994. *Okurasho Tosei no Seiji Keizai Gaku* (The Political Economy of the Ministry of Finance's Control). Tokyo: Chuo Koron Sha.

—— 1995. "Financing Japanese Industry: The Interplay between the Financial and Industrial Bureaucracies," in Hyung-ki Kim, Michio Muramatsu, T.J. Pempel, and Kozo Yamamura, eds., *The Japanese Civil Service and Economic Development: Catalysts for Change*. New York: Clarendon Press Oxford. pp. 288–310.

—— 1997. *Okurasho ha Naze Oitsumeraretaka* (Why the Ministry of Finance Was Pushed against the Wall). Tokyo: Chuo Koron Sha.

Mainichi Shimbun, Keizaibu. (Economic Department) 1997. *2001 Nen Kin'yu Dai Kakumei: Nihon Ban Biggu Ban no Shinario* (The Big Financial Revolution 2001: The Scenario of the Japanese Financial Big Bang). Tokyo: Mainichi Shimbun Sha.

McCubbins, Mathew D. and Gregory W. Noble. 1995. "The Appearances of Power: Legislators, Bureaucrats, and the Budget Process in the United States and Japan," in Peter F. Cowhey and Mathew D. McCubbins, eds., *Structure and Policy in Japan and the United States*. New York: Cambridge University Press. pp 56–80.

McCubbins, Matthew D. and Thomas Schwartz. "Congressional Oversight Overlooked: Police Patrols Versus Fire Alarms." *American Journal of Political Science* 28 (1984), 165–79.

Ministry of Finance of Japan [MOF] web page. http://www.mof.go.jp

Mitsubishi Sogo Kenkyujo [Mitsubishi Soken], Keizai Chosabu. (Mitsubishi Research Institute, Economic Research Department) 1997. *Nihon Ban Biggu Ban no Shogeki*. (The Impact of the Japanese Big Bang) Tokyo: Kindai Serusu Sha.

Muramatsu, Michio. 1981. *Nihon no Kanryosei* (The Bureaucracy in Japan). Tokyo: Toyo Keizai Shimpo Sha.

—— 1994. *Nihon no Gyosei: Katsudogata Kanryosei no Henbo* (Public Administration in Japan: the Transformation of the Activity-Volume Type Bureaucracy). Tokyo: Chuo Koron Sha.

Muramatsu, Michio, Mitsutoshi Ito, and Yutaka Tsujinaka. 1992. *Nihon no Seiji* (Japanese Politics). Tokyo: Yuhikaku.

Muramatsu, Michio and Ellis S. Krauss. 1987. "The Conservative Policy Line and the Development of Patterned Pluralism," in Kozo Yamamura and Yasukichi Yasuba, eds., *The Political Economy of Japan Vol.1: The Domestic Transformation*. Stanford, CA: Stanford University Press.

Nagano, Atsushi. 1997. "Nanimo Shinakuteha Nihon no Shijo, Kin'yu Kikan ni Mirai ha Nai" (Without Doing Anything, There Is No Future for the Japanese Market and Financial Institutions). *Kin'yu Zaisei Jijo*. July 7, 1997, 26–30.

Nakatani, Iwao. 1996. *Nihon Keizai no Rekishi teki Tenkan* (The Historic Transformation of the Japanese Economy). Tokyo: Toyo Keizai Shimpo Sha.

Nihon Keizai Shimbun. Various issues.

Nihon Keizai Shimbun. ed. 1992. *Okurasho no Yu'utsu* (The Melancholy of the Ministry of Finance). Tokyo: Nihon Keizai Shimbun Sha.

—— ed. 1993. *Ginko Futo Shinwa no Hokai* (The Collapse of the Myth of No Bank Failures). Tokyo: Nihon Keizai Shimbun Sha.

—— ed. 1997. *Donaru Kin'yu Biggu Ban* (How Would the Financial Big Bang Be?). Tokyo: Nihon Keizai Shimbun Sha.

—— ed. 1998. *Nihon ga Furueta Hi* (The Day Japan Was Shaken). Tokyo: Nihon Keizai Shimbun Sha.

Nikkei Bijinesu. October 18, 1999. "Atarashii Nihonteki Keiei no Joken toha: Choki Koyo no Zehi Meguri Gekiron Tenkai" (What are the Conditions for the New Japanese Management: Heated Debate Concerning the Merit and Demerit of Long-Term Employment). Tokyo: Nikkei BP Sha. pp. 148–51.

Nishimura, Yoshimasa. 1999. *Kin'yu Gyosei no Hai'in* (Why Financial Administration Lost). Tokyo: Bungei Shunju Sha.

Niskanen, William. 1971. *Bureaucracy and Representative Government*. Chicago: Aldine.

Noguchi, Hitoshi. 1997. "Nihon Ban Biggu Ban no Uchimaku: Goso Sendan Orita Okura no Mekuramashi Senjutsu" (The Inside of the Japanese Big Bang: the Camouflage Strategy by MOF Which Quit the Convoy). *Nikkei Bijinesu*. December 15, 1997. pp. 39–43.

References

Noguchi, Yukio. 1993. *Nihon Keizai Kaikaku no Kozu* (The Japanese Economy—Design of Reform). Tokyo: Toyo Keizai Shimpo Sha.

—— 1995. *1940 Nen Taisei: Saraba "Senji Keizai"* (The 1940 Regime: Farewell to "Wartime Economy"). Tokyo: Toyo Keizai Shimpo Sha.

Noll, Roger G. 1989. "Economic Perspectives on the Politics of Regulation," in Richard Schmalensee and Robert D. Willig, eds., *Handbook of Industrial Organization Vol.2*. Amsterdam: North Holland.

—— 1999. "The Economics and Politics of the Slowdown of Regulatory Reform." Washington D.C.: AEI-Brookings Joint Center for Regulatory Studies.

Noll, Roger G. and Frances M. Rosenbluth. 1995. "Telecommunications Policy: Structure, Process, Outcomes," in Peter F. Cowhey and Mathew D. McCubbins, eds., *Structure and Policy in Japan and the United States*. New York: Cambridge University Press. pp. 119–76.

North, Douglass C. 1990. *Institutions, Institutional Change and Economic Performance*. New York: Cambridge University Press.

O'Donnell, Guillermo and Philippe Schmitter. 1986. *Tentative Conclusions about Uncertain Democracies*. Baltimore, MD: Johns Hopkins University Press.

Okimoto, Daniel I. 1989. *Between MITI and the Market*. Stanford, CA: Stanford University Press.

Okimoto, Daniel I. and Thomas P. Rohlen, eds. 1988. *Inside the Japanese System*. Stanford, CA: Stanford University Press.

Okuno-Fujiwara, Masahiro. 1997. "Toward a Comparative Institutional Analysis of the Government-Business Relationship," in Masahiko Aoki, Hyung-Ki Kim, and Masahiro Okuno-Fujiwara, eds., *The Role of Government in East Asian Economic Development*. New York: Oxford University Press. pp. 373–406.

Olson, Mancur. 1965. *The Logic of Collective Action: Public Goods and the Theory of Groups*. Cambridge, MA: Harvard University Press.

Organisation for Economic Cooperation and Development (OECD). 1997. *OECD Economic Surveys 1996–1997 Japan*. Paris: Organisation for Economic Cooperation and Development.

Osugi, K. 1990. "Japan's Experience of Financial Deregulation Since 1984 in an International Perspective." BIS Economic Papers. No. 26- January 1990. Basle: Bank for International Settlements.

Otake, Hideo. 1997a. *Gyokaku no Hasso* (The Idea of Administrative Reforms). Tokyo: TBS Britannica.

—— 1997b. *Seikai Saihen no Kenkyu* (The Study of the Re-arrangement of the Political World). Tokyo: Yuhikaku.

—— 1999. *Nihon Seiji no Tairitsujiku* (The Conflict Axis of Japanese Politics). Tokyo: Chuo Koron Sha.

Packer, Frank. 1994. "The Role of Long-Term Credit Banks Within the Main Bank System," in Masahiko Aoki and Hugh Patrick, eds., *The Japanese Main Bank System: Its Relevance for Developing and Transforming Economies*. New York: Oxford University Press. pp. 142–87.

Pascale, Richard and Thomas P. Rohlen. 1988. "The Mazda Turnaround," in Daniel I. Okimoto and Thomas P. Rohlen, eds., *Inside the Japanese System*. Stanford, CA: Stanford University Press. pp. 149–69.

Peltzman, Sam. 1998. *Political Participation and Government Regulation*. Chicago, IL: The University of Chicago Press.

Pempel, T.J. 1998. *Regime Shift: Comparative Dynamics of the Japanese Political Economy*. Ithaca, NY: Cornell University Press.

Pempel, T.J. and Michio Muramatsu. 1995. "The Japanese Bureaucracy and Economic Development: Structuring a Proactive Civil Service," in Hyung-Ki Kim, Michio Muramatsu, T.J. Pempel, and Kozo Yamamura, eds., *The Japanese Civil Service and Economic Development: Catalysts for Change*. New York: Clarendon Press Oxford. pp. 19–76.

Powell, Walter W. and Paul J. DiMaggio. 1991. *The New Institutionalism in Organizational Analysis*. Chicago, IL: The University of Chicago Press.

Ragin, Charles C. 1987. *The Comparative Method: Moving Beyond Qualitative and Quantitative Strategies*. Berkeley, CA: University of California Press.

Ramseyer, J. Mark and Frances McCall Rosenbluth. 1993. *Japan's Political Marketplace*. Cambridge, MA: Harvard University Press.

Reed, Steven R. and Michael F. Thies. 1999. "The Causes of Electoral Reform in Japan." Unpublished Manuscript.

Rosenbluth, Frances McCall. 1989. *Financial Politics in Contemporary Japan*. Ithaca, NY: Cornell University Press.

Rosenbluth, Frances McCall and Michael F. Thies. 1999. "The Electoral Foundations of Japan's Financial Politics: the Case of Jusen." Unpublished Manuscript.

Saito, Seiichiro. 1997. "Biggu Ban de Nihon Keizai ha Haretsu suru" (The Japanese Economy Bursts with the Big Bang). *Shokun* June 1997. pp. 76–84.

Sakakibara, Eisuke. 1993. *Beyond Capitalism: The Japanese Model of Market Economics*. Lanham, MD: University Press of America.

—— 2000. *Nihon to Sekai ga Furueta Hi: Saiba Shihonshugi Hokai no Kiki* (The Day That Shook Japan and the World: The Cyber Capitalism in Danger of Collapse). Tokyo: Chuo Koron Shin Sha.

Sakakibara, Eisuke, and Soichiro Tahara. 1999. *Kin'yu—Keizai Nihon Saisei* (Finance and Economy—The Resurrection of Japan). Tokyo: Fusosha.

Samuels, Richard J. 1987. *The Business of the Japanese State: Energy Markets in Comparative and Historical Perspective*. Ithaca, NY: Cornell University Press.

Sanwa Sogo Kenkyujo [Sanwa Soken], Kin'yu Chosa Shitsu. (Sanwa Research Institute, Financial Research Office) 1999. *Tettei Kensho: Posuto Biggu Ban Nihon no Kin'yu* (Complete Examination: Post-Big Bang Japanese Finance). Tokyo: Yamato Shuppan.

Sato, Seizaburo, and Tetsuhisa Matsuzaki. 1986. *Jiminto Seiken* (The LDP Government). Tokyo: Chuo Koron Sha.

Schwartz, Frank J. 1998. *Advice and Consent: The Politics of Consultation in Japan*. NY: Cambridge University Press.

References

Scott, W. (W. Scott) Richard. 1995. *Institutions and Organizations*. Thousand Oaks, CA: Sage Publications.

Scott, Kenneth E. and Barry R. Weingast. 1992. "Banking Reform: Economic Propellants, Political Impediments." Essays in Public Policy No. 34, Hoover Institution. Stanford, CA: Stanford University.

Shiono, Hiroshi. 1991. *Gyoseiho I* (Administrative Law I). Tokyo: Yuhikaku.

Shiozaki, Yasuhisa. 1995. "Kin'yu Kudoka Taisaku Mattanashi" (Measures Against Financial Hollowing-Out Can't Wait). *Chuo Koron* February, 60–9.

—— 1996. "Okurasho kara Kin'yu wo Hikihanase." *Chuo Koron* May, 48–53.

Shleifer, Andrei and Robert W. Vishny. 1997. "A Survey of Corporate Governance." *The Journal of Finance* 52(2), 737–83.

Simon, Herbert A. 1979. "Rational Decision Making in Business Organizations." *American Economic Review* 69(4), 493–513.

Skocpol, Theda. 1979. *States and Social Revolutions: A Comparative Analysis of France, Russia, and China*. New York: Cambridge University Press.

—— (1985) "Bringing the State Back in: Strategies of Analysis in Current Research". pp. 3–37 in Peter Evans, Dietrich_ Rueschemeyer, and Theda Skocpol (eds.) *Bringing the State Back* in. New York: Cambridge.

Steinmo, Sven, Kathleen Thelen, and Frank Longstreth, eds. 1992. *Structuring Politics: Historical Institutionalism in Comparative Analysis*. New York: Cambridge University Press.

Strange, Susan. 1998. *Mad Money: When Markets Outgrow Governments*. Ann Arbor, MI: University of Michigan Press.

Suzuki, Yoshio. 1997. *Biggu Ban no Jirenma* (The Dilemma of the Big Bang). Tokyo: Toyo Keizai Shimpo Sha.

Tahara, Soichiro. 1998. *Kyodai na Rakujitsu: Okura Kanryo, Haiso no Happyaku Goju Nichi* (A Gigantic Sunset: The Eight Hundred Fifty Days of the Ministry of Finance Bureaucrats in Defeat). Tokyo: Bungei Shunju Sha.

Takeuchi, Hiroshi. 1999. *Kin'yu Haisen* (The Day Japan Lost the Financial Wars). Tokyo: PHP Kenkyujo.

Tanaka, Yasuhiro. 1999. *Kaikei Biggu Ban* (The Accounting Big Bang). Tokyo: Nihon Keizai Shimbun Sha.

Teranishi, Juro. 2000. "Showa Kin'yu Kyoko no Keiken ni Manabu—Gurobaru Sutandado to Keizai Seisaku" (Learning from the Experience of the Showa Financial Depression—Global Standard and Economic Policy), in Masahiko Aoki and Juro Teranishi, eds., *Tenkanki no Ajia Keizai* (The Asian Economy in Transition). Tokyo: Toyo Keizai Shimpo Sha. pp. 61–77.

Thelen, Kathleen. 1999. "Historical Institutionalism in Comparative Politics." Unpublished Manuscript.

Tirole, Jean. 1998. "The Corporate Governance." Presidential Address, Econometric Society, delivered in Montreal, Lima, Berlin, and Delhi.

Tsusansho, Sangyo Seisaku Kyoku Sangyo Shikin Ka. (Ministry of International Trade and Industry of Japan [MITI], Industrial Finance Division, Industrial Policy

Bureau) ed. 1997. *Tsusho Sangyo Sho Ban Biggu Ban Koso* (The Big Bang Plan, MITI Version). Tokyo: Tsusho Sangyo Chosa Kai.

Tullock, Gordon. 1965. *The Politics of Bureaucracy*. Washington, D.C.: Public Affairs Press.

Ueda, Kazuo. 1996. *"Nihon no Kin'yu Kudoka to Nihon Keizai"* (The Financial Hollowing Out in Japan and the Japanese Economy), in Kazuo Ueda and Mitsuhiro Fukao, eds., *Kin'yu Kudoka no Keizai Bunseki* (The Economic Analysis of the Economic Hollowing-Out). Tokyo: Nihon Keizai Shimbun Sha. pp. 213–29.

Ueda, Kazuo and Mitsuhiro Fukao, eds. 1996. *Kin'yu Kudoka no Keizai Bunseki* (The Economic Analysis of the Economic Hollowing-Out). Tokyo: Nihon Keizai Shimbun Sha.

van Wolferen, Karel. 1990 [1989]. *The Enigma of the Japanese Power*. New York: Vintage Books.

Vogel, Steven K., 1996. *Freer Markets, More Rules: Regulatory Reforms in Advanced Industrial Countries*. Ithaca, NY: Cornell University Press.

—— 1999. "Can Japan Disengage? Winners and Losers in Japan's Political Economy, and the Ties that Bind Them." *Social Science Japan Journal* 2(1), 3–21.

Waltz, Kenneth N. 1979. *Theory of International Politics*. Reading, MA: Addison-Wesley.

Woodall, Brian. 1994. *Japan under Construction: Corruption, Politics, and Public Works*. Berkeley, CA: University of California Press.

World Bank. 1993. *The East Asian Miracle*. New York: Oxford University Press.

Yomiuri Shimbun. Various issues.

Yoshida, Kazuo. 1993. *Nihon Gata Keiei Shisutemu no Kozai* (The Merit and Demerit of the Japanese-Style Management System). Tokyo: Toyo Keizai Shimpo Sha.

Yoshino, Naoyuki, Yukihiro Asano, and Hidetaka Kawakita, eds. 1999. *Nihon gata Kin'yu Seido Kaikaku: Posuto Biggu Ban no Kin'yu Shisutemu* (Japanese-Style Financial System Reforms: The Post-Big Bang Financial System). Tokyo: Yuhikaku.

Yoshitomi, Masaru. 1998. *Nihon Keizai no Shinjitsu: Tsusetsu wo Koete* (The Truth of the Japanese Economy: Beyond Conventional Views). Tokyo: Toyo Keizai Shimpo Sha.

Young, H. Peyton. 1998. "Individual Learning and Social Rationality." *European Economic Review* 42, 651–63.

Yutani, Shoyo, and Masafumi Tsujihiro. 1996. *Dokyumento Jusen Hokai* (Document: The Collapse of the Housing Loan Companies). Tokyo: Daiyamondo Sha.

Zysman, John. 1983. *Government, Markets, and Growth: Financial Systems and the Politics of Industrial Change*. Ithaca, NY: Cornell University Press.

Index

Note: The letter f denotes a figure and t a table.